MW00834449

I SAW A NEW EARTH

AN INTRODUCTION
TO THE VISIONS OF THE APOCALYPSE

St. John the Theologian

an icon in the chapel of the Monastery of St. John the Theologian.
Patmos.

I Saw a New Earth

AN INTRODUCTION
TO THE VISIONS OF THE APOCALYPSE

PAUL S. MINEAR

Wipf and Stock Publishers
EUGENE, OREGON

Wipf and Stock Publishers
199 West 8th Avenue, Suite 3
Eugene, Oregon 97401

I Saw a New Earth
An Introduction to the Visions of the Apocalypse
By Minear, Paul S.
Copyright©1968 by Minear, Paul S.
ISBN: 1-59244-325-7
Publication date 9/4/2003
Previously published by Corpus Books, 1968

A complete new study and translation of the Book of Revelation.

To
Patrick C. Rodger
and
Lukas Vischer

Acknowledgments

I gratefully recognize the help provided, during the preparation of these chapters, by the staffs of the American School of Oriental Research in Jerusalem and the American Collegiate Institute in Izmir. From the beginning I have had the expert assistance of Mrs. Helen Kent, whose work as secretary merits the citation *magna cum laude*.

Portions of these chapters formed the substance of the Stone Lectures, delivered in November 1967 at Princeton Theological Seminary. I am in debt to President James I. McCord and his colleagues for their hospitality on that occasion.

Table of Contents

List of Illustrations

NOTE: Illustrations have been chosen with two objectives. The first is to indicate how specific artists have interpreted selected texts in the Apocalypse. The second is to suggest in a minimal way how five *different* visual arts have been influenced by the Apocalypse. These intentions do not apply, of course, to the statue of Artemis which is included as an indication of pagan imagination and as a background to John's portrait of the whore in chapters 17 and 18.

Abbreviations

JOURNALS

ALW	*Archiv für Liturgiewissenschaft*
BA	*Biblical Archaeologist*
BE	*Bible and Expositor*
BK	*Bibel und Kirche*
BL	*Bibel und Leben*
Bib	*Biblica*
Bib Sac	*Bibliotheca Sacra*
BZ	*Biblische Zeitschrift*
BASOR	*Bulletin of American Schools of Oriental Research*
BJRL	*Bulletin of the John Rylands Library*
CBQ	*Catholic Biblical Quarterly*
CH	*Church History*
CTM	*Concordia Theological Monthly*
ETL	*Ephemerides Theologicae Lovaniensis*
EQ	*Evangelical Quarterly*
Ev Th	*Evangelische Theologie*
Exp T	*Expository Times*
HR	*History of Religions*
Int	*Interpretation*
JAC	*Jahrbuch für Antike und Christentum*
JBL	*Journal of Biblical Literature*
JR	*Journal of Religion*
JTS	*Journal of Theological Studies*
NTS	*New Testament Studies*
Nov T	*Novum Testamentum*
NRT	*Nouvelle Revue Théologique*
RB	*Revue Biblique*
RE	*Review and Expositor*
RL	*Religion in Life*

RSLR	*Rivista di Storia e Literatura Religiosa*
RSR	*Recherches de Science Religieuse*
RHP	*Revue d'Histoire et de Philosophie Religieuses*
RT	*Revue Thomiste*
Scr	*Scripture*
SEA	*Svensk Exegetisk Årsbok*
SJT	*Scottish Journal of Theology*
ThS	*Theological Studies*
Th STK	*Theologische Studien und Kritiken*
THF	*Theologische Forschung*
ThLZ	*Theologische Literaturzeitung*
ThQ	*Theologische Quartalschrift*
ThR	*Theologische Rundschau*
ThT	*Theology Today*
ThZ	*Theologische Zeitschrift*
VC	*Verbum Caro*
VS	*Vie spirituelle*
VigC	*Vigiliae christianae*
ZATW	*Zeitschrift für die Alttestamentliche Wissenschaft*
ZNTW	*Zeitschrift für die Neutestamentliche Wissenschaft*
ZST	*Zeitschrift für Systematische Theologie*
ZThK	*Zeitschrift für Theologie und Kirche*

REFERENCE WORKS

IB	*Interpreter's Bible*, 12 vols., New York.
IDB	*Interpreter's Dictionary of the Bible*, 4 vols., New York.
P-W	Pauly-Wissowa: *Real Encyclopadie der classischen Altertums Wissenschaft*, Stuttgart.
RGG	*Religion in Geschichte und Gegenwart*, 3rd ed., Tübingen.
S-B	H. L. Strack und P. Billerbeck, *Kommentar zum N.T. aus Talmud und Midrasch*, 3 vols. (München, 1954).
TWNT	Kittel, *Theologische Wörterbuch zum Neuen Testament*, 7 vols. English trans. by G. W. Bromiley, 3 vols. (Grand Rapids, 1967).

Introduction

During the writing of this book I have lived, for long or brief times, in Patmos, Izmir, Jerusalem, and New Haven. In each of these places I have incurred quite definite obligations. The mention of Patmos, where I first saw the icon reproduced here as a frontispiece, reminds me of the need to remember John as a very human individual, impelled by his own purposes, vulnerable to special fears and hopes. Izmir, the modern Smyrna and the center from which I visited the sites of the seven churches, summons each student to deal fairly with those specific congregations, in the midst of their own predicaments and their own horizons of concern. Jerusalem, a city both sacred and defiled, prompts reflections about the holy city of John's vision which will neither minimize nor romanticize the significance of geography. New Haven is the place where I teach, where I am bound to respect both the standards set by historical scholarship and the urgent claims upon parish ministers.

With the publication of this book there comes into view a wider range of places where readers live whom I cannot know. To them also I have an initial obligation, that of arriving at some sort of agreement about what I am proposing to do in this book. I intend it as a companion for their study of the Apocalypse, and I should like here to suggest how it might profitably be used.

Let me first account for offering a new translation of John's work. When I give courses on this subject, at the opening session I ask every student to read Revelation through twice without pause, in a translation he has not seen before. The objective is to exorcise the demon of familiarity which so often blunts the full force of the original and to insure a panoramic view of the whole book before the student becomes absorbed in scenic details. To afford that possibility for all readers, I have provided such a translation. It is not offered as a competitor or substitute for other recent translations, nor for use by ministers or teachers in settings other than that of serious and thorough study. In many cases the Greek text offers a plurality of nuances which justify various renderings in English. The choosing of one of these rather than another gives a particular emphasis which may at times exclude other nuances. Yet I believe that each word of the translation chosen here is justified by the sense of the original. More novel than the translation itself is the typographical arrangement. This is designed to break up long prose paragraphs and to free readers from the lock-step of verses and chapters. The arrangement of the material may also help one to visualize basic units of thought and symmetries of structure. It separates narrative from dialogue and clarifies the roles of various actors and speakers. This typographical device has been helpful to me and may afford similar aid to others.

In Part I the larger blocs of text are divided into consecutive visions, enabling the student to concentrate on each in succession. After reading the translation of a given vision, the student should allow the material full opportunity for superimposing its own pattern on his mind. Why did John begin and end where he did? What major divisions, what sequences, what contrapuntal motifs are intrinsic to the vision? I do not anticipate every student's full agreement with my analysis, but he can more easily arrive at his own sense of the movement of John's thought if he has such an analysis at hand. Let me urge him not to hurry too fast through this work of structural analysis. Each vision must be given a chance to assert its own unitary impact. John was a literary artist as well as a theologian. He should be allowed his rights in both capacities.

In studying each vision, the student may then undertake a consideration of two or three strategic issues. If he has the advantage of class discussions, so much the better. I have chosen problems which are posed by the text and have arranged them in the order in which they may be attacked to advantage. In some cases I have outlined my own conclusions as a foil for the student's own thought. Books sometimes deal with controversial matters by simply providing a list of possible alternatives, the author remaining neutral. At the risk of apparent arbitrariness, I have usually stated my own position, anticipating that the student, well known for his inclination to think otherwise, may find private delight in following a contrary path. The bibliography at the end of each vision provides help in locating treatments of matters which have not been discussed, along with views contrary to those expressed here.

I recommend that each reader spend a major part of his time in Part I, first in active, curious, persistent listening to John himself; then in the effort to recapture the structure and the movement of his thinking; then in exploring various solutions to key riddles posed by the vision; and finally in expanding his range of reading to include relevant antecedents and parallels in the Bible and in other more detailed essays by contemporary scholars.

I have not overloaded Part I with technical data, with material requiring a knowledge of Greek or with elaborate evidence supporting the arguments. Nothing there should prove unintelligible to reasonably intelligent and sophisticated students. This is not so true of Part II. Here I have dealt with questions hotly debated among scholars. In some cases the essays are intended to contribute more directly to the ongoing debate among professionals. This overlap between the two sections of the text produces an excessive amount of repetition. This I regret. But it seems to be necessary in writing a book which will be helpful at the elementary level without avoiding legitimate requests from advanced students for more thorough-going exposition. Some of the key conclusions in Part I must rest on the validity of essays in Part II. The issues are too important to be ignored, too complex to be defined briefly, and too controversial to be treated sketchily. The advanced student may find it preferable to begin with Part II and then move to Part I; most students will, I think, find it better to move in the normal order, but with an occasional detour to consult one of the essays to clear up a particular point. Frequent cross-references guide this shuttling back and forth.

Part III is designed to fulfill still other functions. The reader whose enthusiasm still holds by the time he has finished the first two Parts is invited to complete his study here. First he can read the whole text again consecutively. From verse to verse, questions will now occur to him which may not be vital to the core-message but which may nonetheless be of genuine importance. In locating answers to these more restricted problems, the annotations will prove useful. They are designed to suggest relevant passages in other biblical books and to lead the student to scholarly essays which represent the best current thinking on these topics. Inasmuch as the production of a complete commentary has been beyond our reach, these annotations will serve to answer questions often dealt with in such a commentary.

My chief desire is that each reader will find the Book of Revelation fully absorbing and that this companion volume will both enhance his excitement and guide it toward constructive ends, diminishing some of the frustrations, adding some new discoveries, and in every way furthering the strange conversations which John carries on with his readers.

Archimandrite Nikitaras of Patmos wrote in July 1966: "The Apocalypse . . . has something to show us, some meaning or significance for us . . . but how many appreciate . . . [its] startling and revolutionary message?" Such appreciation is ample reward for our common study.

PART I
The Visions

Part I consists of a consecutive study of the major literary units of the book. Some of these units are long, very long in fact; others are very short. The span of each unit must be determined by its internal structure, and not by the familiar chapter and verse divisions. John neither thought nor wrote in terms of verses and chapters. Those divisions were added centuries later as a device to facilitate quick reference, not to aid in the analysis of thought-patterns. Such analysis requires careful selection of the unit of thought and persistent efforts to detect the author's line of thinking and the rhythmic pulse of that thinking.

Each section of Part I, therefore, has a fourfold structure. First comes a translation of the text arranged on the page in such a way as to suggest the internal patterns and style of the author's thought. Second, there is an analysis of these literary structures. Third, salient aspects of the author's message are selected to serve as the basis for private reflection or group discussion. Fourth, extensive bibliographical materials are provided to enable the student to explore relevant historical or theological problems. The text of John's book remains the focus of concern throughout.

The Triple Introduction (1:1-11)

THE INTRODUCTION TO THE BOOK 1:1-3

1:1 THIS BOOK IS THE REVELATION WHICH GOD
ENTRUSTED TO JESUS CHRIST SO THAT HE COULD
ENABLE HIS SLAVES TO SEE WHAT MUST HAPPEN
2 SOON. JESUS CHRIST SENT THIS REVELATION
THROUGH HIS ANGEL TO HIS SLAVE JOHN WHO,
TELLING WHAT HE SAW, CONFIRMED GOD'S
SAVING PURPOSE AS IT HAS BEEN CONFIRMED BY
JESUS CHRIST.

3 *God bless the Reader. God bless all who hear this prophecy and*
who obey it, for the season is at hand!

Literary Analysis

The title of the book is the place for study to begin. John
selected that title with care, and we should not confuse his selection with that of later editors, such as The Revelation of St. John
the Divine, or The Book of Revelation. Neither of these expresses
the author's own conception of his work. Nearer to the mark
is the title used by the Revised Standard Version, The Revelation *to* John. Actually however, the author's own selection
of a title may be found, in harmony with ancient literary practice, in his opening statement as a whole, the first two sentences
in the translation, which we have set in capitals.

This title shows that John thought of the chain of communication as involving five essential links: God, Christ, his angel, his
slave John, and those slaves to whom John addressed his book.
Of these five links, the most strategic is the second; the document
is the revelation *of* Jesus Christ. The name of John appears, but
only in the third person, as if another speaker, perhaps an editor,

were providing a preface to his work. John plays only a mediating role, that of delivering the message from Jesus Christ to his slaves. The fact, however, that the full statement is the title of the book, indicates that none of the five links can be eliminated.

How does the author speak about what is passed from link to link? Most important are two elements: the saving purpose of God and Jesus' confirmation of that purpose. Only a study of the entire book can fill these phrases with their intended cargo. "Saving purpose" translates the Greek word *logos*, which carried a hundred possible connotations, such as word, speech, message, action, cause, plan, wisdom, etc. To the prophet it expressed everything that God had actualized and promised in Jesus Christ. This is why Jesus could himself be called the *Logos* of God (19:13. The student will find the following uses of the term instructive: 3:8, 10; 6:9; 12:11; 17:7; 19:9; 20:4). "As confirmed by" translates *marturia*, another significant term in John's vocabulary, which can be variously rendered by witness, attestation, validation, verification. Christ verifies God's message and God validates Christ's disclosure of it. John attests Christ's intention and Christ gives his seal to the truth of John's witness. The connotations are complex because the chain of communication depends on the reliability of each link, on the integrity of each witness. "Witness" is a metaphor which derives its meanings from several different situations: a court case in which the defendant is giving his testimony, or where the prosecution or the defence presents witnesses. Or it may suggest the news reporting of events where eye-witnesses are needed. It may call to mind business transactions where a character reference or the seal of a notary is desired. (The student should study the range of possible implications in the following: 6:9; 11:7; 12:11, 17; 15:5; 19:10; 20:4; 22:16-20). An accurate definition of *logos* and *marturia* is not so important at this stage, however, as is the recognition of the author's desire to underline these two phrases as essential to the title, and therefore as clues to the basic message of the book as a whole. (See p. 222f.)

The last sentence (1:3) mirrors the type of occasion for which the book was prepared. We have capitalized "Reader" to call attention to its technical use. The book was intended to be read aloud by the liturgist in a service of worship to the congregation gathered on the Lord's Day. Ordinarily such a congregation would be addressed by its prophets, speaking spontaneously (i.e., in the Spirit) and directly. On this occasion, however, the prophet John was forcibly detained elsewhere. If his witness were to be heard, it must be written *in absentia* and read aloud by someone else. In any Christian gathering, the words of a prophet, whether oral or written, were sure to carry great weight, because they relayed a message from the God who was being worshipped. God's commands must be obeyed; his call to remembrance and hope must be heeded. The listeners would realize that they were being addressed simultaneously by the prophet John, by Christ, and by the Most High God who had disclosed his presence in Christ. The introduction makes it quite clear that all three shared in the authorship of the entire book, although obviously in different ways.

John followed literary convention not only in the preface but also in the conclusion of the book. The alert student will examine chapter 22 to see the artistic rounding-off of the literary intention. The opening beatitude, for instance, is matched by a closing beatitude (1:3; 22:7). The blessing promised to obedient listeners is balanced by a curse on willful alteration of the witness (22:18,19). The writer and the readers are described from the same third-person perspective, and the book is referred to in the same objective ways (cp. 1:1 and 22:6; 1:3 and 22:10). The prophet's care in bringing the whole book to a formal conclusion shows that he planned the whole document as a single unit and that it was designed to be heard as a unit in Christian worship. Since this is true, the student should not be content with his interpretation of any passage unless and until it fits into the message of the book as a whole.

For Reflection and Discussion

After one has grasped the author's literary intention, he should ask whether the message itself comes through clearly, or whether at certain points it encounters resistance in the student's mind. What are the chief obstacles to clear comprehension? These obstacles almost always make us aware of the distance between John's standpoint and our own. What he took for granted we cannot easily assume. His three sentences appear to be based on five assumptions, which we may express as follows:

1. His thought issues from the fundamental conviction of faith in the living presence of God, as well as in God's desire and ability to reveal himself to men. John assumes that his readers will also accept God's presence as the basis for their thought and action.

2. John takes it for granted that God has given to Jesus Christ a disclosure of crucial significance. All understandings of the will of God are therefore inseparable from the understanding of Christ's work. John thinks of that work in terms of the familiar accounts of the ministry of Jesus, as climaxed in his death. He supposes that his readers are already familiar with that story and that they attach decisive significance to it.

3. John assumes that Jesus' disclosure of God's purpose embraces not only the present situation and the events shaping it, but also the whole chain of future consequences. The present, the past, the future (this order is important) are all dependent upon the revelation which God has entrusted to Jesus. John assumes that his readers have already committed themselves to rely on the power of God to determine future developments.

4. John writes under the conviction that his readers identify themselves with "the slaves of Jesus Christ" and that they recognize their kinship with "his slave John." They have already accorded to Christ the right, as their owner and leader, to issue orders. They have already pledged themselves to serve and obey him at whatever cost.

5. John takes it for granted that the visible congregations are constantly engaged in a dialog with the invisible objects of their loyalty (God, Christ, the angel), and that they will therefore welcome the role of a prophet who relays a message from the invisible to the visible partners in the dialog. He and they

believe that a prophet's message, when authentic, will exert power to bless or to curse.

The introduction to the book of Revelation thus clarifies five elements essential to understanding. Whoever does not accept those essentials, or even any one of them, is bound to misconstrue the message, both in the preface and in subsequent paragraphs. Herein lies ample reason why readers, whether ancient or modern, encounter difficulties in understanding this book. Honesty requires an instant recognition of these difficulties. The reader must, above all, preserve that honesty. He must not hedge or hide. He must not force his mind into artificial or superficial conformity to John's mind. An honest opponent may come to terms with John, but not a self-deceived hypocrite. Each student must analyze the degree to which he cannot accept John's presuppositions; such analysis may require not a little time.

For Further Study:

1. THE USE OF THE TERM APOCALYPSE. The Greek word which opens this book—*apokalypsis*—provided a name not only for this document but for a whole class of documents. One detects enough similarities between John's book and the others to justify this classification, but also enough contrasts to warn us of the dangers in such classification. Many critics draw a sharp line between prophecy and apocalypse and insist on applying only the second category to John—a step which would be foreign to John's own intention. The student is urged to read the following with a high degree of independent judgment.

S. B. Frost, *Old Testament Apocalyptic;* H. H. Rowley, *The Relevance of Apocalyptic;* D. S. Russell, *The Method and Message of Jewish Apocalyptic;* J. A. T. Robinson, *In the End, God;* G. von Rad, *Old Testament Theology,* II, 301-315; H. B. Swete, xxii-xxxii; H. Ringgren, RGG, I, 463-466; R. Schütz, RGG, I, 467-469; M. Rist, IDB, I, 157-161; R. H. Pfeiffer, IB, I, 427-432, 435-436; I. T. Beckwith, 166-196; W. Kümmel, 321-324; S. J. Case, 57-159; A. Wikenhauser, 540-547; S. H. Hooke, *Alpha and*

Omega, 94-101; J. Kallas, JBL, 86 (1967), 69-80; J. Moltmann,
Theology of Hope, 124-138.

The meaning of the Greek word itself, during the New Testament period and before it became a technical literary category,
may be examined by reference to the following passages:

Amos 3:7; Isa. 40:1-5; 53:1f.; 56:1f.; I Peter 1:7, 13; 4:13;
Romans 1:17, 18; 2:5; 16:25; 1 Cor. 14:1-30; 2 Cor. 12:1; Matthew 11:25-30; 16:16-20; Luke 2:26-35; A. Oepke, TWNT, III,
573-597.

2. THE LITERARY STRUCTURE OF THE BOOK. It would be of
great help in studying this document if we could recover the
exact literary blue-print John used in his writing. Many scholars
believe they have recovered such a blue-print, although, unfor-
tunately, they rarely receive the approval of other scholars. The
absence of consensus, however, does not spell futility. Each of
the following reconstructions has recaptured certain elements in
the pattern of John's thinking and writing. Even though a student
may not adopt any special hypothesis, he will find it useful to
study them all.

A. Farrer, RJ, 7-23; J. W. Bowman, Int. 1955, 436-453; P. Allo,
lxxviii-cxi; A. Loisy, 21-37; A. Wikenhauser, *ad loc.;* P. Boismard,
9-14; R. Loenertz, ix-xix; A. Feuillet, 26-30; M. Rissi, TH, 1-18;
H. B. Swete, xxxiii-liv; Kümmel, 319f.; D. T. Niles, 99-105;
G. Bornkamm, ZNTW, 1937, 132-149; M. Hopkins, CBQ 27
(1965), 42-47; A. Läpple, 50-57.

Should the student wish to compare the typographical arrangement of the text with an alternative plan, he should consult the
translation into the Dutch language by Prof. A. M. Brouwer (*Het
Nieuwe Testament,* Leiden, Sijthoff, 1949).

THE SALUTATION OF THE LETTER (1:4-8)

**1:4   To the seven Asian congregations John sends grace and peace
from the God who now rules,**

who has always ruled,
and who is coming to rule,
from the seven spirits before his throne,
5 *from Jesus the Messiah,*
who loyally confirmed God's work,
who became the first of the dead to be reborn,
and who is now the ruler of earth's kings.

"*To him be glory and power forever,*
for he loves us,
he has freed us from Sin's bondage by his death,
6 *he has formed us into a kingdom,*
to serve God, his Father, as priests.
"*Amen.*"

7 "*There! He is coming with the clouds.*
Everyone will see him,
even those who pierced him.
All earth's tribes will mourn over him.
I vouch for this!"
"*Amen.*"

8 *This is what God the Lord says:*
"*I, the All-Powerful, am the A and the Z.*
I now rule, I have always ruled, I am coming to rule."

Literary Analysis

The second of John's introductions takes the form of the salutation of the letter. This salutation follows quite closely the pattern of early Christian epistles, such as the opening verses in the epistles of Paul, Peter, and James. First the author names himself—John; then he addresses the churches of Asia; next he wishes for them grace and peace; then he indicates the source of those gifts. In this case, the author describes that source by employing elaborate triadic formulas. The typographical arrangement of the translation may help the student locate several of these formulas: there are three sources of grace, three aspects of

God's power, three explanations of Christ's status, three indica-
tions of his saving work. There are also subtle symmetries to be
noted among these triadic formulas. For instance, the author
matches a triple reference to God (rules . . . ruled . . . is coming)
with a triple reference to Christ (loves . . . has freed . . . is coming). He thus reminds each congregation that its present relationship to its living Lord is the basis for understanding its past
and its future.

When we try to read these verses rapidly as continuous
prose, we encounter certain difficulties. When we analyze the
reasons for those difficulties, we are led to recognize the unusually
abrupt transitions between verse 6 and 7 and between verse 7
and 8. The prose line does not flow smoothly because there are
sudden shifts in speakers (God, Christ, the prophet, the congregation) and in audiences. John did not seek to write continuous
prose but to record an active dialog in which the prophet, God,
and the congregations alternate in their speaking and responding.
As a result, this salutation of a letter could easily be adapted to
the worship services in the Asian congregations. This helps to
explain the hymn-like rhythms of the text.

In the typical letter, the salutation was followed by a thanksgiving (see P. Schubert, *Form and Function of Pauline Thanksgivings*). In the Pauline epistles this thanksgiving expressed not only
gratitude for the readers but also gratitude to God. In John's
letter, this latter motif is dominant and takes the form of a
doxology. He could not recognize Christ as the source of grace
and peace without responding in praise. For this response (vs.
5b, 6) he uses a doxology with which the congregations had
probably become familiar through liturgical use. The thanksgiving section of the letter, designed to be read in worship,
incorporates an act of worship in which the congregation could
join, at least by saying Amen. This doxology, based on the love
of Christ for "us" and his action in making "us a kingdom of
priests," leads into a liturgical expression of confidence in the
coming of Christ (vs. 7), a promise to which the prophet and
congregation could again give their Amen. The pledge of future
vindication then receives its decisive signature, that of God him-

self (vs. 8). The all-powerful Lord, speaking in the first person, vouches for the validity of Christ's credentials (vs. 5a), the truth of the doxology (vs. 5b,6), and the dependability of the promise (vs. 7).

When he comes to the close of his book, the prophet indicates very clearly his intention to treat the whole document as a single letter. The last sentence of the book (22:21) is, in fact, the formal way of ending an ancient Christian epistle. What had begun in 1:4 reaches its end there. Moreover, the pledge of God which the congregation had heard at the beginning is offered again at the end (1:8; 22:20), whereupon the prophet and his people could add their final *Amen*. The student should therefore read the whole book as a letter sent from John to the churches of Asia, which he intended to be read in the context of active worship. As a letter and as an act of worship, John's work invites each congregation to attest for itself the saving work of God, of the Spirit, and of Christ, thus making the chain of guarantors complete.

For Reflection and Discussion

When one asks where, in the first eight verses, the focus of John's interest fell, he can be fairly sure of the answer: on the work of Jesus Christ. The book's title announces that Jesus himself is the Revelation which God sent to his slaves. The letter's salutation also stresses the story of this person. With great care for detail, John identifies Jesus in three adjectival phrases (vs. 5a); then he describes his redemptive work in three clauses (vs. 5b, 6); then he announces his certain but awesome coming in three clauses (vs. 7). Moreover, as we shall soon see, this same person is the one who appears to John in a vision and who conveys whatever messages he wishes relayed to the churches (1:12-20). Whether we think of this document as a book, as a letter, or as a series of visions, Jesus Christ remains the central figure. If we are to understand John, we must understand his relationship to Christ. Of what does John think before he says Christ?

He thinks of a Messiah who had loyally confirmed God's

purpose (vs. 5a). A more literal and familiar translation is "the faithful witness." The special Johannine nuances in the term to confirm or to witness have been examined in a separate essay. At this point we ask only what John had in mind when he used the adjective loyal or faithful (*pistos*). This adjective is used three times to describe the one who testifies or confirms (1:5, 2:13; 3:14). In 3:14, the association with *the Amen* and with *the True* implies the absolute credibility and reliability of the person. He is himself the guarantee and the standard of integrity. In 2:13 Antipas as a witness had been loyal to death. This example of Antipas suggests that in 1:5, as well, John is hailing Jesus as a person who had remained loyal to death; only so is there a smooth transition to the next phrase, "first-born of dead men." This inference is supported by the thought of 11:3 in which the two prophets whom Jesus recognizes as his own guarantors vindicate their fidelity by their death (11:7). In 17:6 also, Jesus' witnesses are described as having been slain. We conclude, therefore, that John's use of the adjective loyal when applied to a person indicates that he has accepted death as the genuine test and measure of faith (2:10; 17:14; 19:11). How could it be otherwise in a situation in which loyalty to Christ provoked violent persecution, placed a person on trial, and forced him to make the ultimate wager (2:10)? To be loyal to death is the climactic test of those who have been called and chosen (17:14). This most rigorous test had been met by Jesus Christ, who was therefore introduced as the confirming witness *par excellence*. By his death he had proved his reliability, his integrity, his loyalty. It was his death which had validated his "testimony" to God's revelation (1:2).

"*The first of the dead to be reborn.*" As Christ had validated his testimony to God by joining the company of the dead, so God had validated Christ's testimony by raising him and making him the first of many dead men to be raised, pledging through him his intention to vindicate all who "washed their robes in the blood of the Lamb." It was for this reason that John could promise grace and peace from Jesus Christ to all who would hear and obey his commands. Their sharing in Jesus' death assured them of receiving his life, his grace, his peace. This, in brief, was one of John's ways of describing salvation—to be reborn from the dead to share in Jesus' grace, peace, and life. The whole revelation of Jesus Christ depended for its validity and power on the actualities of death and rebirth from death. It was entirely appropriate, therefore, that John should identify Christ by these twin actualities.

"The ruler of earth's kings." The power given to the Messiah through his death and resurrection is the power to govern the kings of earth. At this point the student encounters a dominant image in John's mind. Three elements are fused in this description of Christ—Jesus as ruler, the kings as ruled by Christ, and the earth as ruled by these kings who are themselves now subordinated to Christ. If we mistake any of these three elements, we will distort John's message. Moreover, it is difficult to avoid that distortion because of the rich variety in John's vocabulary. The student is referred to the thematic studies for an examination of the separate strands in John's language which deal with rulers and kings, and for a similar examination of his conceptions of the earth (see pp. 228ff., 261f.).

Here let me post a warning signal. One's initial reactions to the term king is almost certain to be misleading. John is most interested in that *kind* of sovereignty or kingly power which has been revealed in Christ's death and resurrection and which therefore is the kind of power exercised by the hidden God, whose ways are not our ways. Along with John, the readers must seek to cope with the ultimate question of how a good God can and does wield final power over all other powers, whether heavenly or earthly.

A study of the essays referred to will reveal three possible identifications of the kings of the earth over whom Christ rules. Whichever identification is adopted, what is entirely clear is that John asserts Christ's power over them. None other is king over all kings (17:14; 19:16). But to which group of kings does John refer in verse 5?

(1) He may have in mind emperors like Domitian, and their provincial delegates, like Pilate, Herod, and their successors. This may be why in verse 7 the prophet calls attention to those who killed Jesus. This is the usual interpretation of the phrase *earth's kings* (as found in other passages: 6:15; 10:11; 17:2; 18:3, 9; 19:19; 21:24). If this be the primary meaning, then it is over such rulers that Jesus received power through his death *at their hands* and through God's vindication of that death.

(2) John may have been thinking of such invisible heavenly rulers as Satan, the Dragon, Sin, and Death. If so, then John is saying that Christ had taken Death itself captive by becoming the faithful witness and the first-born from the dead. He had received the keys of Death and Hades (1:5, 18). He had freed men from their bondage to Sin (1:5. Capitals are used to indicate the inclusive and transcendent character of the reality), creating a kingdom from among those who had been citizens of another kingdom by defeating their erstwhile kings. The kingdom of the earth, once ruled by the destroyers of the earth (11:15-18), had been won back to earth's true lord (11:4). Satan (or the Dragon, or Babylon) had also been King of Kings (ch. 17, 18), but had met the conqueror in Christ.

(3) In 1:5 John may have thought of those faithful servants of Christ who have received from him that sovereignty over the earth which Adam had lost (Gen. 1:27-31; 3:17-24). Students often overlook the incredible audacity of John's picture of true Christians as being rulers of the earth, but this picture is undeniably present (5:10; 20:4, 6; 22:5). This possibility is supported by the immediate sequel in vs. 6 (*a kingdom*, which some manuscripts read "kings"), and in vs. 9 where John and the Christians are described as partners in Jesus' royal power. By their fidelity they have become partners in sitting on his throne, in bearing his name, in wearing crowns and royal garments, and in exercising his authority over his enemies (2:26f., 11:6). To be a king meant to wield power sufficient to overcome enemies. Jesus had given such power to every believer. In my judgment, this third option is the most likely meaning of 1:5; but the independent student will survey the evidence and draw his own conclusions.

"*He loves us.*" One motif in John's thinking is this: a community is the kingdom of that Lord to whom it gives glory and dominion. To say that *the woman* of Ch. 17 has dominion over the kings of the earth is the same as saying that those kings have given authority and power to her (17:2, 12-14, 17, 18). To say that Christ has made us a kingdom is to point to that transfer of power which has been actualized in singing the doxology: "to him be glory and power." The king's power extends wherever he shares that power with his people. Citizens and their rulers share in the same royal realm. This is the measure of the strategic importance of the doxology as sung by the Asian churches. Why are they impelled to sing it? Three answers are given: because of what Christ is doing, what he has done, and what he is about to do.

What Christ is now doing is summarized by the simple phrase, *he loves us.* The actuality of this love was, of course, very far from obvious. Could John think of the conditions of his imprisonment as signs of that love? He did so. Could he speak of the violent persecution of the Asian churches (2:3) as an expression of their king's love? Yes, he viewed the camp of the saints, laid under siege by Satan, as the beloved city (20:9). The power of Christ's love was by no means visible. Enemies of the Church could not recognize it as love; but they would some day be brought to the point of acknowledging it. Such an amazing reversal of their former convictions would be a major component of their punishment (3:9). Because Christ's real, present, and powerful love constituted an ultimate truth, the measure of love on the part of his beloved slaves would always be the measure of their power over his (and their) enemies (12:11). To join in his love was, in fact, what gave authenticity to their testimony and made it possible for them to rejoice, even at the point of death (12:12). It is not surprising, therefore, that Christ's present verdict on his "slaves" is based on the testing of their love (2:4, 19). Their doxology, presented in suffering and in singing, was the instant response to the knowledge of being loved by him. The whole structure of John's thought and the adequacy of our interpretation rest upon this axiomatic conviction: the love of Jesus is the power by which he rules the kings of the earth. Can the interpreter actually accept that axiom?

What Christ has done is set forth in a double act: that of emancipation and of establishing a kingdom. Both are the expression of love's power and of replacing the worship of self by the worship of God. Events in the past have transformed the situation in the present, in as much as the balance of power has been shifted from Satan's Kingdom to Christ's.

"He has freed us from Sin's bondage by his death." Satan's Kingdom represents bondage to Sin, whereas Christ's (and God's) represents emancipation. The shift of men from one to the other bondage had been accomplished by Christ's blood, that is, by his dying for others. (see essay p. 229f.)

In the Johannine vocabulary, as in ours, to free or to release was the opposite of to imprison or to bind. It was the function of the Messianic Kingdom to release or to imprison Satan (20:3, 7). The Messiah closed or opened the door according to his will (1:18; 3:7). In fact, the images of the key and the door were more popular with John than the less dramatic phrase, forgiving their sins. Even more significant to him was the power of Jesus to change human destiny by the fact of his dying. Christ's regal robe, the mark of his kingship, was dipped in blood (19:13). By dying he had bought slaves from all human communities to serve as kings and priests (5:9). To be such a king required the wearing of robes washed in his blood (7:14), since only by such means (the blood of the Lamb as attested by the believer) could the Devil be overcome (12:11). The enemy who had shed Jesus' blood was the same enemy who had become drunk on the blood of his witnesses (16:6; 17:6; 18:24). What had been at stake, therefore, in the dying of Jesus was still at stake in the dying of his followers: the balance of power in the warfare between God and the Devil. Emancipation from sins had become the decisive battle in that war. For a congregation to participate in that battle on the side of Christ's love was to become Christ's army, his Kingdom, his priesthood (19:14-19). All this was implied when the congregation sang the doxology or joined in the Amen to that doxology, for in doing so the congregation was declaring its position in the war.

"*There! He is coming.*" What Christ will do is summed up in this staccato exclamation. We have already noted that in its form this sentence reflects the liturgical practice of the churches. It belongs within the context of that intimate dialog between God and men which is the substance of worship. The introductory word "*There*" (*idou*) is always used in this book to signal a special divine intervention. The speaker is either God (21:3, 5) or Christ (1:18; 2:10, 22; 3:8, 9, 20; 16:15; 22:7, 12) or the angel (5:5), or the prophet speaking in the Spirit and calling attention to his vision of heaven (4:1, 2; 6:2, 5, 8; 7:9). On most occasions this dialog deals with what is about to happen, with how God is enabling men to perceive a different prospect. So, too, the concluding ejaculations "*I vouch for it*" (*nai*) and "*Amen*" are native to the liturgical responses by the various partners in that dialog.

Who, then, is speaking here? If the prophet is speaking, the concluding testimony (*nai*) can be assigned to God or Christ. If God is speaking, that signature can be assigned to the prophet.

Why does this promise follow the doxology of vs. 5b, 6? The sequence may have been suggested by the need to show how for Christ, as for God, the present and the past must be completed by his future coming as Lord of all (see vs. 4). The sequence may have been suggested by the congregational use of the doxology: after the church gives its glory to Christ, it listens for God's promise and awaits his vindication. The sequence may be needed to complete the logic of the preceding affirmations. Has Christ conquered earth's kings? Has his death emancipated his priests? If so, his enemies, those who attack him, do not as yet admit his victory. But they will do so; the prophet and the worshipping congregation are summoned by divine command to see it now. Christ's victory is "the guarantee that others will pass with him through death to Kingship" (G. B. Caird, 17). Christian worship is the celebration of that victory by the coming Lord. (Note how the coming of Christ is linked to the coming of God in verses 4 and 8). There will be no limit to the scope of that victory, for it will become visible to every eye, every enemy, every tribe.

So audacious a promise could be nothing more than a feeble compensation, a gigantic example of wishful thinking, if it were not supported by more than dreams. This promise therefore bears the signature, the *Amen*, not only of the prophet and the congregation (see 1:6; 7:12; 19:4), but also of Christ (16:15; 22:7, 12) and of God.

"This is what God the Lord says." This most decisive signature is provided by God speaking in the first person. (vs. 8) He is the Last, the Omega, the coming one, whose presence is the presence of the Lord of all times and seasons. "All times past and future are embraced in his eternal present" (G. B. Caird, 16). He is the only one to whom the epithet *All-powerful* rightly belongs (4:8; 11:17; 15:3; 16:7, 14; 19:6, 15; 21:22). He exercises all power over other powers, including all those lesser powers who form their own pyramids of authority, and who parade their power by striking Jesus (1:7) and by exterminating his witnesses. Does Sin or Death have final dominion (vs. 5, 6)? God himself says No. The whole of the letter, to which this segment of Christian worship is the salutation, spells out that answer.

The student should not too hastily adopt John's position. And why not? Because to do so would be to separate himself from John's first readers. The modern student's acceptance would be based in part upon the fact that this book has become Scripture, with all the subtle prestige accompanying that status. The first readers did not have this dubious benefit. The student's favorable reaction would probably be based upon underestimating the massive weight of the contrary evidence: the manifest power of earthly, historical forces. The first readers could not so readily ignore that weight. The student who from the outset fully agrees with John has no need to read the rest of the letter. It was because the first readers did not fully agree with John's salutation, in all its implications for daily decisions, that John was impelled to write the whole of the letter. A measure of honest doubt, therefore, is an essential bond between the modern reader and his ancient counterpart.

For Further Study

1. THE PROBLEM OF AUTHORSHIP. The range of current attitudes may be seen in the following: W. Kümmel, 329-331; R. H. Charles, xxvii-lv; I. T. Beckwith, 343-393; E. Stauffer, 39-43; H. B. Swete, clxxiv-clxxxv; E. Allo, clxxxviii-ccxxi; A. Feuillet, 81-91; J. Behm, 5; A. Wikenhauser, *ad loc.*; A. Loisy, 37-54; J. N. Sanders, NTS 9(1963), 75-85; C. Brütsch, 248-256; F. M. Braun, *Jean le Théologien*, 301-395.

2. THE SITUATION OF THE CHURCH IN ASIA. *Primary sources:* 1 Cor. 16:19; 2 Cor. 4:8; Col; Eph; Phm; 2 Tim. 1:15; Acts 2:9; 6:9; 16:6; 19:1-20; 21:27; 24:19; I Peter 1:2; Ignatius; Polycarp; Letters of Pliny to Trajan X.96; Martyrdom of Polycarp. *Secondary sources:* J. Weiss, *History of Primitive Christianity*, II, 774-817; B. H. Streeter, *Primitive Church*, 101-141; S. J. Case, 1-56; W. Frend, *Martyrdom and Persecution in the Early Church*, Ch. 1-3; H. B. Swete, lxvi-xcviii; M. Rissi, ThZ 13 (1957) 241-259; W. Ramsay, *Letters to the Seven Churches in Asia*, 93-184; E. Stauffer, 147-191; R. Schütz, *Die Offenbarung des Johannes und Kaiser Domitian;* B. Newman, NTS 10 (1963-64) 133-139; D. Magie, *Roman Rule in Asia Minor* I, ch. 21-25; A. H. M. Jones, *Cities of the Eastern Roman Provinces*, Ch. 2; A. Satake, *Die Gemeindeordnung in der Johannesapokalypse;* S. E. Johnson, JBL 77 (1958), 1-17; F. M. Braun, *op. cit.*, 331-355.

THE SETTING OF THE PROPHETIC VISIONS (1:9-11)

1:9 I am John, your brother and full-partner with you in Jesus'
agony, in his royal power, and in his loyal endurance. I was on
Patmos Island because of God's saving purpose as confirmed by
10 Jesus. It was the Lord's Day when the Spirit came upon me.
Behind me I heard a majestic voice like a trumpet calling:
11   "Write what you see in a scroll.
Send it to the seven congregations:
Ephesus, Smyrna, Pergamum, Thyatira, Sardis,
Philadelphia, Laodicea."

Literary Analysis

"This book is written for those who have eyes to see; and for
a generation whose mental eye has been starved of imagery it
is in some ways the most important book in the New Testament"
(G. B. Caird, 13). With the latter part of Caird's observation
we must agree. Ours is a generation whose mental eye has been
starved. This is why one recent commentary has been entitled
"A Rebirth of Images." Prof. Farrer was convinced that, apart
from such a rebirth, the modern reader could never grasp John's
message. Another title, "On Seeing the Invisible" (D. T. Niles),
reflects a similar conviction. But should we agree with Caird
when he asserts that Revelation was written for readers "with
eyes to see"? Not wholly. Otherwise those early readers would
not have needed a prophet. A prophet spoke to Christians who
did not see fully or compellingly the invisible operation of God's
design. In every age men's eyes find difficulty in seeing the invisible, the heavenly realm where all events have their origin and
whence they derive their significance. The prophet serves as the
eyes of his congregation to help them see. Moreover, this book
does not rely on only one of the senses. The prophet hears ominous sounds (vs. 10), tastes both the bitter and the sweet (ch.
10), smells the most awful stench and smoke, and is in touch
with both repulsive and attractive animals. His encounter through
the Spirit with the heavenly realms (as inaudible and intangible
as they are invisible) engages all five senses, with any sixth or
seventh sense as well. The mysteries of God involve man as a
whole in his intricate involvement with his world as a whole.

   In literary terms, however, we find in 1:9 the beginning of a
third introduction which gives a single setting for all the prophetic visions that are to follow. John devises this setting with
considerable artistry. With amazing succinctness he outlines the
essentials of the situation:

> his own identity, a name found only in each of the three introduc-
> tions and at the conclusion of the visions (22:8),

his own kinship to his readers,
the place where the visions took place, and why he was there,
the time, linked both to the readers' time and to the Lord's time,
his prophetic credentials—"in the Spirit,"
the form required—a book,
the divinely chosen destination.

Each of these is essential to his literary purpose. Each is also essential to grasping the thought and message, not only of the book as a whole, but of each vision in the book.

Let us note how cleverly John telescopes the introduction of the visions into the salutation of his letter. The transition is so smooth that it almost hides the shift in perspective. The letter begins with John speaking, in the first person, to the Asian churches, in the second person (1:4). So, too, does the vision-book. But when (in vs. 10) the Spirit takes over the stage directions, another dialog becomes primary. Now heavenly voices speak to John and he replies to them. The Asian churches are not forgotten, but they become a third-person reality: "Write in a book . . . and send to *them*." John does not break off his conversation with those churches, for he continues to report to them what happened. "I turned . . . I saw," etc. Yet this reportage is now under the tutelage of the heavenly voices with whom John carries on a genuine two-sided colloquy. This colloquy fits so naturally within the continuing report to the churches that the reader may overlook the dexterity in literary art which is required.

Even more remarkable is the way in which the long sequence of visions preserves, with great though not unbroken consistency, the author's stance. He carries on a rapidly shifting dialog with various heavenly spokesmen within the context of a book addressed by John, at the command of those spokesmen, to the churches (1:11). This book, in turn, is the substance of a letter addressed to the churches by the prophet in his own name. This letter is then edited and published as a book under the title of "The Revelation of Jesus Christ." Such an intricate design must have been devised by the author before he began his composition.

The student can detect the complexity of construction by following closely the shifts in identity of the speakers and hearers. In the introduction to the book (1:1-3), all the characters appear in the third person, with the speaker hiding himself. In the salutation to the letter John addresses the readers in the second person (1:4), an address that is completed in the last sentence of the book (22:21). Here statements about God are in the third person. But since the letter will be read to a congregation gathered in worship, the familiar doxology to Christ is given by the prophet and congregation together (the *us* of vs. 5, 6) with either or both joining in the Amen. This leads to a promise, again shaped by liturgical practice, a promise vouched for by the prophet, by the Spirit, by the congregation, and by God, the whole salutation ending with God's word of validation addressed to the churches, as it has begun with God's grace and peace.

John then returned to direct conversation with the churches (1:9) in order to locate within that conversation the whole report on his visions which the trumpet commanded (1:11). In the command to John the churches are now spoken of in the third person and, for the first time, they are named. Only with 22:8 does the author return to the kind of discourse expressed in 1:9 . . . "I am John, who heard and saw these things." In thus speaking to the churches John gives his signature to the book of visions and completes the tapestry he had been weaving: a series of visions, written down as a book, sent as a book within a letter which would be read as a prophetic message during worship on the Lord's Day, and which would be published as a book to be read by other churches at other times.

One inference from this analysis must not be overlooked. Everything mentioned in the setting of the visions was designed to apply to all of the visions. For instance, all and not only the first (1:12-3:22) are intended for the seven churches. All are presented in the name of John, their partner in the sufferings incumbent on discipleship and in the type of confirmation required of them by the confirmatory action of Jesus (1:9). Unless the interpretation of each vision is kept relevant to this carefully defined setting, it is bound to distort John's intention.

For Reflection and Discussion

If we were writing such an introduction as this, we would
no doubt see the need for giving much the same data—the
author, the time, the place, the audience. But it is not so clear
that we would include other items. Why did John include them?
Especially may we ask this question of two items: the reason
for John's presence on Patmos and the character of his partnership (*koinonia*) with his readers. John's accent appears to fall
upon these items. Why was he writing from Patmos? Because
this was the site of a penal colony in which he had been imprisoned because of his vocation. He had been loyal to the message
of God by giving his testimony to Jesus. Therefore, he believed
that God's design, as attested by Jesus, genuinely was at stake
in his own captivity.

Furthermore, the second item indicates that the prophet was
not alone in this predicament. He and his readers were partners
with one another and with Jesus in three respects. These we have
translated agony (*thlipsis*), royal power (*basileia*), and loyal
endurance (*hupomone*). Jesus had confirmed God's purpose in
such a way that those who joined in that confirmation were made
sharers in these three. These three words are strategic clues to
John's vocabulary and vocation; the student must therefore give
them close scrutiny. Each is significant, as is also their sequence.

The agony—other possible translations are *ordeal* (Caird),
distress (Moffatt), *tribulation* (RSV), and *suffering* (NEB)—
surely included such imprisonment as John's, social ostracism,
slander, poverty, economic discrimination, hostility—both non-
violent and violent—from synagogue, market-place, and police,
disruption of the churches by false prophets, and the constant
threat of death from mob violence or judicial action. To the
prophet this agony was a genuine continuation of Jesus' own
passion. We would, in fact, be justified in translating the phrase
as "full partners in Jesus' passion."

Such partnership was inseparable from a full share in Jesus'
kingdom. John and his readers shared in his royal power (sov-

ereignty, kingship, dominion, etc.). The agony was a result of
the exercise of that power; it became the place where that power
could be verified. Such power creates resistance, but it vindicates
itself by overcoming that very resistance. To be a king is to win
a victory over lesser powers. To share in that kingdom is to share
in that agony and victory. Christ's royal power penetrates that
community which exercises it; it makes that community a kingdom (cp. 1:5, 6). But the sign of victory remains hidden, for
the "kings of the earth" jealously guard their hegemony over the
"dwellers of the earth" (see the essays on kingship and earth-
dwellers). The victory of the disciple remained as hidden as did
the victory of Good Friday.

There was, however, a visible proof of that power: loyal
endurance—*hupomone* can also be translated by patience, steadfastness (Torrey), patient endurance (RSV). Endurance is "the
spiritual alchemy which transmutes suffering into royal dignity"
(R. H. Charles). Endurance connoted not only the stubborn
refusal to give in under fire, but also the alert watchfulness
against deception, the eagerness to make one's testimony credible
to the enemies, the keen discernment of the inner roots of fear
and anxiety, the readiness to forgive, and the joy discovered
within the vortex of pain. Much more than sheer physical stamina
was indicated; a person and a congregation could share in the
stamina of Jesus only by exemplifying that strength which he
demonstrated on the *via dolorosa*. Only thus could his testimony
under fire be confirmed by their testimony to him. Such were
the bonds which bound John to his readers and bound them all
to Jesus.

There is a significant progression in the three items. The
agony was occasioned in large part by external factors, such as
the resistance of social groups to the demands of Christ. It had
an objective visibility. Christians were visible in that society in
the same way that beggars are visible in an exclusive club, or as
Negroes at a segregated church. The *royal power* to accept the
agony and to transmute it into victory was external to the individual Christian and yet wholly invisible, since the source of

this power was "the saving purpose of God as confirmed by Jesus." Yet it was the action of this power which could alone explain the conflict. *Loyal endurance* is an actuality of a somewhat different order. It is both invisible and subjective. The conflict with human antagonists has become internalized. To remain loyal requires a continual wrestling between loyalty to Christ and the pressure of inner doubts and seductions. Over and over again the believer must decide, must choose. External sufferings must now be seen as temptation and trial (*peirasmos*); the royal power has become likewise internalized; the disciple must overcome that trial by willing one thing and serving one master. *Loyal endurance* is therefore the major ethical thrust in John's book, the divinely intended result of the juncture of *agony* and *royal power*. Royal power (the omnipotence of God active in the love of Christ and made available through the love of his slaves) has produced an ordeal comparable to the passion. That power does not crush external opposition, but uses that opposition to test and to purge the loyalty of the slaves. They can become kings by trusting in Christ's endurance. The omnipotence of God is thus channeled into their human strength to endure all things (compare the demand for endurance in Revelation with I Cor. 13:7). Loyal endurance becomes the continuing mode of verifying both his kingship and theirs.

Here, again, the student must beware an over-hasty sentimental acceptance of the assumptions on which John's thought rested. To him loyal endurance required absolute trust in several interdependent convictions: (1) Christ's death had disclosed that God's omnipotence is nothing but "the power of invincible love" (Caird). (2) This omnipotence could be manifested only in conflict with opposing power-structures in society. (3) As king, Jesus required every disciple and every congregation to share willingly in this conflict, a conflict in which "to believe" actually meant "to be loyal to death." (4) His royal power was therefore accessible only to those who "pass with him through death to kingship" (Caird). John's experience as a prisoner enabled him to understand what God was about to do through him and his brothers in Asia. As a prophet he was charged to convey that understanding to them.

Can the modern reader actually accept those axioms and begin to view his own situation as the place for verifying them? Is such acceptance really a live option to him? Even if he can force his mind to adopt them, do they become authentically illustrated by his own existence? Does the kind of agony of which John speaks stand as an inescapable prerequisite for understanding his prophecy and for evaluating its truth? If so, will not that understanding be closed to an affluent church in an affluent society? All these are substantive questions. They are not offered for rhetorical effect or to excite pious sentiments. In them we dig through to the bedrock issues in reading any part of John's book, and more important, in understanding any paragraph in the text of human life.

For Further Study:

LITURGICAL SETTING. According to John, the visions were occasioned by the Spirit's activity on the Lord's Day (1:10), and the book was designed to be read at meetings of the congregations (1:3). From the very first, therefore, we need to visualize a liturgical setting for John's work. The following readings will be helpful:

M. H. Shepherd, *The Paschal Liturgy and the Apocalypse;* Feuillet, 71-74; L. Mowry, JBL, LXXI (1952), 75-84; O. Piper, CH, XX (1951), 10-22; G. Delling, NovT, III (1959), 107-137; S. Laeuchli, ThZ, XVI (1960), 359-378; J. Comblin, ETL, XXIX (1953), 5-40; H. Schlier, ALW, 6 (1959), 43-56; T. F. Torrance, VC, XI (1957), 28-40; P. Carrington, 378-394; D. T. Niles, 99-115; M. J. Congar, *Mystery of the Temple,* 204-235; J. Horst, *Proskunein,* 252-291; F. J. Dölger, *Sol Salutis;* R. P. Martin, *Carmen Christi,* 1-24.

1. The Promise of Victory (1:9-3:22)

We now begin our analysis of the first major vision. Or rather, we continue it, since we have already studied 1:9-11 as John's introduction both to this vision and to all the subsequent visions. Beginning with verse twelve, John describes what he saw and heard. He saw a figure like a man; he heard that figure identify himself and then issue special commands. The writing of the seven letters is in obedience to those commands. It would be better not to separate a study of the letters from a study of their "author," yet we have chosen to do so for reasons which should become apparent.

A. THE SPEAKER (1:12-20)

1:12 **When I turned to see what voice was speaking to me,**	
I saw seven gold candelabra,	
13 **and in the center a figure like a man:**	
a robe came down to his feet	*Dan. 10:5;*
a gold scarf encircled his shoulders	*Eze. 9:2, 11*
14 **his head and hair were white as**	*Dan. 10:5*
snow, or as wool	*Dan. 7:9; 10:6*
his eyes flashed like flames of fire	*Dan. 7:9; 10:6*
15 **his legs like burnished bronze, fired**	*Dan. 10:6*
in a furnace	
his voice had the sound of rushing	*Dan. 10:6;*
rivers	*Eze. 1:24; 43:2*
16 **in his right hand he held seven stars**	
from his mouth came a double-edged	
sword, razor-sharp	
his face blazed like the sun in full	*Dan. 10:6*
strength	

27

The Prophet John and Christ

17 *And when I saw him, I fell like a corpse at his feet. But*
touching me with his right hand, he said:
> *"Have no fear!*
> *I am the First and the Last, the Living One.*
18 *I became a corpse, but look—I am alive forever.*
> *I now hold the keys to Death and to Hades.*

19 *Write down what you have seen, things present and things*
> *to come.*
20 *You saw seven stars in my right hand*
> *and seven gold candelabra*
>> *this is the secret:*
> *those seven stars are angels of the seven congregations;*
> *those seven candelabra are the seven congregations.*

Literary Analysis

Several observations may help the student view the forest
before his gaze becomes fixed on the trees.

1. With 1:12 John begins the report of a vision which was
designed to be a single unit extending through chapter 3. One
sign of this is the fact that the quotation marks which open in
1:17 are not closed until 3:22. This message as a whole is addressed by the Christ-figure to the prophet. Within this continuing quotation there are seven inner quotations addressed to
the separate congregations (the RSV punctuation is very accurate).

2. The setting (1:12-20) covers all seven letters and can be
divided into two sections: the prophet's description of the speaker
(12-16), and the speaker's address to the prophet. In the latter,
Christ identifies himself (17, 18), gives a command (19), and
explains the two symbols which recur in all of the following
letters (20).

3. In constructing his description of the speaking Christ (12-
16), the prophet draws almost exclusively on vivid phrases from
the Old Testament which had become standard ways to suggest

the awesome glory and power of God. (To point this out we have
encumbered the translation with a limited set of cross-references.) He also collects phrases which he will use separately in
the letters as well as later in the book. This description thus
becomes something of an inventory of his repertoire of metaphors.
This kind of picture-language was his way of speaking of the
major attributes of God and therefore of God's Anointed.

4. In the brief verses of self-identification (17, 18), the
speaker appeals, in the most concise way possible, to the Gospel
story, which centered in the passion: "I died." This death and its
triumph disclosed Christ's primal and final status. It guaranteed
his living presence in all times and places. It changed the power-
structure decisively, since Death and Hades had now come under
his control. Few verses could make clearer the intention of John
in the entire book: to proclaim how the lordship of Christ over
every situation had made transparent for the prophet the entire
enigma of human existence. The speaker offered acceptable credentials for dictating messages to the seven congregations.
However, before dictating, he explained the two mysteries which
are directly involved in those letters, since in them all Christ (17,
18) addresses through John (19) the seven angels (stars) of
the seven congregations (candelabra). The *dramatis personae*
are thus introduced in the order of their appearance.

For Reflection and Discussion

Literary analysis has shown that the center of gravity in this
section is located in the Christ-figure, presented first in John's
description and then in self-identification. Therefore, we may
ask at this point what attributes of divinity seemed most apt.
For example, we may substitute for the white hair the terms:
venerable age, dignity, purity, holiness. Or we may say that the
flashing eyes express divine omniscience. There is genuine danger
of distortion, however, in turning picture-language into more
abstract concepts.

Dangers of one sort are indicated by a modern literary critic:

"What do these intellectuals do with literature? Why, they talk about it: they treasure it; they make careers of it; they become an elite through it. . . . It is their material, their capital . . . they project a higher, more valuable mental realm, a realm of dazzling intellectuality. . . . They redescribe everything downward . . . usually making it less accessible. For feeling or response, they substitute acts of comprehension" (Saul Bellow, New York *Times*, July 10, 1966). Critics usually do this under the illusion that success in comprehension is more noble than those subtle responses which the author felt and intended.

Dangers of another sort may be seen in the famous block prints of Revelation made by A. Dürer, one of which is shown at the opening of this section. This is one of fifteen prints which were produced between 1495 and 1498 by the artist before he was twenty-seven years old. With great care for detail, Dürer presents in this picture the Christ whom John describes. The face literally shines with rays like the sun, the hand holds seven stars, and the sword is emerging from the mouth. Yet Dürer's effort to visualize a single figure with all the details mentioned by the prophet adds up to a bizarre ensemble indeed. One must say that, when John's description is turned into a visual replica, it shatters into fragments. The picture conveys neither the prophet's feelings nor his concerns. We can safely assert that John did not intend that his readers try to transfer his words into a single visual collage. This was the risen Lord, whom he and they worshiped. The medley of scriptural symbols had functions other than those fulfilled by this kind of realism.

What are these other functions? We have already suggested them. One is to underscore the full degree to which Christ is to be understood as the Son of God. For John, as for other New Testament authors, sonship is basically that kinship which is established by unity of purpose and work. Jesus is one with God in wisdom, power, steadfastness, and penetrating vision.

Another function becomes apparent when we trace the roots of this symbolic language. John is accenting the extent to which the Speaker in the vision is himself the fulfilment of the Law

and the Prophets. The one who addresses the churches is the
Messiah in whom God's promises to Israel are being accomplished. Christ is God's way of saying *Amen* to the work of Isaiah,
Jeremiah, Ezekiel, and Daniel, and to the hopes embodied in
their messages.

Still a third function emerges when we ask why John placed
his picture of Jesus in immediate conjunction with Jesus' self-
identification. Here the passion story is given as the essential
clue: "I died and came alive." The vision as a whole articulates
the essential interdependence of the eternal (13-16) and the
temporal (17-18), the universal and the particular. Accordingly,
the very specific event of Jesus' death determines the kind of
power attributed to the two-edged sword which issues from his
mouth. It is the cross which enables the Messiah to discriminate
between good and evil. It is the message of the cross which pre-
cipitates final judgment by the Messiah. Do his eyes flash like
fire? This is to suggest how perceptive and penetrating is the
power of his Passion. Does he stand immovable? This is to suggest the steadfast strength of the Crucified. The presence of the
Crucified is perceived to be the awesome and numinous presence
of God himself. The vision illustrates far more than a prophet's
hypersensitive aesthetic imagination. It illustrates a kind of depth-
analysis which perceives invisible implications of the cross within
the contemporary textures of human relations. His language
adroitly introduces those implications into the consciousness and
the sub-consciousness of his readers, seeking to call forth corrobo-
rating echoes from their own earlier responses to "the hound of
heaven." For them as for him, language concerning God had
developed an idiom which had been shaped by God's message
to his people in the Scriptures and in the Gospel story.

The foregoing series of reflections poses a problem worthy
of discussion; how can a modern reader become acquainted with
the idiom of John in a way sufficiently honest to enable meanings
to cross the crevasse between his native land and ours? Does the
Church's experience of the redemptive presence of Christ provide
a sufficiently firm bridge? If it does, should we seek to communi-
cate John's message in our own modern idiom in order to preserve

mental integrity, or should we preserve John's alien idiom and seek to shape our minds by it? Or is this the wrong way of stating the option? Should we perhaps ask whether our own language about Christ manages to serve the functions which John's language served?

For Further Study
JOHN'S VIEW OF CHRIST

1. A catalog of Christological pictures and titles.

Son of man	*the true witness*	*the first born of the*
Son of God	*the faithful witness*	*dead*
Logos	*the Amen*	*the beginning of*
Lion of Judah	*the holy one*	*God's creation*
Lamb	*the true one*	*a male child*
Root of David	*the morning star*	*the Messiah*
Offspring of David	*the living one*	*the coming one*
King of kings	*the Bridegroom*	*one worthy to*
Lord of lords	*the first and the last*	*receive:*
Shepherd	*the beginning and the end*	*glory,*
	the A and the Z	*power,*
		honor,
		praise,
		authority,
		blessing,
		wealth,
		wisdom.

2. Christ is the subject of the following verbs: know, choose, send, give, conquer, fight, walk, sit, wield, search, disclose, hold, love, create, rule, judge, free, come, call, command, confess, redeem, die, guide, travel, comfort.

3. The roles of Christ are intimated by the following symbols: white clothes, sword, keys, horse, book, stars, throne, rod, crown, lampstand, altar, name, manna, stone, fire, temple, city, horns, eyes, angels, spirits, blood, cup, bowl, thief, mouth, feet, wedding-feast, tree of life.

4. Some treatments of John's Christology: T. Holtz, *Die*

Christologie der Apok. des Johannes; J. Comblin, *Le Christ dans l'Apocalypse;* R. Gutzwiller, *Herr der Herrscher;* F. Büchsel, *Die Christologie des Offenbarung;* I. T. Beckwith, 310-317; R. H. Charles, I, cix-cxv; R. Leivestad, *Christ the Conqueror,* 212-238; E. Stauffer, 103-151; R. L. Thomas, *Bib. Sac.,* 122 (1965) 241-247; H. Zimmermann in *Unio Christianorum,* 179-197; G. B. Caird, 289-301; H. M. Feret, 54-81; van der Waal, 19-54; H. Tribble, RE 40 (1943) 167-176; F. Durrwell, *The Resurrection,* 146f., 188f.; A. Läpple, 201-208. Essential to advanced study is the analysis of John's use of each of the "messianic" passages in Scripture. A good starting point for this study is the volume by E. Hühn, or A. Schlatter, 32-56, or A. Läpple, 22-36.

B. THE LETTERS (2:1-3:22)

Let me explain briefly the procedures I have adopted for the study of the letters. First comes a consecutive translation of the letters, in a format which suggests the similarities of structure, with letters placed in the right hand margin to locate these similarities. Then, in the analysis, I will cut across the lines between the letters and examine all seven examples of each structural element, thus enabling each student to see a cross-section of the message to all seven churches. We do not attempt a detailed description of the distinctive features of the separate letters, but we should catch clearer glimpses of the way in which the prophet's mind and pen operated as he delivered a message which, although addressed to seven different congregations, was designed for them all to read, as well as to obey.

2:1   *"Take down this letter for the angel of the congre-*   *a*
       gation in Ephesus:

       'This is dictated by the One who with his right   *b 1:12, 16*
       hand controls the seven stars, who walks among the
       seven gold candelabra:

2   *I know what you have accomplished, your*   c
toil and your loyal endurance. I know you did
not tolerate evil doers, but put to the test
those self-styled apostles and found them to be
3   *liars, as indeed they are. You suffered because*
of me, yet you endured and did not grow
weary.

4   *But this is what I am counting against you:*   d
You have forsaken your first devotion.

5   *Remember the height from which you have*   e
fallen. Repent.
Accomplish again what you did at first.
If you do not repent, I will come to you and
will shift your candelabra from its place.
6   *(You have this to your credit: You hate the*
deeds of the Nicolaitans, which I also hate.)

7   *Let everyone who can hear listen to what the*   f
Spirit is telling the congregations.
I will give to the victor food from the Tree of   g
Life in God's Paradise.' "

8   *"Take down this letter for the angel of the congre-*   a
gation in Smyrna:

'This is dictated by the First and the Last, who was   b 1:17, 18
killed and came alive:
9   *I know your agony and your poverty (in reality,*   c
you are wealthy!) I know the blasphemy of
those self-styled Jews, who are not Jews but
Satan's own synagogue.

10   *Do not fear what you will soon suffer. Look!*   e
The Devil, to put you to the test, is about to

throw some of you into prison, where the
agony will last ten days. Be loyal to death, and
I will give life to you as a crown.

11   *Let everyone who can hear listen to what the*   *f*
Spirit is telling the congregations.
The victor will not be injured by the second   *g*
death.' "

12   *"Take down this letter for the angel of the congre-*   *a*
gation in Pergamum:

'This is dictated by the One who wields the double-   *b 1:16*
edged sword, razor-sharp:
13   *I know that you dwell where Satan has his*   *c*
throne, and yet you remained loyal to me and
did not spurn my own loyalty, even at the time
when Antipas, who faithfully confirmed my
work, was killed there among you, where Satan
dwells.

14   *Yet I am counting a few things against you.*   *d*
Some of you adhere to Balaam's teaching, who
persuaded Balak to set a stumbling-block
before the sons of Israel, leading them into
15   *idolatry and fornication. Some of you adhere*
also to the Nicolaitan teaching.

16   *Repent. If you do not, I will come to you soon*   *e*
and I will fight against them with the sword of
my mouth.

17   *Let everyone who can hear listen to what the*   *f*
Spirit is telling the congregations.
I will give to the victor the bread of heaven,   *g*

*and a white amulet inscribed with a new
name, known to none but the recipient.' "*

18 *"Take down this letter for the angel of the congregation in* Thyatira: a

'This is dictated by the Son of God, whose eyes   b 1:15
*flash like flames of fire, whose legs are like burnished
bronze:*
19 *I know what you have accomplished: your*   c
*love, your faithfulness, your service and your
loyal endurance. Lately you have accomplished even more than before.*

20 *But this is what I am counting against you.*   d
*You tolerate that woman Jezebel, self-
advertised prophetess, who deceives my slaves
and persuades them to commit fornication*
21 *and idolatry. I have given her time to repent
of her fornication, but she will not.*

22 *Look! I am hurling her on to a couch. Those
who consort with her I am hurling into great
agony unless they repent of her deeds. Her*
23 *children I will smite with death. To each of
you I will give whatever your deeds merit. All
the congregations will learn that I am the One
who discerns the innermost secrets.*

24,25 *Until I come hold firm to what you have*   e
*achieved. I add no other obligation for you
Thyatirans who do not follow Jezebel's
teaching and who do not claim knowledge of
what they call Satan's secrets.*

26   To the victor who loyally continues my work   g
to the end,
I will give authority over the nations
just as I received it from my Father.

27   The victor will rule them with an
iron rod,
he will smash them like broken
dishes.

28   To the victor I will also give the dawn-
star.

29   Let everyone who can hear listen to what the   f
Spirit is telling the congregations.' "

3:1   "Take down this letter for the angel of the congre- a
gation in Sardis:

'This is dictated by the One who controls the seven   b 1:4, 16
spirits of God and the seven stars:
I know what you have accomplished. Men   c
think of you as alive, but actually you are   d
dead.

2   Wake up! Rouse what is about to die, those   e
deeds of yours which I have found unworthy
to offer to my God.

3   Remember what you have received and
heard. Hold fast to that and repent.

If you do not awaken, I will come like a
thief and you will be unable to know the
hour of my coming.

4   Among you in Sardis, however, are a few
who have not soiled their clothing. They will
walk with me in white, for they have proved
themselves worthy.

5   *So the victor will walk clothed in white.*   g
       Nor will I cross out his name from the book of
       life.
       I will vouch for him in the presence of my
       Father and his angels.
6   *Let everyone who can hear listen to what the*   f
           Spirit is telling the congregations.' "

7   "*Take down this letter for the angel of the con-*   a
       gregation in Philadelphia:

       '*This is dictated by the One who is holy and true,*   b 1:18
       who holds the key of David. No one can lock what
8   *he opens, or open what he locks. There! I have*
       opened to you a door which no one can close.
           I know what you have accomplished. Even in   c
           your weakness you held fast to my purpose
           and did not deny my name.
9,10   *Because you held fast to the purpose of my*
           own loyal endurance, I will bring members of
           Satan's synagogue, who falsely claim to be
           Jews, to worship at your feet and to admit my
           love for you. I will shield you from that trial
           which is soon to test the earth-dwellers
           throughout the world.

11   *I am coming soon. Hold fast! Let no one seize*   e
           your crown.

12   *I will set the victor up as a pillar in my God's*   g
               sanctuary; never again will he leave it.
           On him I will inscribe the name of my God,
               the name of my God's city,
               (the new Jerusalem which comes down
               from heaven, from my God)
               and my own new name.

13   Let everyone who can hear listen to what the   f
            Spirit is telling the congregations.' "

14   "Take down this letter for the angel of the congre-   a
        gation in Laodicea:

        'This is dictated by the Amen, the True and   b 1:5
        Faithful Guarantor, the Model of God's creative
        work:
15   I know what you have accomplished. You are   c
            neither hot nor cold, when you ought to be   d
16   one or the other. Because you are tepid,
            neither hot nor cold, I will spit you out.
17   Because you say "I am wealthy. I lack nothing."
            and do not see that you are miserable,
            pitiable, poor, blind, naked.

18   This is my advice to you: e
                    Buy from me gold which has been
                        refined by fire, so that you may
                        become wealthy.
                    Buy and wear white clothing,
                        to hide the disgrace of your nakedness.
                    Buy salve for your eyes
                        so that you can see.
19   I discipline and punish all whom I love. Be
            zealous. Repent.

20   Look! I have taken my stand at the door. I am
            knocking. To anyone who hears me calling
            and who opens the door, I will come in. I will
            dine with him; he will dine with me.

21   I will give to the victor a seat on my throne   g
            with me, just as by my victory I have taken a
            seat with my Father on his throne.

²²   *Let everyone who can hear listen to what the*   *1*
         Spirit is telling the congregations.' "

Analysis and Reflection

1. INSTRUCTIONS TO THE SCRIBE   All seven letters are introduced by an identical command, the only variation being in the names of the congregation (indicated by letter *a* in margin of translation). "Take down this letter for the angel of the congregation. . . ." The rhythmic repetition of this command suggests clearly that all the letters were constructed according to the same pattern and were designed to be read as a single unit. For this reason we shall analyze all seven, not *seriatim*, but in accordance with the formal structure of the entire series.

There is nothing especially noteworthy about the dictator's command to his scribe (John) except, perhaps, the address of each letter to the "angel" of a given congregation. What is the referent of this word? How does it affect the thought? There are various interpretations, among which it is difficult to choose with confidence. The Greek word *angelos* may connote simply a human messenger, one who is deputized by a person or a community to carry a message. It is thus used at times in both the Old Testament (Mal. 2:7) and the New Testament (Mark 1:2; Lk. 7:24; 9:52; James 2:25). On the basis of these analogies, the angels in our passage have been identified with the leaders, even the bishops, of the congregations (see Martin, *Seven Letters*, pp. 42f.). One difficulty with this choice is the fact that nowhere else in Revelation does John use the term angel in this sense. Moreover, the symbolic logic of this vision seems to require the device of preserving the heavenly setting for all the characters. The angels are inhabitants of the heavenly world where the whole action takes place. It would be somewhat incongruous to speak of the several bishops of the congregations as being held in Christ's right hand (1:16; 2:1) and as being linked so closely to the seven spirits of God (3:1). Moreover, if the angels simply meant bishops, what would the prophet gain by avoiding the latter term?

I believe something is added by the address to angels rather than to churches. It indicates the unity of the congregation, a unity which cannot be expressed in earthly formulas. It suggests that beneath and above the visible company is a hidden reality, which alone makes a church Christ's people. It intimates the reality of a prior ground for the church's existence, an invisible fountain from which it draws its strength. It preserves the conception of the church as an elect community, whose ontological or theological roots are more decisive than its sociological forms or historical continuities. In saying this, however, we should not suppose that the angel is a purely literary device, less real than the congregation. The angel is a means of communication between that mode of being where Christ can be seen and that mode of being where he cannot be seen. Apart from the need for communication between those two realms, the whole rationale of the vision would evaporate.

Each church has its heavenly counterpart in a lampstand. Each lampstand has a personal focus in an angel. Christ's message is addressed initially to that angel which represents the congregation in its heavenly mode of being; the angel thus becomes the personalized Christic substance of the life of that congregation. Two presuppositions underlie Christ's dialog with these angels: (1) his personal control and government of them and (2) their responsibility to him for the entire life of the congregations. The angel thus becomes an essential personal channel of communication between the transcendent purpose of Christ and the community entrusted with that purpose. All letters, in fact, assume the ultimate reality of that design and the inescapable collision between the design and its earthly execution. The student should give more attention to the dramatic functions assigned to the angels than to their pedigree and status. In doing so, he may be helped by recalling the liturgical setting in which these letters would first have been heard.

2. THE IDENTIFICATION AND CREDENTIALS OF THE SPEAKER
We have already studied the prophet's description of the Christ-figure and Christ's self-identification (1:9-20) and have noted

that the series of attributes in the seven letters are drawn from those summaries. It may be sufficient, therefore, to call attention here to the uniform structure of Christ's address to the seven congregations (indicated by *b* in the margins).

Without exception, the address begins with two Greek words: *tade legei* . . . . "These are the words of" or "Thus says the . . . ." Here we must recognize John's use of an old traditional formula. The Old Testament prophets had established this formula as the appropriate introduction for God's address to his people (compare Rev. 2, 3 with Amos 1, 2, where we also find similar items in a series). This conventional formula, simple and direct, would conjure up in a worshiping congregation the fear and trembling associated with standing before God and hearing his awesome words of judgment and warning. These and many other emotions native to worship would be encouraged by the seven diverse ways of describing the Lord who now addresses them (note the use of present tense throughout, which telescopes within the decisive *now* the pressure of Christ's demands and the congregations' responsibility to him).

"*This is dictated by* . . .

(Ephesus) "*The One who with his right hand controls the seven stars, who walks among the seven gold candelabra.* . . .

(Smyrna) *The First and the Last, who was killed and came alive.* . . .

(Pergamum) *The One who wields the double-edged sword, razor-sharp.* . . .

(Thyatira) *The Son of God whose eyes flash like flames of fire, whose legs are like burnished bronze.* . . .

(Sardis) *The One who controls the seven spirits of God and the seven stars.* . . .

(Philadelphia) *The One who is holy and true,*
who holds the key of David;
no one can lock what he opens
or open what he locks. . . .

(Laodicea)   *The Amen, the True and Faithful Guarantor, the Model of God's creative work. . . ."*

What may be observed concerning this group of self-identifications as a whole? The student may check the following answers to see if the texts support them.

All seven characterizations point to a single person—Jesus the Messiah. All presuppose the basic New Testament story of Jesus' earthly ministry, death, and exaltation (see especially Nos. 2, 7). In all of them Christ asserts an unlimited sovereignty and mastery. This mastery is in this setting a matter of an immediate claim to authority over each congregation. The words of Christ express his mysterious presence with each congregation as the constitutive element in its existence. In its response to Christ, each congregation determines its relation to the living God and therefore its ultimate destiny. The symbolic language which characterizes the speaking Christ is neither esoteric nor novel, but represents a familiar Christian vocabulary for speaking of God and his son, which would be readily understood by John's readers. The accent upon the ability of Christ to discern the true situation in the case of each congregation prepares the reader for the sevenfold assertion which follows: "I know what you have accomplished." Christ's knowledge of those whom he addresses is assumed to be perfect, far superior to their own self-knowledge.

Although we may discern certain common traits in these seven self-designations, we should also note that John adroitly selected for each of the seven letters an aspect of the Christ-figure which would be especially appropriate. The factor of imagistic correlation now takes precedence over verbal rhythm or repetition. Let me give several examples among many. In writing to the Ephesian congregation, the One who travels among the candelabra (2:1) can threaten, on traveling to Ephesus, to remove that candelabra from its place (2:5). In writing to a congregation where imprisonment and death impend, the convict who died and came alive can offer the crown of life to other executed criminals and can protect them from the second death (2:8, 10,

11). In dealing with the Pergamum congregation, divided by deceptive teachings, the bearer of the sword will conduct a war, using the sword to discriminate between the false (Nicolaitans) and the true (Antipas and his supporters) (2:12, 16).

Although the prophet thus brings variety into the address to the congregations, he leaves no doubt that all letters come from the same Author, and all the congregations are united "in heaven" around him. John's concern centers on the intimate invisible relationships between the Lord and the congregations; he assumes that these relationships are either betrayed or honored in the visible behavior of those congregations. When John proclaims Christ's control over the future, he does so in order that every congregation may become fully alive to the temptations and tasks of its day. The vision of Christ rules out any escape from the present into the future and requires total concentration on immediate responsibility.

3. THE SPEAKER'S KNOWLEDGE   Now we may collect those sections of the letters (marked with c in the margins) which present the Messiah's knowledge of the situation:
"I know what you have accomplished:

(Ephesus) *your toil and your loyal endurance. I know*
you did not tolerate evil-doers, but
put to the test those self-styled apostles, and found them
to be liars, as indeed they are. You suffered
because of me, yet you endured and did not grow
weary . . .
(Smyrna) *your agony and your poverty (in reality, you are*
wealthy!). I know the blasphemy of those self-called
Jews, who are not Jews but Satan's own synagogue. . . .
(Pergamum) *you dwell where Satan has his throne and yet you*
remained loyal to me and did not spurn my own loyalty,
even at the time when Antipas, who faithfully confirmed
my work, was killed there among you, where Satan
dwells . . .

(Thyatira)	*your love, your faithfulness, your service, and your loyal endurance. Lately you have accomplished even more than before . . .*
(Sardis)	*men think of you as alive, but actually you are dead. . . .*
(Philadelphia)	*even in your weakness you held fast to my purpose and did not deny my name . . .*
(Laodicea)	*you are neither hot nor cold, when you ought to be one or the other. Because you are tepid, neither hot nor cold, I will spit you out. Because you say 'I am wealthy, I lack nothing.' and do not see that you are miserable, pitiable, poor, blind and naked. . . ."*

Again the student should check the validity of the inferences which may be drawn from these seven statements. He should modify them or supplement them according to his own observations. He should then reflect on what kind of communication is being carried on and what kinds of tests should be applied to determine the credibility of that communication.

The unbroken rhythm of the introductory phrase "I know" stresses above all Christ's unlimited knowledge of the true state of every congregation. In this capacity he shares fully the omniscience of God "from whom no secret is hid." It is assumed that the criteria by which each congregation is judged have already been established by the Speaker. The congregation has already accepted the validity of those criteria by its initial commitment to this Speaker, its first devotion, its earlier deeds of obedience.

His works, as endorsed by the congregation, have become a norm for its own life. His passion has made inescapable for it the acceptance of weakness, poverty, and agony. The ordeals faced by the congregations have been produced by their loyalty to him, and therefore constitute a test of that loyalty. Only by standing this test can they verify his own work and words. His judgments of them are assumed to be an accurate index of their faithfulness to him. His disclosure of the state of the congregation is intrinsic rather than extrinsic to their life as his slaves. His knowledge of their loyalty under fire is far more reliable than their own self-knowledge; in fact, his judgments of them contradict their self-judgments. Self-approval and self-justification are therefore signs of self-deception, which he seeks to demolish.

His enemy, who is the same enemy as theirs, is the hidden source of self-deception. He is Satan, the false claimant to authority, the father of lies. The objectives of Satan are always incompatible with those of Christ. Both lords seek to realize their objectives within and through the conscience of the same congregation. Satan seeks to undermine loyalty to Christ by means of deceit; Christ seeks to strengthen that loyalty by uncovering the deceit.

The basis for Christ's knowledge and judgment of each congregation is furnished by setting the entire story of the congregation's life over against the entire story of Jesus' life; his fidelity in confirming God's saving work functions as the criterion by which he measures their confirmation of that work. His message to the angel of each congregation articulates the degree of conformity to that pattern. He fully recognizes the particularities in the story of each separate congregation, yet he also discloses the universal elements which are embodied in each separate story. Each letter thus helps to inform the conscience of a particular congregation with the distinctiveness of its immediate duties. At the same time, it helps to reinforce solidarity with the entire company of Christ's followers. Every congregation must therefore take seriously what Christ has against other congregations as well as what he has against itself. Each ear must listen to what the Spirit is telling *all* the congregations (John employs this plural in all seven letters).

4. THE SPEAKER'S VERDICT The formulas at the beginning of the several letters are so similar that they can be easily recovered. So, too, there is little deviation in the ending of the letters: "Let everyone who can hear," "I will give to the victor." But the formulas at the center of each letter are more varied and accordingly more difficult to detect. This combination of using and abusing set formulas is often significant. Both repetition and deviation are ways of accenting certain things in the message. So, in this case, the deviation from the use of the same phrases

focuses attention on the varieties of situation. This deviation preserves the distinctive relation of Christ to each congregation. Yet the values of repetition are not wholly lost; for in each letter after the formula "I know what you have accomplished" and before the formula "Let every one who can hear," the Speaker normally deals with two matters—his discernment of the failures of the congregation (we have indicated this structural element by the letter *d*), and the directives issued to cope with these failures (we have indicated these directives by the letter *e*). In what follows we have tried to indicate both the major deviations and the correlation between the situation and the commands.

"But this is what I am counting against you:

(Ephesus)	*You have forsaken your first devotion. . . .*
(Smyrna)	*(Nothing is entered against this congregation.)*
(Pergamum)	*Some of you adhere to Balaam's teaching, who persuaded Balak to set a stumbling-block before the sons of Israel, leading them into idolatry and fornication. Some of you adhere also to the Nicolaitan teaching . . .*
(Thyatira)	*You tolerate that woman Jezebel, self-advertised prophetess, who deceives my slaves and persuades them to commit fornication and idolatry. I have given her time to repent of her fornication, but she will not. Look! I am hurling her on to a couch. Those who consort with her I am hurling into great agony unless they repent of her deeds. Her children I will smite with death. To each of you I will give whatever your deeds merit. All the congregations will learn that I am the One who discerns the innermost secrets . . .*
(Sardis)	*(Everything is counted against this congregation. The verdict is summarized under the "I know" formula as "you are dead.")*
(Philadelphia)	*(Nothing is entered against this congregation.)*
(Laodicea)	*(Everything is counted against this congregaton. The verdict is summarized under the "I know" formula as "you are tepid" and "you say 'I am wealthy.'")*

Perhaps we should not treat as a formula a clause that appears in its complete form only three times: "This is what I am counting against you." Yet there is logic in doing so. To be sure, the formula is entirely appropriate only in the case of congregations where the accounting specifies both plus and minus factors. Yet it is partly appropriate in the other four cases. Even in them the function of this part of the letter is to stress the accountability to Christ of each congregation. Moreover, all of the congregations are expected to give heed to all of the letters. The formula serves to focus attention upon the specific reasons for Christ's condemnation of five congregations (excluding Smyrna and Philadelphia). What are they?

All derelictions are seen as forms of inner betrayals of a prior commitment to Christ. This commitment had been made by the community and also by each individual. Each community and person is accountable because of this previous affirmation of allegiance. Ephesus must recall its first devotion. The analogy of Balaam recalls a situation in which the sons of Israel had compromised their earlier pledge to follow Moses. What does fornication presuppose? The marriage covenant. What does idolatry presuppose? The commitment to worship one God alone.

The existence of these derelictions reveals the fact of self-deception. The greater the sin, the greater the deception. Jezebel, for example, can succeed only by deceiving "my slaves." Evil is not readily recognized but appears in the mask of the good; the good is masked as apparent evil. Satan works through the most attractive channels: the synagogue, the apostles, the prophets. Especially confusing to Christ's slaves are decisions concerning who is to be recognized as true, righteous, rich, or holy, and who are liars, sinful, poor, or blind. The basic problem is to employ dependable criteria for self-appraisals.

Each community is responsible as a community for its individual members *and* for its leaders; each individual member and leader remains at the same time fully responsible for himself *and* his community. This responsibility includes especially an obligation to discriminate between the good and the evil, between the true and the false, between life and death, in a situation where these are readily confused. The escape from self-deception into reliable appraisals of what is living and what is dead (cf. Sardis) requires a new message from Christ, mediated through a true prophet. A community's assumption that it can already discriminate the true from the false is *prima facie* evidence that it is blind. Christ's warning, "but this is what I am counting against you," is intended not to enhance the sense of security, but to destroy it. This principle applies to the use of Old Testament epithets to describe contemporary Christian leaders—Balaam, Jezebel, the Nicolaitans. Ephesus has penetrated their mask; Pergamum and Thyatira have not. It would seem that these instigators of idolatry and fornication were not easily recognized; recognition required intervention by one who could discern the innermost truth of the matter.

5. The Speaker's Commands Modern interpreters readily assume that they can define the shape of each "heresy." They also assume that the original readers could easily identify the "heretics" of whom Christ was speaking. Both assumptions are dubious. The very use of Old Testament labels in the vision was probably intended to warn against those assumptions. The first readers needed help in identifying the sources of infection, for evil always dons the cloak of righteousness. Only thus does the warning "Let everyone who can hear listen. . . ." become intelligible. Jezebel did not call herself by that name, nor did idolators think of themselves as her slaves. For this very reason, the commands which follow each castigation become essential to understanding the varied forms which unconscious idolatry or fornication had adopted.

Each of the seven congregations is the recipient of a direct command from its Lord (marked by the marginal *e*). Because these are so vital to the message of each letter, we must examine them closely, asking their intrinsic meaning and their correlation with the particular form of self-deception which characterized each congregation. There is no common formula to introduce these injunctions, yet they have a common function as orders of Christ. To accent this function we have interpolated an appropriate but imaginary rubric and have introduced each imperative on a separate line.

"*(These are my orders)*

(*Ephesus*)   *Remember the height from which you have fallen,*
Repent,
Accomplish again what you did at first.

(*Smyrna*)   *Do not fear what you will soon suffer. Look!*
The Devil, to put you to the test, is about to throw
some of you into prison, where the agony will last ten
days.
Be loyal to death, and I will give life to you as a
crown.

(*Pergamum*)   *Repent. If you do not, I will come to you soon and*
I will fight against them with the sword of my mouth.

(*Thyatira*)   *Until I come, hold firm to what you have*
achieved. I add no other obligation for you Thyatirans
who do not follow Jezebel's teaching and who do not
claim knowledge of what they call Satan's secrets.

(*Sardis*)   *Wake up!*
Rouse what is about to die, those deeds of yours
which I have found unworthy to offer to my God.
Remember what you have received and heard.
Hold fast to that and repent.
If you do not awaken, I will come like a thief and you
will be unable to know the hour of my coming.

(*Philadelphia*)   *Hold fast. Let no one seize your crown!*

(*Laodicea*)   *Buy from me gold which has been refined by*
fire so that you may become wealthy.

Buy and wear white clothing
  to hide the disgrace of your nakedness.
Buy salve for your eyes,
  so that you can see.
I discipline and punish all whom I love!
Be zealous!
Repent!"

How are we to think of the sins which these commands were intended to overcome? Here the work of interpretation becomes similar to the work of a criminal detective. The good detective first looks for clues, seeking the largest number of them. He will be suspicious of his own initial deductions from the more obvious clues. He will insist upon drawing his own conclusions, as well as upon viewing his own earlier deductions with critical eyes. He will not be wholly content until all the pointers converge in a single direction, however surprising that direction may be.

In collecting and sorting the clues to John's understanding of the crimes of the seven congregations, the commands of Christ assume major importance. The original audience could no doubt recognize what John had in mind, but for modern readers the meaning is often obscure indeed. We may limit our present analysis of the seven letters to a series of tentative deductions, with the expectation of testing these deductions in the subsequent study of the book as a whole. The student is urged to do the same. We turn then to the commands addressed to the several congregations.

Ephesus. What clues can be identified here? This congregation has surmounted real obstacles. It has accepted and endured a difficult situation. It has been able to discern the falsity of certain claims put forward by prominent apostles (are they to be associated with the Nicolaitans—2:2, 6?). In fidelity to Christ's name the congregation has made very real, although unspecified, sacrifices. Yet just because of its success in doing this, it faces the danger of losing everything (its candelabra) which Christ counts valuable. It will in fact lose everything unless—and here the command bites—it remembers, repents, and renews its initial vows. Its vitality depends upon a renewal at its source. This is clear. What is not so clear is precisely what kind of action this renewal entails. What does the "first devotion" connote? What were the initial accomplishments? We should be slow to answer. On the positive side are two clues. The clearest seems to be that archetypal decision with which this congregation had responded to the archetypal Gospel in its commitment to the message of a slain Lamb and its enlistment in the Lamb's mission. This congregation had begun to serve as priests and kings, in response to Christ's love and atonement (1:5, 6), by accepting the agony and the sovereignty and the loyal endurance of Jesus (1:9). The call to remember seems to be a call to re-enact that first response.

Second, each of the three commands throws light on the others. What repentance means is defined partially by remembering and partially by works accomplished earlier. We must infer that the mere feeling of remorse is an insufficient equivalent for repentance. Remembering is an action through which self-judgment (repentance) is linked to new accomplishments which represent a return to the height from which the congregation has fallen. We infer that remembering is to be distinguished from pious adulation of the past. No conception of any of these commands is adequate unless it embraces all three. (See p. 216f.)

On the negative side are two important clues. First, the Ephesians must not allow their accomplishments to induce a feeling of security or complacency. They had been able to win genuine battles, yet those very triumphs could hide their loss of the major war unless the initial motives and objectives remained dominant. Second, in the range of priorities and in the order of values, continued repentance rates above the ability to discern and to repudiate the false apostles and (or?) the Nicolaitans. In this respect the Ephesians were seen as being ahead of Pergamum and Thyatira. In their acceptance of ostracism and persecution they were ahead of Sardis and Laodicea. But such superiority was not sufficient for Christ. All would be lost unless the Ephesian congregation joined in remembering, repenting, and returning. Whatever that triple action entailed, Christ viewed it as more necessary than these other attainments.

Smyrna. The situation at Smyrna illustrates how Christ's judgment reverses what might be called the empirical measurement of prosperity. By any external standard, this community was povery-stricken and harassed by affliction and blasphemy, but by Christ's standard it was prosperous. Christ had nothing to say by way of condemnation. One might expect therefore that it would be unnecessary for him to issue any fresh orders. Yet empirical logic is again reversed. The congregation that was strong and healthy is assured even more arduous tests, including death itself. This command appears to illustrate a double principle: Christ selects his most loyal followers to receive ever more extreme testing; Satan cooperates, as it were, with Christ by providing such a test. If Smyrna is a valid example, we may infer that no congregation, however loyal, can expect from the future anything but maximum ordeals. What is commanded is therefore entirely fitting: a total mastery over the fear of death.

Pergamum. In this case, the Lord gives a divided verdict because Pergamum is a divided church. On the one hand it has accepted the martyrdom of at least one of its members. It has resisted Satan's authority by stubbornly verifying the power of Christ's own death. On the other hand, this congregation had been trapped by false teachers into the practice of idolatry and fornication. The precise meaning of those sins must be analyzed more fully. (See p. 217f.) It may be sufficient here to note that the single command by which Christ parries the danger is this: *Repent.* Let us observe several things about this command.

Even a loyalty which is strong enough to face martyrdom does not obviate the need for repentance. The Smyrnean tolerance for dangerous and false teachers cannot have been based on fear of violence, because that fear had been overcome. This threat must therefore have been much more subtle in its claim to being compatible with faith. Repentance would therefore entail a new awareness of some evil which is masked by its attractiveness. The securing of this awareness depended upon "the sword" of Christ's mouth. Christ's word had power to cut through all deceit and false claims. If the church would not use that sword against the Balaamites, Christ would come and use it. Repentance therefore connoted a readiness to test all pious-sounding intra-church movements by the kind of discretion which was inherent in Christ's message.

Thyatira. Here is another divided congregation. But the logic conveyed by the imperatives is somewhat different than in the case of Pergamum, even though the ostensible sins are the same: idolatry and fornication. Christ strongly commends the accomplishments of this group (vs. 19). His strongest accusation against Jezebel is not her own perversion, serious as that is, nor even her successful deception of fellow-Christians. It is her stubborn refusal to repent. Christ's strongest threat against saints who had been perverted by Jezebel is not called forth by their perversion itself but by the necessity of repentance (vs. 22). His objective in his treatment of these "prostitutes" is to disclose to all the churches his ability to search every heart. Apart, therefore, from his implicit appeal to repentance, he gives them no command. His only command is reserved to those (probably a minority) who have exercised sufficient insight to penetrate the deception. With such proof of their wisdom (which must have been both difficult and rare) they need only to hold fast. This small group within the congregation at Thyatira may thus be nearer to Christ's standard than any group mentioned in Revelation (2:19, 24). If so, it is because they have demonstrated a power to discriminate between what was authentic worship and what was spurious.

Sardis. Everything seems to be counted against this church. Apart from a few members who are worthy (3:4), the congregation is dead and quite unaware of its state. Consequently, the Lord releases a veritable barrage of commands. What is necessary before this congregation can overcome its condition of apparent life but real death? The command to become watchful or to awaken implies a radical reversal of attitudes. The congregation must be alerted to the crisis, since it is an internal one. Its emergency measures will include such steps as establishing firmly what it is that is dying, remembering its charter, fulfilling its covenant, and repenting. One suspects that all these metaphorical expressions are various ways of describing a single command. Since *life* is defined by the Risen Lord, since it is shared only with those who re-enact his passion, this congregation must remember and return to *that* life. Is the death of this congregation tantamount to its avoidance of suffering for Christ? Has it adopted a policy of appeasing the enemy of Christ? Has this church decided that survival rather than self-sacrifice is the first law of life? There is much to ponder in the case of Sardis.

Philadelphia. Because Christ had no condemnation to utter (except to the adversaries of 3:9), his command is similar to the brief "hold fast" which he had given to the faithful few in Pergamum. They had not been led astray by the activity of Satan's synagogue (an obscure factor which must be examined later). They had faced hostility with the strength which is embodied in weakness. Under pressure to recant, they had fearlessly confessed their loyalty. Their enemies had proved unable to close the door which Christ had opened (3:8). They had fully manifested Christ's own endurance (3:10) and had already won his royal crown of victory. Even so, they might still forfeit it if they failed to hold firm. The final struggle still lay ahead. This time of testing would not be the same as that which confronted the earth-dwellers (vs. 10). Loyal disciples must face one type of conflict, the world with its earth-dwellers quite another (See p. 261f.). Christ and his disciples had demonstrated the victory of weakness; in the coming trial the earth-dwellers would demonstrate the emptiness of power. They would then learn the nature of that love which bound Christ to his faithful witnesses (vs. 9d); that is, if the latter held on firmly.

Laodicea. As in the case of Sardis, this Christian community has nothing in its favor. Therefore the content of the "I know" section contains an unqualified condemnation. That verdict is, of course, the exact opposite of Laodicean expectations. Their self-appraisal is totally wrong; their fancied prosperity concealed their real poverty. Chanting their "Lord, Lord," they were more despicable than if they had been outright enemies of Christ. In fact, Christ treats them as more culpable than the anti-Christian populace. He detests them (vs. 16c). That treatment is the reverse of his love (vs. 19). His love is apparent in such chastisement as the Philadelphia community had welcomed and as the affluent Laodicean community had avoided.

The commands correspond exactly to the self-deceptions. The only cure for poverty-stricken disciples was to purchase from Christ gold which is refined in the agonies of the shared passion. For their nakedness (did Hans Christian Andersen find here the theme of "The Emperor's New Clothes"?) the only recourse was to buy such clothes as the naked Christ had won and worn on the cross. The blindness of self-deception could be cured only by understanding the correlation between Christ's love and his discipline. These three purchases constitute a substantial definition of the kind of zeal and repentance which was the burden of all John's prophecies. The thrust of these commands moves in the direction of rigorous warning. They are tantamount to saying "Open your eyes" and "Carry your cross." This letter argues against the widespread assertion of many interpreters to the effect that John's chief concern was to provide consolation to a persecuted church. Nearer the mark would be the opposite assertion; that John, like Jesus, was concerned to bring not peace but a sword.

In the context of the Laodicean situation, the famous promise of 3:20 also takes on unwonted and unwanted meanings. In a congregation whose blindness and poverty took the form of confusing loyalty to Christ with worldly prosperity, to open the door to the excluded Lord would be like buying his gold, his clothing, his salve. It would mean accepting a supper with him as a covenant pledge to die with him.

"Look! I have taken my stand at the door. I am knocking. To anyone who hears me calling and opens the door I will come in. I will dine with him; he will dine with me." While this saying could be taken as a conclusion to all seven letters, it seems to have been John's intention to address especially that congregation which was farthest from accepting the symbolic, yet terrible, significance of the Lord's Table. (A. Ehrhardt, Ev Th [1957], 431-445)

6. A COMMAND TO ALL. *"Let everyone who can hear listen to what the Spirit is telling the congregations."*

Seven times this formula recurs as one element in the conclusion of every letter (2:7a, 11a, 17a, 29; 3:6, 13, 22). In the Greek original there is not an iota of variation in the form or order of the words—a very unusual thing (some translations use an exclamation mark instead of a period, e.g. NEB). The only significant variant occurs in the location of the saying. In the first three letters it precedes the victor-promise, while in the last four letters it follows that promise (see the sentences with *f* in margin). Its function seems to be the same throughout. What should we observe about that function?

It is a warning appropriate to the disclosure of a message from heaven. The message has the power to separate the audience into two groups according to their understanding and acceptance of the message. Many who have ears will be unable to hear and heed the message. They will be quite unaware of their deafness and hence of their resulting disobedience. Yet everyone who hears is fully responsible for how he listens. The message is addressed by the Spirit to all the congregations simultaneously.

The saying operates in support of the commands which precede it. It reenforces those imperatives. It suggests why they are by nature ambiguous and why the help of the Spirit is needed in their correct translation into action. It also operates in support of the promises of Christ to the victors. The speaking of the Spirit and the listening by the congregation are essential if Christ's promises are to produce the kinds of victory he considers worthy. How otherwise would such Christians as the Laodiceans learn to count the poverty they feared as the true wealth?

The present tense of the verbs in this saying creates the sense of an immediate call to test one's hearing now. Commands and promises are designed to bring pressure on the Christian's choices whenever and wherever the letters are heard. Yet the formula enables the prophet to avoid the pretension of defining specific duties. It respects the right of Christ alone to issue the orders and to judge obedience to them on the basis of his perfect knowledge. At the same time it opens the way for Christian communities who are caught in the trap of self-justification to move on their own volition toward the open door of a truer self-knowledge.

7. THE SPEAKER'S PROMISES The final formula in this series of letters (marked by g in the margin) accents the promises attached to victory in overcoming the enemy. In five of the letters the formula begins with a nominative phrase "he who conquers" or "he who wins the victory." In the other two the same phrase appears in the dative case, "to the conquering one" or "to the victor." The verb is the same in four letters: "I will give"; but elsewhere other verbs are used, such as "I will make" or "I will write." There are other variations, which in the interest of showing the basic formula, the following translation submerges.

"I will give to the victor:

(Ephesus)	*food from the Tree of Life in God's Paradise . . .*	*(22:2)*
(Smyrna)	*the victor will not be injured by the second death . . .*	*(21:4)*
(Pergamum)	*the bread of heaven and a white amulet inscribed with a new name, known to none but the recipient.*	*(22:4)*
(Thyatira) *(a compound formula)*	*authority over the nations, just as I received it from my Father. The victor will rule them with an iron rod, he will smash them like broken dishes To the victor I will also give the dawn-star.*	*(22:16)*

(Sardis)	*So the victor will walk clothed in white.*	*(22:14)*
(a variant	*I will not cross out his name from the Book*	*(21:27)*
formula)	*of Life*	
	I will vouch for him in the presence of my	
	Father and his angels.	

(Philadelphia)	*I will set the victor up as a pillar in my God's*	*(21:22)*
(a variant	*sanctuary;*	
formula)	*Never again will he leave it.*	*(21:22)*
	On him I will inscribe the name of my God,	*(22:4)*
	the name of my God's city (the	
	new Jerusalem, which comes down	*(21:2, 10)*
	from my God out of heaven),	
	and my own new name.	

(Laodicea)	*a seat on my throne with me,*	*(22:3)*
	just as by my victory	
	I have taken a seat with my Father on his	
	throne.	

Although John correlated each promise to the content of the letter, we may observe certain features which are common to all seven.

The formulaic repetition of "I will give" stresses the absolute role of Christ as source and donor of every gift. Just as the victory of the slave corresponds to the victory of the Master, so too one notes a complete correspondence between the inheritances of the two. There is an unlimited inclusiveness and solidarity in both victory and heritage. Each reward which involves a share in Jesus' power (e.g. rod, throne, name) links its recipient to God so that an unbroken communion is established from the lowest participant to the highest. This communion clearly provides the essentials of life: food, clothing, home, name, security, power. One basic promise is conveyed in multiple images, since all of them illustrate the principle "where I am, there will the victor be" (see E. Käsemann, *Exegetische Versuche*, II, 80).

As we have seen, the victory has been described in multiple ways according to varying conditions, yet it is a single victory over a single enemy. This enemy manifests his work in different guises, but his power transcends the various earthly agents by which he has tried to deceive and subvert Christ's slaves. The symbol of reward is appropriate to the character of that struggle.

The inheritance of the victors as spelled out in this vision is wholly consistent with the promise given in the later chapters. Not a single promise in this list is missing from the rest of the Apocalypse. Few of them, in fact, are not found in other New Testament writings as well. The most significant concentration of these promises, however, may be found in the final vision of Revelation. To indicate the parallels, the translation above includes cross-references to chapters 21 and 22. After one has studied this series of apparent coincidences he is not surprised to find in that final vision the climactic occurence of the formula itself as a succinct summary of all the promises of the book: "The victor will inherit these things" (21:17). As a subtle contrast to the opening vision, the speaker in the climactic vision is God himself. Furthermore, we notice a striking parallel to the formula which throws light on all its various uses: "I will be his God; he will be my son." Significant also is the appearance in the concluding vision of an antithetical formula which shows clearly the character of those slaves who do *not* become victors. Eight terms are used in 21:8, five of which echo the deceptive threats in the seven cities: the cowards (2:10, 13), the disloyal (2:10, 13), the fornicators (2:14, 20), the idolators (2:14, 20), and finally the liars (deceivers and deceived) (2:2, 9, 20; 3:9). In the final vision, as in the seven letters, Satan remains the ultimate source of these perversions within the life of the Church.

For Further Study

THE SEVEN CHURCHES L. Poirier, O.F.M., *Les Sept Églises* (esp. biblio. pp. 177-201); A. Satake, *Die Gemeindeordnung in der Johannesapokalypse;* Wm. Ramsay, *The Letters to the Seven*

Churches of Asia; H. Martin, *The Seven Letters;* Wm. Barclay, *The Letters to the Seven Churches;* F. J. A. Hort, *The Apocalypse of John* I-III; R. C. Trench, *Commentary on the Epistles to the Seven Churches;* H. M. Feret, *Apocalypse of St. John,* 1-30; C. J. Cadoux, *Ancient Smyrna,* 228-366; A. C. Repp, CTM 25 (1964) 133-147; A. Fabre, RB 7 (1910) 161-178, 344-367; H. Zimmermann in *Unio Christianorum,* 176-197; H. Dallmayr, *Die sieben Leuchter;* G. Dehn, *Urchristliche Gemeindeleben;* F. M. Braun, *Jean le Théologien,* 331-355; A. T. Nikolainen, NTS 9 (1963) 331-361.

2. The Lamb as Victor (4:1-8:1)

A. THE SETTING (4:1-5:14)

4:1   *Afterward I looked: There!*
A door into heaven had been thrown open.
Again I heard the first trumpet-voice telling me:
    "Come up here.
    I must help you see what must happen."

2   *At once I was filled with the Spirit.*

    There!
    In heaven a throne had been placed.

3   *Sitting on it One whose appearance*
      resembled jasper and carnelian.
    Encircling the throne a rainbow, bright as emerald.

4   *Surrounding the throne twenty-four thrones,*
    twenty-four elders enthroned, in white robes with gold
      crowns.

5   *From the throne came lightning, voices, thunder;*
    in front of the throne seven blazing torches (the spirits of
      God);

6   *in front of the throne, a lake of glass, clear as crystal.*
    At the center, around the throne, four living creatures
        full of eyes on all sides,

7   *the first like a lion, the second an ox,*
        the third with human face, the fourth like an eagle in
        flight.

8   *Each of the four had six wings,*
        each was full of eyes, inside and out.
        Day and night, without ceasing they sang:
          "Holy, holy, holy,
          God, all-powerful Lord,

who now rules
who has always ruled
who is coming to rule."

9   *As these living creatures give glory, praise and thanks*
         to the Enthroned who is forever alive,

10   *the twenty-four elders prostrate themselves before the*
         Enthroned, worshiping him who is forever alive,
     they throw their crowns before the throne, singing:

11   *"You are worthy our Lord, our God,*
         to receive glory, praise, power,
         because you created everything.
         You willed everything to exist as your creation."

5:1   *In the right hand of the Enthroned I saw a scroll,*
     with script inside and out, fastened with seven seals.

2   *I saw a powerful angel, shouting with mighty voice:*
         "Who has earned the right to break the seals,
         to open this scroll?"

3   *No one had the power to open the scroll and to look*
     inside, no one in heaven, on earth or beneath the earth.

4   *I was in tears because no one had been found*
         who had earned the right to do this,

5   *but one the elders said to me:*
         "Stop crying! Look!
         David's son, the lion from Judah's tribe, is the
         victor.
         He has earned the right to open the scroll and its
         seals."

6   *Between the throne and the four living creatures,*
     in the midst of the elders, I saw a Lamb!
         He stood as one slaughtered.
         He had seven horns and seven eyes
         (the seven spirits of God assigned to the whole
         earth).

7   *He came and took the scroll from the right hand
        of the Enthroned.*

8   *At that moment
        the four living creatures and the twenty-four elders
        prostrated themselves before the Lamb.
        Each carried a harp and gold bowls full of incense
            (the prayers of holy men).*
9   *They chanted a new hymn:
                "You have earned the right
                    to receive the scroll and open its seals,
                for you were slaughtered,
                    with your blood you purchased for God
                men from every race and language, nation and
                    people;*
10   *you created them priests, a kingdom for our
                    God,—
                as kings they will rule over the earth."*

11   *Surrounding the throne, around the living creatures and
            elders,
        I saw many angels, angels by the thousands and the tens of
            thousands.*
12   *I heard them singing loudly:
                "The slaughtered Lamb has earned the right
                to receive power and wealth, wisdom and strength,
                honor and glory and blessing."*

13   *I heard the song of every creature in heaven,
        on earth, under the earth, in the sea:
                "Eternal blessing and honor, glory and power
                to the Enthroned and to the Lamb."*
14   *"Amen" shouted the four living creatures.
        The elders prostrated themselves in worship.*

Literary Analysis

The vision of the seven seals is quite clearly a single unit, covering over four chapters. It should therefore be read and studied as a single message. This means that the accounts of the breaking of the seals should not be separated, as they frequently are, from the introductory pictures of the heavenly thrones. These throne-pictures should be viewed as dominating the action of the entire vision. The length of the unit, however, virtually forces us to divide the material, since the eye-span of the reader is not wide enough to cover the entire panorama at once. We have therefore separated the setting (Ch. 4, 5) from the account of the seven seals (Ch. 6, 7). Before examining the internal structures of the setting, however, we must determine the place of this vision as a whole within the comprehensive plan of the prophet.

What are the links that connect this vision to the previous one? Each reader should look for clues and evaluate those which he discovers. For example, in the opening sentence (4:1) the prophet himself underscores one link. The voice heard is that of the *first* trumpet, undoubtedly a backward reference to 1:10. By studying the two verses it becomes clear that multiple associations are in his mind: the speaker is the same in the two visions, as is also the listener. In both cases the prophet is "in the Spirit" for the sake of transmitting a message from Christ to the congregation about the impending fulfilment of the divine will. In both instances the prophet is convinced of the inseparability of the saving purpose (*logos*) of God (1:2, 9; 4:1-11) from the confirming work (*marturia*) of Jesus (1:2, 9; 5:1-14). In both cases the vision of the heavenly Christ provides an essential frame of reference for his specific commands to his people. The end of the previous vision is also bound closely to the beginning of the new one. For example, the reference to the door in 3:20 (this is an intrusion into the literary form of the letters) anticipates the opening of the heavenly door in 4:1. The promise of thrones to the Laodicean church deftly links that letter to the dominant image of the new vision: the double throne of God and the Lamb. This illustrates a literary habit of the prophet: he includes near the conclusion of one vision an anticipation of the next. Finally, we should recall that all seven letters ended in promises to the victors; the two new chapters, by presenting the victory of Christ, vindicate his right both to issue and to fulfill those promises.

What links connect the vision of the seals to its successors? Once again each reader should seek to answer this question for himself. At first he may feel that there is virtually a complete break between the silence in heaven (8:1) and the following cacophony of trumpets (8:6f). But let him press further and notice how frequently in later visions he finds backward allusions to the throne, the book, the crowns, the four living creatures, the twenty-four elders, and the victory of the slaughtered lamb. When he locates these continuous, though inconspicuous, threads which bind this vision into the tapestry of the entire book, he will agree that this vision serves to prepare for all the later visions. John viewed the material in chapters 4 and 5 as basic to the understanding of his whole message.

What strategic inquiries may now be most helpful to the reader in his attempt to recover the internal literary structure of the throne scene in chapters 4 and 5? We select two.

(1) Where do the centers of gravity lie? The answer is obvious, but nonetheless important. The details of chapter four, otherwise diffuse and centrifugal, come to a focus in the two hymns, one sung by the four living creatures (vs. 8) and one by the twenty-four elders (vs. 11). Similarly, the four hymns of chapter 5 provide the *raison d'être* of that chapter. When one examines the sequence of these six hymns, he notes that the first two are addressed to God and the last four to the Lamb. There is also a gradual enlargement in the personnel of the choirs. The sequence, too, underscores the interdependence of the two objects of worship and the expanding circles of worshipers. There is an internal momentum of action. It is more important to sense this momentum than to establish a conceptual allegorical equivalent for each detail.

The form of the hymns in these chapters had undoubtedly been shaped by early Christian use and by synagogue antecedents. The first (4:8) echoes the vision of Isaiah 6. The second is reminiscent of many motifs from the Psalms (e.g. 19:1), but finds its closest analogy in the synagogue liturgy (see W. O. E. Oesterley, *The Jewish Background of Early Christian Liturgy*, 44-46). Similarly the first two hymns in chapter 5 call to mind various Old Testament texts, which celebrated the Exodus deliverance, as well as synagogue psalms and doxologies. The Church's familiarity with these hymnic forms would thus enhance their place in John's report.

(2) What kind of action is going on? The character and locus of the action of God is indicated by the two hymns. They celebrate his holiness and power as manifested in his past, present, and future activity (4:8c); his worthiness to be praised is grounded in his creative work (4:11c). The action of the Lamb centers in his historical ministry, and especially his death and its consequences (5:9b, 10). The actions of all other participants are described in terms of worship; they all surrender their crowns and their glory to the Enthroned and to the Lamb. This action of worship binds together heaven and earth, the throne and those who throw their crowns before it. Yet this liturgical scene reflects and corresponds to a type of earthly action which destroys any limitation to what goes on in formal services. The earthly action of the Lamb is embodied in his slaughter (a highly non-liturgical event); the action of his worshipers is likewise embodied in their fellowship in his sufferings (equally non-liturgical in character). Their worship consists of winning the same crown and then of hurling that very crown before the same throne. It is earthly action of this kind which gives specific content to the creative work of God. The slaughter of the Lamb is understood as a supreme instance of that creativity. In reading this section, therefore, we should focus attention on the hymns and notice how earthly and heavenly activities interpenetrate in them.

It is probable, of course, that the liturgical patterns of the churches of Asia provided John with more help than is represented simply by the hymns and the Amens alone. The typical order of congregational worship may have suggested to John the sequence of actions in the vision: the word of invitation (4:1), the coming of the Spirit (4:2), the adoration of God, the prostration of the worshipers, the ceremony of bringing the scroll of Scripture and then its opening and exposition. Whether such a thesis is entirely convincing (see L. Mowry, *op. cit.*), it cannot be doubted that in his choice of symbols John made good use of familiar aspects of congregational worship (e.g., the book, the name, thrones, priests, elders, door, altar, incense, torches). Recognition of such facts should make us all the more impressed by the stunning paradoxes which John presents. In a liturgical setting and using liturgically-shaped materials, he deals with the stark actualities of a judicial execution. As a result, all the theological terms, such as holiness and honor, prayer and incense, must be radically redefined in view of that single mundane event. The sacred and the secular are juxtaposed in such a way as to be mutually transformed. It is this very juxtaposition which marks John's literary craftsmanship as belonging to the order of genius.

For Further Study

THE APOCALYPSE IN VISUAL ART. The choice of readings will depend on whether the focus of interest falls on mosaics, frescoes, manuscript illustrations, or oils. The following items will suggest promising areas of study.

W. Neuss, "Apokalypse" in *Reallexicon zur deutschen Kunstgeschichte* I, 751-782; F. van de Meer, *Maiestas Domini: Theophanies de l'Apocalypse dans l'Art Chrétien;* M. R. James, *The Apocalypse in Art;* L. Delisle et P. Meyer, *L'Apocalypse in Français au XIII⁰ Siecle;* W. Neuss, *Die Apokalypse in der altspanischen und altchristlichen Bibelillustration;* T. Frimmel, *Die Apokalypse in den Bilderhandschriften des Mittelalters;* P. Kristeller, *Die Apokalypsis alteste Blochbuchausgabe in Lichtdrucknachbildung;* N. Petit, *Les apocalypse manuscrites du Moyen*

Age et les Tapisseries de la Cathédral d'Angers; J. Lourcat,
L'Apocalypse d'Angers; W. Dvořak, Dürer's Apokalypse in
Kunstgeschichte und Geistesgeschichte; F. Juraschek, Das Rätsel
in Dürers Gotteschau; A. Dürer, Die Apokalypse; K. Wölfflin, Die
Kunst A. Dürers; J. Snyder, The Trier Apocalypse, Vig C 18
(1964) 146-162; J. M. Carzou, L'Apocalypse; J. Foret, Catalogue
L'Apocalypse, Musée d'Art Moderne de la Ville de Paris; L. P.
Ruotolo, A New Apocalypse, motive, 27, Dec. 1966, 21-36.

B. THE OPENING OF THE SEALS (6:1-8:1)

6:1 I saw the Lamb break one of the seven seals;   a
     I heard one of the four living creatures shout like thunder,
        "Come!"   b
     I looked . . .   c
  2   There! A white horse—   d
           its rider carried a bow,   e
           a crown was given him,   f
           as victor he rode out to win the victory.   g

  3 When the Lamb broke the second seal,   a
     I heard the second living creature shout, "Come!"   b
  4   Another horse came, fiery red—   d
           its rider was given a huge sword,   e
           he was given power to take peace from the earth,   f
           to make men slaughter one another.   g

  5 When the Lamb broke the third seal,   a
     I heard the third living creature shout, "Come!"   b
     I looked . . .   c
           There! A black horse—   d
           its rider carried a pair of scales in his hand.   e
  6   I heard what sounded like a cry from the midst of the   f
              four living creatures:

> "*Charge a day's pay for a quart of wheat or*
> *three quarts of barley,*
> *but do not harm the olives or the wine.*"

7   When the Lamb broke the fourth seal,   *a*
      I heard the fourth living creature shout, "Come!"   *b*
8   I looked ...   *c*
          There! A pale horse—   *d*
          its rider's name is Death;   *e*
          Hades rides with him.
      Authority was given to them over a quarter of the earth   *f*
      to slaughter with sword, famine, death,   *g*
          and by the earth-beasts.

9   When the Lamb broke the fifth seal,
      I saw beneath the altar
      the souls of men who had been slaughtered
      because of God's saving purpose and the confirmation they
          gave to it.
10   They shouted with a loud voice:
          "O Master, holy and true,
          how long until you judge and avenge
          our slaughter by the earth-dwellers?"
11   A white robe was issued to each of them.
      They were instructed to rest a little while longer
      until the count was complete of fellow-slaves and brothers
      who would soon be slain as they had been.

12   When the Lamb broke the sixth seal,
      I looked ...
          There came a great earthquake:
          the sun turned black as funeral smoke,
          the whole moon became like blood,
13   stars fell from sky to ground
          like a fig tree, hurricane-driven, scattering its figs.

14   *The sky was rolled up like a scroll.*
      Every mountain and island was dislodged.
      Taking cover in caves and mountain crevices,
15   *the earth's kings, potentates, generals,*
      millionaires, bosses, freemen, slaves,
      begged the mountains and the rocks:
16   *"Fall on us!*
            Hide us from the face of the Enthroned!
            Hide us from the anger of the Lamb!
17   *The great day of their anger has arrived.*
            Who has the power to stand against them?"

7:1   Afterward I saw four angels standing at earth's four corners,
      controlling the earth's four winds, lest they blow on earth or sea
      or trees.

2   *I saw another angel, rising from the east,*
      carrying the brand of the living God.
      It shouted to the four angels
      who had received power to hurt the earth and sea:
3   *"Don't hurt the earth or the sea or the trees*
            until we have branded
            the forehead of the slaves of our God."
4   I heard the count of those who were branded: 144,000.
      There were 12,000 from every tribe of the sons of Israel,
      12,000 branded from
5   *the tribe of Judah, the tribe of Reuben,*
6   *the tribe of Gad, the tribe of Asher,*
            the tribe of Napthali. the tribe of Manasseh,
7   *the tribe of Simeon, the tribe of Levi,*
8   *the tribe of Issachar, the tribe of Zebulon,*
            the tribe of Joseph, the tribe of Benjamin.

9   Afterward I looked. There!

A huge crowd, too huge to be counted,
from every nation, tribe, tongue, people,
standing before the throne,
standing before the Lamb,
wearing white robes,
palm branches in their hands,
10   shouting with tremendous voice:
      "Salvation to our enthroned God!
      Salvation to the Lamb!"

11 All the angels surrounded the throne, the living creatures, the
    elders—
they prostrated themselves before the throne,
they worshiped God, and sang:
12   "Amen!
    Blessing and glory
    wisdom and gratitude
    praise and power and majesty
    to our God forever.
    Amen!"

13 One of the elders asked me, "Who are those who are wearing
the white robes? Where do they come from?"
14 I replied, "My master, that is something you know."
Then he told me:
    "These are coming from the great agony,
    they washed their robes,
    bleaching them white in the Lamb's blood.
    That is why they now stand before God's throne,
15   worshiping him night and day in his temple.
    That is why the Enthroned dwells with them.
16   Never again will they hunger or thirst.
    The sun does not scorch them, nor any fire,
17   for the Lamb at the throne will be their shepherd.
    He will guide them to the fountain of living water.
    God will brush every tear from their eyes."

8:1   **When the Lamb broke the seventh seal, there was dead silence in heaven for half an hour. . . .**

Literary Analysis

John takes extraordinary pains to show the continuity between the picture of worship in heaven (Ch. 4, 5) and the opening of the seven seals (Ch. 6, 7). Since it is the Lamb who will open each of the seals, it is his qualification to do so which forms the burden of chapters 4, 5. We should also note how the description of the sixth seal (7:9-12) closes a circle which began with the hymns of chapter 5, for the martyrs now join the circle of praise which sounded in the beginning, so that their victory becomes the true completion of the Lamb's victory.

The series of seven seals may be divided into two smaller units, one of four seals and the other of three. Concerning the account of the first four seals the following characteristics are noteworthy: each of the four is initiated by a command from one of the four living creatures. Each of the four commands releases a horse and its rider. The four are shaped to conform to a common model, as the typographical arrangement of the translation should made clear. In the four paragraphs, lines *a* and *b* are identical, except for minor stylistic variations. In all cases, a horse and its rider are mentioned next (lines *d* and *e*). The color of the horse and the object carried by its rider both suggest the character of its assignment. In all cases except the third, line *f* stresses the gift of a particular power to the rider. These literary clues indicate that the work of all four riders should be dealt with together as various descriptions of a single set of consequences released by the Lamb's victory. The brevity of these four paragraphs, in contrast to the length of the last three, suggests that the prophet was more concerned with the latter. In the first four, John is doing little more than creating a collage of traditional apocalyptic symbols. In the latter three, by contrast, he is dealing more directly with the specific situations faced by the Asian congregations.

The center of gravity may be found in the more ample presentation of seals 5 and 6, and especially in the songs of the martyrs in chapter 7. The fifth seal reflects the same ordeals which had been set forth in the letters to the Asian congregations, the apparent frustrations of those who have been slaughtered as a result of their loyalty to God's saving work as confirmed by Jesus. (Compare 6:9 with 1:2, 9; 5:12.) They also are those who have suffered from the release of the four horsemen by Christ, from violence, from poverty, and from Death, all of which are manifestations of the power of earth's beasts, as well as of the power of Christ's passion. There are also very close parallels to be noted between seal 5 and the "interlude" of chapter 7, and strong contrasts between seals 5 and 6, stemming from the conflict which is intrinsic to the very existence of the churches. For example, the call for vindication of the martyrs (6:10) is set over against the cry of despair of their adversaries (6:16). The identity of the two groups should not be too readily or too firmly established, but the incompatibility between them is accented by the literary structure itself. This very incompatibility leads the reader to recognize that a degree of suspense is created by the prophet's introduction of a long interval between the breaking of the seal 6 and seal 7.

This interlude (7:1-17) thus becomes the climax of the whole vision. It discloses the outcome of the very struggle in which the churches are engaged. This is God's answer to the cry of both the martyrs and their opponents; it gives the heavenly verdict on the earthly ordeal (thlipsis) (7:14). Thus, although 7:1-17 interrupts the smooth continuous sequence of the seven seals, the effect of the interruption is to focus attention on the interlude itself. It impels the reader to ask the reasons for the interruption. This in turn leads to a closer scrutiny of how this interlude is a necessary sequel to seals 5 and 6, and how it closes the circle which began with the vision of the throne in ch. 4. Thus it underscores the actuality of God's fulfilment of his promise to Israel (7:1-8) and the emergence of a universal community which comes into existence around its loyalty to God and to the

Lamb (7:9-17). The sequence of seven is thus used as a literary device to focus attention upon that threat and promise which is embodied in the conflict and victory of the slaughtered Lamb.

Looking back over the entire vision, we can now see something of its unity. The setting (ch. 4, 5) tells how by his passion the Lamb became entitled to open the scroll and how by participation in his passion men are entitled to join in his worship. The first four seals describe how that participation involves those men in the ordeals (*thlipsis*) of sword, famine, death through the power of earth's beasts. The fifth and sixth seals then disclose the resulting demand for vindication of the faithful and for the punishment of their adversaries. The "interlude" reveals the identity of those who have loyally endured the great ordeal (7:14) and who thereby established their fellowship with the Lamb in his suffering and victory (7:15-17). The worship of this community, both at the beginning and end (5:11-13; 7:10-12), is authenticated by this fellowship.

For Reflection and Discussion

Let me now advance an interpretation of this vision, an analysis quite different from that of most contemporary exegetes. Then let the reader weigh the evidence for himself. My own understanding of the passage has emerged as I have tried to meet three requirements: (1) Any interpretation must respect the unity and coherence of this vision as a whole (4:1-8:1). (2) It must do justice to John's unique language of image and symbol, observing carefully the special nuances which John gives to certain key words. (3) It must give priority to asking the right questions in the right order and to seeking answers within the orbit of John's own experience. Let me be specific about these questions and then look for acceptable answers to them.

    1. Where and by whom is the action initiated?
    2. What kind of conflict is provoked by this action?
    3. Who are the participants in this conflict?
    4. How is the conflict resolved?

The answer to the first is perhaps the easiest to discover and therefore easiest to forget. The action takes place in heaven. Nothing transpires in the vision that does not originate there. The vision presupposes the open door, the ascension of the prophet in the Spirit. The symbolic source and center of all initiative is thereby traced to the throne of God. Whatever happens is an expression of his purpose. Whatever authority is given to angel or horse is given by him. Nothing happens, nothing exists in the present, past, or future, apart from his intention. The elaborate description of the throne-room functions in a thoroughly conventional way to stress his majesty and power. Yet God's majestic transcendence is fully safeguarded; the prophet does not attempt to describe him.

Some of the specific actions are attributed to the four living creatures (e.g. 4:8; 5:7; 6:1), some to the twenty-four elders (4:10; 5:8; 7:13), some to the seven spirits (4:5), or to various angels (4:1; 5:2, 11; 7:1-3). The stage directions make it clear that all of these actors are always oriented around the throne of God. Everything they do is in response to God's command or is their mode of worshiping him. Their actions are never anything else than manifestations of his action.

Far more decisive, however, than the actions initiated by these heavenly figures is what the Lamb does. It is he who opens each of the seven seals. No other creature is worthy to do so. If these are seals of God's judgment, it is he who exercises that judgment. If they are seals of divine reward, it is he who mediates that reward, shepherding men and guiding them to the living water (7:17). The twelve tribes are carefully listed (7:5-8), but it is also clearly indicated that he is the Lion of the first tribe and the Root of the last (5:4). Moreover, there can be no doubt that he accomplished his most decisive action by his death. That was his victory (5:5). His slaughter was the event by which he was enabled to stand before God. It was the source of his power and wisdom (the seven heads and eyes of 5:6). The hymns of the living creatures and elders indicate the ground of his worthiness to open the scroll: it was by his death that he

purchased his people (5:9). We must not neglect this clue to the
meaning of the whole vision. It is a description of the operation
of forces which were released by the single event of suffering
and victory. This is the action *par excellence*; it becomes the
source and criterion of every other action in the vision.

It is by reference to this event that we can answer the
second question, concerning the kind of conflict. Every element
of conflict in the vision is provoked by this event and disclosed
by it. The prophet is seeking to describe the repercussions, the
echoes, the continuing effects of the passion story. What kind
of conflict reached its climax in the slaughter of the Lamb and
had its resolution in his victory? Several affirmations can be made.
The vision deals with a struggle which is as firmly anchored in
historical experience as is the cross; yet the struggle is also as
universal in its range as the whole creation. Its origin is the
creative work of God, its goal the praise of God by every creature.
It is a conflict so hidden by the cross that victory is seen and
shared only by those who join in the doxologies (ch. 5). Those
who worship the Lamb are plunged into the same conflict. For
example, each of the four horsemen symbolizes sacrifices elsewhere made obligatory by Christ for his followers. He had come
to bring a sword, not peace: he had called on them to renounce
all their possessions. Unless they carried their crosses they could
not join his company. They should not enlist unless they had
resources for this kind of warfare.

The answer to the third question must be a double one. We
have already characterized the personnel fighting on one side.
John views as a single group those who hold firmly to the purpose of God and to the testimony of Jesus. (The *logos-mar-
turia* complex (6:9) is basic, see p. 222f.). This group comprises
those who participate in the agony, the tribulation, and the
patience (1:9, compare with the description of the fifth seal
and of the redeemed, 6:9-11; 7:14-17). Their souls dwell beneath
the altar (6:9). They are a single company of brothers and
fellow-slaves of God (6:11), bearing God's brand on the forehead.
They have had the royal power and the loyal endurance to come

through the great conflict. They have made their robes white by sharing in the Lamb's redemptive action (7:14). Every description of this struggle points to their participation in that same power which he verified by his death.

Thus far the reasoning is easy. But now we come to a more difficult aspect: who constitutes the personnel on the other side in this conflict? Much is at stake here. The evidence is provided mainly by three passages. In 6:10 the opponents are identified as the earth-dwellers. In 6:15 this group of earth-dwellers is divided into seven categories. By implication in 7:14f the enemies are agents of that ordeal which consists of hunger, thirst, scorching heat, and death. This evidence is ambiguous and the interpreter can easily go astray. Let us review the various options.

By earth-dwellers did the prophet mean "all people that on earth do dwell"? Surely not, since chapter 7, as well as 5:9, specifically exempts so many. Given this context, earth is surely a qualitative and not a quantitative term (see p. 261f.). John does not mean all men living now or then. Another option is to suppose that to John the adversaries were non-Christians. Does he invoke Christ's power against those who have never heard or heeded the Christian message? No. The range of God's power mentioned in chapter 4 (vs. 8, 11) does not permit this conclusion. Nor does the personnel of the choir in 5:11-14 permit it, not to mention the constant escalation of numbers in 7:9f. Even more decisively, the character of the Lamb's sacrifice absolutely excludes this objectivist division of human society into a census-like separation of Christians from non-Christians. He did not die for the righteous but for sinners, not for insiders but for outsiders.

There is a further option: by earth-dwellers John may have referred to that company of outsiders who persecuted the Church. Since the state was an agent of persecution in Domitian's day and presumably in John's, he may have had in mind the boundary between State and Church. If this were true, it is strange indeed that John should specify not only the rulers and the generals

(6:15) but also "every free man and slave." Were all of these men engaged in violent persecution of the Church? It would also be strange to speak of such men as being afraid of "the face of the Enthroned" and "the wrath of the Lamb." It would be more reasonable to suppose that this prospect would be feared only by Christians. Yet the decisive objection to this answer is again provided by the character of the Lamb's victory and of the forces released by it. The passion story nowhere leads one to suppose that only the Sanhedrin and its henchmen would encounter the terrible sword of judgment released by the crucifixion. Would the purpose of Jesus' death be fulfilled by turning his wrath solely against these enemies? No. Such an answer would not be congenial either to the Gospel or to John's own experience of its power. (It is significant that although John had been imprisoned, his book reveals no personal animus against those men who were immediately responsible.)

Is there any option left? Yes, at least one. Perhaps the adversaries of the brothers and slaves were false Christians, led by their false prophets and apostles. When we recall the seven letters as well as the general setting and structure of the seven-seals vision, this answer becomes more likely. For it is clear that John was concerned as a prophet with members of Christian congregations in Asia, within which he discerned many kinds and degrees of faithlessness and prostitution. It is also clear that his description of the breaking of the seals would be intelligible only to readers who accepted the worship of God and the saving power of Jesus. Moreover, the concentration of interest in the fifth seal and in the interlude (ch. 7) suggests that John was primarily concerned with the state of the Church. For him the overriding issue was whether the self-confessed followers of Jesus would share in his victory. John sought to force every reader to give priority to the axiological problem. By axiological I refer in this context to the Greek word which appears to be strategic here (*haxios*). In chapter four the basic question is "What makes God worthy to receive glory, honor, power?"; the basic answers being provided by the hymns (4:8-11). In chapter 5 the basic question applies to the Lamb. No doubt is left concerning his

credentials. In chapters 6 and 7 the key question is then applied
to fellow-slaves and brothers. It is simply another way of asking
the questions raised in the seven letters: who will prove that they
have ears to hear? Who will become victors? And the basic
answer is the same: those who remain faithful to God's purpose
and verify it. Those who, like the Lamb, are holy, true, and
patient through every ordeal and temptation. Are they worthy?
Will they earn the right to receive God's brand on their foreheads, the mark of God's true slaves? The vision ends with an
explicit description of those who give valid proof of their
worthiness (7:14-17).

The arena within which this worthiness is to be tested and
established is now clear. The arena is that place where Christian
congregations decide whether or not to wash their robes in the
Lamb's blood (7:14). Here they encounter a wide range of forces
which try to persuade them of the folly and futility of that
action. Since this is the arena, one cannot easily establish the
identity of the adversaries. Persecutors may embody such forces,
but their strength applied externally is not sufficient to decide the
outcome. False prophets and apostles may embody these same
forces, but they will fail unless they win a voluntary following.
The real struggle takes place within the hearts of those who have
heard God's word and have committed themselves to Jesus' victory
and who now, in the setting of today's warfare, decide whether or
not to maintain their first devotion.

Since the conflict is so defined, the answer to the fourth question, "How is the conflict resolved?" becomes a matter of carrying
further the same logic. The Lamb himself will either approve or
reject those who have pledged their allegiance to him. In either
case, his action in breaking the seals (notice the unfailing repetition of "the Lamb" in the first sentence of all seven) is a function of that victory by which he proved his own worthiness. His
conquest *then* had become the criterion of true victory *now* (6:2).
He continues to take peace from the earth and to bring a sword
which turns men against one another (6:4). The conflict can only
be resolved by the loyal endurance of those who fully understand
the mode of Christ's presence within it.

Does such an approach as this also throw light on the third seal with its image of famine and inflation (6:6)? Yes. Loyalty entails real hunger and thirst, poverty and helplessness (7:16). But it also brings the presence of a Shepherd who guides the thirsty to fountains of living water. It does so because loyalty proves that actual wealth may be found in the midst of poverty (2:9), whereas disloyalty discloses the poverty of those who count themselves rich (3:17). The four horsemen are pictures superimposed on the cross; they are reverberations echoing from the initial cry "I thirst." They remind the readers that all values had been reversed and transformed by the redemptive ministry of the Lamb.

Crucifixion had demonstrated the power of Death and Hades over the Lamb, but it had also released the power of the Lamb over Death and Hades (6:7, 8). Now Death and Hades could ride, but only at the command of him who, in giving them authority, had limited that authority to the realm which was still ruled by earth's beasts (the *therioi* of 6:8). Members of the churches in Laodicea or Sardis who appear to be alive but are actually dead (3:1) face condemnation from the Lamb. His verdict takes the form of famine, death, and subjugation by the earth's beasts. But those who in the same situation say "Yes" are worthy to stand before the same throne in the same temple (7:15), with Jesus as their Shepherd. The answer of the Christian bears hidden within it the resolution of the struggle, inasmuch as the Lamb's answer covered both the beginning and the end of the same struggle.

The perceptive student will realize that if this general thesis is adopted, the usual exegesis of the four horsemen must be discarded. Commonly the horsemen are identified with that type of recurring catastrophes which strikes the headlines—such things as world wars, the latest famine in India, or the death of thousands in an earthquake in Turkey. But it is difficult to believe that the prophet John was primarily concerned with explaining such disasters or with showing how the slaughter of the Lamb released such catastrophes on mankind in general or even on the hostile Roman empire. Perhaps the usual interpretation of this vision reveals only how far we stand from John when we assume that a hurricane sweeping the Caribbean is more to be dreaded than such subtle betrayals of the Gospel as characterized the congregations in Sardis or Laodicea.

For Further Study

1. THE SCROLL AND THE BOOK. L. Koep, *Das himmlische Buch;* E. Reissner, *Das Buch mit den 7 Siegeln;* G. Schrenk, TWNT, I, 615-620; J. Weiss, 57ff; A. Schlatter, *Das A T in die Offenbarung,* 62ff.; W. Sattler, ZNTW 21 (1922) 43ff.; H. Langenberg, 137-142; L. Mowry, JBL 71 (1952) 75-84; H. P. Möller, ZNTW 54 (1963) 254-267; O. Roller, ZNTW 36 (1937) 98-113; S-B III, 800; II, 171f.; K. Staritz, ZNTW 30 (1931) 157-170; Dupont, 157-162.

2. THE TWENTY-FOUR ELDERS   The primary evidence: Rev. 4:9-11; 5:5-14; 7:11-17; 11:16-18; 12:10-12; 14:3; 19:4. Possible identifications: (a) 24 hours of day; (b) 24 letters of Hebrew alphabet, from first to last; (c) 24 tones of flute, from highest to lowest; (d) 12 patriarchs (tribes) and 12 apostles; (e) 12 prophets and 12 apostles; (f) 12 judges of O.T. and of N.T.; (g) an image of fullness and wholeness; (h) 24 courses of priestly service, of Levites or of singers (Num. 7:88; 25:9; 1 Chron. 20:6; 23:3-5; 24:3; 27; 2 Samuel 21:20); (i) the high priests as a council (Eze. 8:16; 11:1); (j) a choir of transfigured O.T. saints and patriarchs; (k) heavenly figures corresponding to the elders of Christian congregations; (l) the saints of Israel and the church. The most thorough and persuasive review may be found in J. Michl, *Die 24 Ältesten in der Apok.* See also commentaries of Bousset, Lohmeyer, Hadorn, Swete. Langton, *Angel Teaching of the N.T.,* 196-200; Langenberg, p. 216.

3. THE FOUR LIVING CREATURES.   Primary evidence: chs. 4; 5; 6:1, 3, 6; 7:11; 14:3; 15:7; 19:4. A wide range of identifications has been provided by exegetes; (a) the cherubim of Ezekiel 10:1, their description being influenced by other O.T. passages like Isa. 6: 1, 2; (b) the signs of the Zodiac, as drawn from astrologi-

cal traditions; (c) the fourfold division of the forces of nature or of animate life (e.g., birds, wild animals, domesticated animals, men); (d) the classifications of human societies (e.g., tribes, tongues, nations, peoples); (e) the highest order of angelic beings, agents of divine power and wisdom; (f) symbolic manifestations of divine transcendence and glory. See S-B III, 799, Beckwith, Swete, Charles; J. Michl, *Die Engelvorstellungen*, 5-111; Langenberg, 38-40.

4. THE ANGELIC FIGURES IN THE APOCALYPSE. J. Michl, *Die Engelvorstellungen;* van der Waal, *Priesterlijke Motieven*, 55-86; T. H. Gaster, IDB, I, 128-134; Kittel, TWNT, I, 80-86; J. Daniélou, *Jewish Christianity*, ch. 4, 6; H. Bietenhard, *Himmlische Welt*, ch. 5; A. Satake, 150-155; U. Simon, *Heaven*, ch. 4; A. Mantel, BL, 2 (1961) 59-65.

3. The Prophets as Victors (8:2-11:18)

8:2 *I saw the seven angels*
who have taken their stand before God.
Seven trumpets were given to them.

3 Another angel came and took his stand before the altar.
He was holding a gold censer.
A large supply of incense was given him
that he might offer the prayers of all the holy ones
at the gold altar before the throne.

4 The smoke of the incense with the prayers of the holy
ones
billowed up before God from the hand of the angel.

5 The angel grasped the censer,
filled it with fire from the altar,
hurled it on the earth.
Thunders rolled, shouts,
bolts of lightning, an earthquake.

6 **The seven angels raised their trumpets**
and got ready to blow.

7 **The first blew:**   a
        hail came, and fire mixed with blood;   b
        it was hurled on the earth.
        A third of the earth was burned,   c
        a third of the trees were burned,
        all the green grass was burned.

8 **The second angel blew:**   a
        something like a great mountain on fire   b
        was hurled into the sea.

85

9   *A third of the sea turned into blood,*   c
a third of everything alive in the sea died,
A third of the ships foundered.

10   The third *angel blew:*
a great star, burning like a torch, fell from heaven,   a
fell on a third of the rivers,   b
fell on a third of the springs of water
11   *(its name was Wormwood).*
A third of the waters turned into wormwood.   c
Hosts of men died from the waters,
for they were poisoned.

12   The fourth *angel blew:*   a
a third of the sun was plagued,   c
a third of the moon, a third of the stars;
a third of their light was quenched,
a third of the daylight failed,
       likewise the night.

13   *I saw an eagle flying in mid-heaven.*
I heard him shout with a loud cry:
    "Woe, woe, woe!
Three angels are about to blow three last
    trumpets—
these are the three woes against the earth-
    dwellers."

9:1   The fifth *angel blew:*
I saw a star which had fallen from sky to earth;
to it was given the key to the shaft of the Abyss.
2   *When it opened the shaft of the Abyss,*
smoke poured from the shaft as from a huge furnace;
sun and air were darkened by the smoke from the Abyss.

3 *From the smoke came locusts over the earth,*
Authority was given to them, like the authority of earth's
scorpions.

4 *They were ordered not to injure earth's grass, shrub or*
tree,
but only men who lack God's brand on their foreheads.

5 *They were ordered not to kill them*
but only to torment them for five months,
a torment like the torment of scorpion stings.

6 *In those days men will long for death*
but will not find it;
they will desire to die
but death will flee from them.

7 *The locusts resembled horses groomed for battle;*
on their heads crowns like gold,
their faces like human faces,

8 *their hair like woman's hair,*
their teeth like lion's teeth,

9 *their breastplates like breastplates of iron,*
the clatter of their wings like chariots,
drawn by many horses, rushing to battle.

10 *They had tails and stingers like scorpions;*
in their tails lay their power to wound men for
five months.

11 *Over them as King is the angel of the Abyss.*
His name in Hebrew is Abaddon, in Greek
Apollyon.

12 This one woe has gone.
Attention!
Two woes are yet to come!

13   *The* sixth *angel blew:*
> *from the corners of the gold altar before God,*

14   *I heard a voice command the sixth angel with the*
> *trumpet:*
>> *"Set loose the four angels who are bound at*
>> *the Euphrates, the great river."*

15   *The four angels were set loose. They had been kept ready*
> *for the hour, the day, the month and the year, to kill*

16   *one third of mankind. I heard the count of the cavalry:*
> *two hundred million. This is how I saw the horses and*
> *their riders in the vision:*

17   *Breastplates were fiery red, blue, yellow;*
>> *the horses' heads like lions' heads,*
>> *from their mouths poured fire, smoke, sulphur.*

18   *A third of mankind was killed by these three*
>> *plagues,*
>>> *by fire, smoke, sulphur pouring from their*
>>> *mouths.*

19   *The authority of the horses is in their mouth*
>> *and tails;*
>> *their tails are like serpents,*
>> *tails with heads with which they wound.*

20   *The rest of mankind, not killed by these plagues,*
> *refused to repent their handiwork.*
> *They went on worshiping demonic forces,*
> *idols of gold, silver, bronze, stone, wood,*
> *which have no power to see, hear or walk.*

21   *They refused to repent their murders,*
> *their sorcery, their fornications, their thefts.*

10:1   *I saw another powerful angel*
>> *coming down from heaven*
>> *wrapped in a cloud.*
>> *On his head a rainbow,*

his face like the sun,
his legs like pillars of fire,

2   *holding a little scroll, unrolled.*
His right foot he planted on the sea,
his left foot on the land.

3   *He shouted with a roar like a lion.*
When he shouted, the seven thunders added
     their own voices.

4   *When I heard what the seven thunders said,*
I was about to write it down,
but I heard a heavenly voice saying,
     "Don't write that!
       Seal up what the seven thunders said!"

5   *The angel whom I had seen*
standing on sea and land
raised his right hand to heaven,

6   *took an oath by the One who lives forever,*
who created the heaven and everything in it,
the earth and everything in it,
the sea and everything in it.

7   *"The time for delay has passed.*
In these days of the seventh angel,
when he will blow his trumpet,
the mystery of God will be accomplished
as he promised the prophets, his own slaves."

8   *The heavenly voice which I had heard*
commanded me again
     "Go. Take the unrolled scroll
     from the angel's hand,
     who stands on sea and land."

9   *I went up to the angel,*
asking for the scroll.
He said:
     "Take it. Eat it.

It will turn your stomach sour,
but in your mouth it will be honey-sweet."
10   I took the scroll from his hand and ate it.
It was honey-sweet in my mouth,
but when I swallowed, my stomach turned sour.

11   They said:
"Again you must prophesy
to peoples, nations, tongues
and many kings."
11:1   A reed like a rod was given me with the command:
"Rise. Take the measure of God's temple,
of its altar, and those who worship there.
2   Exclude the court outside the temple.
Don't measure it, for it was given to the
Gentiles.
For forty-two months they will despoil the
Holy City.

3   I will give authority to my two witnesses
and they will have power to prophesy,
clothed in sackcloth, for 1260 days.
4   They are two olive trees, two lamps,
who now confront the earth's master.
5   When anyone tries to wound them,
fire bursts forth from their mouths
and devours their enemies.
When anyone tries to wound them,
he must be killed in this way.

6   They hold authority to shut up the sky
so that no rain fall during their prophecy.
They hold authority over the waters
to turn them into blood.
They have authority over the earth

to smite it with plague
as often as they wish.

7   *When they have completed their testimony,*
the beast which ascends from the Abyss
will fight against them, conquer and kill them,
8   *their corpse on the street of the Great City,*
called in prophetic language Sodom and Egypt,
where also their lord was crucified.
9   *Men from peoples, tribes, tongues and nations*
will stare at their corpse for three days and a
half
and refuse to allow them burial.
10   *The earth-dwellers will gloat over them,*
celebrating, sending gifts to one another,
for these two prophets had been a torment
to the earth-dwellers.

11   *But after three days and a half*
a spirit of life from God entered them.
They stood on their feet.
Terror laid hold of the onlookers.
12   *They heard a loud command from heaven:*
'Come up here.'
They ascended to heaven on the cloud.
Their enemies stared at them.
13   *In that very hour came a great earthquake;*
a tenth of the city was shattered,
seven thousand men perished in the earthquake.
The rest were struck with terror
and gave glory to the God of heaven."

14   The second Woe has passed. Attention!
            The third Woe comes quickly.

15   *The* seventh *angel blew.*
          Loud voices in heaven began to shout:
                    "The kingdom of the world has now become
                    the kingdom of our Lord and of his Messiah.
                    He will rule forever."
16   *The twenty-four elders,*
                    seated on their thrones before God,
                    prostrated themselves.
17   *They worshiped God:*
                    "We thank you, Lord, all-powerful God,
                    you who now rule and have always ruled,
                    you have used your great power,
                    you have established your rule.
18   *The nations were enraged*
                    when your fury came,
                    the time for the dead to be judged,
                    the time for rewarding your slaves,
                    the prophets, the holy ones, those who
                              worship your name, both small and great,
                    the time to destroy earth's destroyers."

Structural Analysis

When we try to read this vision rapidly and consecutively, we notice that certain features accelerate our progress while others impede it. Stages along the way are marked with care. Beginning at 8:6 a rhythm is developed which moves the reader steadily forward from the first trumpet-blast through the sixth, but at two points the reader's progress is delayed. The first detour is short (8:3-5); the second is very long (10:1-11:13). We are impelled to ask why an author, having taken pains to mark out a throughway, should introduce such detours. In both cases he seems to have allowed considerations of content to claim priority over considerations of literary symmetry.

The function of the first detour is fairly obvious: it serves as a prelude to the blowing of all seven trumpets. In this prelude the thunders, which are symbolically akin to the trumpets, are traced to their source in the fire on the altar and in the prayers of holy men. The prophet thus stresses his conviction that it is from this source that the various cataclysms proceed. The judgments are released by prayers. Altar, censer, throne—these are all liturgical symbols with great density of meaning. The cacophony of rolling thunders gives voice to the inaudible clouds of incense. In the earlier vision we noted how the breaking of the seals signified the forces released by a heavenly worship which celebrated the victory of the Lamb. There is a parallel here. From the worship of holy men at the altar are released forces which attack the stronghold of idolatry and murder (9:21). In their prayers the conflicts between God's altar and competing altars reach their maximum intensity. From the gold altar the divine responses to men's worship radiate in the form of trumpet blasts. Here the prophet gives a clue to the function of the following episodes. John is dealing not so much with a philosophical analysis of nature or history as with an appraisal of the forces released by prayer and with the ultimate vindication of those prayers. To ignore this setting is to ignore the prophet's purpose.

After this significant keynote, John allows the reader to listen to six trumpets in rapid sequence. The first four paragraphs obviously belong together, as did the four horses in chapter 6. They are brief, symmetrical, conventional. They are organized on the basis of the four traditional segments of the universe: earth, sea, rivers, sky. They are linked together by the oft-repeated "one-third" and by the initial avoidance of the human realm. One also notices that the agent of violence in all four is fire, the fire which proceeds from the altar (8:5). The mixing of this fire with blood is also significant. It is easy to assume that the heavenly origin and the earthly impact of the thunders are separable, so that in one case John is dealing with the invisible and in the other with the visible. This assumption, however, destroys the integrity of the literary form and the intended message. What happens on earth is no less and no more visionary than what happens in heaven.

The fifth angel moves into the realm of human torment, short of death; the sixth embraces the death of one-third of mankind. The formal symmetry of the first four disappears, yet the steady progression of punishment, finally including one-third of mankind, preserves the continuity of the series. It would be quite wrong to separate the visions of chapter 9 from the series, because John has so deftly labeled them as items in the series. Yet they do serve a somewhat different purpose and may have been drawn from a different source. They seem to say that the heavenly altar is not the only source of human frustration. Some of the penalties of the earth-dwellers (8:13) pour out of the abyss in response to orders from the king of the abyss. Those who serve evil are bound to be punished by the Lord of evil, a torment aptly described in 9:6 as a frustrated desire for death. Idolaters become vulnerable to swarms of locust-scorpions and to the serpent-like mouths of innumerable horses. The descriptions of the locusts and the horses seem bizarre to us and even grotesque, but they were rather conventional in John's day.

> In the Old Testament the scorpion is already coupled with the serpent as a symbol of the spiritual evil by which man is benighted. . . . How does the scorpion express its malevolence? In two stages. The first is in the cunning, deceitful, lying fashion in which it attacks . . . suddenly his tail rises and strikes the unsuspecting face. . . . Then, when their sting has been driven home, what else do they do? . . . Error is the venom which . . . gradually poisons. Its falsehood is injected into you; your discomfort increases until you wish you were dead (H. M. Feret, 120f., quoted by permission of Newman Press).

The introduction of the eagle (8:13) succeeds in separating the first four trumpets from the last three. It accents the importance of the last three, and defines the target of all the thunders as the earth-dwellers. John employs still other devices for increasing the dramatic intensity: the greater length of blasts five and six, the reiterated cries of the eagle in 9:12 and 11:14, and the strong vow of the angel in 10:5-7. One dramatic climax is reached in the termination of the sixth blast in 9:2c, 21, where the objective of all the trumpets is shown to be the repentance of the earth-dwellers. It is God's desire for this repentance, rather than Christian vindictiveness, which motivates the thunders. It is this desire which makes all the more culpable the stubbornness of the rebellion. The inflexibility of the earth-dwellers stands in sharp contrast to the attitudes of the holy men in 8:3-5 and in 11:15-18. It is the contrast between prostitution and chastity, murderous hatred and sacrificial devotion.

Because of the rise in dramatic intensity in the description of blasts five and six, the reader's attention is drawn all the more strongly to the seemingly extraneous interlude of 10:1-11:13. If one deletes this section he can move without apparent loss from 9:21 to 11:14. Why should John insert so long a section at precisely this point? Is there material within this interlude that requires its insertion? I believe so, even though one cannot with certainty recover John's reasoning. This material deals primarily with the vocation of prophets, including John himself. There are several suggestive contrasts between this and the preceding vision (4:1-8:1). In both there are scrolls; one the Messiah opens, the other the prophet eats or seals shut. In the first, judgments are released by the Messiah; here the thunders are more closely linked to the prophet's word (10:4). There, God fulfills his promise to the Messiah; here, to the prophets (10:7). There, the beginning and end of the Messiah's work is described; here, the prophetic vocation (10:11; 11:3-12). There, the worthiness of the Messiah is vindicated; here, the worthiness of the prophets (11:18c). We may conclude that it was the desire to relate the vision of the trumpets to the mission of Christian prophecy that led John to place at this point what is one of the longest unbroken speeches in the entire book (11:1-13). This whole speech can be placed in quotation marks, with Christ as the speaker addressing John.

Proceeding on that assumption, we raise several pertinent questions. Do the thunders, from one to seven, express the ultimate results, in God's eyes, of the varying responses to the prophetic message? Is it the prophet, clothed in sackcloth (11:3), who makes clear what repentance entails, in contrast to the unrepentance of earth-dwellers? (9:20, 21) Since the seven blasts are used to announce the fulfilment of "the mystery of God" (10:7), does the interlude make clear the role of the prophets within that fulfilment? Do the results of the first six trumpets comprise the bitterness of the prophet's task, and the seventh its sweetness? Is the death and resurrection of the two prophets as integral to this vision as the Messiah's passion was the key to the seven seals? Did this vision as a whole enable Christian readers to recognize the criteria which distinguished true prophets from false, a recognition vital to the congregations in Asia? The picture of the two prophets in chapter 11 stands in sharp contrast to the pictures of false prophets in chapters 2, 3 and 13, even as it includes an instructive parallel to the picture of Christ in chapter 5. The reader will find it a challenging assignment to trace the links between this interlude and the rest of the vision, noting stylistic, verbal, and thematic connections.

In their effort to understand the literary structure of this section, exegetes have been led to many radically varied conclusions. It is possible, for example, to treat the olive-tree vision (11:3-13) as quite separate from its context, a prophecy complete in itself. It is also possible to consider the little scroll vision (10:1-11:2) as a self-contained unit, quite unrelated to the seven trumpets. It is my conviction, however, that John intended to organize the series as we have it. The reference to the seven thunders in 10:3, 4 ties together chapters 9 and 10, along with the explicit reference to the seventh angel in 10:7. Chapters 10 and 11 are bound together by the promise to the prophets (10:7), the command to John (10:11), the discussion of the authority of prophets (11:3f.), and the inclusion of the prophets in the hymn of praise (11:18). Other links may be discovered, but these are the most important, and, I think, most persuasive ones.

We should observe how John concludes this vision. The short account of the seventh blast (11:14-18) is a genuine and complete rounding off of the entire series. It not only terminates the sequence of seven, it also closes the circle of worship which was introduced by 8:3-5. It ends as it begins, with prayers in heaven before the altar. It encloses the seven trumpets within the range of God's lordship (compare chapter 4), of Christ's power over the world, and of the worship of the twenty-four elders (compare chapter 5). It shows that the vision of the seven trumpets runs parallel to the vision of the seven seals; it should not be construed as describing later events in history. In both visions the prophet's thought is bracketed by a beginning and an end in the powerful event of God's action in Christ. Here, as elsewhere, John's central concern is to show how that event can be verified by the action of men in a later day. The literary form is subordinated to the requirements of enabling Christians to see the contemporary relevance of that event.

For Reflection and Discussion

We believe that the long interlude (10:1-11:13) provokes important questions, all of which are worth examination. In this vision the interlude is the distinctive element; John himself was interested in drawing attention to it. Moreover, since this is the passage which gives the most complete treatment of the prophetic role, a discussion of that role is in order here. Such a discussion may well begin by summarizing material, found elsewhere in Revelation, which indicates John's conception of prophecy. To cover much ground quickly, we resort to brief tabulations. Aspects of the prophet's role which were shared with his brothers:

the worship of God (19:10)
status as a slave of God (1:1)
participation in the same agony, royal power, loyal endurance (1:9)
exercise of authority as priests and kings (1:6)
the task of confirming and verifying the work of Christ (12:17)
acceptance of death (16:6; 18:20)

Distinctive features of the prophet's role (apart from 10:1-11:14):

a special task in the process of revelation (1:1,2)
a special calling and empowerment by the Spirit (1:10; 19:10)
the obligation to see and to hear
the obligation to write, to tell, to enable others to see and to hear
knowledge of "what is and what is to come" (1:19)
obligation to share that knowledge
a position of leadership in the worship of a congregation (1:3)
authority to issue commands, beatitudes, woes to the congregations
special hazards and sufferings (1:9)
responsibility for testing false prophets

Now we may examine more closely the data provided by chapters 10:1–11:2. This series of episodes appears to concern John's own work. Since he is commissioned to prophesy concerning many peoples, nations, tongues, and kings, his message is viewed as having universal scope. Yet it is primarily addressed to God's own worshipers, for the initial assignment is to measure the temple and the altar (11:1, 2). This mission takes place in the midst of conflict which rages for forty-two months between the trampling nations and the holy city. The prophet's work requires that he distinguish the line between the outer court and the altar itself, or between God's worshipers and the agencies of defilement. That work is destined to be bitter as well as sweet. Presumably these two reactions to eating the scroll are ways of describing the conjunction of blessing and woe in the prophet's message, along with the conjunction of suffering and joy in his own vocation. One element in his message is to announce the fulfilment of "the mystery of God. . . . as he promised the prophets" (10:7). Such a statement presupposes John's solidarity with the whole line of prophetic servants as well as a unique role in celebrating the fulfilment of God's promises to them.

Yet there remains a mystery concerning this fulfilment, for the scroll containing the thunders is to be sealed (10:4) and to be consumed by the prophet (10:9). His oral prophecy is the mode by which the trumpets sound. From the references to the trumpets and the thunders (10:3, 4, 7; the two symbols are coordinated), we may infer that the audition of the seven blasts was intended, initially at least, for John himself. They suggest that during the interim between the prophet's disclosure of God's intention (10:5-7) and the accomplishment of that intention in the blowing of the seventh trumpet (11:15-18), it will be the vocation of prophecy which confronts men with an audible and visible sign of that intention. Idolaters must face not only the judgments proceeding from the altar in heaven and the despair which proceeds from the abyss (chapter 9); they must also confront Christ's delegated prophets and decide how to receive them (11:3-14).

It is my conviction that in 11:3-14 we find a picture of Christian prophecy which is designed to clarify that confrontation. The usual efforts to equate the two witnesses (11:3) with two specific historical figures are doomed to failure. To be sure, the biblical language used in this chapter is resonant with memories of Moses, Elijah, Enoch, Jeremiah, and other earlier prophets. This same language also calls to mind the stories of Christian apostles—Peter, Paul, the "sons of thunder," Stephen, and others. But I do not believe that John expected his readers to select two and only two "originals." Rather, he sets forth with capsule brevity his understanding of the situation and vocation which were shared by all the prophets. The symbolic logic and language of a heavenly dialog enables him to embrace many stories in one. Just as all the promises of God meet in Jesus, so do all the prophetic messages from God meet in the situation which John is facing. In fact, he insists on this coalescence of many times and places by his identification of the city in vs. 8. What G. von Rad makes central in the Old Testament perspective is applicable to John:

> All the prophets shared a common conviction that they stood exactly at that turning point in history which was crucial for the existence of God's people. (*Old Testament Theology*, II, 299).

> A statement made in the Old Testament is initially to be understood as standing in the space between a quite particular past in the divine action and a quite particular future. . . . This is the

only place from which one can determine what faith, unfaith, righteousness or the covenant are in this realm of tension between promise and fulfilment" I, p. vii. (Copyright © 1962 by Oliver & Boyd, Ltd., reprinted with the permission of Harper & Row, Publishers, Inc., New York.)

Taking this paragraph, then, as John's description of the continuing role of prophets during that very interim in which he was standing, we may observe several strategic features of that role. The term of the work is determined by the duration of conflict as set forth in the symbolic period of forty-two months or twelve hundred sixty days (vs. 2, 3). Authority stems from the risen Christ, and is expressive of his light (lampstands) and life (olive trees). Sackcloth (repentance) is their true clothing. Their true weapon is fire from their mouth (i.e., their message). The exercise of this weapon parallels what Revelation says elsewhere about the fire proceeding from Christ's mouth. (The use of this weapon is contrasted with the behavior of the false prophet in chapter 13.) Their Lord gives them immunity to destruction until they complete their confirmation of his saving work, but that confirmation also requires a verification in blood. They are to be killed by the same enemy in the same city as their Lord. This death appears to seal their defeat—good reason for their enemies to gloat. But God's vindication of their work, expressed in terms which echo their Lord's ascension, provides the climactic recognition-scene in which the royal power is actually transferred from Satan to God and the prophets are rewarded by their commander. The vocational cycle—struggle, invulnerability, death, vindication—is completed. The destruction of earth's destroyers (11:18) is an implicate of that cycle, actually a spelling out of God's saving purpose as it had been verified by Jesus.

The prophets were needed to add their contemporary verification in such a way that all holy men could be enabled to see "what is and what is to come," not in the age-long history of cultures and civilizations, but in the manifestation of God's will to nations, people, tribes, and tongues. A bitter-sweet scroll indeed. God's command to John was to "take the measure of God's temple, of its altar, and those who worship there." How could that command be fulfilled except by exercising the kind of vocation which is described in chapter 11?

The prophet's vocation, while unique, did not separate him from the vocation of his brothers, but bound them all the more firmly to the same calling. The vision of the seven trumpets, as illuminated by the interlude, provides an excellent example of that partnership. It is in their verification of their witness that Christian prophets are rightly symbolized by lampstands and olive trees. Participation in their Lord's passion made them instruments of the same kind of judgment and redemption which his suffering had set loose among men.

This interpretation of the two olive trees, however, would be rejected by a majority of scholars, and no reader should accept it without reviewing the alternatives. Most scholars assume that John had in mind two particular heroes from Jewish or Christian traditions, and that he provides sufficient clues to establish their identity. This approach, in effect, formulates the problem in algebraic terms. Given that $x + y =$ two prophets, for whom does x stand, for whom y? Drawing the chief clues from verse 6, many infer that the reference to turning the waters into blood alludes to Moses and to the plagues which helped him deliver Israel from Egypt, while the shutting up of the sky alludes to Elijah's miraculous power. Hence, $x =$ Moses, $y =$ Elijah. This has perhaps been the strongest single hypothesis. At the opposite extreme, at least in chronological terms, is the identification with the two Christian prophets, Peter and Paul. (One wonders if Luke was inclined to identify the trees with James and John, the sons of thunder, Lk. 9:51-55). Between Moses and Paul are other prophetic figures who have been nominated, such as Elisha, Jeremiah, or Enoch. (For arguments and analysis, see books listed below.)

When one begins to correlate clues in the text with these various nominations, several difficulties emerge. John makes no

statement which applies solely to either of the two figures separately. Whatever is done, they do together; whatever is suffered,
they suffer together. The time of their prophecy is a single time,
beginning and ending simultaneously and having the same duration. The place is also the same, for although 11:8 mentions three
separate places, it treats them as one. Moreover, none of these
place-names can be restricted geographically. Sodom is a city
but it is also a typological symbol of God's judgment on all the
cities of rebellion. The behavior of Lot and Lot's wife had become paradigms for Christian decision (Lk. 17:28-37). Response
to the Gospel had made Capernaum and Bethsaida subject to
the fate of Sodom (Lk. 10:12f.). From the time of Isaiah on,
the rulers of Jerusalem had been accused of being, in fact, the
rulers of Sodom (Isa. 1:10; Mar. Isaiah 3:10). The selection of
Sodom was appropriate in this vision of John because of the
calling down of fire in 11:5 and because of the trumpet-thunder
in 9:2, 18 (compare Gen. 19:23f.). Egypt was not a city but a
country, long a synonym for any place of captivity from which
God seeks to deliver his people. Wherever the Exodus had been
adopted as archetype of salvation (and this is the case in almost
all early Christian traditions), there Egypt became a stock-image
for all the kingdoms of the earth which enslave Israel (see Strack-
Billerbeck, III, 812). So, too, even before Christ, Jerusalem had
become a typological symbol not only as the center of true worship but as the center of resistance to that worship. Jerusalem
was the place to which God sent all the prophets and the city
which killed or stoned those prophets (Lk. 13:33-35). The holiest
city was also the city trodden down by Gentiles (Lk. 21:24; Rev.
11:1, 2), the locus of both desolation and redemption. In Christian idiom, therefore, it was natural to view Christian prophets
as united to all the prophets, their adversaries united to all those
who had persecuted the prophets (Lk. 6:22, 26), and to epitomize
this whole history as "the place where their Lord was crucified"
(Rev. 11:8). This one city had become in prophetic terms all
cities—Sodom, Tyre, Egypt, Babylon, Nineveh, Rome (see my
essay in *New Testament Studies* 13 [1966] 93f.). In each epoch,

the vocation of the prophets consisted of appearing in the Holy City (or temple) in such a way that reaction to their work would separate the worshipers of God from the trampling Gentiles (11:1, 2).

It is such difficulties as these which prevent agreement among scholars on the identification of the olive trees with two particular prophets. Since it is impossible to limit the time of the prophecy to one historical epoch or to limit the place to one city, one should not limit the olive trees to two men. John's intention, I believe, moved in another direction. He presented the "transcendental model" of all genuine prophecy, taking as a central clue the story of Jesus' appearance in Jerusalem and describing the common vocation in language drawn from the stories of many prophets. One difficulty with this thesis, however, is that of knowing why John should specify *two* lampstands. The best explanation lies, I think, in recognizing that they serve as witnesses; in biblical tradition any testimony must be validated by two witnesses (Deut. 17:6; 19:15; Mt. 18:16; 2 Cor. 13:1; Heb. 10:28). In John's vision the olive trees provide this double testimony for their Lord and against their enemies. One such testimony would not be sufficient; two are needed. I believe a double testimony appears in Revelation for the same reason as in Luke's account of the mission of the seventy, in which apostles were sent out *two by two* into every place "where he himself was about to come" (Lk. 10:1-24).

For Further Study

1. THE TWO OLIVE TREES AND LAMPSTANDS. The following references will provide knowledge of the range of current interpretations:

D. Haugg, *Die Zwei Zeugen*, Munster, 1937; J. Munck, *Petrus und Paulus in der Offenbarung Johannis*, Copenhagen, 1950; J. S. Considine, CBQ, 8 (1946) 377-392; A. Feuillet, NTS, 4 (1958) 189ff.; E. B. Allo, RB 31 (1922) 572-583; L. Gry, RB, 31 (1922) 203-214; P. Minear, NTS, 12 (1966) 93-100; S. Giet, RSR, 1952,

325-362; H. Langenberg, 33-35; N. Brox, 92-104; S-B, III, 811f.; R. Leivestad, 228-230; A. Satake, *Die Gemeindeordnung*, 119-133; G. B. Caird, 133-140; M. Rissi, 96-104; E. Lohmeyer, 87-94.

2. JOHN'S PROPHECY AND SECULAR HISTORY. Now that the student has examined the visions of John in which scholars have discerned implicit or explicit references to events in secular history, the way is open for an informed discussion of the Johannine conceptions of the relations between the story of redemption and the course of world history. The following selections from a very extensive literature represent the major alternatives.

S. Giet, in *L'Apocalypse et l'Histoire* and RSR 38 (1964) 71-92, 225-264 discerns everywhere in the Apocalypse specific references to successive events in Roman imperial annals, as does L. Herrmann, in *La Vision de Patmos*. By contrast, E. Lohmeyer, in his *Commentary*, vigorously defends a mode of thought quite independent of the externals of secular history, attributing to John a timeless kind of transcendence. M. Rissi in *Time and History* (55-98) expounds a view closer to the theories of *Heilsgeschichte* as advanced by O. Cullmann. Still another perspective, advanced with keen penetration, may be found in the essays of H. Schlier, *Besinnung auf der N.T. II*, 358-373; *Die Zeit der Kirche*, 265-273, and supported by H. Zimmermann in BL 1(1960) 75-86. A survey of the various exegetical positions is given by A. Feuillet, *op. cit.*, 9-17. This problem is illuminated by a comparison of the visions of John with the general pattern of theophanies in the Old Testament and with the more specific pattern of prophetic theophanies: see J. K. Kuntz, *Self Revelation of God*, 52-71, 134-168.

4. The Faithful as Victors (11:19-15:4)

11:19   The temple of God in heaven was opened;
in his temple the ark of his covenant appeared;
lightnings came—voices—
thunderings—huge hail-stones—earthquake

12:1   In heaven appeared a spectacular sign: A_1
        a woman robed in the sun,
        the moon beneath her feet,
        a crown of twelve stars on her head.
2   Pregnant, she cries out,
        tormented by her birth-pangs.

3   In heaven appeared another sign: There! B_1
        A colossal fiery dragon
        with seven heads and ten horns;
        on the heads, seven crowns.
4   His tail swept up and cast to earth
        a third of heaven's stars.

  The dragon took his stand before the pregnant A_1 vs. B_1
  woman,
        to devour her child at birth.
5   She gave birth to a son, a male child,
        destined to rule all the nations
        with an iron rod.
  Her son was snatched up to God, to God's throne.
6   The woman escaped to the wilderness,
        where she receives from God a place
        prepared,
        where they will feed her for 1260 days.

7   War broke out in heaven:
        Michael and his angels fought with the dragon;   *A₂*
        the dragon and his angels fought,   *B₂*
8   but they did not prevail.
        No longer was there room for them in heaven.   *A₂ vs. B₂*
9   Cast down was the colossal dragon, the
            primeval Snake,
        called the Devil or Satan,
        who seduces the whole world.
        He was cast down to the earth;
        cast down with him his angels.

10   I heard a loud voice in heaven: *C*
        "Now has come the salvation and the power,
            the kingdom of our God,
            the authority of his Messiah,
        for cast down is the accuser of our brothers,
        who accuses them day and night before our
            God,
11   for they have conquered him by the Lamb's
            blood
        and by their own work of confirmation,
        for even in death they did not yield to self-love.

12   So be merry, you heavens!   *C*
                    Be merry, you whose homes are
                        there!
                    Woe to the earth and the sea,
                    for the Devil has come down to
                        you!
                    He is furious, for he knows
                    his time is short."

13   When the dragon saw that he had been cast down   *A₁ vs. B₁*
        to the earth,

> *he pursued the woman who had borne the*
> > *male child.*

14 *To the woman were given the two wings of the*
> *huge eagle,*
> > *so that she could fly to her own place, to the*
> > *wilderness,*
> *where she is fed for three years and a half,*
> > *out of the Snake's reach.*

15 *The Snake spouted water from his mouth like a river*
> > *after the woman, to sweep her away in the*
> > *flood,*

16 *but the earth came to the woman's help;*
> > *it opened its mouth*
> > *and drank the river which the dragon's mouth*
> > *spouted.*

17 *Furious with the woman, the dragon went away to* A, vs. B,
> *wage war*
> > *on the rest of her children,*
> > *on those who obey God's commands and*
> > *hold fast to Jesus' work of confirmation.*

18 *And so the dragon took his stand on the seashore.*

13:1 *I saw a beast rising from the sea* B,
> > *with ten horns and seven heads;*
> > *on its horns ten crowns*
> > *on its heads the name 'Blasphemy.'*

2 *Like a leopard was the beast I saw,*
> *like the feet of a bear its feet*
> *like the jaws of a lion its jaws.*
> *To it the dragon gave his own power,*
> > *his throne and great authority.*

3 *One of its heads was as slaughtered*
> *but the plague of its death was healed.*
> *The whole earth was hypnotized by the beast;*

4   *they worshiped the dragon because he gave authority*
         to the beast;
    they worshiped the beast, saying:
                "Who is its equal?
                Who has power to resist it?"

5   *It was given a mouth to speak arrogant blasphemies;*
    it was given authority to operate for forty-two
         months;

6   *it opened its mouth in blasphemies against God,* A_3 *vs.* B_3
                it blasphemed his name,
                it blasphemed his temple,
                those who dwell in heaven.

7   *It was given power to fight against the holy men and*
         to conquer them;
    it was given authority over every tribe, people,
         language and nation.

8   *All the earth-dwellers will worship it,*
         all whose name appears not in the Life-Book of
                the Lamb
                     who was slaughtered ever since the
                          world began.

9   *Let everyone who can hear listen to this:*
10   *"Whoever goes into slavery, into*   C
                          slavery must go.
                Whoever kills with a sword, with a
                     sword must be killed.
         This is the key: the loyal endurance, the
         faithfulness of holy men."

11 *I saw a second beast rising from the earth;* B_4
         it had two horns like a lamb, but it spoke like
              a dragon.

12   *It exercises the whole authority of the first*
          beast in its presence;
      it causes the earth and the earth-dwellers to
          worship the first beast,
              whose death plague was healed;
13   *it works spectacular signs, even making fire*
          descend before men from heaven to earth;
14   *it deceives earth-dwellers by the signs it was*
          allowed to work in the beast's presence,
      inducing earth-dwellers to make an idol to
          the beast, who received the sword-plague
          and yet came alive.
15   *It was allowed to impart breath to the idol of*
          the beast, so that
              the beast's idol might speak
      and sentence to death as many as would not   *A, vs. B,*
          worship the beast's idol.
16   *Unknown and famous,*
                      rich and poor,
                      free men and slaves,
      it causes them all to be branded on their right
          hand or on their forehead,
17   *so that no one is able to buy or sell unless he*
          has the brand, the beast's name or the number
              of its name.

18   *This is the key:* Wisdom
                  Whoever has intelligence should cal-
                      culate the number of the beast.   *C*
                  It is a human number. Its number
                      is 666.

14:1   **I looked:**   *There! The Lamb has taken his*
                                   stand on Mt. Zion

with him a hundred and forty-
 four thousand,   *A₃*
having his name and his father's
 name
inscribed on their foreheads.

2 I heard a voice from heaven:
   like the voice of many rivers,
   like the voice of great thunders,
   a voice like harpists playing on their
    harps.
3   They sing a new hymn before the throne,
   before the four living creatures and
    the elders.
   No one is entitled to learn that hymn,
   but the hundred and forty-four thousand
   whom he purchased from earth.

4   These are virgins, they have never *C*
    been defiled with women.
   These are men who follow the Lamb
    wherever he goes.
   They have been purchased from men
    as a first installment
     for God and the Lamb.
5   They are blameless; no false confes-
    sion was found on their lips.

6 Flying in mid-heaven I saw another angel *B₃*
with an eternal gospel to proclaim to the earth-
 dwellers,
7 and to every race, tribe, language and people,
  shouting loudly:
     "Fear God! Give glory to him! *C*
     The hour of his judgment has come!

Worship him who created the heaven,
the earth, the sea, and
the sources of the rivers!"

8   A second angel followed, shouting: B_5
"Great Babylon has fallen, fallen.
All nations have drunk the wine
of [God's] fury on her fornication."

9   A third angel followed them, shouting loudly:
"Whoever worships the beast and   C
its idol,
whoever receives its brand on
forehead or hand,

10 he will drink the wine of God's fury
poured out straight in the cup of
his wrath.
He will be tormented by fire and
sulphur
before holy angels, before the
Lamb.

11 The smoke of their torment rises
forever,
day and night they have no
rest,
those who worship the beast and its
idol,
who receive the brand of his
name."

12 This is the key: The loyal endurance   C
of the holy ones,
who obey God's commandments,
who hold to the faithfulness
of Jesus.

13   I heard a command from heaven: "Write!
           From now on, blessed are those who   C
           die in the Lord.
           They shall now receive rest from
               their travail, for
           their works accompany them.
           The Spirit says 'I guarantee it.' "

14   I looked:
           There! A white cloud!   A vs. B₈
           On the cloud sits a figure like a man
           with a gold crown on his head,
           a sharp scythe in his hand.

15   Another angel came from the temple,
           shouting loudly to the one who sat
               on the cloud:
                   "Send your scythe! Harvest!
                   Harvest time has come,
                   the crops of earth are
                       withered."
16   He who sat on the cloud sent his scythe to the earth,
           and the earth was harvested.

17   Another angel came from the temple in heaven,
       he also had a sharp scythe.

18   Another angel came from the altar
       who held authority over the fire.   A vs. B₈
       He shouted loudly to the one with the sharp scythe:
                   "Send your sharp scythe!
                   Gather the grapes from
                       earth's vineyard,
                   for the bunches are ripe."

19 *And the angel sent his scythe to the*
earth;
he gathered earth's grapes;
he cast them into the great wine-
press of God's fury.
20 *The wine-press was trampled outside*
the city.
Blood flowed from wine-press, as
deep as horses' bridles,
for two hundred miles. . . .

15:2 *And I saw what looked like a crystal sea, mixed with fire.* A_3 *vs.* B_6
Standing at the crystal sea, the victors over the beast,
its idol, and the number of its
name.
3 *They play God's harps and sing the hymn of Moses,*
God's slave, and the hymn of the Lamb:

"Lord God of all power, C
your works are majestic and
marvelous.
King of the nations,
your ways are just and trustworthy.
Lord, who will not fear you?
4 *Who will not glorify your name*
for you alone are holy?
All nations will come and worship
before you
for your justice has been vindicated."

The Structural Analysis

We have already noted how the trumpet-thunders prepared the way for this new vision. Amid the reverberations of the thunders the prophet had received his mandate to prophecy concerning peoples, nations, tongues, and many kings. (10:11. The unusual choice of the word kings may be significant.) His task included the measurement of the temple (compare Eze. 40:3). This would bring him into direct confrontation with the beast (10:7) who exercised his sovereignty over the court outside the temple (11:2). It would, in fact, result in an apparent victory of the beast and his cohorts, as a stage necessary in the ultimate vindication of the royal power of God and of his Messiah.

If there is a center of gravity in 8:2-11:18, it falls on the war between the two prophets and the beast (11:7); in 11:19-15:4 the center of gravity falls on the issues at stake between the earth-dwellers and the holy men, between the two armies commanded by the Dragon and the Lamb. To help the reader find the evidence, I have added in the right hand margin of the translation several letters, which seek to isolate, for purposes of comparison, the adversaries (A and B) and the calls for decisions (C).

A_1 is the woman and B_1 is the dragon (12:1-6)
A_2 is Michael with his angels, B_2 the dragon with his angels (12:7-9)
A_3 is the children of the woman (12:17, 18)
B_3 is the sea-beast (13:1-7)
B_4 is the earth-beast (13:11-17)
B_5 is the company of earth-dwellers, including Babylon (14:5-11).

If we study these in sequence we can see that John relies upon a recitative-like narrative to describe the battle. The recitative carries forward the account of the warfare in terms of a steady shift in personnel:

The Woman vs. the dragon
Michael vs. the dragon
The woman's children vs. the dragon
The woman's children vs. the sea-beast
The woman's children vs. the earth-beast

The whole of chapter 14 then resounds with alternating voices which declare the verdict of heaven upon the virgins (14:4) and upon the beast-worshipers (14:5-11).

The recitative materials are punctuated regularly with what we have termed calls for decision on the part of the readers of the Apocalypse. Here we detect John's main purposes for writing. Some of them, in fact, have the form of asides which are directed by the prophet to the Christians in Asia. Two of them call explicitly for loyal endurance and one for discernment (13:9, 10; 13:18; 14:12). Two or three are in hymnic form, with the intimate *you* and *our* of congregational worship (12:10-12; 15:3, 4). Others express exhortation and warning by way of beatitude and woe (12:12; 14:13) or by way of angelic explanations (14:4). All of these imply that the real issue at stake in the warfare, at whatever stage or with whatever opponent, is whether the followers of Jesus will endure or will become earth-dwellers. The closing scene pictures those who endure (15:1-4).

Many exegetes treat all the material from Ch. 12 to the end of the book as a single unit. They observe that in chapters 12 and 13 are identified, in descending order, the line of command in Satan's army: first the commander-in-chief, then the sea-beast, the earth-beast or false prophet, Babylon, and finally, all the beast-worshipers. The series of pictures showing their defeat, however, is given in reverse order: the beast-worshipers (14:9-11, 14-19), then Babylon (18:1-24), then the beast and false prophet (19:20), and finally the arch-monster himself, with his associates Death and Hades (20:14). We should keep in mind the forward momentum provided by this double sequence.

Recognizing that all these chapters narrate stages in the fulfilment of the prophet's task (10:11), we must, however, divide the text into smaller units. This is desirable for practical purposes, since one's mind can hardly cope with so large a body of material at once. But it is also desirable for scientific purposes. As a literary architect, John had a conception of the whole temple before he began constructing its various arches. Care in that construction was necessary, for each arch needed a symmetry of its own if the whole temple were to be seen in its unity.

Our first task, a difficult one, is to conjecture the beginning and end of this particular arch. We have selected 11:19 as the beginning for two major reasons. First, it is the practice of the prophet himself to choose heaven for the locale of each vision, thus showing how everything that happens is consequence of the release of power from heaven. Here as elsewhere we are dealing with what appears in heaven (12:1), with what emanates from God's temple, and with the ways by which God fulfils the covenant with his pilgrim people on their Exodus through the wilderness (11:19; 12:14. This motif continues that of 11:8). God has made a covenant with his holy ones; wearing the name "Blasphemy," the Dragon seals a parodic covenant with his deceived ones. The vision unfolds both the parodic triumph of the beast-worshipers and the real triumph of the Lamb-worshipers. All of this is an index to the real power which God exercises in his temple in defence of his covenant. The second reason for choosing 11:19 as the beginning of a new vision is the awkwardness of attaching it to the previous vision. Elsewhere John never terminates a vision with a verse like this. The song of the twenty-four elders (11:17, 18) is itself both a typical and an adequate ending of the vision of trumpet blasts.

Where does this vision end? Surely not at 13:18, where some commentators locate it, inasmuch as that verse does not conclude anything; 14:5 might serve, since the action appears to stop there and another series of angels seems to take charge. A still better choice is 15:4; 15:3, 4 is a hymn of triumph which is liturgically homogeneous with the scene of 11:19. In 15:5 the temple is opened again, the sign for a new set of plagues. Finally, and most important, 15:2-4 is in its content an effective summary of the previous chapters. Here as elsewhere the prophet is unwilling to close a vision on the note of wrath (14:17-20); always it must be paired with a note of victory. From the beginning to this end, the struggle proceeds between the nations (Gentiles might be a better translation here: see 11:2, 9, 18; 12:5; 13:7; 14:6, 8; 15:3, 4) and those who conquer "the beast, its idol, and the number of its name." (This threefold series, often repeated, is significant.) The sea of glass mingled with fire is the symbolic counterfoil to the sea from which the beast rises (13:1); so, too, the rejoicing of the Lamb-worshipers is the antithesis to the songs of the beast-worshipers (11:10; 13:4; 14:3). In fact, every line of the song of Moses, the slave of God, is an artistic rebuttal to the lies which have deceived the slaves of the beast. Accepting, then, the whole passage from 11:19 to 15:4 as a unit in the prophet's literary outline, let us examine the sequence and the functions of the various paragraphs within it. We are not helped by any septenary device, a proof that John did not feel bound to a seven-fold division. It would not have been of much use, since the prophet wishes to distinguish various echelons in a complex power structure.

The sequence is easy to recover from 12:1 through 14:5, for there is, as we have seen, a noticeable progression in the *dramatis personae*, in the location of the warfare, and in the threats and assurances given to the readers. Let us examine the paragraphs successively.

12:1-17. The woman and the dragon are introduced as the ultimate antagonists. The arena is heaven. The initial focus of conflict is the birth of the woman's child. When God saves this child the woman flees to the wilderness. Now war breaks out in heaven. Michael and his angels contest the place of the dragon and his angels. The latter army loses and is evicted from heaven. So the battle scene shifts to the wilderness where Satan struggles to destroy the woman. He fails. If we assume the stance of John's readers and assume that they would grasp the identity of the actors, we can more easily trace the sequence of the accents in John's appeal to those readers. The first accent comes in vs. 5 and falls upon God's rescue of the woman's child and his enthronement to rule the nations. The second accent comes in vs 11-12 and falls on the weapon which is powerful enough to enable the Lamb to overcome, along with those whom he frees from self-love. The third comes in vs. 17 and is most significant of all. It identifies the rest of the woman's offspring as those who, accepting God's design, seek to verify in their own lives the power of Jesus. Satan's war has shifted from heaven to the wilderness and then to any place where the woman's offspring could be found. Its target has shifted from the Messiah (12:4) to the mother (12:13), to her other children (12:17). The stake remains the same and the weapons the same. It is clear that John is most concerned with the current phase of the war between the dragon and these other children; this is also the phase in which John's readers are engaged.

13:1-10. 12:17c effectively introduces the later phases of the war, for the dragon is also now most concerned with those children. How shall he regain the initiative? He needs reinforcements. Standing on the beach, he therefore summons a beast from the sea, his first *alter ego*. Although the origin of this beast is the sea, the locus of his battle is the earth. The literary form is designed to accomplish several functions: first, to indicate the collusion of dragon and sea-beast as powers that share the same throne and authority (vs. 3, 4); second, to indicate their joint unqualified success in persuading the earth-dwellers to worship them (vs. 3, 4, 8); third, to indicate their temporary and qualified success in blaspheming against God by overcoming those among whom he dwells, the heaven-dwellers (vs. 6, 7a). The message of the prophet required those three functions in order to reinforce his appeal to his readers, who were potential beast-worshipers among the offspring of the woman. The prophet wished to elicit their loyal endurance (13:10). So to endure in worshiping the Lamb required on their part an understanding of how the beast had been killed and how he had then been returned to a position of power (vs. 3; see p. 247f.); this understanding, in turn, required that they remember how the woman and her child had overcome the dragon (12:5, 11, 16). To dissuade those who might obey the prophet's appeal in 13:9, 10, the dragon and the sea-beast realized the need for a more deceptive *alter ego*.

13:11-18. That *alter ego* appears now as a beast summoned by the dragon (who since 12:17 is the apparent master of ceremonies) from the earth (in John's vocabulary the realm under Satan's control, see p. 261f.). In describing this phase of the war, where the action must in the nature of the case be more deceptive, the earth-beast must fulfill more subtle functions. On the one hand, his identity with his superiors must be maintained. This is done symbolically (a voice like a dragon) and also quite directly by his assertion of the same authority and objectives. But, on the other hand, the earth-beast must display similarity to the Lamb (vs. 11) sufficient to seduce Christians, a display which required the use of signs similar to those of the true prophets (compare 13:13 with 11:5). He must even give persuasive evidence of the resurrection of the beast, thus converting men into worshipers of that beast. He must be able to convince men that their life or death depends upon worshiping the beast.

The progression of action in chapter 13 describes the application of greater and greater pressure to those who keep the commandments of God and who loyally endure in their witness of Jesus (12:17). The degree of pressure, although steadily becoming more intense, also becomes more internalized. More and more discernment is needed (13:18), to detect the ever more circuitous lines of attack. At the end, Satan's attack must be launched from a beachhead within the Church, where the earth-beast not only carries on priestly activities but displays the credentials of a prophet. The readers are called to discern the criteria which will enable them to separate the lamb-like beast (13:11) from the Lamb himself (14:1).

14:1-5. This paragraph belongs in the same sequence of battle scenes, even though it describes the resolution of the battle. Now the prophet answers the question of how to discern the name which is written on men's foreheads (14:1 is a complete rebuttal of 13:1, 6, 8, 17). Over against the dragon who stands on the beach is the Lamb who has taken his stand on Mt. Zion. Over against the sea and its baleful power, the prophet can hear the voice that sounds like many waters. Before the throne of God (not the throne of the beast) sing those who have been purchased from the earth (not purchased by the beast). This paragraph appears to complete the action of the warfare by presenting a picture of victory comparable to that of the Lamb at the beginning (12:11), thus showing how completely John was concerned

"Blessed are the dead who die in the Lord" (Rev. 14:13)
a tapestry (number 5) in the Museum of Tapestries. Angers
(Fourteenth Century)

throughout with the problem of whether those who claimed to follow the Lamb would be persuaded to belie their confession (14:5) or would follow "wherever he goes."

We earlier suggested that 15:1-4 is a more fitting conclusion to the vision. How, then, are we to explain the prophet's addition of 14:6-20? Is it another interlude? What is its thematic function, representing as it does a change from the closely-knit fabric up to this point?

We hazard this guess: in 14:6-20 the prophet wished to summarize the certain and just enforcement of God's judgments (15:4d) upon the dragon's henchmen; 14:5 assures the faithful of divine mercy, but it stops short of describing the fate of the opposing army which had been allowed "to make war on the saints and to conquer them" (13:7). John must also answer the question of their fate. One angel addresses a warning, really a gospel, to the earth-dwellers. Another proclaims the curse on Babylon, an anticipation of the next vision, but also an indication that Babylon and the nations of beast-worshipers are allied in John's mind. A third declares a terrible doom for those who worship the beast. Another voice assures life for those who die in the Lord. Finally, earth itself as a whole is harvested, both the grain and the wine—a judgment inclusive of all the others combined, since earth itself was an image which included earth-dwellers, earth's kings, and earth's beasts. There is no neat line of thought in these sentences and no detailed pattern of arrangements. But two accents seem to dominate the whole: (1) the identity of the two communities which the warfare serves to separate, the earth-dwellers vs. the servants of the Lamb; and (2) the appeal to the Christian readers for such discernment and endurance as would furnish means by which they could confirm and verify the victory of their Lord.

Questions for Reflection and Discussion

Each vision poses two problems for the reader: what constitutes John's distinctive purpose in that specific vision and, in view of that purpose, on which features of the vision should the reader concentrate? In analyzing the structural features, we have already answered the first question. In the vision of the seals, John presented the victory of the Lamb and the vindication of his worthiness to rule. In the vision of the trumpets, John concentrated on the victory of the two prophets and the vindication of their worthiness to mediate the promises of God. In the present vision he is more directly concerned with the victory of those "who follow the Lamb wherever he goes" (14:4) and who thereby attest their worthiness to sing the hymn of Moses (15:3). Although the warfare engages all echelons of authority in the opposing armies, it is seen from the perspective of the private soldiers. It is viewed as the struggle between those who are deceived and conquered by the beast, on the one hand, and those who conquer the beast, on the other (13:8; 15:2). The whole vision becomes a call for the holy ones to verify their faithfulness by acute perception of enemy strategies (13:18) and by loyal endurance (13:10; 14:12). The first issue for discussion is whether this analysis is accurate.

The second issue, in turn, is the selection of those features of the vision most germane to the prophet's purpose. It is in this process of selection that many commentators lead the student into various detours which, although they may be interesting enough, are not strategically vital. For example, hundreds of essays and even books have been written to deal with the precise identity of the woman clothed with the sun (12:1-6). Most of these are motivated by the mariological debates of the past four centuries and not by the strategic demands of the prophetic vision itself. What are those demands in this case? It would seem to be essential to the prophet's argument to give full weight to the double role of the woman as that community which is mother at once of the Messiah and of those who share the Messiah's work (12:5, 17). I do not think it is so decisive for understanding John's message to determine the degree to which he identified this community with the person of Mary. The same observation should be made with reference to the work of

Michael and his angels, which has also provoked a flood of writing, much of which is not really germane to the original line of communication between John and the Asian churches.

A great deal of scholarly work has also concentrated upon the identification of the two beasts of chapter 13, and upon what the prophet intended to convey by the wound of the beast (13:3) and the number 666 (13:18). This cluster of concerns is undoubtedly vital to John's central purpose, although I think that the obsession with decoding the numeral 666 often leads to a gross distortion of emphasis, since John used this numeral in one verse only. He is greatly concerned, to be sure, with the power of the beast; but he does not rely upon this numeral alone to convey his message to his original readers. And it must be said that even after most expositors have translated the cryptogram 666 into some historical equivalent satisfactory to themselves, this solution is of little help in understanding John's vision as a whole. In this study we have recognized the strategic importance of comprehending what John had in mind when he wrote about the sea-beast, the earth-beast, the wounded head, and 666. We have sought to give in the essays of Part II our solutions of this whole complex of symbols. There is no need to repeat our conclusions here, even though they constitute the basis for formulating what now seem to be the most fruitful topics for discussion.

The struggle which is described in this vision is best grasped by collating the various descriptions of the combatants, whom we may call the heaven-dwellers vs. the earth-dwellers (12:12). Those who dwell in heaven are known by their verification of the Lamb's love through their conquest over self-love (12:11). Thus they prove their ancestry (12:17), their holiness and sainthood (13:10) and their powers of discernment (13:18). Thus they reveal whose name is inscribed on their foreheads (14:1-5), how permanent are their deeds (14:12, 13), how fruitful their vocation (15:1-4). It is clear from these descriptions that their victory is both subjective and objective, both internal and external, both sub-conscious and conscious, both empirical and transcendent.

Drawn in sharp contrast are the pictures of the earth-dwellers, who accept and worship "the beast, its idol, the number of its name" (15:2). They exemplify the wrath of the devil (12:12) and his success in his warfare against the messianic mother (12:17). They marvel at the sea-beast's recovery from the plague of death and are thereby induced into assuming the omnipotence of the beast (13:3, 4). They are taken captive (13:10) and they yield to all sorts of deceptive political, economic, and religious pressures which are exerted by the earth-beast (13:12-18). They become vulnerable to the scythe of the harvester (14:9-11, 14-19), their torment providing the full antithesis to the joy of the heaven-dwellers (15:2-4).

Having thus identified the antagonists, we select one topic for more detailed examination. This is what we may call the dynamics of deception. The victory of the heaven-dwellers stems from their refusal to be deceived, whereas the earth-dwellers succumb to that deception. The immediate agent of deception is the dragon-like, lamb-like earth-beast of 13:11-18. What is it that gives him his power to deceive? John later speaks of him as the false prophet (16:13; 19:20; 20:10). John has already outlined the role of the true prophet (11:1-13). May we learn something of the dynamics of deception by observing the antithetical descriptions of these two roles?

For elucidation of this topic I am indebted to an article by E. Watson and B. Hamilton ("Lumen Christi-Lumen Antichristi: The Exegesis of Apoc. 11:5 and 13:13 in the Mediaeval Latin Fathers," in *Rivista di Storia e Literatura Religiosa*, II [1966], 84-92). The central thesis of this essay is this: "The image which is common to both texts (11:5, 13:13) is fire as a symbol of power: the contrast lies in the use to which that fire is put. Fire proceeds from the mouths of the two witnesses to the greater glory of God; the Second Beast brings down fire from heaven in the sight of men to the greater glory of Anti-christ." In the essay may be found a long, detailed, and cogent support for this thesis. First comes a survey of the early interpretations of 11:5. The fire of true prophecy is the power of God's word, the power of that word to inflame hearts with the love of God, the pentecostal power of the Holy Spirit to produce the glorification of God within the church, the power of the double love-commandment to overcome self-love. Second, the authors review early interpretations of 13:13 which find in the beast's use of fire a parody of Pentecost, a use of God's word to do the devil's work, a false preaching which brings Christians into the service of the antichrist. The devil uses pseudo-charismatic gifts in order to test the faith of Christians and to create a community which will resemble the true Church in possessing the marks which distinguish that Church. The parody of Pentecost and the parody of the true Church accomplished by the parodic prophet causes men "to confuse good and evil, by making them mistake the followers of antichrist for the true church and the worship of antichrist for the worship of the true God" (p. 88). Third, the authors trace (p. 89) the fire of the beast to the natural human desire for signs from heaven (see Mt. 16:1). Finally, the authors collect the iconographical evidence from the Middle Ages (e.g., the tapestries of Angers) which shows that the artists, like the exegetes, interpreted as a parody of Pentecost the fire which the second beast brought down from heaven.

This line of exploration is highly rewarding. Students of Revelation, once given this link between the pictures of the true and the false prophets in chapters 11 and 13, should seek for other links. How much importance should be given to the following items, separately and cumulatively?

- There are two prophets; the beast has two horns.
- The duration of witness is 1260 days; of deception, 42 months (12:5).
- The power and authority of both false and true prophets are derived from their "lords."
- True prophets stand before the lord of the earth; the false prophet before the beast.

- In each case, the word of the prophet carries power to slay his adversaries.
- In both cases, death is followed by life, apparent or real, temporary or permanent.
- In both cases, the result of the work of the prophet is the fear and worship of God.
- In both cases, the *name* is an important symbol of the issues at stake (11:18; 13:17).
- In both passages, the result of the prophetic signs on the earth-dwellers is stressed (11:10; 13:14).
- God retains full right to vindicate or repudiate both prophecies.
- In both passages the writer accents the inclusion of all men in the struggle (11:9; 13:16).

Readers will give differing weight to the separate items in the list above. Some entries are dubious, but other items are difficult to attribute to sheer coincidence. Readers will also differ in the weight they give to the cumulative evidence.

Those who are persuaded that John consciously drew each portrait to correspond to its opposite should return to the prior question. Does the double portrait throw light upon the dynamics of deception in the work of the sea-beast as a false prophet? John's views of both true and false prophets were, of course, shaped by his views of their respective lords. A comparable contrast may be found in the dual portraits of the Lamb and the earth-beast, both of whom had been killed and restored to life. This contrast may provide essential criteria for distinguishing false prophets from true, since the vocations of prophets stem from their respective lords. Other helpful data may be located in John's warnings against false apostles, teachers, and prophets in the seven letters. There can be no doubt that John consciously stressed the solidarity in doom of the dragon and the two beasts, as well as the solidarity in blessedness of the Lamb and his prophetic witnesses. The dynamics of deception are therefore inseparable from the dynamics of punishment. Slavery to deception bears ineluctable penalties designed to fit the crime (13:11-18; 14:9-11), just as victory over deception produces a commensurate reward (14:1-5).

If one follows out the implications of this mode of analysis he will move steadily away from the current interpretation which is content to locate in the earth-beast only a reference to priests of the imperial cult and in the sea-beast only a reference to Nero. He will ask why the imperial cult could appear to Christians so deceptively masked in the robes of prophecy, and how the legend of Nero's suicide and return could become an effective rival to the worship of God. Watson and Hamilton, with whose essay we began the study of this topic, are correct in insisting that the effort to find literal, historical equivalents for the sea-beast, an effort which recurs in every century of exegesis, weakens and debilitates the whole force of the image of fire (*op. cit.* p. 89). That effort, when successful, drastically restricts the message of John to a single moment in the history of the church. By contrast, the awareness of the functions of the two kinds of fire in John's day preserves the continuing relevance of the vision without in any way denying the urgency with which John was addressing himself to a specific situation.

For Further Study

1. CHAPTER 12 AND THE ROLE OF THE WOMAN. The most extensive Protestant study is P. Prigent, *Apocalypse 12, Histoire de l'Exegese;* the most thorough Catholic examination is B. J. Le Frois, *The Woman Clothed with the Sun* (with bibliography, xii-xiv). The student should in addition consult a sampling of the following: A. Feuillet, *L'Apocalypse*, 91-98, a bibliography; A. Feuillet, RB 66 (1959) 55-86; J. Michl, BZ 3 (1959) 301-310; J. E. Bruns, CBQ 26 (1964) 459-463; F. M. Braun, RT (1955), 639-669; L. Cerfaux, ETL (1955), 7-33; P. Rigaux, RB 61 (1954) 321-348; A. M. Dubarle, in *Mélanges biblique* (Festschrift for A. Robert) 512-518; A. Th. Kassing, *Die Kirche und Maria;* G. H. Dix, JTS 1925, 1-12; A. Kassing, BK 15 (1960) 114-116;

P. Minear, *Christian Hope*, 149-162; K. Rahner, *Mary, Mother of the Lord;* F. M. Braun, *La mère des fideles;* M. Thurian, *Mary, Mother of the Lord;* O. Semmelroth, *Mary, Archetype of the Church;* E. B. Allo, 187-199; L. Legrand, *Biblical Doctrine of Virginity;* M. Rissi, TH, 35-40.

2. CHAPTER 13 AND THE NUMBER 666. R. Schütz, *Offenbarung des Johannes und Domitian;* H. Langenberg, BA, 225.; P. Minear, JBL 72 (1953) 93-102; H. Schlier, *Die Zeit der Kirche*, 16-28; E. Watson and B. Hamilton, RSLR 2 (1966) 84-92; A. Farrer, *Rebirth*, 294f.; R. H. Charles, I, 332f.; S. Lägerlof, *Miracles of the Antichrist;* B. Newman, NTS 10 (1963) 133-139; E. Stauffer, *Coniectanea Neotestamentica*, 11 (1947) 237-241; H. A. Sanders, JBL 37 (1918) 95-99; W. Hadorn, ZNTW (1919) 11-29; A. H. McNeile, JTS 14 (1913) 443-444; E. Stauffer, TNT, 213-219; U. Simon, ENY, 159-187; E. B. Allo, 232-236; C. Brütsch, 237-246.

3. THE ANTICHRIST. The two beasts with the dragon constitute a demonic trinity of antichristic forces. The mode of interpretation has troubled scholars from the beginning. The following list has been selected to show the range of possible conceptions. H. Schlier, *Principalities and Powers;* B. Noack, *Satanas und Soteria;* W. Bousset, *The Antichrist;* R. Leivestad, *Christ the Conqueror*, Pt. IV; Halver, *Der Mythos;* K. Heim, *Jesus the Lord*, Pt. III; P. Minear, *Eyes of Faith*, Ch. 4; *Kingdom and Power*, Ch. 5; *Horizons*, Ch. 2; G. B. Caird, *Principalities and Powers;* J. Danielou, *Jewish Christianity*, Ch. 6, 14; H. Gunkel, *Schöpfung und Chaos;* B. Rigaux, *L'Antechrist*, 318-382; L. Cerfaux, *Numen*, Supp. 4 (1959) 459-470; E. Stauffer, 64-68, 213-219; E. G. Selwyn, 313-362; J. Horst, 263ff.

4. THE APOCALYPTIC THEME IN FICTION. Readers of the Apocalypse must constantly be warned against the tendency to equate Christ and Antichrist with objectively defined historical entities (Church vs. State) or with simplistic conceptions of moral behavior (chastity vs. sexual promiscuity). Novelists and dramatists are effective teachers of the complexity of the apocalyptic conflict and of the subtlety needed for its interpretation. An introduction to the apocalyptic theme in modern fiction may be found

in R. W. B. Lewis, *Trials of the Word* (New Haven, 1965), 184ff. and G. Dudley III, *The Recovery of Christian Myth* (Philadelphia, 1967). Examples, widely varied, of notable fictional treatments of apocalyptic motifs: F. Dostoevsky, *The Possessed;* S. Lagerlof, *Miracles of the Antichrist;* G. Bernanos, *Star of Satan;* T. Mann, *Doctor Faustus;* F. Buechner, *The Final Beast;* N. West, *Day of the Locust;* H. Böll, *Billiards at Half-Past Nine* and *The Clown.*

5. Victory Over Babylon (15:5-19:10)

A. THE PANORAMA (15:1, 5-16:21)

15:1 I saw another sign in heaven, great and spectacular—seven
angels with seven plagues, which are the last, because with
them God's fury is ended. . . .

5   Afterward I looked:
> thrown open was the sanctuary of the Tent of Witness in
> heaven,

6
> out of the sanctuary came the seven angels with the seven
> plagues,
> robed in shining white linen, with gold scarves around
> their chests.

7
> One of the four living creatures gave to the seven angels
> seven gold bowls full of the fury of the God who lives
> forever.

8
> The sanctuary was so filled with smoke from God's glory
> and power that
> no one was able to enter the sanctuary until the seven
> plagues of the seven angels were ended.

16:1
> From the sanctuary I heard a loud command to the seven
> angels:
>> "Go! Empty over the earth the seven
>> bowls of God's fury."

2
>> The first went and emptied his bowl over the
>> earth.
>> A foul, devilish ulcer appeared on those men
>> who bore the brand of the Beast,
>> who worshiped his idol.

3 *The second emptied his bowl over the sea.*
   it turned to blood, like the blood of a corpse.
   Every living thing died,
   everything in the sea.

4 *The third emptied his bowl over rivers and*
      water-springs.
   They turned to blood.
5 *I heard the angel of the waters say:*
            "You are just in condemning
               these things, O holy one,
                  you who now rule and have
                     always ruled.
6   *They have poured out the blood of*
               holy men and prophets,
                  so you have given them blood to
                     drink.
            They deserve it!"
7 *I heard the altar approve:*
            "Yes, O Lord, all-powerful God,
               your verdicts are reliable and just."

8 *The fourth emptied his bowl on the sun.*
   It was allowed to scorch men with fire;
9 *men were seared with great blisters.*
   They blasphemed the name of God
            who authorized these plagues;
   they would not repent by giving glory to Him.

10 *The fifth emptied his bowl on the Beast's*
      throne.
   His kingdom was plunged into darkness.
   They gnawed their tongues with pain.
11 *They blasphemed the God of heaven for their*
      pains and ulcers,
   but they did not repent of their deeds.

12   *The sixth emptied his bowl over the* Euphrates,
        the great River.
        Its water was dried up to prepare the road
        for the kings to come from the East.

13   *I saw three polluted spirits like frogs*
                    from the mouth of the Dragon
                    from the mouth of the Beast
                    from the mouth of the false
                        prophet.
14   *These are demonic spirits, working*
                        miracles,
                    sent to summon the kings of the whole
                        world
                    to battle on the Great Day of God,
                        the all-powerful. . . .

15   *(Attention!*
                    I am coming like a thief!
                    Blessed is the alert watchman
                    who guards his clothing,
                    lest he walk naked
                    and men stare at his shame.)

16   *. . . and they gathered them at the place*
                    called Armageddon in Hebrew.

17   *The seventh emptied his bowl over the* air.
        From the throne, out of the sanctuary, came a
            loud voice;
                    "It is ended."
18   *Lightnings, voices, thunders, a great earthquake*
            came.

> *Never since men have lived on earth has any*
> *earthquake been so violent.*
> 19   *The Great City broke into three parts.*
> *The cities of the Gentiles fell.*
> *Great Babylon was remembered before God;*
> *he gave her the cup*
>   *with the wine of the fury of his anger.*
> 20   *Every island fled; every mountain vanished.*
> 21   *Hailstones, heavy as hundred-weights, fell on*
> *men from heaven.*
> *They blasphemed God for the plague of hail,*
>   *so terrible was that plague.*

The Structure of the Panorama

This vision begins, like the others, with certain stylized features. Heaven is thrown open (4:1; 11:19; 19:11). The prophet sees the inner sanctuary where God has his throne (16:17) and from which he authorizes the attack on the throne of the beast (16:10). The angels are garbed in white and gold. They receive the bowls from one of the four living creatures, who have served as agents of God's glory and power. The contents of the bowls suggest that all seven are to execute verdicts of wrath. There are perhaps two novel features in this opening paragraph. The Tent of Witness is mentioned as a reminder of Israel's stay in the wilderness, of God's covenant which had been sealed there, and of the plagues which accompanied the rebellions against Moses. Furthermore, an explicit warning is given that no one can enter the temple until these plagues have been executed, a sober warning indeed for pilgrims to the Promised Land.

In the literary structure of this particular septenary there are other distinctive features. Most notable is the fact that, having begun the series of seven, John moves through to the end with only very brief interruptions. This fact is connected to another: none of the seven deals explicitly with God's merciful promises to the faithful, but all deal with the threats of doom to blasphemers. The picture of destruction is unrelieved in its bleakness. Why does the prophet vary his pattern in this way? Probably because he wished to depict in this first section a telescopic view of the entire panorama of plagues, so that thereafter he could devote himself to a microscopic and detailed treatment of the seventh plague—God's verdict on Babylon. It is for this reason that we have divided our analysis of structural elements into two sections: 15:5-16:21 and 17:1-19:10. This allows us to study at the outset the entire series of bowls.

We discern again a distinction between the first four and the last three items. The first four, appearing in mathematical sequence, cover the traditional divisions of nature: earth, sea, rivers, sky. In each case, however, the plague on nature is immediately translated into suffering for mankind. Each plague is described in language reminiscent of the Exodus from Egypt. There is an ominous ring to the rhythm, a ring which becomes explicit at the end of the fourth plague (16:9): "they blasphemed . . . they would not repent." This very rhythm conveys the sense of a steady escalation of guilt and acceleration of penalties. There appears to be only one interruption to the smooth flow of thought and symmetry of stanzas: the dialog in 16:5-7 between the angel and the altar. This dialog clarifies the logic which permeates the whole series: the blood which sinners drink, which is poured out on them, is just requital for the blood of holy men (15:1-4) and prophets (11:3-13) which these sinners have poured out. With blood God vindicates the martyr's self-sacrifice of blood. God's wrath is exercised in recognition of their love; this recognition affects the language as well as the logic of the prophet.

In the last three items, thought shifts from nature to the human scene as represented by the kingdom of the Beast, by the Euphrates (traditional site of an attack upon the imperial power), and finally by the heartland of enmity, the Great City itself. The plagues move relentlessly forward until they reach a climax in the verdict of God on Babylon. In its fall is included the ruin of all the cities of the Gentiles. This is why of all the earthquakes that had destroyed cities in the past (and the archaeologists' spade has uncovered many of those ruins), none had been so violent as this final earthquake which would embrace them all. The fifth plague strikes that kingdom of which Babylon is the archetypal embodiment. The sixth releases those demonic spirits which sound the tocsin for the final battle against Babylon. The seventh celebrates the doom which falls inexorably on the Great City, epitome of all enemy empires.

The forward momentum is broken by one quite surprising and sudden halt. Verse 15 stops the flow of thought like a lightning bolt from another world. Did John mean to destroy the artistic integrity of his scheme of seven bowls? Or did he mean to interject a clue which would reveal the intention of that scheme? We must discuss this point after analyzing the rest of this vision. The forward momentum is less obviously broken by another interruption, the episode of the three frogs in vss. 13, 14, 16. Why did John speak of frogs in this particular sequence? He may have wanted to link this vision to the earlier description of the warfare between Christ and these three embodiments of antichristic forces (ch. 12, 13), a vision in which the fall of Babylon and the destruction of the Beast's throne had been promised (14:6-11). He may also have wanted to point ahead to the later account of Armageddon, in which the three mouths out of which the frogs came would be destroyed after aiding God in his destruction of Babylon (19:17f.). In any case, it is worth noting that in these three strategic episodes (ch. 14, 17, 19) God uses demonic spirits in the final destruction of the forces of evil.

B. THE MICROSCOPIC DETAIL (17:1-19:10)

17:1   One of the seven angels with the seven bowls came to me
         and said:

2   "Come. I will enable you to see the verdict on the
            great prostitute, who sits on the many waters. Earth's

A Statue of Artemis
discovered *1956–57 in Ephesus (First Century)*

kings have committed adultery with her. The earth-
dwellers have got drunk on the wine of her adultery."

3   *He carried me in the Spirit to a wilderness where I saw*
                a woman sitting on a scarlet Beast,
                which was full of the names of blasphemers,
                with seven heads and ten horns.
4   *The woman was robed in purple and scarlet;*
                she was gilded with gold, jewels, pearls.
                She carried in her hand a gold cup
                filled with abominations,
                the pollutions of her adultery.
5   *On her forehead was inscribed a name, a*
                    mystery:
                        "Babylon the Great,
                        mother of prostitutes,
                        mother of earth's abominations."
6   *I saw her drinking the blood of holy men,*
                the blood of Jesus' guarantors.

7   *On seeing her I was astounded, but the angel asked:*
                "Why this astonishment?
                I will explain to you the mystery of the   *d*
                    woman
                and the mystery of the Beast which carries   *a*
                    her,
                with his seven heads and ten horns: *b,c*

8   *"The Beast which you saw did rule, but rules no*   *a*
            longer.
      He is about to ascend from the Abyss and to go to
            perdition.
      When they see the Beast, that he ruled but rules no
            longer
                and is to come,
      the earth-dwellers will be astonished,

those whose names have not been inscribed
in the Book of Life since the world began."

9   (This is a call for the intelligent man to use his wisdom.)

         "The seven heads are seven mountains, on which   b
             the woman sits.
         They are also seven kings—
10   *five have fallen,*
                   one is ruling, the other has not yet
                      come;
                   when he comes he must remain a
                      short while—
11   *The Beast which did rule, but rules no longer,*   a
         is himself an eighth, yet one of the seven;
         he is going to perdition.

12   *"The ten horns you saw are ten kings*   c
         which have not yet received a kingdom.
         With the Beast they will receive authority
         to rule as kings for one hour.
13   *They agree in a common cause, to give*
         to the Beast their power and authority.
14   *They will wage war on the Lamb*
         but the Lamb will conquer them,
         for he is Lord of lords, King of kings;
         those on his side are the called, the chosen, the loyal."

15   He said to me:
         "The waters which you saw,
         where the prostitute is sitting,
         are peoples, crowds, nations and tongues.
16   *The Beast and the ten horns which you saw—*
         they will hate the prostitute,

they will make her a wilderness,
they will strip her naked,
they will devour her flesh,
they will consume her with fire.
17 For God planted his purpose in their hearts
to join in a common cause,
to give their kingdom to the Beast
until God's purposes are realized.

18 The woman which you saw is the Great City   d
which exercises sovereignty over earth's kings."

18:1 Afterward I saw another angel coming down with great
2 authority from heaven. The earth was alight with his glory.
With a powerful voice he shouted:
"Babylon the Great has fallen, fallen.
She has become the haunt of demons,
the prison of every polluted spirit,
the cage of every polluted, hateful bird,
3 for all nations have drunk the wine
of the fury of her adultery.
Earth's kings have committed adultery with her,
earth's merchants have fattened on the power
of her affluence."

4 I heard another voice calling from heaven:
"O my people, come out of her,
5 lest you share in her sins
and receive a share of her plagues,
for her sins have risen to heaven
and God has remembered her injustices.

6 Give her tit for tat!
Whatever she has done; double it!
Pour her a double portion of the cup she mixed!

7 *Give her as much torment and grief*
as she gave herself of arrogance and luxury.
Because she gloats in her heart:
  'I now rule as queen,
  I am no widow,
  I shall not know grief,'
8 *therefore her plagues will fall in a single day:*
  famine, grief, death.
She will be consumed by fire,
for mighty is the Lord God who condemns her."

9 *When they see the smoke from her burning, earth's kings,*
those who shared her adultery and affluence, will weep and
10 *wail over her. Standing far off from dread of her torment,*
they will cry:
  "Woe to you! Woe to you!
  O great city, O mighty city, Babylon!
  In a single hour your condemnation has come."

11 *Earth's merchants will weep and grieve over her, for*
no one buys their merchandise any more:
12 *gold and silver, jewels and pearls,*
  cloth of purple and silk and linen,
  scented wood and ivory dishes,
  precious carvings, bronze, iron and marble,
13 *cinnamon, spice, incense, perfume and frankincense,*
  wine and oil, flour and wheat,
  cattle and sheep, horses and chariots,
  the bodies and souls of men.

14 *"Fled from you are the objects of your soul's lust;*
  vanished from you all the glamour and splendor,
  never again to be found."

15 *Traders in these things, who had grown rich off the city, stood*
far off from dread of her torment, weeping and grieving:

16   *"Woe to you! Woe to you!*
    O Great city!
    City robed in linen, purple, scarlet,
    city gilded with gold, jewels, pearls,
17   *in a single hour so much wealth was made*
     wilderness."

18 *Pilots, travelers, sailors and all who worked at sea*
stood far off when they saw the smoke of her burning.
They kept wailing:
    "What other city is like the great city?"
19 *Weeping and grieving they threw dust on their heads, wailing:*
    "Woe to you! Woe to you!
    O great city,
    where all ship owners
    grew wealthy from her splendor!
    In a single hour the city was made wilderness."

20   "O heaven, O you holy men,
      O you prophets and apostles,
      rejoice over her, for from her
      God has claimed justice for you."

21 *A mighty angel lifted a stone, heavy as a millstone, and*
hurled it into the sea, saying:
    "With such violence as this
    will the great city, Babylon, be hurled down,
    no longer to be found.

22   *No longer in you will be heard*
     the music of harps and singers,
     of flutes and trumpets;
    No longer in you will be found
     the artists of any craft;

No longer in you will be heard
the sound of a mill;
23   no longer in you will be seen
the light of a lamp;
no longer in you will be heard
the voice of bride and groom,
for your merchants were earth's potentates,
by your sorcery all nations were deceived,
24   in you was found the blood of prophets and
holy men,
the blood of all who have been slaughtered on
the earth."

19:1   Afterward I heard what sounded like the roar of a great
multitude in heaven:
"Alleluia!
The salvation, the glory, the power of our God!
2   His verdicts are just and sure.
He has brought to judgment the great prostitute,
who polluted the earth with her adultery;
from her hand he has claimed justice
for the blood of his slaves."
3   Again they shouted:
"Alleluia!
Her smoke is rising forever."

4   The twenty-four elders and the four living creatures prostrated
themselves
and worshiped the God who is enthroned, saying:
"Amen! Alleluia!"

5   A message came from the throne:
"Praise our God
all his slaves,
you who fear him,
whether unknown or famous."

6   Like the roar of a huge multitude,
    like the rushing of many rivers,
    like the rolling of mighty thunders,
    I heard them shouting:
            "Alleluia!
            Our Lord, the all-powerful God
            has established his kingdom!
7   Let us rejoice, let us celebrate,
            let us give him the glory,
            for the wedding of the Lamb has come!
            His bride has prepared herself;
8   she has been given pure white linen to wear;
            this linen is the vindication of holy men."

9   He said to me:
        "Write this down: Blessed are those invited to the
        Lamb's wedding supper!"
    Again he said:
        "This is the sure purpose of God."

10 When I fell at his feet to worship him, he said to me:
        "Don't worship me. Worship God!
        I am your fellow-slave,
        fellow-slave of your brothers,
        who verify Jesus' work of confirmation.
        That very work is the spirit of prophecy."

Literary Structure

This major segment of this important vision may be divided
into consecutive sections, each of which fulfills different functions
and is composed of different types of literary forms.

17:1-6. In this brief paragraph the prophet accomplishes a number of objectives. He announces his theme in the opening verse.
He indicates the associations between the prostitute and the

Beast, earth's kings and earth-dwellers, and, on the other hand, the faithful witnesses to Jesus. His lurid description of the prostitute is designed to combine various details from Old Testament prophecies with the strongest possible contrast to the woman of chapter 12 and the bride of chapter 21. The following correspondences are typical:

17:1	prostitute	21:2	bride
1	many waters	22:1	river
2	earth's kings	21:24	
	adultery	21:8	
	wine	21:6	water of life
3	Spirit	21:10	
	wilderness	21:10	mountain
	scarlet beast	19:11	white horse
	name	20:15	
4	jewels	21:19	
	forehead	22:4	

17:7-18. In this section the angel explains to the prophet the various mysteries to be treated in the remainder of the chapter. His explanation moves from the beast (vs. 8) to the heads (9b, 10), to the horns (12-14), to the waters (15), and finally to the city (18). It must be confessed that what is purported to clarify the initial riddle only makes it more opaque. According to this paragraph, John is more concerned with the Beast than with the city and more concerned to link this vision with other visions than to make this one self-sufficient and self-explanatory. He stresses several features in the Beast's role which appear contradictory. As one instance, the Beast (with heads and horns) makes war against the Lamb (vs. 14); even so, he acts in line with God's purpose (vs. 17). Again, the Beast appears at the outset as an ally of the prostitute, but at the end he hates her and is instrumental in her downfall (vs. 16). The most frequently recurring motif in the role of the Beast is the phrase "was, is not, is to come," which I have translated in terms of ruling (vs. 8, 10, 11, 12). The understanding of this motif indeed calls for every

intelligent man to exercise his wisdom (vs. 9). Here and elsewhere it is helpful for the reader to remember that John's perspective is that of a prophet struggling with the Beast and
dealing with the Beast's power from the standpoint of faith in
God.

18:1-24. The fall of Babylon, announced on earlier occasions, is
celebrated with appropriate language and lament. Reading the
chapter consecutively but omitting vss. 4-8 and vs. 20, we note
that the funeral litany begins and ends with angels who exercise
great power. In both cases the prophet utilizes a dirge-like
rhythm, in vss. 2, 3 stressing by six lines of synonymous paral-
lelism the accusations against the city, and in vss. 21-24 describing her desolation in terms of five parallel couplets followed by
the repetition of the basic charges which justified her destruction.
Between are the poignant laments and curses of those groups
who have been polluted by the city's adulteries: the kings of the
earth (the lament comes in vs. 10, but is based on vs. 3), the
merchants of the earth (the laments are in vs. 14, 16, anticipated
in vs. 3 and echoed in vs. 23), the sea-going traders (vs. 19). Set
over against these laments, this funeral litany, are two messages
addressed especially to God's people. The first calls for them
to break loose from their attachment to the city and justifies the
vengeance which is her lot (vs. 4-8); the second is a hymn of
rejoicing which, coming after the last lament, stands in very
sharp contrast to it. The form of both the dirges and the hymns
of joy are shaped after Old Testament models and saturated with
typical prophetic irony and savage humor. At important points
the portrait of the city is painted in colors opposite those of the
new Jerusalem (Ch. 21, 22).

19:1-10. Never does John end a vision on the unrelieved note of
doom. Here again allelulias replace dirges. The scarlet dress of
the prostitute is replaced by the white linen of the bride. Echoing
here are the songs of a huge multitude of holy men, prophets
and apostles, groups which in 18:20 had been addressed by the

salutation "O heaven." They constitute the choir in 19:1-3, 6-8. They respond with praise to the message from the throne (vs. 5) and receive the hearty approval of the elders and living creatures (vs. 4). The vision ends with the disclosure that the angels are themselves fellow-slaves who find their vocation in worshiping God by ratifying the revelation of Jesus Christ. The fusing of all these things together—hymns of victory, beatitudes, injunctions to worship God, the command to write—justifies the selection of this paragraph as the intended conclusion of the vision.

Questions for Discussion

As a means for organizing the discussion of this vision, we have selected two issues which seem to be strategic to John's purposes. Both are so repellent to modern taste that few readers relish this section and even fewer preachers base sermons upon it. The first deals with the recovery of John's purposes, the second with his conception of God's wrath. The two are, of course, woven together; but discussion may be enhanced by separating them.

(1) John's purposes. We begin by outlining the exegetical position which has dominated recent studies. At the risk of caricature, we may summarize that position thus: Babylon stands for the Roman empire, the avowed and powerful enemy of the Church; in John's day that empire required Christians to worship the emperor as divine. The line between refusal and willingness to worship the emperor is the line on which John has chosen to fight. He seeks to arouse in his readers an intense hatred and loathing for everything Roman and he promises them eternal happiness in exchange for their readiness to be killed. His double appeal thus constitutes a prime example of hate-literature and of the attempt to maintain social control over a ghetto community. He pursues this objective by extreme use of both carrot and stick. Drawing a sharp line between the in-group and the out-group, a line which is impossible to maintain in actual life, he encourages the members of the in-group to gloat over the

anticipated suffering of their enemies (which did not in fact
come to pass) and to invest their fortunes in the impending
vindication of their own dreams (which also failed to materialize).

I have elsewhere challenged the essential assumption on
which this exegesis is based, the assumption that Babylon is a
simple, unambiguous code-word for Rome and that John is
writing as a self-appointed spokesman of the Church in its battle
with the State (see p. 235f.). It is, of course, clear that John
is addressing insiders, not outsiders, and that he desires to produce positive action on their part. How, then, does John conceive
the options confronting those churches? And what kind of actions
does he wish to encourage?

The first strand of evidence may be located in what we have
called the brackets of the vision, its beginning and its end. In
15:5 we have noted an explicit warning. None of the readers can
enter God's temple until the plagues are finished, i.e., until they
have passed the examination which has been set for them. The
pouring out of the bowls represents not the vindictiveness of the
Church against its enemy but the trial of its own faithfulness.
Such an inference, which may seem unjustified at first, is
strengthened by the concluding bracket, 19:1-10, in which victory
in that trial on the part of the faithful is presupposed. Several
aspects of that victory are stressed. To conquer is to praise God
and to give him the glory. The greatest danger to such worship
is the development of idolatry in their own hearts. They had
been in doubt of the dependability and justice of God's judgments. Is he in fact the ruling king? If so, his kingship can be
verified only by guarantors who hold firm to the type of verification attested by Jesus (19:10). John uses the vision in an appeal
to Christians to wash their linen in his blood. Their justice and
holiness must correspond to God's standard, their faithfulness
must conform to that of the Lamb. The blessedness of those
invited to the Lamb's supper (analogous to Mt. 25:31-48) is
wholly contingent upon their readiness to worship God in his
way, i.e., by his Passion. John intended his readers to hear this

appeal, not to gloat over their human adversaries. The only alternative is their rejection by the Lamb (analogous to Mt. 22:1-14).

A second strand of evidence is provided by several nuances woven into the account of emptying the seven bowls. Implicit in 16:2 and 10, for example, is John's warning against worshiping the idol of the Beast. Presumably Christians were tempted to do so. One form of this temptation was the feeling of resentment over the apparent impotence and injustice of God (16:5-7) and the related refusal to repent (16:11). We may recall similar appeals and refusals in the seven letters. The plagues serve as the Lamb's way of waging war against the Beast, but that war involves the testing of the Beast's hold over the Lamb's followers. Would those whom he had called prove themselves worthy of being chosen? (17:14. Compare Matthew 22:14; see K. Stendahl, *Root of the Vine*, 63-80.) More than a test of strength is involved here. It was primarily a test of discernment, for Christians were more vulnerable to unconscious than to conscious treasons. They were susceptible especially to demonic spirits (parody of the Holy Spirit) which performed miracles (parody of genuine charismata) through the work of false prophets (16:13-16). There is considerable evidence, therefore, that in telling his readers about the seven bowls John adopted a strategy to counter the insidious arguments being used by leaders within the Church to reduce the rigor of Christ's demands.

A third strand of evidence is provided by the location and rationale of the beatitude in 16:15.

> "*Attention!*
> *I am coming like a thief!*
> *Blessed is the alert watchman*
> *who guards his clothing,*
> *lest he walk naked*
> *and men stare at his shame.*"

Far too little has been made of this beatitude as a clue for interpreting the whole vision. R. H. Charles has analyzed the problem and has decided that the beatitude could not have originally been located at this point. I should like to hazard another solution. I accept the Greek text as it stands and reject any conjecture of gloss or interpolation. If this verse interrupts the flow of thought, and it does, John intended to interrupt it, as he frequently did in other visions. He broke into the stream of consciousness in order to jolt his readers into becoming as mentally alert as the beatitude itself demands. They are at the point of falling asleep. Christ threatens their drowsiness with his own thief-like coming. Christ wants them to realize where they are standing, precisely between the call to battle and the assembling of the soldiers. The issue is whether they will answer the frog's call or the Messiah's. For them neutrality is impossible. If we assume that the rest of the paragraph deals only with forces external to the Church, the interjection makes no sense. But if we adopt the opposite assumption—that the paragraph deals with forces which penetrate the internal life of the Church—the interjection makes full sense.

This line of reasoning is supported by the normal use of beatitudes by Jewish and Christian prophets. Although teachers often used them to embody proverbial wisdom on the more conventional ordering of life, it was the habit of prophets to use them to support an emergency appeal. Often in prophetic discourse they epitomized a long section of eschatological teaching or formed the climax of an apocalyptic hymn. In a capsule-size axiom they made explicit what was only implicit in a longer parable or vision. To God's people, gathered to hear a message from him, they conveyed his promise in the face of critical tests. Sometimes they were conjoined to a woe which voiced God's threat; at other times this threat was implicit in the beatitude itself. A beatitude had this advantage: only the hearer could determine by his action whether he accepted the promise (or warning) as applicable to himself. It had also the advantage and the weakness of paradox. Assuming a sharp either-or, it asserted the divine reversal of human evaluations: "Blessed are you poor." The prophet could therefore effectively use the beatitude in forcing believers to re-examine their own alertness. The one who said "Blessed" was assumed to be God; the word was assumed to be addressed to those who wanted his blessing; yet the desired word must surprise them. (See, for example, in addition to the familiar beatitudes in Revelation and the Synoptics, Dan. 12:12; Tob. 13:14; Psa. Sol. 4:23; 17:44; 18:6; James 1:12; 4 Ezra 7:13. K. Koch, *Was ist Formgeschichte*, Neukirchener Verlag, 1964, 8f., 20f.)

Most of these aspects of the prophetic use of the beatitude-form are illustrated in Rev. 16:15. It is located at a highly dramatic moment, between the sixth and seventh items in the series and between the call to battle and the response. There could not be a sharper contrast between blessedness and the work of the demonic spirits. The saying reveals the terrible danger in which the unsuspecting Christian stands. If one asks with R. H. Charles, "How could any one sleep through the cosmic earthquakes which were happening?," one may answer, "That is just the point." There were Christians asleep, so John believed, quite undisturbed by din of doom, unaware that anything was happening that could threaten their treasure or leave them exposed and naked. To be asleep was to be unconscious of the urgent necessities of the time. (Compare the disciples in Gethsemane, Mk. 14:26-42.) The beatitude was designed for sentinels who had forgotten that a war was being fought. It served to internalize and to demythologize the elaborate imagery of the apocalyptic conflict, so as to disturb congregations that felt secure (3:1-6). Far from being an easy and cruel speech, it constituted a penetrating warning against the smooth and cruel speeches which were coming from false prophets (16:13).

A final strand of evidence concerning John's purposes may be found in the direct injunction from heaven: "O my people, come out from her" (18:4ff.). Quite obviously the intent of this command depends upon the meaning of Babylon and the nature of her sins. It is wise not to try to substitute for the name Babylon the name of a human institution or agency. It is wiser to collect all that John says about her and to allow this to give the term its content. The very form of the command carries certain implications. For example, it implies that Babylon is a realm into which one may enter, in which one can dwell, and which one may leave. All this is clumsy indeed if Babylon be made simply a code-word for the non-Christian segment of humanity or for the Roman empire. The command presupposes the possibility of choice; in fact, it presupposes that choice has already determined the realm in which one is dwelling. Departure is made synonymous with abandoning a share in her sins. (The Greek term for "share" is the same as in 1:9!) What, then, are the sins which constitute such a partnership? The list is long and lurid, but a profuse and vivid vocabulary should not lead us to suppose that the sins themselves were so obvious as all that. The three most frequent categories are idolatry, adultery, and blasphemy—three sins which were universally recognized by Israel as deserving maximum punishment. But other categories are to be included—self-glorification, self-sufficiency, pride, complacency (18:7), reliance on luxury and wealth, avoidance of suffering.

The best procedure is not first to locate Babylon as a particular city, and then to attribute these sins to that city, but first to grasp the character of the sins, and then to infer that where they are found, there is Babylon. Where demons dwell, where foul spirits congregate, where prostitution and luxury-seeking thrive, there is Babylon. And from that city John calls his readers to come. Babylon is the mother of earth's abominations, the source of every evil intent and deed, the queen of those believers who prostitute their faith, who accept the deceptive wiles of compromisers and appeasers. To blaspheme the Bride is to become degraded by the whore, whose scarlet and purple robes contrast so vividly with the white robes of the Bride. Blasphemy thus defined presupposes an earlier verbal commitment to holiness. It is from every hidden form of this blasphemy that Christ calls his people. Obedience to the call makes them vulnerable to Babylon's violence, but invulnerable to the plagues with which God requites her (18:4, 5).

This concept of "coming out" makes intelligible the frequent reminder that Babylon's doom takes place in a single hour. We have observed that the holy man can and must decide in which city to dwell—Jerusalem or Babylon. The sudden effectiveness of this choice corresponds to Babylon's vulnerability. The lure of her self-sufficiency, of her immunity to mourning, of her secure affluence, can burst suddenly like a bubble. Her sins are such that those who break loose from them receive the power to join in inflicting the plagues. They rejoice in the execution of God's judgment "in a single hour." Babylon's kingdom depends for its very existence upon the continued allegiance of her subjects; their exodus marks her doom.

To sum up, then, the prophet seeks to change the attitudes and actions of readers who have been enticed into fellowship with Babylon's sins. He warns them that they have been deceived in their reading of the balance of power in human affairs. He calls them to awake, to dissociate themselves from the prostitutions of faith which make them residents of Babylon and, by a fresh act of repentance, to join in celebrating the doom of the great city. The foregoing analysis does not exhaust the possible interpretations of this vision; but it does supply an outlook whereby we may understand the rationale of the vision.

(2) John's conception of God's anger. Central in John's descriptions of God's anger is the image of bowls of blood and wine which intoxicate men. The choice of this image is far from casual and its meaning may be far removed from that of our first reactions. When we envisage the Apocalypse as an emergency measure to keep Christians faithful in a time of persecution, it seems that the prophet is voicing all the pent-up frustrations and hostilities of a helpless minority. His promise of a gory death for persecutors, combined with his pledge of glorious rewards for the martyrs, is the measure of his own vindictiveness and, worse, his own betrayal of Christ's love of his enemies. The accuracy of such a reading is debatable. Let me outline an interpretation which may be more cogent, even if more complex.

Why should John select bowls as instruments of divine

wrath? During the first century, as archaeological excavations have demonstrated, bowls were a part of the daily life of every household. Nothing was more common, more ordinary, more necessary. Because they had so many uses, there was a wide variety in types of bowls. Bowls were also a part of every kind of religious function, a fact which enhanced their symbolic value. No temple, no altar, no priesthood, no festival could do without them. Especially bowls made of silver or gold were closely related to the cultic expression of "man's ultimate concern," to use Paul Tillich's phrase.

It is to this sacred context that John appeals by his choice of this image. The first reference to it comes in 5:8, where the twenty-four elders are described as carrying bowls as instruments of adoration and praise. The material is gold, sure sign of their dedication to divine worship. They are filled with incense, immediately explained as the prayers of holy men. In adopting this idiom, John takes his place in a long-standing Jewish tradition. The altar furniture for Moses and for the twelve tribes during the Exodus had included bowls (Ex. 27:3; Num. 4:1-14). The covenant with God had been sealed with bowls of blood, poured half on the altar and half on the people (Ex. 24:1-8). Solomon's temple with its altar had required an elaborate set of gold utensils (I Chron. 28:17). When Babylon despoiled Jerusalem, all the gold bowls had been removed from the temple and taken to Babylon (Jer. 52:18), poignant proof of the totality of the desecration. Zechariah had referred to bowls in two prophecies with which John almost certainly was familiar. In one, the sacredness of the altar-bowls (14:20) had symbolized both the plagues inflicted on rebellious nations and the bringing of the wealth of the nations into the Holy City, when they came to join in worship of the Lord of hosts. In the other (9:15) the sons of Israel had been pictured drinking the blood of their enemies like wine, "as full of it as altar-bowls" (Moffatt). It is not therefore a novel thing to find John using this same syndrome of bowls, blood, wine, altar, and drinking to celebrate the triumph of God's people over their adversaries.

We should notice how John develops this imagery in his picture of the final conflict. The scene is heaven, the Tent of Witness, the sanctuary (15:5f.). The bowls are given to the seven angels by one of the four living creatures, linking this scene to the worship of the Lamb in 5:8. The bowls are carried by angels in white linen, marking their kinship to the holiness both of the Lamb and of his loyal followers. The air is heavy with incense, redolent of God's power and the prayers of his slaves. The content of the bowls is the blood which men are given to drink in punishment for their sin. But what is the sin? It is the killing of holy men and prophets (16:6). Their blood had been poured out as self-sacrifice on the altar. Therefore it is the altar itself which proclaims the justice of the plague. Blood for blood. Heaven-dwellers poured out their own blood; earth-dwellers shed that blood; God pours out that blood on rivers and seas. The wrath of God is his justice at work, vindicating the self-sacrifice of his servants and frustrating the strength of men who worship the Beast (16:3, 4, 10). The bowls become the cup which Babylon must drink (16:19). But as it is her sin which constitutes her prostitution (17:2), the blood becomes wine; this wine brings on drunkenness for the harlot, for all kings and great men of the earth and for all earth-dwellers (17:2, 6). The bowl, now a cup, is filled with all of her abominations (17:4; 18:3). Yet the justice remains constant. She herself must drink from the brew which she has mixed (18:6). The seven plagues represent the effect on earth and its residents of the emptying out of the blood of prophets and holy men.

In view of this survey of the complex of bowls of blood, what can one say about John's views of God's wrath? Are those views compatible with the love of God as manifested in Jesus' passion? Without trying to arrive at a neat and complete answer, we may affirm the following observations as germane to a discussion of the issue.

1. Interpreters should ignore neither the character of this document as a prophetic vision of heaven, nor the intentional use of irony, nor the conventionally hyperbolic language habitually used by a prophet.

2. Full weight should be given to the fluidity of the imagery and to its traditional meanings in the literature of Israel.

3. John's language and message should not be distorted to solve problems which he did not have in mind (e.g. the problem of a theodicy).

4. It is not strange that a prophet, so strongly convinced of the love of God as was John, should speak so bluntly of the wrath of God against those who, having affirmed their commitment to love, later prostituted their vocation by compromising in subtle ways with self-serving. John would have recognized as a betrayal of love any tendency to minimize the wrath of God in this situation.

5. The plagues of blood may therefore be not John's way of calling for retaliation against external enemies of the Church, but his way of warning avowed worshipers of the criteria by which their own hypocrisy is detected and punished. His use of mythological materials is his way of saying with Paul "We wrestle not against flesh and blood, but against principalities and powers. . . ."

6. The penalties for the iniquities of Babylon are ultimately self-chosen and self-inflicted. The sins of blasphemy are of such a nature that they carry along their own reward. A man cannot worship demons without being possessed by the demons he worships.

7. If one affirms the truth that he who seeks to save his life will lose it, is he not under some obligation to describe how that loss takes place and how to avoid it? Did not Jesus also have a lively sense of how all self-seeking resulted in death as an expression of God's wrath? (Compare Rev. 19:20 with Mt. 25:41.)

8. The line between insiders and outsiders was not frozen. John did not believe that his readers were immune to the plagues. He offered no preferential treatment for them. No sin or punishment is mentioned in this vision which was not present in one of the seven churches.

9. Even in this vision of doom, the possibility of repentance is affirmed; refusal to repent is seen as more culpable than the previous adulteries.

10. Even if a reader finds such considerations insufficient to clear John of vindictiveness, he would still be left with the same problem: how, then, does God vindicate his justice and his power if such terrible prostitutions are allowed to avoid a final accounting?

Consideration of such factors leads me to applaud the wisdom of the following conclusion of G. B. Caird: "John makes no attempt to usurp the judgment seat of God, either by a dogmatic universalism or by an equally dogmatic particularism. There would be no point in a last judgment unless the final decisions lay in the hands of the Judge; and John is content to leave them there" (*op. cit.*, 260).

For Further Study

1. THE ANGER OF GOD AND THE CHRISTIAN ETHIC.

A. T. Hanson, *The Wrath of the Lamb*, 159-180; D. H. Lawrence, *Apocalypse;* R. Leivestad, 212-238, 300-310; R. Schnackenburg, *Moral Teaching of the New Testament*, 378-388; *God's Rule and Kingdom*, 329-347; M. Rist, IB, XII, 347f; E. Stauffer, CC, 147-191; N. Turner, *Peake's Commentary*, 1043-1044; Kümmel, 331-333; F. X. Steinmetzer, BZ, 1912, 252-260; A. Strobel, NTS (10) 1964, 443-445; H. Schlier, *Besinnung auf das N.T.* II, 358-373; H. P. Müller, ZNTW, 51 (1960) 268-278; L. Cerfaux, Numen Supplement 4 (1959) 459-470; M. Rissi, Th.Z., 21 (1965) 81-95; Charles II, 74f., W. Klassen, CBQ, 28 (1966) 300-311; L. Morris, *Biblical Doctrine of Judgment*, Ch. 3,4.; L. Brun, 70-100; G. Caird, 90f.

2. BABYLON IN JEWISH-CHRISTIAN THOUGHT. John's thought and diction is so permeated by the Old Testament pictures of Babylon that the student needs to read extensively in those primary sources: Isaiah 21, 47, 48; Jer. 25, 50, 51; Eze. 26-28; Daniel 2, 7. Undoubtedly, these earlier prophecies were in John's mind as he wrote. There is also little doubt that specific verses from Scripture formed the models for John's descriptions of the plagues

and the laments over Babylon. As sample passages where study may focus upon the alterations in context and content, the following are worth close scrutiny: Rev. 16:2—Exodus 9:8-10; Rev. 16:21—Exodus 9:22-26; Rev. 17:14—Deut. 10:17; Rev. 17:16—Ezekiel 16:37-41; Rev. 18:7, 8—Isa. 47:8-11; Rev. 18:22, 23—Isa. 24:8-13; Jer. 16:9; Ezekiel 27:27-32. After a student has examined these literary data, he should explore the symbolic significance of the picture of Babylon as a whole.

A. Vanhoye, Bib, 43 (1962) 436-476; J. Cambier, NRT, 1955, 113-123; J. Bruns, CBQ, 26 (1964) 459-463; K. Kuhn, TWNT, I, 514-517; Lohmeyer, 135-144; O. Cullmann, State in the New Testament (1956), 71-85; P. Minear, IDB, I, 338; H. Langenberg, BA, 21-24; A. N. Wilder, Healing of the Waters, 3-10; Strack-Billerbeck, III, 812; W. Neuss, Das Buch Ezechiel in Theologie und Kunst zum Ende das XII Jahrhunderts; J. Dürr, Die Stellung des Propheten Ezechiel in der israelitisch-judischen Apokalyptik, Münster, 1923; E. Hühn, I, 256-260.

6. *Victory over the Devil (19:11-22:7)*

A. THE BURNING LAKE (19:11-20:15)

19:11   I saw heaven thrown open:
        There! A white horse!
        Its rider, loyal and trustworthy!
        He judges and fights with justice,

12   his eyes like flaming fire,
        on his head many crowns,—
        no one else knows what Name is inscribed—

13   wearing a robe spotted with blood.
        He is God's saving purpose in person.

14   The armies in heaven follow him
        riding white horses,
        wearing pure white linen.

15   From his mouth comes a razor-sharp sword
        with which to smite the nations;
        he will rule them with an iron rod;
        he will tread the wine-press
        of the fury of the anger of God the all-powerful.

16   On his robe and on his thigh
        his name is inscribed:
        "King of kings. Lord of lords."

17   I saw an angel standing in the sun. He shouted with a loud
    voice to all the birds flying in mid-heaven:

18   "Come! Gather for God's great feast,
        to eat the flesh of kings and generals and armed men,
        the flesh of horses and their riders,
        the flesh of free men and slaves,
        the unknown and the famous, all of them."

19 I saw the Beast gathered with earth's kings and their armies to
   do battle against the rider and against his army. The Beast was
20 taken prisoner, and with him the false prophet who faked
   signs before him, by which he deceived those who accepted the
   brand of the Beast and worshiped his idol. Both were hurled
21 alive into the fiery lake burning with sulphur. The rest were
   slaughtered by the sword coming from the mouth of the rider.
   All the birds were glutted with their flesh.

20:1 I saw an angel descending from heaven
   carrying in his hand the key of the Abyss and a great chain.
2 He captured the Dragon, the primeval snake who is the devil
      or Satan,
         he chained him for a thousand years,
3   he threw him into the Abyss;
         he shut and locked the door on him
         so that he would no longer deceive the nations
         until the thousand years are over.
         Afterward he must be released for a short while.

4 I saw thrones, and enthroned I saw
         the souls of those who had been murdered
         for their loyal witness to Jesus, to the saving purpose of
            God;
         they worshiped neither the Beast nor his idol;
         they refused his brand on their foreheads and arms.
         They were installed as judges;
         they came to life and shared Christ's royal power
         for a thousand years.
5   (The rest of the dead did not come to life
         until the thousand years were over.)
6   This is the first resurrection.
            Those who share this first resurrection
            are blessed and holy;
            the second death wields no authority over them.
            They will be priests of God and priests of Christ,
            sharing his royal power for a thousand years.

7   *When the thousand years are over, Satan will be released*
8   *from his prison. He will come out to deceive the nations at*
    earth's four corners,—Gog and Magog,—summoning them to
    battle. They are as numerous as the sand of the sea. They
9   *ascended to the broad surface of the earth. They built*
    siege-camps around the beloved city, the holy ones. But fire
10 *came down from heaven and devoured them. The devil who*
    deceives them was hurled into the lake of fire and sulphur,
    to join the Beast and the false prophet. Day and night will
    they be tormented forever.

11 *I saw a great white throne, and One enthroned*
        from whose face earth and heaven fled away,
        they vanished utterly.
12 *I saw all the dead, the famous and the unknown,*
        standing before the throne.
        The books were opened.
        (Another book, the Book of Life, was opened.)
        The dead received verdicts according
                to their accomplishments in the books.
13   *The sea surrendered its dead,*
        Death and Hades surrendered their dead;
        each received a verdict according to his accomplishments.
14   *Then Death and Hades were hurled into the burning*
            lake.
        (This is the second death, the burning lake.)
15   *Into that lake was hurled everyone*
        whose name was not entered in the Book of Life.

Literary Analysis

In few places has reliance upon the chapter divisions of the
Bible played greater havoc in interpretation than in chapter 20
of the Book of Revelation. Many interpreters separate this chapter from its context, then give it the title *The Millennium*, trying
to place it in the long history of millenial schemes both before

and after the epoch of John. Such arbitrary division, combined with theological scholasticism, has produced a spate of temporal schemes, always changing but never convincing. If such havoc is to be avoided, every effort must be made to respect the units of John's thought and the mode of his thinking.

We are persuaded that study should begin with 19:11, for the vision begins there. The first indication of this fact is a stylistic one. John says "I saw heaven opened." In every other place in the book where this phrase appears, John uses it to initiate a new vision (4:1; 11:19; 15:5). Only in the case of the seven letters and the seven trumpets is this formula absent. The second clue is more dramatic. In the two opening paragraphs the antagonists in the final warfare are introduced: on the one side the Beast, the kings of the earth, and their armies; on the other side God, his commander, and the armies in white. This careful portrayal of the enemies, in their corresponding echelons, is more than a coincidence, inasmuch as the whole vision represents an effort to proclaim ultimate doom on the mystery of rebellion. A third clue is more theological. In John's perspective each vision must begin with a recognition of the righteous power of God and end with the full vindication of that power. That requirement is fulfilled if we establish the brackets of this vision at 19:11 and 22:7. A fourth clue is the sequence of divine verdicts which John orders in terms of the increasing magnitude and depth of the force of rebellion: the earth-dwellers, Babylon, the Beast and the false prophet (19:20), the devil himself (20:10), and finally Death (21:4, 8). Within this sequence the story of the final doom of the Devil (20:1-10) forms only one episode. Finally, in this vision as in all the others, John is primarily concerned with the choices confronting his Christian readers; the shape of these choices is made most clear in the beginning and the end of the vision as a whole.

Let us observe the sequence of episodes and their central accents. Paragraph 1 (19:11-16) introduces those who provoke the war and who demonstrate their victory. Two elements here are essential: the manifest unity between the Messiah and his army, and the character of their weapons—loyalty, truthfulness, and righteousness. The sword, the rod of iron, the winepress are vivid metaphors for stressing, by extreme paradox, the inexorable power of those weapons. If there is a war on (and there is), it is between fidelity and infidelity, truth and lie, righteousness and rebellion. This is the kind of internal warfare, which, although occasioned by external forces, must be settled within man's soul. The intangible stakes must be made tangible by grotesque language, and the results must be projected on a universal screen.

Paragraph 2 (19:17-21) is a gory and gruesome picture of the fate of those proximate enemies, the Beast and the false prophet (the two beasts of chapter 13). The definitive index to their character is provided in vs. 20: it is by the deceitfulness of their power that they succeed in inducing treason among men. This makes them the wielders of weapons exactly opposite those used by their opponents (19:11). But it also makes them vulnerable to the word-sword which proceeds from the Messiah's mouth, a weapon which everywhere in Revelation signifies his witness to God's saving purposes.

Paragraph 3 (20:1-6) deals with the initial defeat of the dragon and the corresponding victory of his enemies. It is essential to keep both defeat and victory in mind, for their interdependence constitutes the reality of the situation. The deceit of the Devil is ended (vs. 3b) by men who refuse to be deceived (vs. 4b). In the devil's hands this deceit has been expressed supremely by his use of death to nullify their testimonies to God's work. But they have made this mask useless by accepting death at his hands. In overcoming the Devil's deceit they have overcome death itself, and have thus become worthy to begin their rule with Christ (vs. 6). John is portraying the dynamics of the release of that royal power. The references to the thousand years (vs. 3, 4, 5) is an effective way of establishing the correspondence between the devil's imprisonment and the exercise of power by these guarantors. The truth of the Gospel can be verified only by victors over the devil in this subtle battle between deceitfulness and faithfulness. The prophet here accomplishes his task, assigned at the outset (1:19), of revealing "what is."

Paragraph 4 (20:7-10) is John's way of revealing to Christians the character of "what is to come." God will release the dragon for a climactic campaign in which he will deceive the nations and incite them to join him in an attack upon the "beloved city." The refusal of the holy ones to be deceived will mark the final defeat of the dragon, who will at last join his minions, the Beast and the false prophet (vs. 10), forever consumed by fire from heaven. (For the symbolic weight of this concept, see 11:5; 13:13 and our discussion p. 124f.)

Paragraph 5 (20:11-15) extends the range of God's victory to include Death and Hades. Death and Hades are emptied of men (vs. 13); they lose their power to judge men, along with their power to deceive men by the judgment which they have fraudulently exercised. Men are to be judged only by God and only in terms of their own deeds, i.e., not in terms of their earthly fortunes and fates. When this purpose has been accomplished, Death and Hades are banished into the lake of fire. They no longer exist for those who are not deceived by them (vs. 14). All the evidences of their power over men (crying, pain, separation from God) vanish utterly from God's presence, i.e., where God dwells with men, Death has lost his power (vs. 11).

What links all of these paragraphs together is the lake of fire, the second death, which is the permanent home of all the superhuman agents of rebellion against God. All have been subjected to the devil; he, in turn, has been subjected to God.

B. THE NEW CREATION (21:1-22:7)

21:1   I saw a new heaven and a new earth!
                The first heaven and the first earth had disappeared,
                the sea had lost its power.
  2   I saw the Holy City,
                New Jerusalem, descending from heaven, from God,
                like a bride, beautiful for her husband!
  3   I heard a loud voice from the throne:
                "There! God's home is with men;

he will dwell with them,
they will be his people,
God will himself live with them.
He will end their weeping:
4   no more death, no more grief,
no more wailing or suffering,
for the first things have vanished."

5   The Enthroned spoke:
"There! I am making everything new . . .
Write it down. This saving purpose is faithful and
reliable."

6   Then he told me:
"It is done.
I am the A and the Z, the beginning and the end.
To the thirsty I will freely give water
from the fountain of life.

7   These things the victor will inherit:
to him, I will be 'God';
to me, he will be 'Son.'

8   But the second death,
inheritance in the lake afire with sulphur,
will be for cowards and traitors,
perverts and murderers,
prostitutes and sorcerers,
idolators and all liars."

9   Then came one of the seven angels with the seven bowls full
of the final plagues. He called to me:
"Come! I will show you the virgin-wife of the Lamb."

10   In the Spirit he took me away to a huge, high mountain.
He showed me the Holy City Jerusalem descending from
heaven, from God.

11   God's glory filled it;
its light like a precious jewel,
like crystal jasper.

12   It had a broad high wall with twelve gates,
at the gates twelve angels,

13   to the east three gates,
to the south three gates,
to the north three gates,
to the west three gates,
inscribed the names of the twelve tribes of
Israel.

14   The city wall rested on twelve foundations,
on them twelve names,
the twelve apostles of the Lamb.

15   The angel who spoke to me was carrying a gold rod to measure
16   the city, its gates, its walls.

             The city had four corners,
its length equal to its width.
The city measured twelve hundred kilometers,

17   its length, width and height were equal,
its wall measured one hundred forty-four times
the length of the forearm

18   (This is a man's measure, an angel's measure.)
The walls were constructed of jasper.
The city itself was pure gold,
transparent as crystal.

19   The foundations of the city-wall were beautiful
with all kinds of jewels:

20   the first foundation jasper, the second
sapphire,
the third chalcedony, the fourth
emerald,
the fifth agate, the sixth carnelian,
the seventh yellow topaz, the eighth
beryl,
the ninth topaz, the tenth apple-green
quartz,
the eleventh blue sapphire, the twelfth
amethyst.

21
     The twelve gates were twelve pearls,
     each of the gates made out of one pearl.
     The city's street was pure gold,
          like transparent crystal.

22
     Within the city I saw no temple,
     for its temple is the Lord,
23
     the all-powerful God and the Lamb.
     The city has no need for sunlight or moonlight,
     for God's glory floods it with light,
24
     with the Lamb as its lamp.
     In its light the nations walk.
25
     Into it the earth's kings bring their glory
          with the glory and praise of the
               nations.
     There is no night,
26
     so the gates are never closed day or night.
27
     Into it will come nothing unclean,
          nothing corrupt, nothing false;
     only those included in the Lamb's Book of Life.

22:1
He showed me a river, flowing from the throne of God and the Lamb,
     the water of life, sparkling like crystal.
2
     The tree of life, in the middle of the city street,
     on both sides of the river, producing twelve
        harvests,
     every month yielding its harvest.
3
     The tree's leaves give health to the nations.
     (No longer will anything be damned.)

     In it God and the Lamb will be enthroned.
     His slaves will worship him;
4
     they will look on his face,
     his name will be on their foreheads.
5
     There will be no more night,

no need for lamplight or sunlight,
for the Lord God will shine on them,
and they shall be kings forever.

⁶ *He said to me:*

"These promises are trustworthy and true!
The Lord, God of the prophets' Spirit,
sent his angel to show his slaves
what must happen soon"

⁷   *"There! Soon I am coming.*
Blessed is the man who obeys
the prophetic commands of this book."

Literary Structure

Just as in separating chapter 20 from its original setting,
exegesis has complicated its own task, so, too, the interpretation
of chapter 21 has been emasculated by disjoining it from chapter
20. Of all the sections of Revelation, the vision of the new creation has been most frequently used in art, in hymns, and in
preaching. Almost always in funeral services one hears extracts
from this vision. But these extracts very rarely begin with chapter
20 and they normally delete from chapter 21 itself all reference
to the lake of fire (vs. 8, 27). The expurgated version often then
encourages that sentimental euphoria in which, to use H. Richard
Niebuhr's words "A God without wrath brought men without sin
into a kingdom without judgment through the ministrations of a
Christ without a cross" (*The Kingdom of God in America*, 193).
With the original bond broken by chapter headings, chapter 20
tends to become the monopoly of millennial pessimists and chapter 21 the monopoly of innocuous optimists. John tried to prevent
the separation of the chapters by inserting in his account of the
death of Death a clear reference to the flight of the first heaven
and earth (20:11, a motif to which he returns in 21:1).

To some extent, however, John is himself responsible for this

"The Adoration of the Lamb"

Altarpiece, Cathedral of St. Bacon, Ghent. Hubert and Jan Van Eyck.

misunderstanding, for in this last vision he has expanded the length of the treatment of God's promises. Why should he have done so? As a prophet, of course, he was obliged to balance the account of the punishment of the devil and death with an account of creation freed from their corruptions. But I think that editorial factors are also present. As an editor, compiling a series of visions into a single book, he was obliged to include a composite picture of the city of God which would establish contact with each of the preceding visions and which would be an appropriate conclusion to them all. We noted earlier that in chapters 4 and 5 he provided an introduction not only to the opening of the seven seals but to all subsequent visions as well. Now we find at the end a similar editorial accomplishment. Let us observe some of the ways in which John does this.

What John sees and hears, as narrated in 21:1-8, is a direct sequel and a fitting conclusion to the final battles of 19:11ff.; 21:9 establishes an explicit connection to the prophecy of the seven bowls. The seven angels, having shown John a picture of the great prostitute, here enable him to picture more clearly her antithesis—the bride of the Lamb. As the prostitute had been identified with one city, so here the bride is identified with another. In a similar fashion, John may have intended 21:15ff. to serve as sequel to the angel's instructions in 11:1, 2 to measure the temples or city. The details of the measurements in chapter 22 fulfill the chief requirements of 11:1, 2: the need to mark the boundary between the purity of the altar and the profane forces surrounding it.

In similar fashion the picture of the blessedness of the faithful (22:1-5) brings together many rewards which had been promised to the victors in the seven letters. (see above, p. 6of.) Place is also found within the city for those armies of the Lamb which had engaged in the battles of chapters 12 and 13 (21:24-27; 22:2, 3). Surely it is fitting for a collection of prophecies to conclude with a final orientation of all things around the throne of God and the Lamb, where the slaves are pictured as simultaneously ruling and worshiping. No major vision fails to be echoed in this inclusive vision of the completion of God's saving work. If we think of the prophet as having used the separate visions on various earlier occasions, we can better understand why, in editing them into a collection, he should provide coherence by weaving together all the promises into a single majestic summary.

How does the vision end? Not alone with a scene around the throne where all the celebrants are kings, but also with a recognition of all those who had shared in the communication of revelation (see above p. 3f.). In 21:6 four are mentioned: God, the angel, the prophet, the slaves. And in 21:7 the fifth adds his verifying word "I am coming" with his direct appeal to the reader "Blessed is the man." The vision ends with the reader himself facing a call to obedience, a call which had motivated the entire sequence of visions.

For Reflection and Discussion

We have chosen for discussion two matters: John's treatment of the death of Death and his conception of the coming of Christ.

1. THE DEATH OF DEATH. As already noted, comments upon this vision usually become obsessed with the problem of the Millennium, the thousand year period which is mentioned some seven times in close succession (20; 2, 3, 4, 5, 6, 7). That this is an important feature of the vision no one should deny. But one should reject the idea that it was as important to John as it has since become. That it was indeed less important to him than other aspects of this vision is proved by this fact: never elsewhere in the book does he refer to the Millennium, although every other feature in this vision does appear elsewhere. It therefore seems fair to discuss the more important issues first and only then to ask about the thousand years.

There is one issue which has pervaded the whole Revelation, from beginning to end: the power-struggle between what we may call the christic and the antichristic forces. John seeks to deal with that struggle in its full complexity, subtlety, and magnitude, all the while emphasizing the victory which the christic force has won and is destined to win.

Christic force is a term by which we point to the full magnitude of that power released into human affairs by "the revelation which God gave to Jesus Christ to enable his slaves to see" (1:1). This force stems from God, from the saving word-deed of God; it is the *logos* of God in action. Put simply, it is the love by which an all-powerful God seeks to redeem his whole creation. The power of this love was disclosed and confirmed by Jesus the Messiah in his passion and victory. The verification took the form of creating a kingdom of priests, a community whose cohesion was continually being created by God's love in Christ. This community, in and through each of its members, was called into being to give contemporary confirmation to the reality and power of the christic force. This work of verification embraced all the places and times in which the community worshiped God by holding firm to the work of Christ.

By the term antichristic force we refer to that total structure of power which God's revelation had released and which continually expressed itself in hostility to Christ and his kingdom. God's love in Christ was hated, a truth of which the passion story had given ample evidence. Christ's love in his Church was hated, a truth of which the story of prophets, apostles, and holy men had given ample evidence. The rebellion against the christic force was no less constant, no less violent, no less deceptive in John's day than earlier. The whole scenario of John's visions underscores the depth and magnitude of the conflict between God's love and the violent rejection of it. This hatred bound together men from different places and times, men from many nations, peoples, tongues, and tribes. The King of kings was opposed, from beginning to end, by another king of kings (17:14, 18; 19:16). The nearer he came to the end of his book the more emphasis did John put upon the full magnitude of this warfare.

The warfare had already received both its clearest definition and its climactic resolution in the victory of Jesus. His agony (*thlipsis*, 1:9) had proved the measure of incompatibility between God's love and the hatred of that love. Jesus had met the enemy without acts of retaliation against his human adversaries and traitorous friends. Had he met hate with hate he would have lost the battle. Nor had he met the enemy with appeasement or compromise, by trying to serve two masters or reducing the cost of victory. The reality and finality of his victory had been for John the absolute conviction on which every other conviction rested. The contemporary verification of that victory was the important task of every prophet and believer in Asia. Such verification was possible by undertaking the same battle. The prophet must enable his brothers to see why their warfare was inevitable, why they should fight with confidence and joy. He must enable them to understand that the antichristic hatred of their love warranted neither retaliation nor compromise but only the verification of Jesus' power through their own victory.

We should not, however, minimize the difficulties which John's argument must meet. Such events as the martyrdom of Antipas appeared to accentuate the weakness of love and the strength of doubt and despair. To many Asians, including Christians, these events must have seemed to prove that superior power did indeed rest with the massive weight of antichristic forces. Must there not come another kind of verification in which God not only defeats but visibly destroys those forces? Must not the prophet disclose both what is and what is to come? Where lies the ultimate power to overcome? When and how will God destroy the hidden source of antichristic rebellions?

Let us here formulate in an abstract way some of the problems John faced and then observe how he describes the final defeat of the Devil.

Christic love would be betrayed if men viewed their particular human adversaries as the source of evil. To do so would turn love into a hatred of such adversaries, whether conceived as persons, agencies, or institutions (e.g., Pilate, Judas, the synagogue, Rome). But love would also be betrayed if the terrible action of the wrath of God were minimized. His love is the most fearful judge, more terrible to confront than any other judgment, at least for those who have pledged to serve it. Love would also be betrayed if this wrath should be so separated from love as to spring from self-love and self-defensiveness. This would be true if wrath were directed primarily against the outsiders, all the while special privileges and comforts were accorded to insiders. Finally, love would be betrayed if its proponents accepted the existence of a power which could forever withstand it, or if they supposed that some natural process or historical institution could provide immunity from its claims. Unless the christic force actually proves itself able to overcome all opposition, faith in it loses credibility.

With this as a transcript of the inner logic of John's position, we may be able to see why in this particular vision he must carry further the sequence of judgments described in the earlier visions. In these last two visions he describes the operation of God's wrath upon a sequence of three major concentrations of superhuman forces: Babylon, the Beast-and-his-false-prophet, the Devil himself.

In the preceding vision the prophet had announced the ruin of Babylon, which, although allied to the Beast and the false prophet, was ultimately weaker than they and subject to their hatred. Babylon, the mother of prostitutes, was left desolate. The successive dirges which bewailed her demise were filled with the irony of her false pretensions. What is Babylon? That particular configuration of power, whether political, military, economic, or cultural, which in every generation sets itself against the christic way. Babylon is a "spatial and temporal universal" which is manifested by the pyramiding in every society of the will to power. The cohesion of this city is provided by individual and corporate desires for self-determination, self-security, and self-glorification (H. Schlier, *Besinnung auf das N.T.*, 364). Much of what is called Roman imperialism may be suggested by Babylon's portrait, but there is nothing to limit the portrait to this one entity. She was the first of the major mythological figures to succumb before the wrath of God.

The second concentration of forces is represented by the beast and the false prophet. These are less reducible to specific historical embodiments than Babylon. It is in response to their call that the great prostitute begins her seductions. They stand nearer the ultimate source of hatred; therefore they yield less quickly to the fury of God's anger. They can be overcome only by the Messiah in person, in his power as King of kings. This is his war, waged by his weapons of righteousness; this is his judgment, executed in his truth. His robe, white though dipped in blood, defines the kind and degree of holiness. With him are heaven's armies, whose clothing denotes the same kind of holiness and power. Thus the christic force comes in full panoply, ready for the battle which had been anticipated in the sixth bowl (16:12-16). The result of this battle is the casting of the Beast and the false prophet into the lake of fire. The last-but-one source of idolatry is brought under the permanent control of the christic army. The last source—the ancient snake—remains to be dealt with. It is with his doom that chapter 20 deals.

It is not surprising that any story which presumes to narrate the death of the devil should present complications. He is not only primeval and primal; he also has as his allies Death and Hades. Victory over Satan must include victory over these allies, releasing from their grasp all the dead. John discerns a significant difference between two deaths, the first and the second. This difference is more crucial to his argument than the measurement of a temporal span between them. Satan, Death, Hades—these antichristic forces have control over the first death, i.e., they can crucify the Messiah and destroy those who refuse to worship the Beast (20:4). But that appears to leave Death itself finally in control. Death loses this control only when it is forced to surrender all whom it holds, so that they are judged not in terms of their having died but in terms of their deeds (20:12, 13). Defrauded of its booty, Death itself then receives God's penalty. Although Christ is seen as exercising the power to overcome the beast (19:11-21) and to chain the Devil, it is only God (20:11) who has the final power to issue the verdict against Death. The prophet associates this event with the passing away of the first heaven and earth (20:11; 21:1, 4).

One should not overlook the fact that the second death is the destiny of cowardly and faithless disciples (21:8; see p. 44), but faithful followers have overcome every form of antichristic power, including that of Death and Hades. Moreover, John is careful to point out that this escape is not contingent upon future events. Having proved themselves immune to Satan's deceit (20:3), they become channels as well as recipients of Christ's power to judge, to live, and to rule.

Thus the prophet presents the character of God's final justice, comprising both wrath and love. The only way for men to verify their confession of the power of Christ is by actions which reveal that the love of God has fully overcome self-love (12:11). God then overcomes every hostile force, including the Devil, Death, and Hades. This happens through his action of dwelling with men in the new city (not Babylon), in the new creation where Death is no more. We see, then, in the whole vision from 19:11-22:7 a single complex conception of the ultimate resolution of the struggle between christic and antichristic forces.

Within the context of that struggle, what functions does the notion of the Millennium fulfill? The division of the defeat of the Devil into two stages served to distinguish his penultimate defeat by Christ and his army from his ultimate defeat by God. The penultimate defeat represented the provisional termination of his power to deceive the nations, while the ultimate defeat represented the final surrender by Death and Hades of their power over men. It also separates that first death which falls within Satan's power to inflict from that second death which only God can inflict. It represents a full recognition of victory which is won in the first resurrection (20:6), along with the necessity of extending that victory to all who are held captive by Death (20:13). It distinguishes God's vindication of the christic force (20:4) from his final judgment on the whole creation.

John cannot accept any limitation on the blessedness and holiness of those who join Christ on his throne. The Millennium

does not set a temporal limit to their power. Yet neither can
John accept a future consummation which sets limits to the re-
newing power of God. God is the last as well as the first, the
Z as well as the A. His love, as released through the work of
Christ, will extend its scope until it is unlimited by space or time.
It will not only deliver men from the fear of Death; it will also
accomplish the elimination of Death's power to separate men
from judgment and redemption. It will therefore provide a final
verification of God's work as all-powerful creator, so that all
creation will bear the mark of that redemption which is borne
already by those who have his name on their foreheads. It also
serves notice on these victors that their victory is not complete
until it has become all-inclusive. For this reason, the vision which
holds before them the promise of realized sonship (21:7) simultaneously warns them against the potential loss of sonship
through cowardice and hypocrisy (21:8). They have yet to face
the final efforts of the Devil to deceive them through the manifest power of Death and Hades. At its deepest level, the distinction between the earlier binding and the later loosing of Satan
may make greatest sense when related to the actualities of worship. The worship of the true and holy God makes the worshiping
congregation aware that the christic force which now rules has a
mission which will not be complete until the final deception
(20:8) is overcome and the Book of Life is opened (20:15).

If the preceding argument is sound, we infer that the idea
of an interim is more than incidental to John's thinking. But the
idea of an interim is one thing, and its measurement by calendar
time is another. What are we to make of the figure of a thousand
years as it appears in chapter 20? Its significance should not be
exaggerated, yet neither should we ignore its presence. Those who
are acquainted with other apocalypses are aware that the conception of a millennium is encountered in them. The appended
bibliography will enable the student to check on the major literary antecedents as well as certain modern interpretations. Here
we may distinguish several plausible options.

Viewing the expectation from the perspective of John himself, one school dates the beginning of the Millennium in the future, when Christ shall have come again to establish his kingdom on earth. Saints will then join Christ in a thousand years of earthly bliss, after which the kingdom of God will be established. The Millennium is the term for the kingdom of Christ, yet to be ushered in by the first resurrection, and then to be ended by the second.

There is a second school which associates the Millennium with "the time of the church," the beginning of which is to be dated from the time when Jesus, by his dying, chained the Devil and when, by their baptism, believers joined him in the first resurrection. Those who accept this beginning usually conclude either that John's expectation of the end was mistaken (it is now 1968) or that the figure one thousand measured a different type of year than is customary in temporal reckoning.

A third school is inclined to spiritualize the temporal and spatial references, viewing the reality of Christ's kingdom as a timeless and spaceless order which cannot be so measured.

Without attempting to force a choice among these, it is well for us first of all to recognize the difficulties which confront all of them. One of these stems from our own ways of formulating the options. In this process we tend to trust our own conceptions of time and we use them to mark out mutually exclusive alternatives. Then we insist upon limiting the choice to one of these. Our own conceptions of time, which obviously are not the same as John's, complicate the problem.

Another difficulty is posed by the symbolic use of numbers in Revelation. Especially comparable to the "thousand years" image of chapter 20 are the following symbols of duration: times and times and half a time, 42 months, 1260 days, the interim between binding and loosing, the period in which the beast "is not." These other symbols of duration fulfill comparable functions; in dealing with none of them can we arrive at a fixed measure of solar years.

A third difficulty arises when we locate the beginning of the Millennium in any particular year. John explicitly relates this beginning to the victory of Christ *and* to the victory of those who had not worshiped the Beast (20:4-6). Both in chapter 20 and in every other vision of the book, John views the share in Christ's royal power as a contemporary reality in his own day, not as postponed to some temporal future. The "beginning" therefore covers many distinct places and dates (e.g., 11:5). It bears the character of a spatial and temporal universal. It is not timeless, but neither is it restricted to a single date or place. Human language as such is poorly adapted to express such an order of beginnings. Our measurements of temporal duration require a single fixed beginning; otherwise they are thrown into confusion.

A corresponding difficulty arises from the effort to establish the year of an *end* which by its intrinsic character (the death of Death, the passing away of the first heaven and earth, the new creation) transcends chronology. A chronology can date the deaths of men. It helps us to order the successive episodes or events within human history; but it was never designed to cope with such an End as that of which John speaks. How can man measure on his time-line an epoch which has its beginnings and its endings in God's warfare with the powers of evil?

All these difficulties stem from the fact that John speaks within the context of a prophetic vision of events which have their primary locus in heaven before God's throne. All these events have, to be sure, a strategic relevance for man's existence on the plane of history, whatever we may mean by that term; but we do not establish that relevance by precise translation from a heavenly tongue into earthly predictions which can be reduced to chronological exactitude. The kind of translation which prophetic vision encourages is the translation of suffering into joy, of passion into endurance, of the worship of the Beast into the worship of God, of deception into truthfulness, of verbal confession into verification in deed. Any interpretation of the Millenium which does not advance John's prophetic vocation is certain to distort his language. In the churches of Asia there appear to have been prophets who spiritualized the Gospel and others who historicized it. The motivation for both appears to have been the desire to escape the struggle between christic and antichristic forces and thereby to relax the rigor of the requirements for participating in Christ's victory. Such interpretations John branded as the work of the false prophet.

In my judgment the difficulties mentioned leave the exegete in a position where he must recognize that even the best available translation of John's message into an alternate idiom is bound to fail. His only consolation comes through admitting that such failure has the merit of leaving the last word with the prophet himself. John, in turn, leaves the last word to him who holds the keys to Death and Hades. In the end it is Christ's criteria for distinguishing true prophecy from false that the Christian must accept. He is thereby delivered from judging John to be a false prophet either because a thousand years have passed "and all things have continued as they were" (2 Peter 3:4), or because modern theories of the end of the cosmos (a term which in our day carries a very different meaning) seem to make silly the whole substance of John's vision.

2. THE COMING OF CHRIST. In his opening sentence John had stated clearly one aspect of Christ's assignment: "To enable his slaves to see what must happen soon." (The verb *deiknumi*, usually translated here as *show*, normally bears the fuller connotation "enable to see." H. Schlier, TWNT II, 26-33) One aspect of the prophet's assignment was to tell what he had seen, under the conviction "the season is at hand." Each command to the prophet to write had been prefaced by a vision. Accordingly, his commission to write covered three things: what he had seen and heard, "what is," "what is about to happen" (1:19). Each vision in the book is structured to include all three.

Now one line of interpretation of John's book goes astray almost at once. It concentrates upon the third aspect alone. It moves on the assumption that John conceived his task as one of consoling tormented Christians and of threatening the enemies of the Church by predictions concerning events in the political realm which would happen in the decades immediately following

95 A.D. By contrast, we would insist that all three aspects of 1:19 must be considered as a single unit. John was enabled to see into heaven. What he saw enabled him to understand "what now is," and that vision of the present enabled him to foresee what was about to happen.

How is the exegete rightly to distinguish John's reference to things present from his reference to things to come? Some readers believe they can do this by observing the tenses of the verbs. A verb in the past or present tense described what John visualized as having happened or as taking place when he was writing; the future tense indicated what he expected to happen. This expedient fails to solve the problem. It ignores the complex requirements of the visionary mode of communication and it fails to recognize that for John what was expected to happen on earth had already taken place in heaven. The translator simply cannot mechanically use an English present or future tense to render every present or future tense in the Greek.

Other readers scan the Apocalypse carefully to locate that single point where John turns from a description of the situation in his own day toward a prediction of coming events. Everything following that point is called prediction. But this entails equally great difficulties. For example, it treats 22:6f. as wholly future, and chapters 4 and 5 as wholly present or past, a distinction which does not do justice to either passage. In both there is a baffling compresence of the times.

Another expedient is to look for that point in each successive vision where the thought shifts from "what is" to "what is to come." This point may be located where the prophet moves from one item to another in a sequence of seven. In the opening of the sixth seal, for example, we can infer that the fifth seal applies to events before 95 A.D., but that the sixth seal does not (6:12f.). Or in the trumpet blasts, the introduction of the eagle's woes (8:13) marks the movement from memory to anticipation. In the account of the warfare between the dragon and the woman, either 12:17 or 14:7 or 14:14 seems to mark a similar shift from present struggle to predicted course. John's text, however, does not allow us to persist in this sort of arbitrary division. However plausible at first we may find such a shift, we soon find predictive material before it and reminiscent material after it.

Many interpreters find one exception to this rule in 17:10-12. If we can discover which Roman emperor is the sixth, then we can safely date John's writing and assign to predictive status what he says about the seventh, including the beast who is to come and the ten kings who will rule for one hour. We have elsewhere examined the evidence for this interpretation and found it too weak to support these conclusions (p. 235f.).

Where, then, are we to look for a sounder approach? A good place to start is to observe in 22:6, 7 the conjunction of the formula "what must happen soon" with Christ's word "I am coming soon." Since the most frequently repeated clue to things to come is the affirmation that he is coming soon, we should recall the typically Johannine contexts for that latter affirmation, noting the extent to which these reflect a single pattern of expectation.

We have already noted the dependence of Christ's coming upon God's coming. Consider the familiar formula concerning God. Strict logic leads us in such passages as 1:4, 8, to expect the sequence "was, is, and will be." Instead we find the sequence: "is, was, and is coming," or, as we have translated it, "who now rules, who has always ruled, and who is coming to rule." Two alterations are significant: John places the present tense in the first and more emphatic position, and instead of "will be" (*esomenos*) he writes "is coming," an important parallel to the two phrases "what is" and "what must soon happen." Whatever is to happen soon will be a manifestation of God's coming.

Similar observations should be made with regard to the formulas used for Christ as the coming one. In 1:5-7 we note the same sequence of present, past, and future. Moreover, this promise is usually expressed in the first person (22:7; 16:15). The most important thing that will happen is the coming of Christ in fulfilment of his promise. Christ's coming thus becomes the effective future horizon for every decision of believer and congregation (2:5, 16, 25; 3:3, 11).

Whatever it is that will happen soon is a corollary of this

coming. Does Judgment lie ahead? Yes, but it is the judgment of
God and the Lamb (6:17; 14:7, 15; 18:10). Does salvation lie
ahead? It is by their joint action alone (12:10; 19:7) that this is
accomplished. It is congenial to this pattern to describe the riding
of the four horsemen as the response to their command (6:1f.).
We must observe, too, how in his coming the Messiah is accompanied by the elect who have proved themselves worthy of him.
Not only do they receive from him the symbols of kingship and
priesthood (7:9-17); they *come with him* as armies of heaven
(19:14, 19). His "future" is theirs as well. Furthermore, the coming of Christ is clearly inseparable from the coming of the holy
city, the new Jerusalem, with its personalized gates, walls, and
foundations. What is to come is the consummation of fellowship
in this city, to which the kings of the nations will bring their
glory and honor. In Christ's coming all the christic forces will
cohere in a single community with its new name (3:12). Here
lies a major part of John's message concerning what is to happen
soon.

But does this part of the answer overlook the bitter woes
which are to fall on the earth? The notion of coming is applied
to the antichristic forces as well. One function of the Millennium,
as we have seen, is to set forth the mystery of the Dragon who
was in power, who no longer has power, but who will be released
for a little while (20:1-10). John anticipates his coming from
the Abyss. So, too, the Beast is described as one who will ascend
from the Abyss (17:8, 11, 12). It is the coming of the demonic
trinity (16:13, 14) and of the nations whom they summon to
war which John predicts. They will come from the Abyss, but
after a little while they will go to perdition, when they have
yielded their power over men to one who is stronger than they.
The concluding chapters make very clear the kind of community
which derives its existence from their deception. It is a city which
embraces all the cowardly, the adulterous, the idolators, the liars
(21:8, 27).

What, then, is about to take place, according to John? The
final conflict between the christic and the antichristic communi-

ties. Over and over again in the concluding summary the prophet stresses the ultimate incompatibility of those two cities. Yet he stresses even more the assurances that the gates of the holy city shall never be shut and that all men may enter the city by those gates. Note how this paradox is present both in 21:24-27 and in 22:14, 15.

Here we see that the logic of John's thought focuses attention upon the decisions to be made in the present by those who read his prophecy. The visions of what is to come articulate the dimensions of the struggle for power which is already proceeding by way of those inconspicuous choices which congregations make as they listen to the prophet's message. Eschatological predictions thus operate as logical corollaries of the prophet's insights into the moral dilemmas of the churches. The concluding vision simply writes large what had been written small in each of the letters to the congregations in Asia. Their whole existence, from beginning to end, is condensed in the Lord's promise to come and in their prayer for him to come. His verification of God's love and his servants' verification of his love will mark their entrance into this city whose gates never close.

Whether or not the foregoing analysis is an acceptable version of what John thought about coming events, readers of the Apocalypse should test alternate versions, to see if they are compatible with "what is" as John saw it and with his understanding of how the churches should translate into obedience their hope for the future. For the heart of the matter is contained in the choice which is posed by the coming Christ in his final beatitude (22:7).

For Further Study

1. THE MILLENIUM AND THE DEATH OF DEATH.

H. Bietenhard, *Das Tausendjahrige Reich*; A. Feuillet, *L'Apocalypse*, 98-101, with bibliography; J. Danielou, *Theology of Jewish Christianity*, 377-403; W. Bauer, *Reallexicon für Antike und Christentum* XV, 1073-1078; M. Rist, IDB, III, 381-382; S. J.

Case, *The Millenial Hope;* E. Stauffer, *N. T. Theology,* 213-225; J. W. Bailey, JBL, 53 (1934), 170-187; E. Allo, 315-329; J. Michl, *Lexicon für Theologie und Kirche* II, 1058f.; G. E. Ladd, RE, 1960, 445-466; R. Summers, RE, 1960, 176-183; B. Noack, *Satanas und Soteria,* 50-137; K. Kuhn, TWNT, I, 789-791; S-B, III, 823-831; C. Brütsch, 271-294.

2. THE NEW CREATION, THE HOLY CITY, THE TEMPLE.

M. J. Congar, *The Mystery of the Temple,* 107-247; S. H. Hooke, *Alpha and Omega;* J. A. T. Robinson, *In the End, God . . .,* 44-128; E. Stauffer, *N. T. Theology,* 222-233; J. Michl, BK, 16 (1961), 113-115; N. Pohlmann, VS, 1963, 637-659; N. W. Porteous, "Jerusalem-Zion," in *Verbannung und Heimkehr,* 235-252; F. M. Braun, *Der christliche altar in seiner geschichtlichen Entwicklung,* Munich, 1924, I; A. Causse, RHP, 18 (1938), 377-414; J. de Young, *Jerusalem in the N.T.;* M. Eliade, *Sacred and Profane;* R. Knopf, "Die Himmelstadt" in *Neutestamentlichen Studien* (G. Heinrici), 213-219; W. Müller, *Die heilige Stadt;* R. Patai, *Man and Temple in Ancient Jewish Myth and Ritual;* K. L. Schmidt, *Jerusalem als Urbild und Abbild,* Eranos Jahrbuch 18 (1950), 207-248; H. Wenschkewitz, *Angelos* 4 (1932), 70-230; J. Comblin, ETL, 1953, 5-40; R. Harrisville, *Newness in the N.T.,* 93-105; S-B, III, 840-847.

The Triple Conclusion (22:8-21)

22:8   *This is John speaking. I am the one who heard and saw these things. When I heard and saw them, I fell down to worship at the feet of the angel who showed them to me. But he said:*

9   *"Don't do that! Worship God!*
I am only a slave along with you and your brothers,
the prophets and all who obey the commands of this
book."

10   *Then he said to me:*
"Don't seal up the prophetic commands of this book,
for the season is at hand.

11   **"Let the unjust go on doing injustice,**
Let the filthy go on being filthy;
Let the just go on doing justice,
Let the holy go on becoming holy."

12   *"There! I, Jesus, am coming soon,*
bringing my reward with me,
to repay everyone according to his work.

13   *"I am the A and the Z,*
the first and the last,
the beginning and the end.

14   *"Blessed are those who cleanse their robes,*
in order to receive authority over the tree of life,
and to enter the city through its gates.

15   *"Shut out are the dogs, sorcerers, prostitutes,*
murderers, idolaters, and every one who loves and
serves the Lie.

16   "It is I, Jesus, who sent my angel to confirm these
            things to you, for the sake of the congregations.
      I am of David's tree, its root and its fruit.
      I am the bright star of the dawn."

17   "The Spirit and the Bride say 'Come.'
      Let the man who hears say 'Come.'
      Let every thirsty man come.
      Let every one who wishes receive free
            the water of life."

18   I promise every hearer of the prophetic commands of this book:
            if any one adds to them,
                  God will add to him the plagues described in
                        this book;
19   if anyone subtracts from the prophetic commands of
                        this book,
                  God will subtract his share in the tree of life
                        and in the holy city, as described in this book.

20   It is one who confirms these things who says
            "I vouch for it.
      I am coming soon."

            "Amen! Lord Jesus, come!"

21   The grace of the Lord Jesus be with all.

Comments on Structure

This section is not an easy one to read smoothly or quickly.
The transitions from one speaker to another and from one audience to another are abrupt and unexplained. It is difficult to recover John's intention and far from easy to translate it into
anything resembling continuous prose. Why should we find such
a jumble here? Two conjectures are worth examining.

The first is based on the assumption that the time when
John assembled the book as a whole was not the first occasion

when he had used the several visions. He may have delivered them separately at different times when he had been summoned to prophesy. On such occasions each address to a congregation would have called for concluding remarks. These would probably include such things as (1) an affirmation of the reliability of the message, as in 22:6; (2) a blunt command to worship God, as in 22:8, 9; (3) a beatitude or woe addressed to the congregation by Christ, as in 22:14, 15; and (4) an assertion by Christ of his intention to come soon, as in 22:20.

As an editor weaving together the whole series of visions, John would require a somewhat different technique. He would need to revise the introductions and the conclusions of the separate visions. He would delete because of redundancy some of these four items from earlier addresses. When he had then completed the job of splicing all the visions into a whole, he would have some clippings left over. Rather than discarding those beatitudes and warnings, he deposited them at the end. A conjecture of this sort might explain why some of these sayings seem to apply to the whole book (22:18, 19), whereas others echo the separate visions: 22:8, 9, for example, is a virtual repetition of 19:10; 22:10 could be intended after the vision of the two prophets to countermand the orders in 10:4; 22:14, 15 might have been related originally to the vision of Babylon's fall and have then been located at 10:8. The adoption of this conjecture would affect the interpretation of the earlier visions, for it would show how at every point John had been concerned with implications for the churches' obedience.

A second conjecture is based on the assumption, adopted in our treatment of chapter 1, that John was trying to bring to an appropriate end each of the three modes of discourse which he had chosen. He had begun a letter to the Asian churches (1:4); he must now complete it. This he does (22:21).

He had begun in 1:9 his introduction to a series of visions which was not finished until 22:7. His first task in 22:8, therefore, is to return to the same stance as in 1:9f. Again he must assume his own identity, no longer speaking in the Spirit. He must speak now, in retrospect, of what he had seen. When he reports further dialogs with the angel, they must take place within the context of his own direct dialog with the churches. The angel at the end is the same one, repeating now the same command (1:10, 11; 22:10). As the initial appearance had been designed to produce a message for the congregations, so the last appearance must refer explicitly to them (1:11; 22:16). Christ's last word must conform to his first (1:17, 18), and the response expected from the congregations must be made very clear (22:17). Thus the sequel to the last great vision (22:8-17) can be made intelligible by a careful comparison with the stage setting for the first.

It now remains to explain 22:18-20. This may be regarded as the place where the editor of the book adds his signature and rounds off that different type of document. He had begun with a third-person reference to the book and its contents, including a beatitude for those who listened while it was being read (1:1-3). He now ends with a curse on wilful modification of the text and he appeals to the coming Jesus as ultimate sponsor of his message.

Both of these conjectures are of dubious certainty. Neither explains all the phenomena satisfactorily. But what is so striking is the repetitiveness of certain themes. Again and again the different participants in the revelation join in speaking. All wish to underwrite the dependability of the message. The alternation of speakers fits more naturally into the antiphonal character of Christian worship than into the prose report of a single narrator. Most frequently it is Jesus who breaks in with his pledge to his followers that he will come and complete the work which he had begun.

For Reflection

In his concluding comments on the series of visions which he had received through the angel, the prophet reestablished direct contact with his readers. He again addressed them simply as his fellow-slaves. He asserted that the truth of his message had been fully endorsed by the angel, by the Spirit, and by the

Messiah. He appealed to every reader and every congregation to join in the circle of endorsement. Presumably this appeal succeeded; otherwise his book would doubtless have joined many other early Christian documents in oblivion.

Even though the churches of Asia responded by preserving the book, the question remains as to how a modern congregation will respond. Wherever the book is read today, the response to it, whether positive or negative or a confused mixture of the two, reveals the fact that the conversation which John initiated still continues. But is the response the same? One may doubt whether, if forced to make the decision afresh, the modern church would include this book in the canon of sacred scripture. Nevertheless, it continues to be read and to provoke all kinds of questions.

Throughout our study thus far some have doubtless found themselves asking whether they could themselves accept John's view of things. Let us try to force these doubts into the open in order to deal with some of them in a more or less systematic way, by proposing and answering four questions:

1. What was the essential core of John's message to the churches of his own day?
2. Can temporal and cultural distances be bridged so as to make possible a genuine communication of that core to men today?
3. Assuming a positive answer, just what does acceptance or rejection of the message actually signify for us today?
4. Within the modern situation how does a congregation which accepts John's message confirm its validity?

The whole of our analysis of the Book of Revelation constitutes an attempt to answer the first of these questions. Whatever the student may feel about the adequacy of that attempt, he is obliged to arrive at some articulate summary of the core message as he himself understands it. This is a minimum goal of all serious study. Until we are clear about the content, it makes no sense to talk about accepting or rejecting it.

The second question poses problems which appear to become

more complex and less soluble to the degree that one becomes immersed in contemporary debates in historiography, philosophy, or hermeneutics. How can we fully understand in our own unique context *anything* which someone else thought or wrote in an entirely different context? Even to use the same words may be to say a different thing. The idea that we mean the same things by them is often an illusion. The modern analysis of language, which stresses the degree to which all linguistic meanings are contingent upon their immediate contexts, throws doubt upon the possibility, not to mention the efficacy, of any conversation between ourselves and someone from another century.

Although I do not wish to ignore the dilemmas in this area, I feel that it would be all too easy to get permanently bogged down in them. If we are to stick to the distinctive problem which is posed by a particular book, we are obliged to recognize that such difficulties are common to the reading of all ancient documents. If a radical scepticism is valid, then it is valid for all conversations across the boundaries of time and culture. I believe, however, that the presently exaggerated form of scepticism is too popular to be permanent. Most contemporary readers will be able to agree that at least some ancient writers have in fact spoken effectively and convincingly to them. The issue at hand is whether John is able to do so.

To take up the third question, what does it mean for a modern person to accept or reject John's message? This query is carefully phrased. It assumes that both options are equally possible. It is not slanted polemically or rhetorically in order to urge the reader to accept rather than to reject; some rejections are, in my judgment, far better grounded than some acceptances. We are calling rather for an examination of the grounds for the reader's response. The implications of what he accepts or rejects must be understood. Only then will we know what he means by his yes or no. Let me try to illustrate the problems in several different ways.

A. John's message appears to be inseparable from the use of certain conceptual and linguistic idioms in speaking of space.

His spatial categories include such terms as heaven, earth, Hades. He distinguishes the above from the below. His visions presuppose the existence of a curtain between heaven and earth, between invisible and visible reality. They presuppose that this curtain has been cut at certain points by the initiative of heaven and by such earthly events as the passion of Jesus. Consequently, the invisible can at times be seen and the inaudible heard, at least by prophets "in the Spirit." The meaning of John's message thus seems to be contingent upon a very definite perception of space. *What*, then, does it *mean* when readers reject John's message because of this spatial idiom, and others accept it for that same reason? Either response may be justified by sound reasons or by false; either becomes to some degree an index to the reader's own perceptions of space. Moderns are sometimes so certain of one cosmology that any reference to heaven, any thought of "up there," is automatically ruled out. Other moderns, by contrast, are so aware of man's bondage to spatial categories, a bondage disclosed all the more sharply by interplanetary travel, that they all too quickly accept any promise of emancipation into an "other-worldly" or heavenly realm. In rejecting or affirming John's message for these reasons, persons of both views may be deceiving themselves. What they reject or affirm is not his message but their own prior views of space.

B. John's message appears to be equally contingent upon his use of certain conceptual and linguistic idioms in speaking of time. He utilizes temporal categories based on the distinction between before and after. He relays as a message from Christ the announcement "I am coming soon." Such a message presupposes the normal existence of a curtain between things present and things to come. It asserts that this curtain has been penetrated by events in the past or the present which afford dependable knowledge of the future. John is a prophet charged with communicating this advance knowledge of coming events. Does such a message have meaning for us? Many who say no, do so because their views of temporal and historical process will not tolerate such interruptions. Many who say yes greet those very interruptions as dependable omens of a very real future. In either case, we must ask what such acceptance or rejection really means. Unless we have the same perceptions of God's relation to the temporal process as John did, our acceptance or rejection may be quite deceptive. We need to ask, furthermore, whether the focusing of attention upon these time-factors may not obscure the core-issues with which John was concerned.

C. Of even greater importance than categories of space and time in determining John's message was his conception of a continuing warfare between God and Satan, between God's justice and the infinitely complicated structures of injustice, between the active embodiments of love and the corresponding embodiments of hate. He saw the ultimate issues as gravitating around the defeat or the victory of the christic forces, a struggle in which all men are sooner or later, more or less consciously, involved. The validity of his message appears, therefore, to be dependent upon the validity of this complex way of perceiving and describing the conflict. Is Christ the victor? What does it mean to say that? What does it mean to affirm today that God has initiated a struggle with Satan by sending Christ to create an army of holy men who can now share in his victory and thus testify to others that Christ is coming soon? Or, conversely, what does it mean to deny all this? If there is meaning in either affirmation or denial, that meaning must apply to a level of reality deeper than the level on which much of our thinking and talking and acting usually proceeds. The visible face of the universe and the tangible flux of social process do not in themselves disclose the existence of a warfare of this sort. Yet that fact by itself neither proves nor disproves the pictures drawn by John.

D. John's message makes strategic use of another idiom which may be even more vital: the contrast and conflict between the first creation and the new (21:1f.). Here the curtain may be described as marking the division not between heaven and earth (both may be aspects of the first things), nor between things present and things to come (both Satan and Christ are coming), nor even between battle and victory (even in the new order John sees idolaters excluded from the holy city); but between the whole of one creation (the above *and* below, the before *and* after) and the whole of another creation, the transcendence of which is not diminished by its descent from God, the newness of which is not lost in its embodiment among men. His message confronts the reader with the choice as to whether or not to affirm the reality of this new creation where God is now making all things new, where Christ is the first and the last, and where his slaves share in his eternal sovereignty over all things. What does it mean for a modern congregation to accept or to reject such a message? The point is not whether this idiom is more difficult for us to adopt than the others (in some respects that is certainly true) or more easy to adopt than the others (in some respects that is also true). The point is simply to ask in what context it would be meaningful to say "I saw a new heaven and a new earth."

Reflection upon such problems as these is incumbent upon John's readers. It is not enough for them to say, "Yes, I agree with John" or "No, I can't follow him." They must analyze the reasons for one statement or the other. I suggest to those who say *no* that they all too easily buttress their negation by such disclaimers as "John is too naive a thinker for us to take seriously." The area of his naïveté may vary—his conceptions of space, of time, of conflict, or the new creation—but the accusation seems so obviously justified that the nay-sayer rarely feels any need to reopen the matter. To those who say *yes* I suggest that they all too easily allow their thinking to stop there. They may support their response by eulogies of the prophet: "John was a profound seer, very profound indeed." But this eulogy may itself be no more valid than the accusation of naïveté. The eulogy implies that they are at least profound enough to recognize such greatness. Yet their own thought may actually be too shallow to cope with either those issues which are faced by contemporary nay-sayers or those issues which were decisive for the initial readers of the Apocalypse.

Is there any exit from the impasse into which such reflection leads? Does John indicate any guidelines? Had his own idioms perhaps been changed during the process of his reflection? If so, what force had produced that change? Like all of us, he could only think with the conceptual tools available to him. Yet his mind was not totally bound by his use of these instruments, nor need ours be. As we recall his total message, we may be able to discover certain truths which transcended the customary patterns of his own mentality. Presumably he shared the same linguistic idioms and thought patterns as his false-prophet antagonists. Yet John's thinking deviated radically from theirs. What forces had reshaped his mind but not theirs? Such a question could only be answered in a booklength essay; here there is only space to mention two considerations.

1) All the evidence available supports the conclusion that one factor which dominated John's thinking was the revelatory power of the Gospel of Jesus the Messiah. It had been the *marturia* of Jesus which had revealed and verified the purpose and design of God. If one thinks in terms of a spatial curtain between heaven and earth (and John did), that curtain had been penetrated by Jesus in such a way as to transform those *categories* of thought. If one thinks of a temporal curtain between what is and what is to come, as John did, Jesus' death had penetrated that curtain in such a way as to alter the use of temporal *categories*. If one thinks of men as being involved daily in a conflict between superhuman Good and superhuman Evil, for John the slaughter of the Lamb had forced a drastic change in all *conceptions* of that warfare—antagonists, weapons, defeats, victories. If one holds the possibility of new creation (e.g., with Isaiah 65), the events reported by the Gospel had both corroborated that possibility and had revolutionized its meaning. Not long ago a perceptive theologian called for such an appraisal of the resurrection event as would enable us to utilize a new kind of "historical reason" (R. R. Niebuhr, *Resurrection and Historical Reason*, esp. 2-4). I believe that the Book of Revelation constitutes one of the earliest efforts to accomplish that task. John assumed that a man had not really listened to the word of God until that word had produced radical changes in his previous

understandings of himself and his universe. Pascal was not the first to recognize that it is only by knowing Jesus Christ that man can learn who God is and what man and the world and life and death really are. Our linguistic tools, our mental patterns are not John's, nor need they be. But when we encounter a prophet whose mind had been so illuminated by God's revelation in Christ as to break through the very forms of his thinking, we are impelled to ask whether a similar illumination may recur in the twentieth century for men who utilize entirely different patterns and idioms of thought. It may be impossible for men today to find in contemporary language the precise equivalents for John's ideas and yet possible for them to allow their own language to be renewed and changed by the same revelation of God's power and wisdom.

2) Our study supports a second conclusion: John's writing makes it clear that to him the truth of Jesus' *marturia* can be verified only by those who accept the same ordeals and win the same victories. The ultimate problem to John was not whether the meaning of a verbal confession in 95 A.D. in Smyrna coincided with that of Jesus' teaching in 29 A.D. in Jerusalem, but whether or not the witness of a follower coincided with the witness of his Master. Followers must hold fast to Jesus' testimony. The justice and reliability of God's purpose could be comprehended and validated only by that type of self-sacrifice for which Jesus would vouch before God's throne. *Meaning*, then, is a term which in this context may apply less to conceptual statements than to interpersonal relations and to ethical decisions. To John, truth inhered in action—not just any action, but action which conformed to the model of Christ's action. Every moral imperative in the Apocalypse conveyed ontological significance, whether John was speaking of repentance or of loving or of waking up. And every ontological presupposition or affirmation conveyed a moral thrust which was intrinsic to it, whether the assertion of a new creation or the picture of Jesus as the bright star of dawn. In connection with this latter image we can note that Thoreau was not the first to teach that "only that day dawns

to which we are awake." The verbal use of the term "awake" is not what determines the matter, but the kind of wakefulness expressed by it. For John himself it was a wakefulness prompted by the grace of God (1:4). It was oriented toward the grace of a coming Lord (22:20, 21); it was occasioned by the dread of practicing falsehood (22:15). He believed that the test of true prophecy was its being fully awake to the gracious work of Jesus as that work was continued among the churches by the Spirit (19:10).

For Further Study

The interpretation of the message of the Apocalypse as a whole and of each separate vision presents every reader with multiple problems of hermeneutics. These problems are too varied and the literature is too vast to be covered in a single list, but the following list may suggest potential starting points.

1. THE PROBLEMS OF DEFINING THE RELEVANCE OF APOCALYPTIC THOUGHT.

E. Käsemann, *Exegetische Versuche und Besinnungen*, II, Göttingen, 1964, 82-130, 268-289; R. Bultmann in *Apophoreta* (Festschrift for E. Haenchen) Berlin, 1964, 64-69; NTS 1 (1954) 5-16; M. Eliade, *Myth of the Eternal Return*, N.Y., 1954; L. Goppelt, ThLZ 1952, 513-522; H. Günkel, *Schöpfung und Chaos in Urzeit und Endzeit*, Göttingen, 1921; R. Halver, *Der Mythos in Letzten Buch der Bibel*, Hamburg, 1964; S. H. Hooke, *Alpha and Omega*, London, 1961, 94-108, 265-288; W. Kamlah, *Apokalypse und Geschichtsbewusstsein*, Göttingen, 1931; R. Leivestad, *Christ the Conqueror*, N.Y., 1954; P. Minear, *Eyes of Faith*, St. Louis, 1965, 131-151; 253-359; *Kingdom and the Power*, 83-114, 215-245; *Horizons of Christian Community*, 44-102; *Neutestamentlichen Studien für R. Bultmann*, Berlin, 97, 15-23; J. A. T. Robinson, *In the End, God*; C. G. Rossetti, *The Face of the Deep*; H. H. Rowley, *Relevance of Apocalyptic*; D. S. Russell, *Method and Message of Jewish Apocalyptic*; P. Schütz, Gesammelte Werke, Vol. 3: *Parusia, Hoffnung und Prophetie*; U. Simon, *The End is Not Yet*; P. Vielhauer in E. Hennecke, *N.T. Apocrypha II*,

581-626; A. N. Wilder, *Eschatology and Ethics;* NTS 5 (1959) 229-245; "Social Factors in Early Christian Eschatology" in *Early Christian Origins,* Chicago, 1961; "Kerygma, Eschatology and Social Ethics," in *The Background of the N.T. and its Eschatology,* 509-536.

2. THE INTERPRETATION OF THE SYMBOLS AND PICTURES.

C. Clemen, in *Festgabe für J. Kaftan;* J. Danielou, *Primitive Christian Symbols; From Shadows to Reality;* E. Goodenough, *Jewish Symbols in the Greco Roman World* (12 vols.); M. Eliade, *Images and Symbols;* E. Cassirer, *Philosophie der symbolischen Formen,* Pt. 2; H. Langenberg, *Die prophetische Bildsprache der Apok.; Schlussel zum Verstandnis der Apok.;* P. Minear, *Christian Hope and the Second Coming,* 1954; Int. 19 (1965), 3-15; K. L. Schmidt, ThZ 3 (1947) 170f.; *Eranos Jahrbuch* 18 (1950), 207-248; E. Stauffer, ZST 8 (1930), 203-215; F. W. Dillistone, ed., *Myth and Symbol;* G. Dudley, *Recovery of Christian Myth.*

3. THE INTERPRETATION OF THE COMING OF CHRIST.

C. H. Dodd, *The Coming of Christ;* A. Winklhofer, *The Coming of His Kingdom;* J. A. T. Robinson, *In the End, God; Jesus and His Coming;* P. Minear, *Christian Hope,* 85-114; 201-211; E. Stauffer, TNT, 205-234; O. Cullmann, *Christology of the N.T.,* 109-190; H. Schlier, *Die Zeit der Kirche,* 265-273; *Besinnung auf das N.T.,* 1964, 358-374; K. Heim, *Jesus the World's Perfecter,* Part III; T. Holtz, 166-211; P. Minear, SJT 6 (1953) 337-361; M. Rissi, *Die Zukunft der Welt;* N. A. Dahl, in *Background of the N.T. and Its Eschatology* (C. H. Dodd), 422-443; C. K. Barrett, *Jesus and the Gospel,* 82-99; J. Moltmann, *Theology of Hope,* 194f., 224f.

PART II
Issues in Interpretation

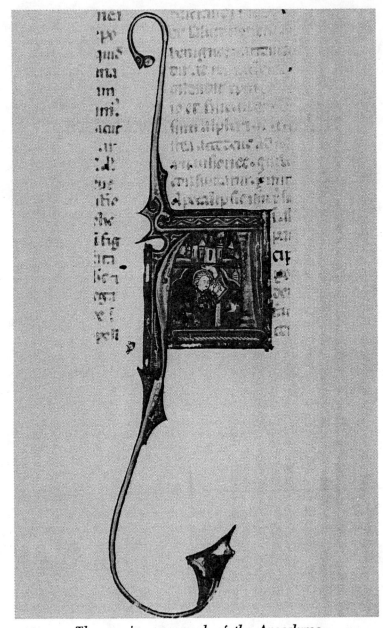

The opening paragraph of the Apocalypse
An illuminated Ms. Southern France (Thirteenth Century)

1. The Significance of Suffering

As the prophet laid the groundwork for his first vision of Christ, he found it desirable to speak both of his own captivity on Patmos and of the agony (*thlipsis*) his readers shared with Jesus. "I am John, your brother and full-partner with you in Jesus' agony, in his royal power, and in his loyal endurance" (1:9). This is an obvious clue to the fact that the book was written during a period of great external hostility toward the Christian movement. Knowledge of that hostility and of its origins should enhance our understanding of the visions. It is quite obvious that John considered this animosity as entirely normal; many modern interpreters assume that it was more or less abnormal. Which is right? Much hangs upon the answer. Let us review the evidence.

Virtually the whole of the New Testament provides positive support for John's position. The evidence begins with the earliest period. Jesus had been reared in Galilee, a province which during his early years had been the vortex of seething unrest and violence. John the Baptist, to whose message Jesus had been strongly attracted and in whose baptism Jesus had been included, was imprisoned and killed soon after Jesus endorsed his movement. The Gospels leave little doubt that Jesus had taken full notice of John's fate, and had decided to continue his inflammatory message. They leave even less doubt that Jesus' own work aroused even deeper antagonisms among an even broader spectrum of the power structures of his day: the Roman overlords, the Sanhedrin and the priesthood, the synagogue leaders and huge sectors of the public. The passion story in all four Gospels stresses how these usually opposed groups reached full consensus in their desire for Jesus' execution. Moreover, the same Gospels speak with one voice in treating the acceptance of a death like his as normative for his disciples. He had set the carrying of the cross as the inescapable cost of discipleship. The Gospels agree in showing that none of the twelve had initially been ready to pay that price, assertions of loyalty notwithstanding. But the death of Jesus had changed them. Of the twelve disciples, those three whose deaths are credibly reported in the tradition (apart from Judas), were all martyred: Peter, James, and John. It is significant that it was these three who had been closest to Jesus during his ministry. Nor is the martyrdom of his chief disciples strange when we recognize that public animosities would almost inevitably have shifted from a crucified leader to those followers who, subsequent to his execution, had hailed him as savior and publicly accused his adversaries of fighting against the Most High God. Anyone converted to this cause would obviously have invited the same opprobrium which had greeted Jesus. The list of martyrs is a long one. Some were killed, such as James (the "brother" of Jesus), Stephen, Paul, John the elder, and Antipas. Many more followers knew prisons from the inside: Silas, Timothy, Titus, Epaphras, Andronicus, Junias, Aristarchus, Aquila, Priscilla. The stigma attached to participation in this movement was such that no member could escape. Guilt by association was virtually automatic.

The letters of Paul give ample evidence of varying types of hostility which were encountered in the line of apostolic duty: imprisonments, beatings, lashes, stonings, hunger and thirst, exposure, "danger from my own people, danger from Gentiles, . . . danger from false brethren" (2 Cor. 11:23-28). Paul also makes it clear that he expected other apostles and companions in the ministry to accept with joy a similar, if less extreme, kind of testing. Persecution was by no means limited to radical proponents of the Gentile mission. Paul's earliest letter tells how the churches in Judea had suffered from the Jews who had "killed both the Lord Jesus and the prophets and drove us out" and also how the believers in Macedonia had "suffered the same things" from their own countrymen (1 Thes. 2:14, 15). Those who were summoned to accept Jesus as Lord were warned in advance that they should expect suffering as an inescapable consequence of faith. Paul's letters offer a vivid documentation not only for his own story but also for that of his churches.

At least five books of the New Testament were written in prison; others in the intervals between prison terms. Many books were addressed to congregations which were even then undergoing severe ordeals. It can be said without exaggeration that every writing during the first or second generation (30-90 A.D.) either recalls or anticipates periods of severe stress. The injunction of 1 Peter is entirely typical: "Beloved, do not be surprised at the fiery ordeal which comes upon you to prove you, as though something strange were happening to you" (4:12). Even the objective secular historian cannot deny that the new movement aroused from the beginning violent antipathies on the part of outsiders. And this is the unanimous verdict on the part of ancient non-Christian writers, the Jewish compilers of the Mishnah and Talmud and such Roman authors as Tacitus, Suetonius, and Pliny. Their verdict is fully corroborated by leaders and writers of the second-century church, such men as Ignatius, Polycarp, Justin, and Irenaeus.

> Suffering and tribulation belonged to the very nature of the primitive Church. The Christian, like the Jew, was expected to confess and if need be to suffer for the Name. "Whosoever shall confess me before men, him will I confess before my Father which is in Heaven. But whosoever shall deny me before men, him will I deny before my Father who is in Heaven" (Mt. 10:32-33). In this passage of Scripture Christianity follows current tradition. Death was to be preferred to the breach of the new Covenant implied in denial of the Name just as it had been of the Old, and he who persevered would be rewarded at the Day of Judgment. The plain word of Scripture was the Christian martyr's source of inspiration. To endure "the great persecution that is coming," Hermas urged, was to be blessed, but to deny was to court rejection by the Lord Himself. It is hardly accidental that St. Luke associates denial with "blasphemy against the Holy Ghost" (Lk. 12:10). (W. H. C. Frend, *Martyrdom and Persecution in the Early Church*, 79; cited by permission of Blackwells Books).

To be sure, the New Testament writings imply that it was very hard to secure unanimity among churchmen on the best ways of responding to enemies outside the Church. Many apostles, prophets, and teachers wished to avoid danger by taking the path of moderation. The continuing debate which Paul carried on with such leaders was often acrimonious on both sides. The presence in the Synoptics of the demand for total sacrifice may, in fact, reflect the strength of the opposite tendency in the Church on the part of leaders who wished to call Jesus "Lord" without following his path of self-sacrifice. Even so, it is difficult to discover any early Christian writer who defended *as normative* a less strenuous pattern of obedience. The Evangelist Luke is sometimes selected to illustrate such a tendency, with his picture of the Jerusalem church as the strongest evidence of the less "heroic" norm. Let us briefly test that evidence.

Luke's story of Pentecost tells us that three thousand auditors of Peter's sermon were so "cut to the heart" that they repented and were baptized. Such a story appears to contradict the picture of universal hostility at the crucifixion of Jesus, which had occurred in the same city only a few weeks earlier. What could explain such a total transformation? An even more amazing contrast appears in Luke's accounts of the apparent popularity of the Pentecostal church. "Day by day attending the temple together and breaking bread in their home, they partook of food with glad and generous hearts, praising God and *having favor with all the people*" (2:46, 47). In a later summary we read that "the church throughout Judea . . . had peace and was built up" (9:31). To be sure, Luke did stress the hostility of the rulers, elders, and scribes toward the apostles, yet he says that this hostility was restrained by their fear "of being stoned by the people" (4:21, 5:26). In such honor did "the people" hold the apostles that "more than ever believers were added to the Lord" (5:13, 14; paradoxically, the same verse says that "none of the rest dared join them"). Moreover, in spite of severe threats, imprisonments, and beatings, the apostles continued their preaching in the temple itself. Even when a violent persecution arose over the preaching of Stephen, the apostles were not forced to flee, a fact presumably implying that they were acceptable to the religious and political authorities (8:1). On the basis of such evidence, many interpreters have concluded that Jesus' earliest followers in Jerusalem were far less incendiary than Jesus himself and were therefore more popular among their neighbors. "The church . . . had peace." Such interpreters conclude that discord arose only when Stephen and Paul, more iconoclastic than Peter and James, launched direct attacks upon the temple or the Law or upon the cautious conservatism of Judean Christians. We cannot advance here a full rebuttal of this set of conclusions, but we suggest three major lines along which that rebuttal might move.

A. Such a hypothesis ignores or minimizes the contrary evidence within the Book of Acts itself. The apostolic sermons directly accuse the "house of Israel" of primary responsibility for the murder of Jesus (2:36, 3:13). Moreover, the very sermons which produced repentance among "thousands" also produced corresponding and continuing hatred. Even Luke tells how imprisonment was the immediate sequel of Pentecost (4:1f.). The earliest songs and prayers of the Church celebrated the power of God to overcome the rage of such enemies as "Herod and Pontius Pilate, with the Gentiles and the peoples of Israel" (4:25-31; the hymns in Acts reflect as much conflict as those in Revelation!) It was such enmity which impressed Luke with the boldness of believers and the audacity behind their confessions to the power of the Holy Spirit. If the Church had peace, Luke did not view this peace as entailing a high degree of social prestige, but as a manifestation of internal cohesion and unity, all the more effective as proof of divine power when seen against the background of public hostility.

B. The picture of a community "having favor with all the people" is to be attributed in part to the late date of Luke's writing. Distance had begun to lend enchantment to the view. By the end of the century most Christians were inclined to describe the beginnings of the Church in both a stylized and an idyllic fashion. The pictures in Acts of the power of the apostolic word quickly to produce a community of 3,000 and then of 5,000 are to be attributed, at least in part, to the romantic halo produced by pious memories. The letters of Paul are far more realistic and more dependable, written as they were from the vortex of struggle. Furthermore, Luke was writing at a time when he believed that the best strategy called for minimizing the conflict with Rome, for maximizing the responsibility of synagogue leaders, and for stressing the miraculous growth of the Church. Such editorial motives colored his description of the first church in Jerusalem, written some forty to seventy years after the event, inducing him to forget the bitterness of conflict and to recall the speed with which the earliest church established a secure anchorage in the Holy City.

C. Luke was concerned not so much with producing an objectively accurate historical record as with suggesting the theological significance of that history for his Christian readers. It is wrong, therefore, to treat his vocabulary as if it were the matter-of-fact literal prose of the secular historian. His references to places, for example, are often instances of a theological geography. Jerusalem signified much more to him than a place on the Roman map. The temple as the place of God's presence connoted multiple symbolic meanings, not unlike those expressed in John's visions (chs. 18, 21). Pentecost was a religious festival, with rich historical, typological, and archetypal values. The accounts which stress the peace of the church in Jerusalem are distinctively Lucan in aroma and flavor. Peace itself was, in his view, a unique mark of salvation. "To have favor (*charis*) with all the people" was a formula drawn from the Septuagint, which he had already applied both to John the Baptist and to Jesus (1:30; 2:40, 52), for whom such favor had, even in Luke's account, brought no immunity to violent hostility. In fact, such phrases as "the house of Israel" and "all the people" do not indicate numerical or quantitative measurement. Misuse of his vocabulary is bound to produce distortions in reading his story. In short, the evidence from Acts serves to strengthen rather than to weaken the conclusion that social hostility was considered entirely normal by the New Testament writers.

Whether or not this hypothesis should be extended to cover

the whole Christian movement during its first two generations, certainly it does apply to the churches in Asia during the generation preceding Revelation, as well as during the succeeding generation. The earliest document from Ephesus speaks clearly of the many adversaries Paul had encountered there (1 Cor. 16:9). The affliction he experienced had been so great that he had despaired of life itself (2 Cor. 1:8-10). In all probability several of the lashings, beatings, imprisonments, and dangers which he detailed in 2 Cor. 11 had taken place in the cities of Asia. The degree of probability is smaller, although in my judgment still substantial, that it was during an imprisonment in Asia that Paul wrote Colossians, Philemon, and Philippians—letters which add circumstantial evidence to the picture of almost unremitting conflict.

The Pauline evidence is strengthened by Luke's narrative, which may have been edited in Asia during the period of the Apocalypse itself. According to Acts, it was Jews from Asia who had been among the opponents of Stephen who had instigated the riot in which he was killed (6:9). Later on the hostility of the synagogue in Ephesus had forced Paul to withdraw (19:8-11); he had narrowly escaped death when pagan craftsmen aroused the populace against him (19:23-41). Paul's farewell address to the elders had clearly anticipated not only his own imprisonment and death, but continuing external and internal stress among the churches of Asia (20:18-35). Nor is that the end of the record. Jews from Asia had instigated the riot against Paul in the Jerusalem temple from which he had been saved in the nick of time (21:27-36). The people of Asia had been as violent against the apostle as they had been earlier against Jesus and Stephen. Paul and Luke agree, then, with the evidence of Revelation 2, 3 that those who faithfully witnessed to Jesus in Asian churches were regularly confronted by dangers from the Gentiles, from the synagogues, and from false apostles and teachers.

Later documents (e.g., Ignatius, Polycarp) show how these dangers persisted beyond the first century. In fact, even as late

as 177 A.D., the letter sent to the churches of Asia from persecuted churches in Gaul reveals how closely those in the west
were linked by their sufferings to their mother churches in Asia.

> Not only was the letter sent to the Churches in Asia Minor
> written in Greek, but any statements spoken in Latin were spe-
> cially noted. A reading of Eusebius and of the names of the mar-
> tyrs preserved in the Martyrology of Jerome (early fifth century)
> and the later, ninth-century Martyrology of Ado shows that the
> leaders and about half of the forty-eight known martyrs were
> probably Asiatics. Pothinus, the aged bishop, is likely to have
> been himself an immigrant, his senior presbyter and famous suc-
> cessor, Irenaeus, had been brought up in Smyrna. Attalus, de-
> scribed as a "pillar of the Church" at Vienne, was a Roman
> citizen from Pergamum. Alexander, another prominant Christian
> at Lyons, was a physician who had emigrated from Phrygia. The
> name Vettius Epagathus suggests a Greek or Asiatic freedman,
> and among the more humble Christians, Biblis, Elpis, Ponticus,
> and Alcibiades are names that indicate Greek or Asiatic origins.
> The spiritual home of the two Churches was Asia Minor, for it
> was to the Churches of the provinces of Asia and Phrygia more
> than a thousand miles away that they addressed themselves in
> their hour of need. Here were "the brethren who had the same
> faith and hope of redemption." Their links with these provinces
> must have been strong indeed (W. H. C. Frend, *Martyrdom and
> Persecution in the Early Church*, 2-3. Used by permission).

We may conclude, therefore, that all available evidence
makes it highly probable that the congregations in Asia lived
in the midst of acute hostility from their founding until long
after John's day. They experienced recurring explosions of that
hostility in violent form. They were inured to conflict. If there
was a crisis at the time John was imprisoned, it was by no means
unprecedented.

Another feature needs to be stressed even more, however,
than the normality of violent persecution as the response of outsiders to the Church. This is the degree to which Christians
recognized such persecution as intrinsic to the redemptive pur-

pose of God, as comprehended within the *dei*, the divinely willed necessity, which had dominated the mission of Jesus and his apostles. They not only experienced the *thlipsis* (to use the term of Rev. 1:9); they also accepted it as being an inescapable consequence of entering the kingdom. But it was also more than consequence; it was the door for entering, and the mode of proclaiming that kingdom. The introduction to the kingdom required that men share in the "messianic woes."

These woes marked the upheaval occasioned by the collision between God's kingdom and Satan's. This is why New Testament writers located their ultimate adversary not among Roman governors or Jewish priests, but in the invisible power which aroused and used this hostility as a trial of Christian faith. The unmasking and defeat of this transcendent enemy was God's objective. Victory in that war required the staging of battles in which God's rule was demonstrated as more powerful than Satan's rule. This demonstration required the "unleashing of Satan" so that he could bring maximum pressure to bear on God's witnesses. It required a demonstration of wealth in poverty, strength in weakness, glory in shame, joy in suffering. Only such a demonstration could suffice to show the emptiness of the Devil's reliance on wealth and power to mete out shame and suffering to men. Only through death could victory over death be vindicated. The arousing of hostility to the cross was thus built into the Gospel of the cross.

Early Christians believed that this factor explained why the Messiah had been crucified as a sign to all men of the contrast between God's ways and Satan's. This was why the Messiah had laid upon his apostles the same yoke and why every Christian had to be baptized with the same baptism (Paul's vocabulary), or to wear clothing washed white in the Lamb's blood (the vocabulary of John). There was a single ultimate vocation, grounded in God's saving purpose, which required that men should learn through the experiencing of weakness the power of their king. Imprisonment, therefore, became not a fearful and unforeseen threat, but a normal opportunity to proclaim the

Gospel in a mode which would correspond to its archetypal expression in the passion story. The faithful witness would use that opportunity to testify to Christ's power over Satan, a power which became apparent in the very boldness with which he spoke. Only in such fashion could the human enemies whom God loved in Christ be emancipated from the tyrannies of the Devil. Mission theology and strategy alike demanded witnesses of this calibre in situations of this kind.

> Behind their action lies the whole theology of martyrdom in the early Church. They were seeking by their death to attain to the closest possible imitation of Christ's passion and death. This was the heart of their attitude. Christ himself suffered in the martyr. Love of Christ and hope of salvation through Christ alone was their inspiration and the essence of their faith (W. H. C. Frend, *op. cit.*, 15).

Or, to phrase the point in the words of S. Laeuchli, "eschatology in its apocalyptic form was the poetry of expensive grace" (*The Serpent and the Dove*, 181). The expense was so great because the serpent was present in the midst of the Church (*ibid.*, 129) making it difficult to discern the dividing line between traitors and saints (*ibid.*, 193).

We need not labor the point here, for any perceptive reading of Revelation will provide an extensive and varied elucidation of this rationale. But since modern readers find this rationale so foreign, it may be well to ask why it is so foreign. What is the source of our notion that the resistance to early Christianity was an exceptional and passing phenomenon, due to the peculiar blindness of the Jewish religion and the Roman state, rather than a normal and continuing reaction to the intrinsic demands and character of God's revelation itself?

One factor is our hasty classification of Christianity under the category "religion," so that we assume that it is as "harmless" politically and socially as are the chief alternate options, such as Judaism and Islam. Another source is our usual notion that religion is on the whole a conservative, innocuous, self-protective force, applicable to man's inner life but not to the powers which control historical destiny. Another source is our penchant for discovering crises only in the extraordinary tides of historical development and not in the ordinary sequences of daily life. The Church has so emasculated the Gospel that it threatens no other power-structure. The Church no longer arouses hostility among the same elites and to the same degree as in the first century, but this is due not so much to a change in the operation of power-structures as to the Church's betrayal of the Gospel itself. In fact, in reading Revelation, we may discover that the prophet was alive to that very betrayal in the churches of Asia and that he traced such betrayal to Satan's deceptions. This is why he describes the Great Prostitute as he does, because he discovers whoredom among Christians themselves. This is why his parodies are so caustic and cutting: the Prostitute as a parodic image of the Church, Babylon as parody of the New Jerusalem, the Beast as parody of the Lamb, the slaves of the Beast as parody of the slaves of Christ. Such an interpretation of John brings him within the succession of the great prophets, like Isaiah, Jeremiah, and Ezekiel, whose vocation under God was to make God's people aware of their own apostasy.

For Further Study

Granted the origin of the *Book of Revelation* in prison, granted that imprisonment has conditioned its outlook, how is the modern reader to increase his empathy for it? One answer is to consult modern writings which have been produced by Christians under similar circumstances. As examples, let me mention: D. Bonhöffer, *Letter and Papers from Prison;* R. DePury, *Journal from My Cell;* P. Dumitryu, *Incognito;* P. Geren, *Burma Diary;* H. Lilje, *The Valley of the Shadow.*

For explicit theological treatments of the relation between Christian suffering and the apocalyptic message, I suggest:

K. Kitamori, *Theology of the Pain of God;* S. Kierkegaard, *Gospel of Suffering;* R. Leivestad, *Christ the Conqueror;* P. Minear, *The Kingdom and the Power;* H. Schlier, *Besinnung auf des N.T.*, 358-374; W. H. C. Frend, *Martyrdom and Persecution in the Early Church.*

2. The Prophet's Motives

No interpreter of the Apocalypse should minimize the actualities of social animosities that beset the Christian congregations. As W. H. C. Frend has stressed: "The intense fury of the people and their fear that somehow or other the Christians might triumph over their gods stand out on every page of the confessor's story" (p. 9). Even more remarkable, as we have seen, was the reaction of Christians to this popular fury. The same author has well characterized this reaction: "In the interim before the Second Coming, the Christian was called upon to suffer rather than to inflict suffering. His citizenship was truly in heaven. . . . If this involved him in the hatred of the world, that was to be expected and was a cause of rejoicing. He would be avenged, but not by the warrior's sword" (p. 98f.).

When the modern exegete reconstructs the full scale of the conflict between the Church and its neighbors, he is almost bound to exaggerate one thesis concerning John's purpose in writing. The prophet is seen as an agent of "social control," who helped to allay the fears and to calm the nerves of frightened Christians. His objective was to produce a heroic willingness to accept death and to warn against the penalties of apostasy. His use of carrot-and-stick was successful in proportion to the number of brothers whom he induced to accept martyrdom.

There is evidence in the Apocalypse to support this hypothesis. The prophet did in fact seek to produce certain changes in the attitudes and actions of his audience, and one of these changes was the replacement of terror by courage in the face of persecution. But when one isolates the hortatory sections of his book, and analyzes the thrust of those sections, he is impressed with the diversity of external conditions, the variety of Christian response, and the manifold shape of the author's purpose. It is clear that the document would never have been written apart from John's desire to produce changes in thought and behavior. It is true that no vision is intelligible apart from this desire, and that the recapture of purpose is essential to every student's work. But the expert literary critic becomes rightly sceptical of any neat formulation of an author's intention, especially when the author is not available for interview. Let us begin then by reviewing the evidence.

John expressed a distinct hortatory intention in at least eight different literary forms. Let us briefly scan these, noting in each case that the readers are invited to define the "specific gravity" of the command and to determine its applicability to their own situation.

A. The first form to be mentioned occurs four times, all in connection with the warfare with the beasts and Babylon. The verbal tag is the introductory phrase *hode estin*, which shows the enigmatic character of the preceding vision and provides a key to its riddle. What follows this phrase is the clue which the reader needs to decipher a heavenly mystery (13:10, 18; 14:12; 17:9). Twice the call is for wisdom, twice for endurance. In all cases, the call presupposes that a war is on. Discernment is needed to identify the antagonists; courage is needed to persevere against an enemy who appears to be irresistible. The prophet seeks to arouse in his readers that insight and that stamina.

B. A second, easily recognized, form is the beatitude, which appears seven times (1:3; 14:13; 16:15; 19:9; 20:6; 22:7, 14). In an earlier section we have called attention to the difference between the use of beatitudes to reinforce conventional wisdom and their use to epitomize the radical choices produced by apocalyptic crisis (above, p. 149). John illustrates the second type. His exhortations in the beatitude-form bring pressure upon the readers both to perceive the crisis and to act with total resolution. Yet it is left to those same readers to determine the kind of communal action which will embody that resolution.

C. In at least a dozen cases the prophet exerts admonitory

pressure by using a conditional clause (*ei tis*) followed by a definition of the resulting reward or penalty. "If any one (*ei tis*) worships the beast and its image, and receives a brand on his forehead or hand, he also shall drink. . . ." (14:9). The conditional clause can usually be translated "When any man. . . ." (3:3, 20; 11:4; 13:9, 10; 20:15; 22:18). Frequently, as in the example given, the condition is defined in several somewhat ambiguous ways. This form of sentence gives the reader a rather wide latitude in determining what specific actions constitute a worship of the beast, as well as in deciding whether he is himself covered by the saying. The penalty seems at first to be stated more "objectively" than the sin, but actually both are fully indigenous to the world of the prophet's imagination.

D. In some seven instances John uses a hortatory subjunctive. In other writers of his day this form of the imperative occurs frequently, but not in John. It appears mostly in his final chapter (22:11, 17) as a way of stressing his affectionate desire:

> *"Let him who hears say 'Come.'*
> *Let him who is thirsty come."*

We notice, however, that the prophet does not clearly specify which actions are embraced by such coming.

E. The hortatory impulse often appears in a more diffuse and vague way in sentences which are introduced by a participial phrase used substantivally. A familiar example is the promise given in each of the seven letters: "He who conquers" or "To him who conquers." The same type of clauses also appears as descriptive of beast worshipers and harlots. Whether followed by threat or promise, the clause is equivalent to a strong appeal from Christ to the churches. This grammatical form appears more frequently than any other and is one of John's ways of bringing pressure to bear on his readers. Very few imperatives are not found expressed in this way: fear, dwell, hear, follow, hold, repent, etc. It is assumed that the reader will want to be among those who obey, hold, follow, etc.

F. Developing out of such participial phrases, sentences are detected in which substantive nouns or adjectives appear without the participle, yet with the same emotive force. Those who are worthy are mentioned in such a way as to impel the readers to obedient action. They are, for example, spoken of as the called, the chosen, the faithful, the virgins, the holy, the true. They wear white robes. They are brothers, holy men, slaves. Each of these suggests a goal so desirable as to elicit action. For each of them John (or his readers) can easily provide a pejorative antonym. If one studies 14:4-5, he will discover how easily John can move from one of these grammatical forms to another, without diminishing the hortatory impulse.

The seventh mode of exhortation is provided by lists or catalogs of the saved or the damned; the eighth is provided by explicit commands in the imperative mood. To these we will now give closer scrutiny.

G. Lists of virtues and vices may be found in the following passages: 9:20, 21; 13:4-8; 14:4, 5; 21:8, 27; 22:15. Let us look closely at the first of these with its concentration on five vices: idolatry, murder, sorcery, fornication. and thievery.

> *"The rest of mankind, not killed by these plagues,*
>   *refused to repent their handiwork.*
> *They went on worshiping demonic forces,*
>   *idols of gold, silver, bronze, stone, wood,*
>   *which have no power to see, hear or walk.*
> *They refused to repent their murders,*
>   *their sorcery, their fornication, their thefts"* (9:20,21).

Before examining the five specified sins, we should comment upon the fact that the prophet appears to say that there is something worse than all five—the refusal to repent. Like a funeral lament comes the phrase "they refused to repent." If men had repented of those sins, presumably they would have been forgiven and would have escaped the torments of further plagues. Here lies the prophet's primary concern. To repent is to worship the true God. Refusal to repent is to prefer the worship of demons and idols. What then distinguishes worship of false gods from worship of the true? Demons and idols are constructions of man's own hands, representing a trust in his own works, his self-won securities. Demons and idols lack the power to see, to hear, to move. In worshiping them, men think their gods can see, but men fool themselves by arranging a set of mirrors. If idols seem to hear, it is only because men have set up bugging devices. If they seem to move, it is like puppets on a string which men pull. This is not true of God.

All this, however, while clear in principle, may be very obscure in practice. How does John understand that practice? The answer becomes evident as we examine his use of such key terms as *daimonia* and *eidola*, along with four other words: murder, sorcery, fornication, theft. As in our own day, these terms were epithets which men hesitated to apply to themselves. Especially heinous did these offences appear to men with Jewish background, who revered the Old Testament. Each of them was forbidden by the Decalog. "There are only three fundamentals of Judaism for which a man or woman must prefer death to transgression—the worship of idols, adultery, and the shedding of innocent blood" (S. Grayzel, *A History of the Jews*, 1947, 201. Cited in E. Goodenough, *Jewish Symbols* I, 11). John seems thus to have been condemning sins which his readers already recognized and condemned as evil. Then, as now, that was a rather superficial way for preachers to talk. It is a way which insured maximum agreement and minimum controversy, that is, unless the preacher is engaged in laying an ambush, to catch his readers unaware with the startling accusation "You are the man."

Was John laying this sort of ambush? Because his readers agreed that idolatry is always wrong, was he using this agreement as the basis for attack upon their unsuspected idolatries? Because they already condemned murder, must this become his accusation? Had their reliance upon self-protective definitions of murder (in criminal and religious and common law) prevented them from recognizing their own unwitting murders (see Mt. 5:21f.)? I believe that these questions must all be answered in the affirmative.

Let us now examine seven terms which represent John's attack, indicating the frequency with which each appears:

repentance (*metanoein*) 2:5, 16, 21, 22; 3:3, 19; 16:9, 11
idolatry (*eidola*) 2:14, 20; 21:8; 22:15
demonism (*daimonia*) 16:14; 18:2
murders (*phonos*) 21:8; 22:15
sorcery (*pharmakia*) 18:23; 21:8; 22:15
adultery (*porneia*) 2:14, 20, 21; 14:8; 17:1-5, 15, 16; 18:3, 9; 19:2; 21:8; 22:15
thefts (*klemmata*) 3:3; 16:15

These frequencies are not in themselves impressive. But the number of passages would be doubled if we were to consider the antonyms for each (e.g., the symbols of chastity as over against adultery), the equivalent expressions (e.g., blasphemy, which in various passages is a form of idolatry), and their strategic locations (e.g., 9:20, 21 is a summary covering two chapters. With these considerations in mind, let us study four passages within which we find the greatest concentration of cross-references.

The first of these passages comprises two lists of those men who are excluded from the Holy City (21:8; 22:15). Four of the terms mentioned are included within both of these catalogs. Very clearly these lists mark the boundary between the two communities which we have tried to describe on p. 171f. This boundary runs between the repentant and the unrepentant, between those who love or hate the lie (the climactic criterion in 22:15). The standard of judgment is provided neither by criminal nor by codified religious law, but by the prophetic disclosure of the truth and faithfulness of the creator God and the victor Christ (21:5). Repentance is so decisive, so revolutionary, and so powerful because it is the only appropriate way for man to respond to the eschatological event. It is his response to the primal and final purpose of God which makes man either a son of God or a worshiper of the Beast. Repentance marks the moment when either self-deceit or self-knowledge triumphs. Only by repentance can man recognize his own identity as murderer, sorcerer, adulterer, idolator. The prophet does not say to his reader, "You are a murderer." But he arranges the dialog in such a way that the listener hears Christ announcing, "Blessed are those . . ." and "Excluded from the gates are those. . . ." This message compels every listener to examine himself, to recognize his own condition and to repent before the throne.

This mode of communication clearly presupposed as an audience those who had already made a confession of loyalty to Christ. Adultery betrays an earlier wedding covenant; cowardice and infidelity derive their meaning from the requirements of courage and faith; blasphemy and idolatry point to the guilt of those who have affirmed faith in one God. John sees the boundary between the Holy City and the "outsiders" as cutting through the company of those who confess the name of God. "The boundary is to be located at the center" (J. Bosc). This is why self-appraisals are so deceptive and subtle, and why, if treason is to be recognized, it must be labeled with names of sins which these men had come to abhor. To draw the boundary between Christian and non-Christian would be insufficient, because within the congregations to which John was writing there were Christians whose true name was Jezebel or Balaam. Christ must therefore reveal what distinguishes his name from the name of the Beast in such a way as to destroy the complacent self-image of Christians.

H. We now should examine samples of those passages in which John relies upon explicit commands in the imperative mood. Of these there are some thirty cases in which the prophet (usually speaking for Christ) orders his readers to hear, to repent, to remember, to hold, to be zealous or faithful. The greatest concentration of these appeals is to be found in the seven letters. Let us recall the kinds of action which are enjoined there. In Laodicea self-deception had reached the point where the congre-

gation had almost lost its powers of discernment. The church's
real state had become the opposite of its fancied state (3:15-17).
Its eyes needed healing salves. John's threats were therefore as
severe as any in the book (vs. 16). Yet those threats were based
upon one fixed axiom: Christ's chastening is motivated by his
love. John appealed to the Laodiceans to recognize the punishment which Christ had exercised, to discard the false self-image
which had concealed their guilt, and to accept the love which
had prompted the penalty. Their pitiable poverty, nakedness,
blindness must be overcome by the refining fires which discipleship entailed. Such a pattern of appeal would be unintelligible
to men who had never known or confessed the power of Christ.
The act of repentance was grounded in what they could remember, in what they had heard and received (3:3). It was a matter
of their becoming worthy of joining Christ in white robes (3:4,
5). John believed with the author of 1 Peter that judgment begins
within God's household (4:17).

The same motifs are central in the letter to Ephesus. Repentance was a matter of remembering the first devotion, the
first vows, the height from which they had fallen. Christ would
hold accountable those who did not allow their present behavior
to be determined by that memory. They would be excluded
from their heavenly home, a threat as unqualified as any in the
book. Yet their repentance would make accessible the tree of
life. John's objective here is the same as in 9:20, 21 or in 22:15.

The letters of Smyrna and Pergamum offer an interesting
variant, in that these congregations had been able to penetrate
some of the disguises of Satan. In Smyrna, Satan had been able
to enlist a community which thought of itself as Jews, i.e., as
worshipers of the true God, whereas they were really guilty of
blasphemy. Satan's use of this community to incite an ordeal of
poverty and suffering had not, however, misled the faithful (2:9,
10). The Pergamum disciples also lived where Satan was enthroned. Yet the fear, the anxiety, the cowardice, the betrayal
which Satan sought to produce through intimidation and external
violence had not appeared (2:13). If John was referring to sys-

tematic persecution by the State, as is likely, then this letter shows how other trials had proved to be more dangerous. Teachers within the church had succeeded where Roman officials had failed. Some Christians had begun to follow the Balaamites and Nicolaitans into idolatry and adultery. The prophet saw the locus of these sins as within the church, and launched as dire a threat as any in the whole book: Christ will fight against them with his sword. The symbolic reference to Balaam reinforces the conclusion that we are dealing with unconscious subversion. Whatever the external forms their action had taken, its inner meaning was adultery. One may doubt whether there was in fact any group within the church which called themselves Balaamites or Nicolaitans. John was probably using obnoxious epithets to lead the readers to look for unrecognized adulteries.

In writing to the Thyatirans, John dealt with the same two sins—idolatry and adultery (2:18-29). The presence of these sins, however, did not prove the decadence of the congregation; on the contrary, John acknowledged their unusual strength and endurance (2:19). The effectiveness of Jezebel may have been due to this vitality. Jezebel claimed to be a prophetess and these claims had been recognized by others. Her charismatic gifts had deceived both herself and them. Christ's previous disciplinary action had been designed to lead her to repent, but she had refused, and it was this refusal which had become more culpable than her sins. It is very doubtful if she called herself Jezebel, so obnoxious would that label have been. John was surely using it to strengthen his condemnation of a group whose self-image was much more innocent. Jezebel and her clique could probably have presented a strong defense in Christian terms, whatever "the deep things of Satan" may have been. In any case her punishment was very severe. None of the more elaborate woes of later chapters is more terrible. But there remained one escape: repentance. That action is viewed as strong enough to transform curse into blessing. Any conception of repentance which reduced this power would fail to capture the term's meaning to John.

As we recall the eight different ways in which John exerted

pressure upon the attitudes and actions of his readers, we are bound to conclude that he visualized many different situations, each exerting upon the congregations multiple temptations, with each temptation evoking the need for discernment. Moreover, the prophet accorded to his readers a wide range of latitude in determining which actions would embody their loyalty to Christ in their own dilemmas. In almost every situation, however, he was certain of the need for repentance. In the words of Victorinus, one of the earliest commentators:

> Whether writing to them who labor in the world and live off the frugality of their labors . . . he admonishes them by love that in what respects their faith is deficient they should repent; or to those who dwell in cruel places among persecutors, that they should continue faithful; or to those who under the pretext of mercy, do unlawful sins in the church and make them manifest to be done by others; or to those who are at ease in the church; or to those that are negligent, and Christians only in name, or to those who are merely instructed that they may bravely persevere in faith; or to those who study the Scriptures, and labor to know the mysteries of their announcement and are unwilling to do God's work that is mercy and love: to all he urges penitence, to all he declares judgment.
>
> (Ante-Nicene Fathers VII, 345, comment on 1:16)

In addition to the command to repent, we may specify another constant element underlying all the commands of the prophet: the call *to witness* (*marturein*) or, as we have usually translated this verb, *to confirm* the work of Jesus and the word of God. Briefly stated, God's word (*logos*) had provided the basis and the motivation for Jesus' mission; Jesus' work had provided the basis and motivation of the prophet's book; the prophet's objective, in turn, was to establish Jesus' *marturia* as the effective norm for the *marturia* of each congregation and each of its members. We will see this if we explore fully the multiple implications of the pregnant phrase in 1:2, "the word of God and the testimony of Jesus."

Logos is a notoriously flexible term because it bears so many nuances. It is capable of many translations, yet none is adequate. It is *what* God gave to Jesus to show to his slaves (1:1). It represents his speech and speaking, his act and acting, his purpose, design, and plan. It is his covenant-promise to his people, his royal edict with its authoritative threat and assurance. It points to God's participation in history, the mode by which he governs the world, his specific and cumulative conversations with his people. It is his creative and redemptive work, as a whole or in any of its manifestations. All rendering of *logos* must remain tentative because none really suffices; yet we must choose one and use it wherever it fits the context. Our choice for most contexts is "God's saving purpose."

An essential link between God's purpose and man's participation was furnished by Jesus Christ and his testimony (*marturia*). Here again the usual translations, such as witness or testimony, are too thin and threadbare to carry the full cargo of associations. The word was used here to embrace Jesus' whole work. It included Jesus' success in showing to his slaves what God had given to him (1:1). He had been the mediator of the grace and peace of God (1:4). As *martus*, his whole story had been a testimony to God's saving purpose. He had made that purpose visible and audible. He had guaranteed its truth, ratified its factuality, and proved its dependability, vindicated its claims, verified its power. Although it is difficult to make one rendering equally serviceable in all settings, we have chosen as basic "the confirmation of Jesus." John is himself centrally concerned with God's saving purpose and with its confirmation by Jesus (1:2, 9; 12:17; 20:4).

But Jesus' contribution required a more contemporary mediator: the angel whom Jesus sent to give various messages to the prophet (1:1). One of the functions of this angel was to convey and to confirm the message from God. In doing this the angel exemplified his own status as a fellow-servant of all who hold fast to Jesus' *marturia*. He served all the links in the chain of communication by convincing each human witness of the truth of God's saving purpose (19:1, 10), until that purpose should be realized (17:17. I believe that the plural of *logos* does not signify in Revelation anything different from the singular.) The angel's confirmation became very explicit in the concluding chapter, where the Spirit did precisely what had been indicated in the prolog (compare 22:6 and 1:2), where Jesus commissioned the angel to ratify what had been said and done (22:16), and where the angel joined in the confirmatory prayer: "Come" (22:17). We may observe that the use of the Greek verb *deiknumi* was limited in Revelation to the action of the angel (6 examples) or of Christ (2 examples), by which the purpose of God was disclosed to the prophet. The act of disclosure was in itself an act of attestation by which the angel enabled the prophet to see and then to attest to the divine work (see H. Schlier, TWNT II, 28).

Again the contribution of John himself is described in terms of confirming that confirmation of the saving work of God which had been given by Jesus. This is the activity which had led to John's imprisonment (1:9). John's motivation for writing the book itself had arisen from this same source (1:2). He exemplified the kind of confirmation which Jesus expected of his two witnesses (11:3) whose prophesying constituted both his gift and their faithful response (11:7). They would complete their verification of God's purpose as it had been confirmed by Jesus by dying at the hands of the same enemy (11:8). In John's lexicon, the true prophet is one who by word and deed throughout the time of his prophesying guarantees the truth of God's saving work in Jesus' death.

It is, however, in the confirmation by all Jesus' slaves that the purpose of God finds its consummation. To be his slave is, in fact, to confirm the confirming work of Jesus in the only way that such verification is possible. This is described as hearing and obeying the confirming word of the prophet (1:3). It is described as holding firm to Jesus' own purpose, by imitating his endurance (3:8, 10), and by ratifying in action the conviction that Jesus is the saving purpose of God personified (19:13). Under the altar the prophet saw the souls of those who had been slain because

of the saving work of God and of the confirmation to it which
they had given (6:9). Few verses could more clearly indicate that
the form of verification which Jesus had adopted remained the
form by which his followers could verify the same *logos* of God
(12:11, 17). Through their victory they became credible witnesses
to others (2:13). Such dependable verification of the purpose of
God is what united them to the prophet, to the angel, and to
Jesus. It was this kind of underwriting which was demanded by
God's saving deeds (19:9, 10), and which he in turn would
underwrite with his own gift of life and kingly power (20:4).
The beatitudes guaranteed this gift, as the plagues guaranteed
the destruction of every faithless and false witness.

John's purpose in writing is to produce this vindication and
verification of the revelation of God's design in the mission of
Jesus. Or, negatively put, John was seeking to help the congregations in Asia unmask their failures in witness. As there were
mouths in which no lie was found (14:5), so there were deceived
and deceiving mouths, worshipers of the Lie. Some Christians
wore robes washed white in the Lamb's blood, others wore the
scarlet robes of the harlot. Some were virgins, some whores.
Some congregations had become Satan's synagogues; some prophets and apostles had become Jezebels and Balaams. Experience
had shown that the great betrayal was possible at any moment
in any place by anyone. The Beast and the Dragon had succeeded in scattering idolatry and adultery throughout their
dominion. That is why John underscored the terrible reality of
the wrath of God, why he had presented as the touchstone of
fidelity the saving work of God as guaranteed by the slain Lamb
to those who remained true and trustworthy witnesses.

It may appear from this discussion that martyrdom in the
modern sense of the term was for John the primary denotation
of *martus*. There can be no doubt that to John the atoning love
of Jesus had been disclosed supremely in his death as a martyr.
Moreover, John was deeply concerned with the problem of
whether those who had joined their Lord in such martyrdom (e.g.,
Antipas) would be vindicated. In that situation, death by mar-

tyrdom actually constituted a "normal" *terminus ad quem* for the faithful verification of Jesus' power (12:11). Yet the primary meaning of *marturia* in Revelation remains that of confirmation and witness. This conclusion is too involved to permit elaboration here. H. Brox has thoroughly explored this problem and has arrived at a judicious set of conclusions (*Zeuge und Martyrer,* Studien zum A. T. und N. T., München, V (1961), 92-109; also H. Zimmermann in *Unio Christianorum,* 185f.; H. Strathmann, TWNT IV, 499).

I find deficient another line of interpretation. It is advanced in the recent book of L. Vos. Vos recognizes the strategic significance of the phrase in 1:2 (pp. 196-214), but I believe he stresses unduly the extent to which John intended to require a verbal confession to the status of Jesus and a dogmatic conceptualization of that status. I think this is an error to which Protestants readily succumb. I believe that there were many Christians in the Asian churches in whose verbal confessions John would have found no dogmatic deficiencies but about whose faithfulness John was deeply concerned. In this respect I am more attracted to the position of a contemporary Catholic novelist.

In his recent novel *The Clown* (New York, McGraw-Hill, 1965) Heinrich Böll quite clearly addresses himself to a Christian audience, respectable and good citizens who are adept in using conventional morality and theological orthodoxy to deceive themselves about their own status. Böll's protagonist is a clown, a confessed unbeliever, who, although an adulterer by objective standards, remains an honest and faithful lover, a monogamist of high integrity. As the novelist unfolds the story of this clown and his beloved Marie, the story progressively unmasks virtually all the other characters, disclosing the truth that they (as Christians) are polygamous liars. "There are some strange unrecognized forms of prostitution compared with which prostitution itself is an honest trade" (p. 216). One central function of the novel is the elaboration of such a definition of prostitution that many good people will detect these forms in themselves. It is not easy to realize such an objective in a situation in which the "safest

hypocrisy" is to gamble on the Catholic side, where every number is a winner (p. 222). There is almost nothing in this novel
to suggest that Böll was consciously modeling his work according
to biblical patterns (although he does admit his indebtedness to
Kierkegaard's theory of the clown). Yet his earlier explicit em-
ployment of apocalyptic motifs in *Billiards at Half Past Nine*
makes it probable that he was quite aware of the congruities
between the clown's reflections on prostitution and John's call
for repentance from fornication.

3. Sovereignties in Conflict

The image of the king is without doubt central to the repertoire of prophetic symbols and a key to the way in which John's
mind worked. If this image is misinterpreted, the message of the
visions will be distorted. This is not an isolated metaphor but a
master-image, since in it a whole congeries of symbols is subtly
woven together to produce a complex pattern. In this essay we
are primarily concerned with grasping that pattern as a whole
rather than with establishing the identities of the separate royal
figures.

Concern for the pattern requires that we survey the whole
body of evidence. This evidence is not limited to those words
which are normally translated by the nouns king (21 times) and
kingdom (7 times) or by the verb to rule (5 times). In John's
thinking the function of the king blends with the function of the
priest, the judge, the shepherd, and the conqueror. Words con-
noting these functions must therefore be included, whether as
nouns or verbs. The work of ruling is also connoted by many
supplementary symbols, such as sword, crown, robes, keys, rod,
horns, and heads.

Most significant of these is the throne, which H. Langenberg
with ample justification calls the central image of the *Apocalypse*.
It appears no less than forty times. In using all these symbols,
the prophet achieved allusive richness rather than analytical pre-
cision. He welded together tangible and intangible components
so tightly that it is extremely difficult for the analyst to define
the conceptual or empirical equivalent of a particular king or
sword. The student who searches for a simple code by which to
translate symbols into objectified meanings is sooner or later
baffled by failure.

We have therefore chosen another approach to this elaborate
configuration of symbols. The prophet found it necessary to dis-

tinguish between two hierarchies of sovereignty. He pictures each of these hierarchies in terms of at least three echelons of authority, and he views each hierarchy as the predestined antagonist of the other. We shall for convenience label these two hierarchies A and B, and analyze first their vertical cohesion and second their horizontal antagonism. Hierarchy A indicates the structure of the divine kingdom and B of the demonic kingdom.

A	B
The All-powerful (God)	Satan
The King of kings (Christ)	The Beast (or other antichristic figures)
Those who rule on earth	The kings of the earth

In examining the structure of A, the proper place to begin is the picture of God as king. This picture dominates and determines all other royal symbols, just as it is his throne which is the absolute center from which to view all other thrones. To him alone does the title Pantocrator or All-powerful belong. The reality of his kingdom serves as the criterion by which to measure the truth or falsehood of all other kingdoms. The First Commandment is the absolute axiom underlying John's thought. Much depends, therefore, on whether we consider John's notion of God's power as the projection to the nth *degree* of imperial political power or as the manifestation of a different *kind* of power. Has John's view of God's omnipotence been transformed by the cross? Has it been Christianized? In other words, does John's conception of God's power derive from the kind of power which the Lamb released through his slaughter? If so, God's sovereignty as King of kings will be defined by Christ's sovereignty as such a king.

John uses this title to refer to both God and Christ (15:3; 17:14; 19:6, 16). To be sure, he insists upon a distinction between God's kingdom and Christ's, but this distinction does not negate their unity (11:15; 12:10). This fact is made clear by his description of their throne (5:13; 7:9f.) and their city (22:1, 3). Why can one symbol of sovereignty serve for both? The whole book gives the answer, or rather a kaleidoscope of answers, for each of the symbols of royalty is shared by God and by Christ, whether it be the rod, the crown, or the white robe. One verse specifies seven more abstract bonds of unity: "worthy is the Lamb to receive power and wealth, wisdom and strength, honor, glory, and blessing" (5:12). All the varied royal symbols may be viewed, in fact, as explications of this tribute to the Lamb who was slain (5:9).

Christ is King, but over what kings does he rule? "The kings of the earth" (1:5). What constitutes the essence of this kingdom whose citizens are themselves kings? First of all, this kingdom is constituted by the loyalty of its subjects to the king. Second, it is also constituted by the fact that these loyal subjects themselves come to share their Master's throne, to rule with him. Here the notion that the metaphor is a projection from earthly governments collapses. Not only do Christ's slaves constitute the realm over which he is sovereign (1:5, 6, 9); they also themselves become kings and rule *with him* (5:10; 20:4; 22:5). In terms of the regal insignia, they will sit on his throne (3:21) and receive his robes, his rod and name. Their kingship is promised on a double condition, which is really a single condition: first, they must obey and worship the Lamb, and join in singing the new song; second, they must conquer his enemy "by the Lamb's blood and by their own word of confirmation" (12:11).

Where this double condition is fulfilled men enter a realm which is dominated and permeated by "the salvation and the power, the kingdom of our God, the authority of his Messiah." As kings of the earth they share with the Pantocrator and his Messiah the same name, throne, crown, and city. The term kingdom thus embraces the whole pyramid of royal power within which God's saving authority is manifested whenever "the Accuser" is defeated (12:10). God's kingship is inherited by conquest of his enemy. The only door into this realm is the exercise of the same power (3:21). In this respect John's symbolism of sovereignty is common to the whole New Testament. The Church knew that it was engaged in "a fight between two claims of salvation that could not endure co-existence." In that fight the confession "Christ is Lord" was a subversive battle cry which both precipitated war and distinguished the two sides (S. Laeuchli, p. 34).

The three echelons of Hierarchy B discloses an amazing degree of correspondence to those of Hierarchy A. When the prophet speaks of the demonic realm inclusively, he refers to the sovereignty of Satan, or of Death and Hades (1:18). Distinction among the various echelons of demonic authority becomes necessary in two separate yet correlated visions. The first is the vision of the warfare in heaven and on earth (ch. 12-14). Satan is the Commander-in-chief of the army. He is "the great dragon . . . the ancient Snake . . . the deceiver of the whole world." His chief activity, after his defeat in heaven, is prosecuting the war on earth against those who bear testimony to Jesus (12:17). For this purpose he summons up a subaltern, a sea-beast, who is equally blasphemous and deceptive. The prophet is very explicit about the interdependence of the dragon and this first beast—they share the same power, throne and authority (13:2), the same goal in making war on the saints (13:7) by enticing them into blasphemous worship (13:8). The horns, heads, crowns, and names of the first beast symbolize this blasphemy, this defiance of the First Commandment. Precisely the same marks characterize the second beast, the earth-beast (13:11-18). It succeeds in persuading earth-dwellers to worship the beast, and thereby to worship the Dragon. The skeletal structure of this kingdom is a parodic imitation of the structure of God's kingdom.

The second vision in which the several echelons of demonic authority are distinguished is that of the Great Prostitute. She claims to be a queen (18:7), and with her "the kings of the earth" have committed fornication (17:2, 18:3). She is "Babylon the Great, mother of harlots, and of earth's abominations" (17:5). She has "become drunk with the blood of the saints" (17:6), while all "earth-dwellers" have become drunk with the wine of her fornication (17:2). She has a kingdom over the "kings of

the earth" (17:18), a parodic correspondence to the true "King
of kings." Moreover, the cohesion and unity of her kingdom is
very similar to that of the beasts in chapter 12, 13 (a vision with
which the harlot-image coalesces with some awkwardness in
ch. 17). There is one mind and one royal power (17:17), one
wine and the resulting drunkenness, one blasphemous collusion,
and one war—the battle against the Lamb (17:6, 14; 18:24).

Sketching this battle "horizontally," it is obvious that, at its
highest and most inclusive level, the warfare proceeds between
God and Satan; it is a warfare that can be conceived only in
primal and eschatological terms. With his victory over Satan,
Christ becomes enthroned as King of kings, including Satan and
all lesser figures in Hierarchy B. In the idiom of chapter 12, the
war now shifts to earth, because the enemy has been evicted once-
for-all from heaven. Now, on one side, fight the saints who have
been given a share in the agony, the royal power, and the loyal
endurance of Jesus (1:9). On the other side fight the beasts and
their blaspheming worshipers, the harlot and her consorts. In this
hierarchy the kings of the earth share their power and authority
with their queen or with the beast on which she sits. The battle-
line is drawn in terms of accepting or rejecting "the commandments of God as confirmed by Jesus." Men must choose whether
to drink the blood of the saints or to wear robes dipped in the
blood of the Lamb. The kind of power which is wielded determines the army in which one fights. Saints do not win their battle
apart from the power of Christ. On the other side, the beast and
the harlot are wholly dependent upon demonic power in their
work of deception.

Why does the prophet utilize such a grandiose and complex
pattern of thought? Because his vocation as a prophet required
that he help the Church to identify sins which otherwise would
remain hidden. The source of the competing sovereignties
remained invisible, yet the conflict between them was as deadly
as it was ambiguous. Each soldier needed help in identifying the
antagonists and in determining his own immediate duties. Each
congregation needed guidance in determining its strategies. Each

element in the traditional apocalyptic myth had to be redefined because the concept of divine power had been transformed by the death of the Messiah. Christians had not invented that myth, but their conception of the mode of warfare had been transformed by the passion story. The prophet was one of the agents who was needed to keep the transformation up-to-date.

In this respect John continued the vocation of the prophets of Israel, whose books, in which John had saturated himself, were replete with similar pictures of warfare. Those earlier prophets had celebrated God's sovereignty over both Israel and the Gentiles. Every attempt to usurp that sovereignty or to repudiate it had been challenged in the sharpest terms as blasphemy, idolatry, and adultery. In some of these earlier prophecies there had been the anticipation of the advent of a particular messianic figure, but far more central and dominant had been the assurance of an accelerated conflict between God and his adversaries until in the end, after the greatest of all battles, the whole earth would come to recognize God's sovereignty. Interpreters of this whole body of literature confront similar difficulties in identifying specific empirical equivalents for each of the prophetic images. In very few cases should the divine-demonic conflict be construed either as a highly spiritualized fantasy about another world or as a transparent allegory describing particular historical persons and governments. The prophetic master-image of warfare between the rival kings points to realities of a primordial and eschatological order, an order which is more determinative of contemporary actualities, and more effective in defining the issues at stake in human decisions, than the order of political history. It is quite true that the issue of earthly sovereignty is raised by almost every prophet, yet this issue is rarely reducible to the normal range of political choices.

Whatever may have been true of John's prophetic ancestors, however, it is clear that for him the victory of Christ over Satan had served to provide the essential definition of that kind of power by which God established his sovereignty. Moreover, this definition had determined the character both of that kingdom where all holy men joined God and Christ on their thrones and of that rival kingdom which could be traced back to the primeval sin of Adam and forward to the death of Death. It is the power of the Lamb that is symbolized in the sovereignty of the Lion of Judah, and it is this very sovereignty which is at stake in the warfare with the bestial figures. Consequently, the very elaborateness of the mythological constructions is a way of accenting the paradoxical understanding of the Lamb's power. As W. Koester has written, the essential key to every vision of the *Apocalypse* is neither the hazard of violent death facing the Church nor the appearance of God concealed in the form of a servant, despised and rejected by men, but the truth that a creature whose contingency and mortality is signified by the form of a slaughtered Lamb should be exalted to the position of power at God's right hand. "John has experienced the death of Jesus, his atoning sacrifice and his epiphany, more intimately, more strongly, longer than Paul: on Golgotha, during the forty days, and again as prisoner on Patmos" (in *Vom Wort des Lebens* [M. Meinertz], 157). The substance of Koester's conclusion remains valid even if one rejects the apostolic identity of the author.

4. The Kings of the Earth

The purpose of this essay is to examine the evidence concerning the meaning in John's vocabulary of the phrase *the kings of the earth* and to evaluate the arguments identifying those kings with the succession of Roman emperors. The evidence may be located first of all by including passages where the phrase explicitly appears (1:5; 6:15; 17:2; 18:3, 9; 19:19; 21:24). To these passages should be added 16:14, in which the reference is to the kings of the *oikoumene*. Also to be considered are cognate references to those who destroy the earth (11:18), and to the merchants and powerful men of the earth (18:3, 11, 23). The kings of the earth are associated frequently with other "earthly" figures—the earth-dwellers, the beast (6:8; 10:5, 8; 12:9; 13:3, 11), and possibly the scorpions which wield authority over the earth (8:5). More important, however, than these texts which make explicit use of the phrase, are the symbols of royal power: heads, horns, crowns, and thrones. These symbols link the kings of the earth to their lords, the beast, and to the mother of earth's pollutions, their queen. It also links the kings to inferior echelons of obedience and worship, i.e., to the "earth-dwellers."

We may survey the arguments which make the kings equivalent to the Roman emperors by focusing attention first on chapters 17 and 18 where that identification receives its strongest support. These chapters are connected by the prophet to the vision of chapters 12, 13 through the image of the beast with seven heads and ten horns (17:3; 13:1). It is on this beast that the Great Whore sits. In chapter 17 the prophet appears to decode this allegory for the sake of his readers. The woman "is the great city which has dominion over the kings of the earth" (17:18). The seven heads on which the woman is seated receive a double explanation; they are seven hills and seven kings (17:9, 10). The ten horns of the beast are ten kings (17:12).

Unlike his practice in dealing with many other riddles in the *Apocalypse*, the author seems here to provide his own solution. With the help of this solution, interpreters have here arrived at a broad consensus covering a number of points. The woman Babylon stands for the city of Rome. The beast represents the Roman Empire as a whole, with its subject-provinces and peoples. The seven kings refer to a selected dynasty of Roman emperors. The ten kings are heads of puppet and restless states, eager to escape their slavery to the colonizing power. In predicting doom for the Whore and the beast, John is simply forecasting the imminent destruction and dissolution of the Roman Empire, an expectation which was later disappointed.

For this prevalent conception of John's anti-Roman polemic there seems to be ample supporting evidence. The term Babylon had often, in fact, been used by both Jews and Christians to refer to Rome. Rome had ruled as mistress of many peoples and nations and tongues (17:15). It had frequently been described as a city set on seven hills. It had become notorious among its enemies for its power to corrupt native governments (17:13), to persecute illegal religions like the Church (17:6), and to arouse the passionate hatred of occupied countries (17:16). Plots by subject peoples to throw off the hated dominion were endemic, and success was possible if enough kings could be united in their hatred of the harlot (17:16). Over her hoped-for demise many peoples would rejoice along with "saints and apostles and prophets" (18:20). It may be said that many interpreters adopt these equations as an adequate basis for dating the book, for explaining the occasion for its composition (official persecution of the Church by Rome), and for decoding the prophet's chief prediction (the imminent destruction of the persecuting power). These clear identifications in chapter 17 may readily be transferred to the warfare vision of chapters 12, 13, and thereafter to the enigmas of the other visions as well. In this way, the interpretation of chapter 17 comes to control the interpretation of the whole book.

Many scholars of undoubted competence are fully convinced

of the accuracy of these equations. Yet there is evidence which casts doubt on this line of interpretation and which impels us to look for a more adequate, if also a more subtle, understanding of John's intention.

We may consider first the claim that John intended the Whore to represent Rome because of his identification of the seven heads with seven hills. Do these hills so clearly point to the city on the Tiber? We begin by observing that the seven hills do not belong to the woman but to the beast. One can readily visualize an image of a city set on seven hills, but it is much more difficult to visualize those seven hills as heads (symbols of ruthless sovereignty) which belong to a beast which comes *from the Abyss*. John views these *hills* as instruments of diabolical power, but it is difficult to see how the hills along the Tiber served as such instruments. It is also difficult to think of the *same* heads as denoting *both* kings and hills, that is, if each hill signifies a specific geographical locale and each king signifies a specific emperor. R. H. Charles recognized this incongruity but evaded its implications by adopting his frequent device, asserting the presence of a later gloss, even though there is no textual evidence of it.

Let us look more closely at how John elsewhere used the term hill. The Greek word, *oros*, appears eight times, but only in 17:9 do most translators adopt the English *hill;* elsewhere they use *mountain*, as in RSV. This is an example of how previous exegesis often determines even the best translations. Does John use this word allegorically (i.e., with a specific empirical equivalent in mind) or symbolically (to suggest invisible forces and realities)? In Revelation, as elsewhere in the Bible, mountains symbolize strength and stability. For a mountain to be cast into the sea was a proverbial way of pointing to a stupendous miracle (8:8); for it to be shaken was a sign of drastic revolution in human security (6:14); for men to call on the mountains to fall on them was a measure of frustration and despair (6:15f.). To indicate the sudden disappearance of the usual securities, the prophet speaks of a situation in which no mountain was left standing

(16:20). It is unlikely that this writer would use the term else-where with this symbolic elasticity and only in one verse (17:9) make it apply to a specific place. To be sure, he used the term in references to Mt. Zion, but even there the theological component outweighs the geographical. It is much more likely that the mountain-heads of the beast allude to the contrast between the apparent security of Babylon and the real security of the heav-enly Jerusalem.

This probability is strengthened when we notice John's habitual ways of using the number seven. To identify the seven hills of Babylon with the seven hills of Rome seems utterly plausible until we notice that he rarely elsewhere uses this num-ber to denote an exact numerical measurement. In his mind, seven connotes completeness or wholeness, whether of good or evil. To be sure, John addresses seven congregations in Asia, but there were more Christian communities in Asia than that. If he did not use the exact number of the churches of Asia, he would hardly have done so for the hills of Rome. It is true that secular Roman writers had long associated the city of Rome with its seven hills, but it is doubtful if John and his readers would have been conversant with that literature. And it is quite fantastic to suppose that they would have seen in the Tibertine hills a symbol of awesome imperial power as exercised in the province of Asia. Their minds were dominated by biblical idioms more than by pagan, and the Bible provided ample precedents for the use of mountains to symbolize the fusion of political and religious power. Isaiah 2, for example, on which John draws elsewhere, visualizes the future in terms of the conflict between "the moun-tain of the house of the Lord" and "all the high mountains" (study especially 2:2-4, 12-19). To sum up, then, the reference to seven mountains in Rev. 17:9 does not require the usual equation of Babylon with the city of Rome.

How about 17:10, with its apparent reference to the suc-cession of Roman emperors? "The seven heads [of the beast] . . . are also seven kings, five of whom have fallen, one is, the other has not yet come, and when he comes he must remain only a

little while." Exegetes seem to be fully justified in supposing that
John had in mind precisely seven emperors, no more and no less,
when he spoke of the seven heads. But again we must not neglect
to recognize difficulties.

If elsewhere John used the number seven as a symbolic
rather than a numerical measurement, we should assume that his
habit persists in this instance. Moreover, if elsewhere he speaks
of kings who were not rulers of political entities (cf. the preceding essay), we should assume the possibility of the same
metaphorical habit in this instance. We observe that those "kings"
belong to the beast and not to the Whore, and that the Whore
is pictured as sitting on the heads/kings, which is a distorted
image indeed if John has in mind the city of Rome sitting on,
that is, maintaining secure mastery over (14:14-16; 17:1, 3, 15;
18:7; 19:11, 18-21) the successive emperors. It would be far
more logical to picture the emperors as sitting on the hills or on
the city. Such a precise equation of kings with specific emperors
also leads to other incongruities. For example, what can it mean
for the alleged emperors to commit fornication with the alleged
city (17:3)? And what can it mean to speak of these Roman
emperors as hating the harlot (17:16), if the harlot represents
their capital city or their empire? On such terms we cannot make
sense of God's use of the beast as an instrument of his judgment
on the harlot. And how do the kings survive her destruction to
such a degree that they can be pictured as mourning over her
demise (18:9)? John takes pains to separate God's punishment
of Babylon (18:1-19:10) from his punishment of the beast *and*
the kings (19:19-21), but this would be nonsense if all three
(Babylon, beast, kings) stood for the same historical entity. We
are also at a loss to explain how the beast itself could be identified as an eighth *emperor* who is also one of the series of seven
(17:11). If one interprets 17:10 as specifying seven Roman emperors in succession as heads of the beast, there is simply no
satisfactory explanation of 17:11 in which the beast itself becomes an elusive eighth emperor. This becomes both an arith-
metical and a chronological impossibility—sure sign that, instead

of decoding the prophet's supposed allegory, the exegete has failed to grasp the prophet's mentality and his use of symbols. Every commentator knows how useless this supposed key actually proves to be in practice. It does not enable the exegete to know with which emperor John's counting began or how he counted the three emperors of 68-69 A.D. What appears to be a dependable key turns into a source of endless confusion, and one must suppose that the first readers must have been just as confused by John's enumeration, that is, if he intended them to go to the trouble of calling the roll of emperors, a very unlikely intention when one considers the state of the churches in Asia. (How many Americans can immediately name the last seven presidents?)

A convincing interpretation of the seven kings of 17:10 must do justice to three considerations. (1) Since these kings are heads *of the beast*, the interpretation must make clear the symbolic relationship of these heads to this beast, rather than to Babylon. (2) Since the primary imagery of kingship in Revelation is a feature of the power-conflict between the Lamb and the beast, and between those who share the rule with those two enemies, the kind of sovereignty described in 17:10 must be the true antithesis to the kind of sovereignty exercised by Christ. (3) Since these kings are immediately related to the seven hills and to the Whore, the nature of this relationship must be clarified.

The prevailing equation of these kings with seven successive Roman emperors may, with minor concessions, fulfill the third of these stipulations, but it falls far short of the first and the second. Perhaps it has been so persuasive because of the explicit statement that of the seven "five have fallen, one is, and one has not yet come." Does this not refer to the process of dynastic succession to the imperial throne? The first factor which forces us to be cautious in answering that question in the affirmative is this: in chapter 17, as elsewhere in the Apocalypse, John is describing the process of judgment on the beast, and therefore on its heads. Those heads fall in response to divine judgment, not to normal dynastic succession.

A careful reading of chapter 17 itself shows that the seven heads are more clearly an aspect of the beast than of Babylon. Since their first appearance in 12:3 and later in 13:1, 3, they had been inseparable from the description of the *dragon* and his agent, the sea-beast. The same careful reading also reveals that while the relationship between Babylon and the beast is close, it is by no means essential to either. The horns and heads are intended to help in the identification of the dragon and beast, not the Whore, and even to help in distinguishing the dragon from the Whore.

Even more significant is the fact that in chapter 17 that aspect of the beast which is most frequently stressed is the sequence of his entrances and exits. These are so strategic that they should be seen together. (Here I use the more familiar RSV text):

> vs. 8a "The beast . . . was, and is not, and is to ascend from the bottomless pit and go to perdition. . . .
> vs. 8d "it was and is not and is to come. . . .
> vs. 11 "the beast . . . was and is not . . . and it goes to perdition . . ."

We should not overlook the fact that in this chapter there is a double mystery, that of the woman and that of the beast. To the explication of the mystery of the beast the prophet devotes ten verses (17:8-17); to the mystery of the woman, only one (17:18). In this explication, the major element that causes astonishment (vs. 8d), and which requires "a mind with wisdom," is this three-stage history of the beast. To the prophet it is this element which explains the power exerted by the beast over the earth-dwellers and also the power by which the beast makes war on the Lamb (vs. 14). This sequence "was, is not, is to come" is related to the dynamics of Satanic deception. That is why it is a mystery.

The fundamental requirement in the exegesis of vs. 10 is to retain its basic consistency with this pattern of thought, for what is said there of the *heads* links that verse to what is said of the *beast* in the other three verses. *Stage one* in the sequence of the heads is the clause: "five have fallen." This is so closely parallel to the thrice repeated "the beast was" as to indicate a basic kinship in meaning. *Stage three* in the sequence of the heads is the clause: "the other has not yet come, and when he comes he must remain only a little." This expectation conforms in substance to the predictions concerning the beast who will ascend from the Abyss and go to perdition. Even the phrase "a little while" or "one hour" is elsewhere associated with this impending activity of the beast (20:3). Where two of the three stages so closely conform to the "life-cycle" of the beast, we may expect the second stage also to conform. Yet, as a matter of fact, there seems to be a direct contradiction. *Stage two* says of the kings *one is*, whereas in the case of the beast there is an emphatic *is not*. We must note, however, the curious (and I think intentional) double-talk in vs. 11 which says of the beast that it both "is not" and "is." Moreover, this "isness" is relative to the beast's activity as one of the seven heads! Verses 11 and 10 are thus locked together, for the prophet goes out of his way to distort his formula in order to connect them. Moreover, verse 12 is also involved, for there the "little while" of the seventh king becomes defined as the "one hour" when the ten kings will receive authority before they go with the beast to perdition. To the prophet, the function of the seventh king is identical with the function of the ten kings and the beast in the final showdown with the messianic kingdom (19:17-21; 20:3, 7-10).

How can John speak of this beast as both "is" and "is not"? The function of the *is not* assertion appears to indicate that the Lamb has conquered him, that he has been banished to the Abyss, and that the slaves of the Lamb refuse to recognize his power or to worship him (17:8c). The function of the *is* assertion is to indicate that to the beast-worshipers or the earth-dwellers, the power of the present head and the present beast is a very real thing. In other words, we are dealing with an ambiguous and dialectical reality. Subjective human factors are involved in any appraisal of the existent authority of this type of demonic power.

Those who worship the beast verify the fact that he *is;* those who do not so worship verify the fact that he *is not.* But even these latter must anticipate his future ascension from the Abyss for a short time (compare the promises given to the Smyrneans [2:10 and p. 221] and to the Philadelphians [3:10 and p. 56]). Such a way of thinking about the beast enables us to recognize the central thrust of the formula which John applies to both God and the Lamb: "He is . . . was . . . and is to come." Both the Lamb and the beast have been killed (5:9; 13:3). Both live again (1:5; 13:14). Each has slaves who have been killed (5:9; 13:3). Each has slaves who worship their risen Lord. Each must pay the price of that worship. (See next essay.)

We may find further help by locating in the other visions the analogies to the 5-1-1 sequence of 17:10. These seem to indicate that in the vocabulary of John, the community whom Christ addressed is standing near the end of the process of God's judgment. In the case of the seals, five seals have been opened, while the sixth and seventh deal with present and impending wrath and mercy. When seven trumpets are sounded, the sixth poses most sharply the existential decision of the present, while the seventh marks the consummation of warfare and victory, after the "little while" when the beast ascends from the Abyss (11:7f.). In sum, the sequence of 5-1-1, in visions in which John uses seven to cover the total span of God's judgment, exemplifies a dramatic focusing upon the present stage in the messianic struggle.

There are two other aspects of the earlier myth that must be considered before one can accept the usual rendering of 17:10. If it can be shown that the *beast* (and not Babylon) stands for the Roman Empire, or if it can be shown that in chapter 13 its wounded head stands for the emperor Nero, our thesis can not be sustained. We will examine those issues in the next essay, where we arrive at negative conclusions. There we will seek to show that neither can the beast be identified with the Roman Empire as a political entity nor can its wound be identified with Nero's suicide.

There yet remains the possibility, however, that for John the figure Babylon should be associated with the imperial authority of Rome. It is easier to justify this interpretation if the allusions to the hills and kings are detached from the thesis and made subordinate to the mystery of the beast. To be sure, John never uses the name of the city or the empire. In fact, never in the New Testament do we find Rome explicitly identified as the enemy of the Church, a fact which is often ignored. Yet it would probably be quite wrong to dissociate the imperial rule entirely from the mythological entity of Babylon. Indeed, the prophet attributes many traits to Babylon which do seem to reflect the conflict between Empire and Church. Yet, his full description of the eschatological city of rebellion does not allow us to construct a one-one correlation with Rome. The two realities may be related but they are not identical.

In this respect let me suggest a parallel offered by a modern poet. Consider the following lines from Edith Sitwell's *Still Falls the Rain**

Still falls the Rain—
Dark as the world of man, black as our loss—
Blind as the nineteen hundred and forty nails
Upon the Cross.

Still falls the Rain
With a sound like the pulse of the heart that is changed to the
    hammerbeat
In the Potter's Field, and the sound of the impious feet

On the Tomb:
            Still falls the Rain
In the Field of Blood where the small hopes breed and the human
    brain
Nurtures its greed, that worm with the brow of Cain.

---

* Reprinted by permission of the publisher, The Vanguard Press, from *The Collected Poems of Edith Sitwell*. Copyright, 1948, 1949, 1954, by Edith Sitwell.

Still falls the Rain
At the feet of the Starved Man hung upon the Cross.
Christ that each day, each night, nails there, have mercy on us—
On Dives and on Lazarus:
Under the Rain the sore and the gold are as one. . . .

Those lines were actually written under a specific historical emergency. Yet the poem does not require from its readers knowledge of what that emergency was. The poet does not allow the details of place and date to dominate the imagination. The rain which still falls binds together all the centuries since Golgotha. The cross encompasses the whole world of man. Knowledge of the poet's immediate situation is not essential to the communication of a vision which so completely transcends time, place, and particular circumstances. Yet this fact does not turn the falling of the rain into some timeless or spaceless process, but helps to accent its universality. The symbols are more inclusive than any single set of historical factors could be. The meaning, the message, the reality—all are there in the poem itself. In future centuries, after all memory of recent events shall have been lost, the poem, if extant, will continue to speak simultaneously of both ancient and modern actualities.

When the reader now is told the sub-title of the poem, *The Raids*, he will immediately broaden his perception of the symbol of the rain to include the falling of bombs. This perception will supplement and enrich the scope of his understanding. He may, as he hears the poem, recall the terrible sounds of explosive violence, so native to modern warfare. But this enrichment will not induce him to cancel out all other nuances of meaning in the image of rainfall. If it did, the result would not enhance the poet's intention but would be a radical and unjustified contraction of the horizons of meaning.

To learn that the date of the raids was 1940 will enable the reader to endow the poem with even greater specificity. Miss Sitwell was writing during the crisis of the German bombardment of London. This additional knowledge of the occasion will contribute both realism and richness to the imagery of the poem. Yet it would be sheer vandalism to *limit* the sensitivity of the poet to one specific date, place, and set of conditions. So to restrict the reach of the poem would mutilate and truncate the event which the poem "celebrates."

The comparison with *Revelation* is, I think, a valid one. For us to *equate* Babylon with Rome would be literalism and historicism of the worst sort. The figure Babylon can convey the prophet's message and mentality without such an explicit association. We do not first require an exact knowledge of his immediate circumstances to grasp his message. The evidence that he was in a Roman prison and that his brothers had encountered official hostility will enrich our perceptions of the inclusive and realistic thrust of his images. But to substitute Rome where he meant to say Babylon would lead to vast distortion and reduction of meaning. The Whore, the beast, its horns and heads, the seven hills and the seven kings of 17:9 are realities which must not be subjected to such arrogant and self-confident violence. The invisible struggle among transcendent powers is for the prophet himself a fully contemporaneous reality, yet the struggle itself could not be compressed within the bounds of specific circumstances.

As a Christian poet, Miss Sitwell refused to identify the rain with the Third Reich and the cross with besieged Britain. The uniquely Christian character of the myth would have been corrupted and destroyed by that identification. There is no reason to suppose that John was any less sensitive to the dangers of such identification (although this cannot be said of his interpreters). He would have betrayed the redemptive power of the cross by too hasty an identification of God's enemies with specific men or institutions.

5. Death and Resurrection of the Sea-Beast

It is the purpose of this essay to discuss the special role of the sea-beast of chapter 13 and the significance within that role of his curious injury (13:3). We have already appraised the armies engaged in warfare and the central trio of antagonists, which have been called the satanic trinity (p. 229f.). John has taken rather unusual care in identifying the first and third animals in this trinity. The Great Snake is Satan himself, onetime resident of heaven. The earth-beast is later thrice called a false prophet, which links him to such figures as Jezebel in the Asian congregations (2:20) and to all who commit deception or love it (14:5; 21:27; 22:15). The sea-beast stands between the others as the object of worship by the earth-beast and as the servant of the Snake. Let us examine the three key references to its wound.

Of the sea-beast it is said:

> One of its heads seemed to have a mortal wound, but its mortal wound was healed, and the whole earth followed the beast with wonder (13:3 RSV).
> The earth-beast exercises all the authority of the first beast in its presence, and makes the earth and its inhabitants worship the first beast, whose mortal wound was healed (13:12 RSV).

By working wonders which impress and deceive men, the earth-beast induces them to "make an image for the beast which was wounded by the sword and yet came to life" (13:14). What is this wound? How and by whom was it inflicted? These are surely germane questions for those who would grasp the message of the prophet.

The student of *Revelation* is accustomed to find sharp disagreements among commentators in their solutions to the enigmas of this book.[1] He is therefore amazed to learn that at this point current exegetes achieve an almost complete agreement.

C. A. Scott comments:

> It is one of the points in the interpretation of the *Apocalypse* on which most modern scholars are agreed, that in this legend of "Nero redivivus" we are to find the explanation of the "wounded head" of 13:3 . . .[2]

H. B. Swete is equally confident that John had in mind the Neronic legend, using it to represent the revival of Nero's policy of persecution by Domitian. He traces this explanation back to Victorinus, the earliest of the Latin commentators. A dissenting opinion, to be sure, is offered by some important scholars,[3] but a clear majority supports the Neronic hypothesis.[4] Where such amazing consensus exists, it may be futile to re-examine the evidence. Nevertheless, such an examination should confirm the hypothesis, if it actually is a sound one.

Let us first summarize the Neronic legend itself. Toward the end of his reign, Nero's unpopularity among Roman citizens had assumed huge proportions. In 67 and 68 A.D., open revolts had broken out against his authority in Gaul and Spain. At length he had been repudiated by the Praetorian Guard and by the Senate. Fleeing from soldiers sent to arrest him, he had taken refuge in a friend's suburban villa, where he had received word that the Senate had proclaimed him a public enemy and had approved Galba as his successor. Having been warned that the pursuing soldiers were approaching his hideout, he had cut his own throat with a sword (June 9, 68).[5]

After his death a rumor spread abroad that he had not

---

1. Part of this essay is based on an article published in JBL 72 (1953) 93–101.
2. *Revelation*, 57.
3. A. Farrer (*Rebirth of Images*, 294) prefers the Caligula identification.
4. Among others, I. T. Beckwith, 635ff.; R. H. Charles, I, 332f.; E. F. Scott, 78ff.; J. Weiss, 92.
5. A. Momigliano, *Cambridge Ancient History*, X, 739ff.

actually died but had escaped to Parthia, whence he would soon return to regain his throne. This rumor circulated most quickly in the eastern provinces, and it assumed strange forms. At one stage, popular expectation envisaged the return of Nero from Parthia, with a huge army subduing all opposition. "And to the west shall come the strife of gathering war and the exile from Rome, brandishing a mighty sword crossing the Euphrates with many myriads" (Sib. Or. 4:119f., 137f.). On the basis of this rumor, impostors arose in the east who assumed the name of Nero in the effort to exploit the legend. There are records of at least two such claimants.[6] There seems to have been a later stage in the legend in which Nero's figure had become invested with supernatural status. Now his return from the Abyss with hordes of demons is anticipated as an omen of the "last days." Among the oracles of the Sibyl we find an extensive reference to this expectation:

> There shall be at the last time about the waning of the moon, a world convulsing war, deceitful in guilefulness. And there shall come from the ends of the earth a matricide fleeing and devising sharp-edged plans. He shall ruin all the earth, and gain all power, and surpass all men in cunning. That for which he perished he shall seize at once. And he shall destroy many men and great tyrants, and shall burn all men as none other did (Sib. Or. 5:361f.).

So much for the legend. Undoubtedly it was current in the first century and was absorbed into various apocalyptic traditions, both Jewish and Christian. It is not strange, therefore, that scholars have identified the wounded beast of John's prophecy with *Nero redivivus*. They believe that the blasphemous claims of the sea-beast include the assertion of divine authority for the Roman empire and its rulers. Among the rulers, Nero was notorious for his cruelty; his execution of Christians was presumably widely known. What would be more natural than that Christians

---

6. In addition to A. Momigliano, *op. cit.*, see Tacitus, *Hist.* I, 78; II, 8; Suetonius, *Nero,* 57; Ascension of Isaiah 4:2.

should see in his policies the hand of the devil? When one reads *Revelation* 13:3, therefore, and asks, with H. B. Swete, "whether any of the earlier Roman emperors received a death-blow from which he recovered or was supposed to have recovered," a positive answer is found in Nero.[7]

Yet we must object to this way of putting the question. It presupposes an identity in the prophet's mind between the sea-beast and the Roman Empire, an identity which cannot be maintained in chapter 13 and which is specifically repudiated in chapter 17 (see previous essay). It assumes that the "seven heads" in 13:1 denote a chronological series of Roman emperors, an assumption which we have challenged in the previous essay. In assuming this, it supposes that *seven* in the prophet's language was John's way of measuring quantity; it leaves unexplained the *ten horns* in the same verse; it fails to account for the seven heads of the Great Snake (12:3) or the two horns of the earth-beast (13:11), not to mention the seven horns of the Lamb (5:6). It assumes, finally, that the death-blow and the recovery referred to such events as would leave a record in the annals of the emperors. Apart from the validity of these assumptions the conclusion would be threatened. Having already examined the others, let us first focus attention upon the notion of the wounding itself, then on the number of the beast (13:18), and finally on the supplementary evidence in chapter 17. We must deal carefully with the meaning of each term in the prophet's own vocabulary and context.

We note, for example, that the wound, although first assigned to one of its heads, is later assigned twice to the beast itself (13:12, 14). Most commentators recognize this, but few give it sufficient weight. *If* the beast represents the empire and its head an emperor, it is obvious that the two may be interchangeable, for an empire's authority is vested in the emperor. But this is true only so long as the emperor exerts his delegated power in the administration of his office. It ceases to be true when an emperor

---

7. Swete, *op. cit.*, 163.

has been deposed, when he dies, when a successor has been vested with the crown. A wound inflicted on a *former* and rejected ruler is not a wound inflicted on the empire. In the *Apocalypse* the wound of the head is so clearly a wound of the beast that in two out of three cases it is the latter whose wound is mentioned. But actually, the wound inflicted by Nero on himself did no harm to the beast. R. H. Charles recognized this difficulty. He admitted that only when Nero returns from the Abyss in the last days will the head become the complete antitype of the beast that was wounded (*op. cit.*, I, 350). The *Apocalypse*, however, speaks as if this identity were already established. Other commentators meet this problem by arguing that what weakened the empire was not Nero's wound but the anarchic conditions following his death, the civil unrest which was terminated by Vespasian's succession. In this case 13:3 cannot refer to Nero's suicidal wound at all, because the civil unrest precedes his death, and the healing of the wound has nothing to do with his reported reanimation.

We note also that to the prophet this mortal blow which affected the sea-beast injured the dragon as well. Such power and authority as the head possessed it had received from the dragon; the use of this power had been devoted to extending the worship of the dragon. The horns and heads of the beast corresponded to those of the dragon, sign that each shared power with the other. Ten and seven are numerals that signified the completeness of this delegated power, and therefore the degree of kinship between dragon and beast. A mortal wound simultaneously destroyed the authority of head, beast, and dragon by terminating the blasphemous adoration by men. It is difficult to maintain that Nero's suicide fulfilled such specifications. His death did not jeopardize the power of the empire, because he died as a fugitive and enemy of the state. Imperial authority was not threatened by his death; rather, his death demonstrated the superior power of the state. Nor should we consider the rivalries of Galba and others for the throne as a mark of diminished authority. Whether morale was low or high, whether the conditions were auspicious or ominous, these factors did not affect the *dynamis* or *exousia* conferred on the beast by the dragon. Nor did they diminish the dragon's sovereignty.

Still another factor should be carefully weighed: according to John the *healing* of the wound enhanced the prestige of the beast. It led people to yield greater wonder and reverence in the presence of the beast (13:3). It induced them to acknowledge the invulnerability of the beast (not of the head), by exclaiming "Who can fight against it?" (13:4). The cure encouraged the beast to greater blasphemy; it increased his ability to deceive men. It enabled the beast to renew his war against the saints (13:7). The cure also impelled men to worship the *dragon* by the greater devotion and fear which they accorded to the *beast*. Now there is absolutely no evidence that the rumored resuscitation of Nero actually had such effects as these. It did not induce either Roman citizens or Christians "to follow the beast with wonder." It did not enhance the seductive worship of the dragon, nor did it aid the dragon in his deadly war against the saints. The legend of Nero's pending return from Parthia was even considered a threat to the empire and its rulers. If we are to grasp the meaning of the wounded head, therefore, we should look not so much for an emperor who died a violent death, but for an event in which the authority of the beast (and the dragon) had been both destroyed and deceptively restored.

Because it was a wound unto death, we may first ask what was the instrument by which the injury was inflicted. It was, of course, a sword (13:14). Superficially considered, this may seem to refer to Nero's dagger, used in self-destruction. But such a hasty inference is ill-advised. We have already observed that Nero's sword did not actually wound the beast, nor did the legendary healing of his throat enhance the authority of the beast. Apart from this inference, we would naturally assume that the wound was *not* self-inflicted, but given to the beast by its enemy. Can we find any case in apocalyptic literature in which the beast intentionally commits suicide? In thinking about the weapon, we should consider John's typical usage of the term sword. This is one of his favorite symbols, which he uses in three distinct connections: (a) The sword is the instrument by which the Messiah executes judgment and wages war on his adversaries. From his mouth comes a sharp sword (1:16; 2:12, 16; 19:15, 21). (b) The rider of the red horse is given a great sword (6:4, 8). Here the word refers to a plague which God sends upon men; it is a heaven-sent punishment executed on earth. (c) The sword is a weapon turned against the Lamb and his followers by the beast. It is the beast's means for gaining vengeance on his divine adversary (13:10: the other connotations may be present in this aphorism).

Was the beast, then, wounded by one of these swords? An answer is given in the word that is translated as wound—*plēgē*. When one studies the appearances of this term in the *Apocalypse*, he discover two things. In the first place, while the RSV translators have chosen the rendering "wound" in chapter 13, *every other* occurence of *plēgē* (twelve in all) is rendered by the English word "plague." In all these other contexts, the plague is an episode in that war in heaven which overarches the conflicts on earth between the dragon and the messianic community. It is a divinely-ordained and messianically-administered punishment for sin. It is a drastic punishment that spells death in the prophet's vocabulary; such a wound is always mortal. In the second place, the appearances of *plēgē* in chapter 13 may all be translated in consonance with the apocalyptist's vocabulary, albeit with some awkwardness for our non-apocalyptic prose. The beast received the *plague* of the sword and yet came to life (vs. 14); "the first beast, the *plague* of whose death was healed" (vs. 12); "one of its heads as slain unto death, and the *plague* of its death was healed" (vs. 3).

If, then, we are guided by the vocabulary of the prophet, we must conclude that the sword was the symbol of God's wrath (for a likely antecedent, see Isaiah 27:1). The wound was a God-inflicted plague which simultaneously destroyed the authority of the head, the beast, and the dragon. It was a wound from which the beast could recover only by using deception, by succeeding in that deception, and by making absolute his blasphemous claims to ultimate power over human destiny. We return, then, to the question: What plague was inflicted on the beast which actually marked his death but which was deceptively used to enhance "his power and his throne and great authority" (vs. 4)?

The correct identification of the beast's enemy enables us to answer this question. To John, Christ alone has been the enemy able to defeat the beast. His conquest had been accomplished in "the blood of the Lamb and the word of their testimony" (12:11). Through his faithfulness unto death he had received the keys of Death and Hades (1:14; 2:7). He alone had received the right to release the plagues, and to use the sword of judgment. His authority had been sufficient to evict Satan from heaven. It was this eviction of the dragon that provided an image whose function is the same as that of the wounding of the sea-beast. The defeat of the dragon in chapter 12 is followed by renewed activity against the saints, just as the killing of the beast in chapter 13 is followed by the intensification of the same war. The dragon, like the beast, was killed and yet came to life. This death, then, was much more than the suicide of a human emperor. It was the plague of death released through the Messiah in his own crucifixion and exaltation.

Such an interpretation explains why the wound of the head also injures the beast and the dragon. Such an interpretation is in line with other New Testament descriptions of the war between the servants of God and "the principalities and powers" (e.g., Eph. 6). In the words and acts of Jesus during the days of his humiliation, Satan had received a deadly blow (Luke 10:17-24; 11:14-22). In his death the "powers of darkness" had had their hour (Luke 22:53; John 19:11); the "rulers of this age" had "crucified the Lord of glory" (I Cor. 2:8). But in demonstrating their power over Jesus, they had unwittingly signed their death-warrant, for God had used this very cross to disarm the principalities and powers and to make a public display of their impotence, "triumphing over them in him" (Col. 2:15). This same power over the King of darkness had been granted to these servants of Christ who "loved not their lives even unto death" (Rev. 12:11 RSV).

The wound inflicted by the Lamb, however, could appear to be healed in the very event which had marked the real failure of the beast. To all but the faithful, the beast's power to kill the saints enhanced its authority; its ability to blaspheme was increased; its temptations became more deceptive. So great did its prestige become that men everywhere were induced to cry "Who can fight against it?" (13:4). By successful war against the saints the beast continued to hide the fact that it had been killed. To aid him in concealing his vulnerability, the dragon called upon the sea-beast with all its manifest glory and power to demonstrate the powerlessness of the saints (13:5-10). The sea-beast, in turn, called upon the earth-beast, with its lamb-like appearance, to tempt with its words and signs those men whom violence had not subdued. The goal of all three remained the same: the worship of the beast and the dragon. The means varied, since not all saints were deceived by the same illusions; but whatever the means used, the continued life of the mortally wounded beast depended upon the worship men gave to it. We discover in verses 15-17 an explicit reference to the "resurrection" of the beast. Its image received life (*pneuma*) through that worship which had been sponsored by false prophets within the Church. It was by such sorcery that it was enabled to speak, to exercise its authority, and to compel the obedience of men. Such obedience presupposed deception concerning which of the two enemies, the Lamb or the beast, was actually dead and which was alive. The *Apocalypse* sought to disclose the dimensions of this deception by a fresh message from the martyred Lord and from those servants who had already conquered the dragon.

In the prophet's mind, therefore, there was more than a formal, rhetorical antithesis between the slain Lamb and the slain beast. Both wielded swords. Both had followers on whose foreheads were inscribed their names (13:16-14:1). Both had horns (5:6; 13:11). Both were slain, the same Greek word being used to describe their death (vss. 3, 8); both had arisen to new life and authority. The point of greatest conflict, the death of the martyrs, became the point of greatest illumination and power. At this point both antagonists claimed victory. To the servants of Christ, the beast was mortally wounded in this encounter; to the servants of the beast, the wound was healed.

We must not fail to remember that John was concerned about the loyalty of self-confessed slaves of the Lamb. He was concerned with the subtle work of false prophets within the congregations of Asia. On what terms could the reported wounding and healing of Nero be used by false prophets to fool Christians? Would it help them in their disguise as a Lamb (13:11)? No. Would the report of Nero's resuscitation be one of the "great signs" to which they could appeal (13:13)? No. Would that report induce them to build an idol of the sea-beast (13:14), or to endow that idol with life or to kill those who would not worship (13:15)? Did any group in John's day wear Nero's brand on their heads (13:16)? Positive answers would be quite incredible, whether one takes the false Lamb figure as applying to priests of the imperial cult, as do most interpreters, or to the inroads of deceptive prophecy within the Church, as I do.

Two verses in chapter 13, however, are sufficient in the minds of many exegetes to outweigh all the above difficulties. In these verses the number of the name of the sea-beast is explicitly given as 666 (in some mss. 646 or 616). The list of conjectures concerning the meaning of this number is almost endless, and although many exegetes have become quite certain in their own minds of their own solutions, the variety of solutions makes them all problematic. Let me first point out several specifications of the problem which the desire for a definite equivalent often leads the student to ignore.

The use of a number here must accord with John's use of numbers elsewhere in the book. It must be the number of the beast and not merely of one of his heads. It must be such a number as to require special insight (*sophia* or *nous*, vs. 18a), an insight which was needed by his readers to detect deceit and to overcome temptation. The figure must represent both the

name of the beast and his brand (*charagma*) as they were inscribed on the heads and hands of the earth-dwellers (vss. 12-16).
The same name and brand must apply to all who are thus described in the whole book. The name and brand must be intelligible as *antonyms* to the name and brand worn by those who
refused to worship the beast. The name must therefore be
integral to the syndrome of deception, idolatry, blasphemy,
adultery—in fact, to all the sins which were believed to exclude
men from the holy city.

It is difficult to see how the name of Nero fulfills these
specifications, least of all in the period some thirty years after
his death. Nowhere else does John use *gematria*, that is, a device
to conceal a human name within a number. Nowhere else does
he call for wisdom in order to decipher a purely mathematical
puzzle. Nowhere else does he identify either Satan or the sea-
beast by referring to an individual ruler like Nero. Nowhere
else does he limit to so restricted a number the company of
beast-worshipers or earth-dwellers. The brand of Nero's name
it quite insufficient to serve as an adequate antonym to the name
of God or as a definition of the final conflict. "It is the number
(*arithmos*) of a man (*anthropou*)." How does John conceive such
a phrase? Is this the one place where he leaves the realm of
vision for the realm of stark historical fact? Is this the one place
where Satan and the beast cease to be primordial, mythological
forces? Does symbolic language here give way to a cheap and
unnecessary allegory?

Number (*arithmos*)[8]—how does John use this word elsewhere? Always in connection with visions of heavenly reality and
with the contrast between the size of the conflicting armies.
Where the count is not specified, the purpose is to stress an
ineffable magnitude (which no one can number); where it is
specified, the prophet uses such symbolic images of completeness
as 144,000 (7:4f.) or ten thousand times ten thousand (5:11).
That the prophet had such a symbolic meaning in mind is sug-

---

8. See Rühle, TWNT, I, 461–464.

gested by the fact that in 15:2 the phrase "the number of his name" recurs as one of the three enemies which are overcome by the choirs and orchestras in heaven. It appears in sequence with the beast and his idol, strongly suggesting a central component of idolatry and blasphemy.

The number *of a man* (*anthropou*)—how does John use such a phrase elsewhere? In 21:17 we find a striking example. Here the measurement of the wall, a clearly symbolic and mythological datum, is called both the measurement of a man *and* the measurement of an angel (or of a man who is an angel). No one has, so far as I know, attempted to say that in this later context John is referring to a particular historical figure comparable to Nero. Yet the combination of angel and man in 21:17 is quite similar to the combination of beast and man in 13:18.

What is especially noteworthy about the human number in 13:18 (and it would be quite in order to translate the phrase "The brand, the name of the beast, or the number of its name . . . is an *ordinary human number*. His number is 666") is the heaping up of the number 6. Because of its contrast to 7 we may be content with an interpretation which sees in 666 an allusion to incompleteness, to the demonic parody on the perfection of 7, to the deceptiveness of the almost-perfect, to the idolatrous blasphemy exemplified by false worshipers, or to the dramatic moment between the sixth and the seventh items in a vision cycle (compare the cycles of seals, trumpets, bowls, and kings, 17:10). In short, none of the key terms of 13:18—name, number, man, 666—requires the effort to find an emperor the letters of whose name will add up to a total of 666. Moreover, that effort leads to a serious distortion, not only of the way in which the prophet used these terms, but also of his basic purposes and messages. In no sense would knowledge that 666 = Nero have enhanced the wisdom of his readers or enabled them to penetrate the fraudulent claims of the Dragon, the sea-beast, or the earth beast. It would not have strengthened the intended contrast between the self-styled Lamb of 13:11 and the true Lamb of 14:1, *the number of whose name* was inscribed on the foreheads of 144,000 loyal slaves (14:1). Those who are able to learn the song of 14:3 because of the Lamb's purchase (*agoradzo*, 14:3) are the precise opposite of those who are unable to purchase unless they wear the beast's number (13:17).

One other line of evidence is often cited to support the interpretation of 666 as Nero. This is found in 17:8-10. It is often supposed that Nero is the sixth king who both is (his ascension) and is not (his suicide), or that his expected return from the East is alluded to in the seventh king whose rule is to be short, or that he is the eighth who is one of the seven, or that he will lead the ten kings in their war against *both* the Whore (17:16) and the Lamb (17:14). There are many unresolved difficulties in any of these equations, some of which have been discussed in our essay on earth's kings. Here again the prophet calls for wisdom, but I doubt if by wisdom he meant the mathematical and calendrical ingenuity to assign to each head and each horn its equivalent ruler from the annals of the Empire. It is better simply to recall the promise concerning man and the serpent in Genesis 3:15. "He shall bruise your head" is the prophecy which John the prophet saw to be fulfilled in Christ's wounding of the Serpent. In addition to the reference in the Genesis story to the double wounding, we note other links to the *Apocalypse:* the deceitfulness of the Serpent and his success in temptation, the continuing enmity between him and the woman, the curse that falls on him and all beasts, and the travail of the woman in child-bearing.

However we may interpret the numeral, we should at least try to do justice to John's own clear emphasis. He chose to refer to 666 only once, whereas the other key phrases, such as the name of the beast, his brand and those who bear them, recur with almost monotonous rhythm (14:9, 11; 15:2; 16:2; 20:4). Surely this shows that he was primarily concerned with the alternative confronting Christians, whether they would worship the Lamb or the Beast, or, in the symbolism of numbers and names, bear the imprint of one or the other on their foreheads. The operative word in 13:17 seems to be *name* rather than *number*, and there

is abundant evidence in the Apocalypse concerning the significance of the name of the beast (12:3; 13:1-6; 14:11; 17:3f.).
Wherever there is blasphemy, there the beast's name is found.

If it be objected that this interpretation of 666 is too radical
an innovation, it should be remarked that it constitutes a return
to one of the earliest interpretations, that of Irenaeus (*Against
Heresies*, V, ch. 29-30). Irenaeus contends that the prophet chose
this number as a recapitulation of all kinds of deceit and iniquity
so that the beast might represent "all apostate power," a distilled
concentrate of "six thousand years" of false prophecy. "The digit
six, being adhered to throughout, indicates the recapitulations
of that apostasy, taken in its full extent, which occurred at the
beginning, during the intermediate periods, and which shall take
place at the end." Irenaeus also warns against the dangers to
faith when curious Christians try to equate the figure of the
Antichrist with some political ruler. Moreover, Irenaeus develops
the thesis that the reference to the wound, which is so central to
the *Apocalypse*, must be understood as an appeal to Gen. 3:13f.
At the beginning, Satan had inflicted the stroke of death upon
disobedient man in Adam (V, 34, 2) and in John's day he
wounded men unto death "by teaching blasphemy" (IV, Pref. 4;
also V, 25, 4; V, 28, 4). In response, the Messiah had freed men
from this wound by wounding Satan and by giving them the
power also to inflict wounds on the beast (I, 31, 4; V, 34, 2)
through overcoming his blasphemy.[9]

---

9. See B. Newman, NTS 10 (1963), 136–139. For a fuller bibliography dealing with the issues, see above p. 128.

6. The Earth

We have reviewed the evidence supporting the thesis that all the references to kingship and to earth's kings are symbolic in character, rather than literal or allegorical. We have seen that John was primarily concerned with the continuing struggle between two opposing power-structures, the christic vs. the antichristic forces, inherently incompatible but empirically co-existent. However we may interpret the term king, our interpretation must be equally applicable to both sides in this war, and also to the various echelons of authority—God, Christ, holy men vs. Satan, the beast, the beast-worshipers.

Thus far we have concentrated on John's conception of the higher echelons. We should now look at his ways of speaking of the lower echelons. One such expression by which he refers to antichristic forces is "those who dwell on earth" (*hoi katoikountes epi tēs gēs*), which we have translated as "the earth-dwellers." We must seek to define the exact reference on this phrase. John uses it eleven times in four separate visions (3:10; 6:10; 8:13; 11:10; 13:8, 12, 14; 17:2, 8). Our modern tendency is to suppose that so general a phrase refers in a general way to all men, without any qualification or discrimination. This I believe to be quite wrong. On the one hand, these dwellers are to be known by their dependence on the beast: "earth-dwellers" is synonymous with "beast-worshipers" (13:8, 12, 14; 17:2, 8). They constitute the citizenry of Babylon who get drunk on the wine of her adulteries (17:2, 8). They are deceived by the false signs paraded by the beast. As such, they are the object of the eagle's woes (8:13) and must confront the hour of trial (3:10). On the other hand, these dwellers are known by their hostility to the faithful. The category does in fact exclude all whose names are in the book of life (13:8). It excludes the prophets who are a torment to the earth-dwellers (11:10). Indeed, it is the earth-dwellers who are re-

sponsible for the slaughter of both prophets and holy men (6:10).
We may conclude that John conceives of an important boundary
separating the two groups, a boundary which coincides with the
distinction between the woes and the beatitudes (H. Feret, *op.
cit.*, 99f.).

John was, of course, not the first to employ the phrase "earth-
dwellers" in the qualitative, emotive, semi-technical sense. The
idiom had long been current among Israel's prophets. We cite
three of these, all of whom influenced John and all of whom
left other traces of that influence. First is the vision of God's
judgment in Isaiah 24. In this vision, the earth, polluted by its
inhabitants, becomes subject to terror, the pit, the snare. It is
to be shaken and its city turned into a wilderness, for the Lord
will become king on Mt. Zion and will punish all the kings of
the earth. Second is Jeremiah's short parable of drunkenness
(13:12-14), in which bowls of wine become symbols of the drunkenness, the idolatries, and the destruction of kings, priests, prophets, and all the citizens of Jerusalem (see also 1:14; 9:26; 10:18).
Third is Ezekiel's cycle of funeral dirges against Tyre and Egypt
which in various ways served John as a model for his laments
over the fall of Babylon (ch. 26, 27). In all these cases the prophets of Israel were primarily concerned with God's sovereignty
over his own people in the face of that people's rebellion; in
none of them does the phrase earth-dwellers refer literally to all
men. The currency of this idiom in the first century is supported
by the Qumran Thanksgiving Hymn (8:19-36) in which "dwellers
on earth" are opposed to "the army of the holy ones, the congregation of the sons of heaven" (see M. Burrows, *Dead Sea Scrolls*,
404f.).

How, then, does John describe the opposing community, the
servants of Christ? He explicitly exempts them from the kind of
trial which earth-dwellers must face (3:10). They have been
redeemed from that earth which had become the habitation of
destroyers (11:18). They are branded with another seal (13:8),
and therefore do not live on that earth whose fateful harvest is

blood (13:3, 8, 12, 14; 14:7-20). To be sure, they must stay awake (16:15), otherwise their place of residence is changed. But as long as they remain citizens of Jerusalem, they do not live on the same earth with citizens of Babylon. Where they live depends upon their own decision. Where, then, do they live so long as they stand firm? Several answers must be given. They dwell in Jerusalem, although this does not exclude other towns. They also dwell in a wilderness prepared by God, the place where Jesus was tempted and where Israel lived during the Exodus (12:6, 14). They also dwell in heaven before the throne of God, shepherded by their King (5:9-13; 12:12; 13:6), where they present their songs and prayers (5:9; 14:3). As congregations, their lampstand is in heaven (1:20), their existence wholly oriented around the altar (7:10-15). They are citizens of that city where their true names are written. These various answers, far from being contradictory, reinforce each other.

How far is it, then, from Babylon to Jerusalem? By what mileposts does one measure the distance? The clear implications of 11:8 makes useless any physical calculations. The two prophets and their enemies obviously meet on the same streets, and yet this city can be called Sodom, Egypt, or Jerusalem, and one should add Babylon, Rome, or Smyrna. Heaven-dwellers and earth-dwellers are in immediate contact and conflict with each other, since the clue to their identities is provided by their diverse loves and hates, decisions and deeds, prayers and names. Mutually incompatible forces co-exist, and the focus of collision and divergence is located in the decisions of men in response to the word of the prophet. The prophet's task is to help his readers see both "what is" and "what is to come soon" as the result of this inescapable collision.

To grasp John's idioms of conflict, therefore, we must be careful to catch the nuances in his use of such ordinary terms as earth (gē). It is this term which forms the common denominator for all the antichristic forces—beasts, kings, potentates, millionaires, merchants, and dwellers (see especially 6:15 for a sevenfold series). Yet John does not limit himself to one denotation in his use of this word. Here are four which we may distinguish.

A. In some contexts, gē is used with the term heaven to point simply to the entire range of God's creation (14:7) over which he maintains sovereignty. Occasionally this dual concept is expanded to include the sea (10:6). In this sense John can speak of the time since man appeared on *earth* (16:18).

B. In other contexts, gē points to the realm where God is making all things new. Here again earth is usually matched with heaven as a single realm (21:1), where God is worshiped by every creature. This same totality can be described in tripartite or quadripartite fashion (5:3, 13).

C. Earth most frequently points to that realm which has been corrupted and destroyed by false sovereignties and loyalties. It is the dominion of the beasts (6:8; 13:11) which is filled with their abominations (17:5). This dominion embraces peoples, nations, tongues, tribes which are deceived into worshiping the devil or his various aliases (11:10; 13:3; 19:2). Along with its corresponding heaven, this earth represents the "first" realm which "passes away" when God's new heaven-and-earth comes (21:1).

D. A corollary of the third meaning is this: the earth is that realm on which God inflicts his punishments. Angels are sent into the whole earth (5:6; 18:1), destroying its peace (6:4), striking it with every plague (16:1, 2), and driving its dwellers to despair. They harvest earth's grain and its grapes (14:15f.). The processes of condemnation are as extensive as the scope of deception and corruption, *but no more extensive.* They extend to this earth's heaven—sun, moon, stars—and to its Abyss. It is this earth on which the prophets call down fire (11:6), and which flees before the great white throne (20:11). It is over such an earth that the Messiah makes those men kings who share in his victory over the devil (1:6, 19; 5:10; 11:15; 12:10; 20:4, 6; 21:24; 22:5).

If this is a correct analysis of the different uses of the term earth, we should ask whether these four have any common component. Such a component is not to be located in any geological or geographical core, but rather in the reference to God-relatedness. Each of the four conceptions makes primary the activity of God and his competitors; each makes primary the loyalties of men to God or to those competitors. In John's lexicon, if not in ours, it is entirely natural to speak of a new heaven and a new earth, and in so speaking to have in mind the actualities of God's dwelling with men (21:1-3). We are therefore bound to distort his thought if we substitute for his word *earth* our own concept of a geological entity as something which can be conceived quite apart from any reference to God or man, and quite apart from the struggle between God and Satan. Similar distortions follow corresponding interpretations of the meaning of "the earth-dwellers" or "the kings of the earth."

The implications of this principle are far-reaching indeed. For example, it is a custom among exegetes to speak of apocalyptic prophecy as announcing "the end of the world." Usually this phrase is taken to speak of *end* in a modern sense (e.g., the end of the road, the school year, the game, etc.) and also of *world* in a modern sense (e.g., the geophysical universe, humanity, civilization, etc.). Taken in this sense, I insist that John said nothing at all about "the end of the world." He was concerned with quite a different ordering of things. To him "earth" had no autonomous existence, with its own beginning and ending. The significance of a particular earth derived from its relation to God and to God's redemptive work. The problem of identifying the earth-dwellers is therefore inseparable from that of understanding who are the heaven-dwellers.

It is no doubt audacious to challenge so openly the prevailing conception that the *Apocalypse* contains a set of predictions concerning the end of the world. Nevertheless, whatever the degree of audacity, I feel that I must issue that challenge. This is not the place, however, to parade the full scope of evidence to support the challenge. Let me instead summarize a single line of evidence which runs counter to the prevailing stereotypes.

I have in mind the Johannine use of the tradition of the four horsemen in chapter six. The riding of these four has usually been interpreted as features of an expected future judgment of God on the wicked world, a judgment which will take the form of terrible cosmic disasters, such as warfare, famine, and pestilence. When, however, we inquire more closely into the dramatic structure of John's vision and the function of this quartet in that vision, another picture emerges.

Briefly, this picture is this: the four horsemen describe the various ways in which the conquered and conquering Lamb chastises and disciplines his congregations in Asia and thus enables them to verify God's saving purpose (6:9) for his people.

First, we examine the role and function of these four seals in the vision as a whole. The vision begins at 4:1 and ends at 8:1. The first two chapters provide the necessary setting for the seven seals. The opening of these seals is therefore one of the objectives of the throne-room scene, of the hymns sung by all the choirs, of the worship of the Lamb, and of his worthiness to be worshiped. Chapters 4 and 5 answer the question, "Who is worthy to be worshiped?" Chapters 6 and 7 answer the corollary, "Who is worthy to join in that worship?" Without the opening of the seven seals, the purpose of the throne-room drama would remain unfulfilled. As we have stressed in our earlier analysis, it is Christ who commands the living creatures to open the four seals. Whatever the riders do is done in response to this command. The mission of the four horsemen is, in fact, a consequence of the Lamb's redemptive work (5:9-12). In the opening of the seals the seer describes events which are released by the Lamb's death and which are involved in the Church's worship. Interpretations which do not point to events of this order would be foreign to John's intention.

Let us now examine how the four seals are related to the other seals. As we have already shown, the first four form a unit which can be separated from the last three. The four have identical introductions and a single summary in verse 8c. They are similar in length and in form, and this form is highly traditional.

There seems, in fact, to be nothing distinctively Christian about them. The author does not dwell long on them. The fifth and sixth seals are different at many points. They are longer; they are distinctly Christian. They present as the cardinal problem the complaint of the saints in 6:10. The sixth seal is obviously dependent on the fifth because it deals with the Lamb's punishment of the antichristic forces. The whole of chapter seven constitutes the answer to the complaint of the fifth seal, giving in detail the Lamb's reward to his faithful witnesses and closing the circle of worship which had opened with chapter 4. The four seals, therefore, occupy a strategic place between the victory of the Lamb in chapter 5 and the victory of the saints in chapter 7 by serving as the prelude to seal five, where the fate of the saints is at stake.

Within this literary structure, then, the four seals describe the forces which have been released by Christ's death (5:5, 9, 10). They explain the urgency and the anguish embodied in the Church's prayers and hymns (5:8; 6:10; 7:10). They prepare the way for the fifth seal by indicating how the holy men had been slaughtered by the earth-dwellers (6:9, 10). They constitute the great ordeal (7:14) through which the followers of the Lamb vindicate their calling. They indicate the conditions in which as Victor he opens to them the opportunity of becoming victors, thus obeying the central imperative of the seven letters.

John was seeking not to present pictures of cosmic disasters to fall on the world as a whole or even on evil men in particular, but rather to show how the contemporary sufferings of Christ's followers were related to the power-struggle released by his death. One may notice various details which support such an hypothesis. For example, the clearest single antecedent in prophetic literature for the horsemen is Ezekiel 5:12-17, where God also executes judgment not on Gentiles but upon his own people, "a divine mission, which, like every divine action, accomplishes a triumph over evil" (A. Feuillet ZNTW [1967], 247). In the account of the first horse, the decisive verb is *to conquer* which is used always in the *Apocalypse* in referring to the fateful struggle between christic and antichristic forces (e.g., 5:5; 11:7; 13:7; 17:14). The same may be observed of the term for *crown* (2:10; 9:7). In the description of the second horse, again, the key words are significant. The word for slaughter links the work of this rider to the martyrdom of Christians (6:9) as well as to the death of Christ (5:6, 9, 12). The sword which he uses is the same as that used by antichristic forces (13:10, 14) as part of the warfare in which the Church is already engaged. This rider, in fact, fulfills the word of Jesus that he came to bring not peace but a sword. So, too, the work of the third rider releases the kind of poverty which, according to the seven letters, represents real wealth in heaven (2:9), the kind of hunger and thirst which qualifies loyal slaves for heavenly sustenance (7:16; 21:4-7).

Most clearly of all, the fourth horseman represents what we should recognize as the "last enemy" of the Church. In the *Apocalypse* Death and Hades are twin realities over which the final victory must be won. Having won the victory over them (1:18), Christ releases them to test the fidelity of his followers (2:10) and to enable them to share in his triumph (7:14). Death and Hades must be vanquished before the appearance of the new creation (20:13, 14). It is significant that John traces all four conditions to the beasts of the earth (6:8). Our analysis of the role of the *beasts*, combined with the current study of the *earth*, should clarify the force which this phrase held for John and his readers. These beasts are everywhere the avowed enemies of the Church, yet Christ uses them to manifest his power by providing the resources by which his followers can overcome these enemies.

In summary, then, each of the four riders contributes to the ordeals currently faced by the seven churches; each prepares the way for the cry of the slain in 6:9f. In this respect the ordeal of the witnesses corresponds to the ordeal of Christ as witness, and this ordeal is commanded by Christ as part of the process by which their witness is authenticated. As the Son of Man had had to suffer, so too must his followers. The righteous must bear the sins of the world. The four horsemen had been released by

Christ to kill his followers with sword, famine, and death (6:8). Small wonder that those who had been so slaughtered should cry out from beneath the altar (6:9; note how the context of worship is retained here). Yet the decisive factor for John was this: their death at the hands of the beasts of the earth had been occasioned by their efforts to verify God's saving design (6:9). We conclude that John was not speculating about the general future of the world; he was describing the struggle which pervaded the doxologies, prayers, and daily ordeal of the churches of Asia.

7. Heaven

The whole of John's book consists of visions of "heavenly things." In each of the visions he tells of seeing a series of events taking place in heaven. Everything which transpires on earth is first seen as happening in heaven. But the locale of the action does not affect the integrity of the vision or the reality of the event. He does not shuttle back and forth between an imagined heaven and a real earth, but everything he says is equally real and equally visionary. He remains consistent in maintaining the integrity of the visions as visions. Each interpreter must accordingly seek to do justice to those modes of thinking which were indigenous to John's outlook when he was speaking in his role as a prophet "in the Spirit." We may well believe that when John was not speaking in that role he would have employed a different vocabulary.

It would be wrong, therefore, to attribute a non-visionary substantiality to the various objects which John saw in heaven. When he speaks of the first heaven and earth he is not, as we have noted, writing as a historian or a sociologist, let alone an astronomer or a physicist. Nor does he do so when he tells of the descent of the new heaven and earth, for these two "creations" were interacting aspects of the same vision. Yet if we can analyze the interior logic of that vision, we may be able to make more sense of his treatment of those phenomena which we call space and time. "Then I saw a new heaven and a new earth; for the first heaven and the first earth had passed away and the sea was no more. And I saw the holy city, new Jerusalem, coming down out of heaven from God. . . ."

If we want to speak of space-time events, should we begin with a text like this which appears to be an example of the most extreme kind of futuristic eschatology? Was not John's final vision the most futuristic of all and therefore the least relevant to today's problems? I wish to offer three answers to this objection. (1) To reject this vision as basic to the prophet's thought on the ground of its thoroughgoing futurism is to make normative our own conception of time and our notion that things present are more real than are things to come. When we do this we replace the prophet's conception of heavenly realities by our own conception of temporal futurity. (2) Critical study of the final vision of the prophet (ch. 21, 22) has revealed increasingly the multiple correlation between this vision and all the earlier visions. Neither the literary structure of the book nor its thought structure can justify the isolation of the closing chapters from the earlier chapters. (3) When we examine the morphology of John's imagination, we are justified in beginning with the clearest expression of that imagination, providing that we test that expression by other expressions to prove that it is in fact typical.

Let us therefore examine the prophet's various references to heavens and earths. "The first heaven and the first earth had passed away." Immediately one axiom of the prophet's thought becomes clear. A heaven belongs to its earth and vice versa. The two are inseparable. Together they constitute a single, interlocking reality. Note: this collocation of a heaven with its earth is a familiar phenomenon in biblical thinking, found not only in the Apocalypse (10:6; 14:7) and in the prophets (Isa. 65:17; Hag. 2:6) but also in historical (Gen. 1:1), legal (Deut. 5:8; 10:14; 32:1), and liturgical (Psa. 96:11; 19:1f.) traditions (see U. Simon, *Heaven*, 126f. and H. Sasse, TWNT I, 677-681). Furthermore, the text suggests that to the prophet the first heaven and the first earth are bound together in a common transiency. One could not grow obsolete or pass away without the other. The first heaven may be distinguished from its corresponding earth. It may, in fact, hold a degree of transcendence over it. Nevertheless, where God's action comes into view, as in this text, their interdependence is asserted. They had been created through God's will (10:6; 14:7); they remain subordinated to his will; they pass away in response to his action.

This principle remains valid whether this first creation be

described as bipartite (heaven and earth, 6:13; 12:9), as tripartite (heaven, earth and sea, 21:1; 10;6) or as quadripartite
(heaven, earth, sea, the fountains of water, 14:7). The basic unity
of the first creation is not destroyed by such subdivisions. The
use of these subdivisions merely enables the prophet to depict
dramatically the successive extensions of God's judgment and
to incorporate into his symphony a large repertoire of traditional
motifs. The image of the first heaven and the first earth embraces
all "the first things" (*ta prota*) which pass away. The "first things"
of the prophet's vision include, of course, more elements than
such celestial, terrestrial, and marine phenomena. Mourning,
crying, pain, and death are explicitly mentioned. Moreover, the
prophecy declares that the fate of the first heaven and the first
earth will be shared by the liars, the cowards, the faithless, the
fornicators, and the idolators (21:8). When one tries to find a
single category which will include the fate of these people, along
with the trials of the saints (pain and death) and judgments upon
seas and suns, perhaps the term *ta prota* is more adequate than
the phrase "the first heaven and the first earth." The adjective
first is more definitive than the nouns *heaven* and *earth*. We are
dealing with a symbol which embraces this whole range of first
things, which is defined by a given power-structure: false gods
who provide the object of man's allegiances and thereby supply
the cohesion of his communities.

"I saw a new heaven and a new earth." The passing away
of the first things does not leave a void, but a new creation. The
passing away and the coming down are interlocked yet opposing
movements. In this respect the new earth and the new heaven
are components of a single reality. The new creation as a whole
is the locus where all things become new (21:5). The choice of
the adjective is not fortuitous. If the relation of the new to the
old were one of simple temporal succession, the use of the ordinal
the second would be sufficient. The term *new* negates the idea
of a continuing and perhaps endless series of heavens and earths.
The new heaven and earth is not a thing that can become old
and pass away. The accent therefore falls not upon its temporal

novelty, but upon its qualitative newness. Throughout the New Testament *kaine* is an eschatological term, related to an eternal life in a kingdom which has no end (compare *Rev.* 2:17; 3:12; 5:9; A. Richardson, 254f).

Precisely in the same way that *ta prota* indicated the inclusive range of the first creation, so here *panta kaina* indicates the inclusive range of the new creation. Moreover, the decisive determinant of this newness is this: "The dwelling of God is with men. He will dwell with them and they shall be his people" (21:3). It is this new situation which is the key to the other symbols of newness: the holy city, the bride, the death of death, the water of life, the sonship of the conquerors. It is the city which binds this new heaven and its earth together, for it is the place where God dwells with his people. The strategic difference between the first and the new creation is thus defined by the community which dwells there. The mark of one community is idolatry (vs. 8), of the other victorious faithfulness (vs. 7).

Let us now note a third use of the term heaven by the prophet. "I saw the holy city . . . coming down *out of heaven* from God" (21:2). Which heaven is this? It is possible to think of it as the new heaven from which the new Jerusalem descends to the new earth. It is, however, preferable to think of this heaven as the source of the new creation as a whole (heaven-and-earth). This would constitute a distinctive use of the term heaven as referring to that realm which is the source of all creative and redemptive work. The phrase *from God* seems to underscore the ontological ultimacy of this heaven. As the throne-heaven from which the Most High speaks and from which eternal life flows (vs. 5, 6), it is a symbol of unconditioned primacy. As the sphere of God's glory (vs. 11, 23), it is the source of that light which needs no darkness for its definition (vs. 24, 25). It would be wrong to speak of a *third* heaven, with its suggestion of astronomical hierarchy. This image connotes no simple concept of transcendence, such as *the above*, but a much more complex concept, "the above-the-above" (see Simon, *Heaven*, 62-68, 96f.).

All the visions presuppose an orientation around this throne (ch. 4), yet John preserves the element of pure transcendence by his reticence in describing the Enthroned. John is concerned to speak of God's transcendence not in terms of a philosopher's analysis of nature or history, but in terms of a prophet's role in Christian worship. God is to be known most surely through the doxologies and prayers of his servants. The throne-heaven is the realm where the unlimited power and love of God are fully known and fully operative. Here burns the eternal fire, here dwell the seven spirits of God. Here is no conflict, no battle for supremacy; yet there is unceasing action. This action can be described in the language of worship, as in ch. 4, 5, 7. Or it can be described in the related language of the sounding of the trumpet-thunders or the emptying of bowls of blood.

In chapter 5, a scene in the throne-room, John describes what is to him the most decisive of all actions. This is the event of Jesus' death and enthronement. It is important to note just how John introduces that action; for, although the event took place at a particular place and time, John discerns in it an authentic degree of universality and transcendence. The action is introduced by the insistence upon impotence and unworthiness. "No one in heaven or on earth or under the earth was able to open the scroll" (5:2). But this reference to frustration only serves to accent the climactic answer. There is one who is able, though only one: the Lion of Judah, the slain Lamb. Immediately the prophet explains what it is that enables the Lamb to do what no other power can do: "thou wast slain and by thy blood didst ransom man for God" (5:9). The frustration in heaven gives way to worship: "every creature in heaven and on earth and under the earth" (5:13) joins in the new song, the new priesthood, the new kingdom. The unlimited character of this song is the sign of its ultimacy. Yet the song is simply the declaration of what has happened in the death of the Lamb and in the verification of that death by his servants. It is this temporal victory which constitutes the theme of the heavenly choirs.

It is, then, this very event in time and space which marks the transition between the two creations, between the realm of

crown-casters and the realm of drunken idolators. In one creation
all creatures worship God and the Lamb; in the other all give
glory and power to the Dragon (compare 5:13 with 13:4-8,
14-17). In one creation the kings of the earth bring their glory
into the virgin city (21:24); in the other they commit fornication
with Babylon (18:3). The prophet does not speak of the servants
of God as inhabiting the same earth as the servants of Satan,
yet they do meet in crucial conflict. Their specific decisions,
taken on particular days in particular places, constitute the
Archimedean point where the two competing forces find leverage.
It is by the word of their testimony that the Lamb's servants
overcome Satan (12:10-12); their worship in heaven is God's
vindication of their worship on earth. They are slain by earth's
kings, yet they themselves rule on earth.

We are clearly dealing with visions which disclose how
transcendent powers operate within the context of ordinary human existence. Earth-dwellers (citizens of the first creation) accord to their many lords a primary glory, power, and longevity.
The first heaven is a mode of transcendence integral to their
existence. Holy men likewise accord to their Lord the glory and
power which they believe belong to him. The new heaven is a
mode of transcendence implicit in their existence. Both modes
of transcendence are features of the prophet's vision.

In the vision of the throne-room, however, John affirms a still
more ultimate kind of primacy and finality. As sign of this he
retains a distinction between the throne of God and the throne
of the Lamb, even while stressing their unity. God is the only
one whom the prophet calls all-powerful. He alone creates
everything (4:11). From his throne all judgments proceed; he
is the only ultimate source of grace and peace (1:4). He alone
sets the standards of worthiness which the Lamb fulfilled (4:11;
5:5). The revelation comes through Christ, but only because
God had first given it to him (1:1). The fire which alone was
powerful enough to burn the devil, death, and Hades came directly out of heaven from God (20:9), as did the Holy City itself.
The final command is simply this: "Worship God" (22:9). Such

evidence as this supports the conviction that John's vision was that of a radical monotheist.

John also preserves the transcendence of the Holy City over the churches, never using the latter term to refer to the former reality. The movement of the new Jerusalem is a descent from God, not an ascent of man. The new city continues to bear the marks of its place of origin and to point men in that direction. God has come with his eternal glory, so there is no need for sun and stars. Yet he remains God, the sole ruler of this city. He dwells with his people, but his government does not resemble an ecclesiastical oligarchy or a town-meeting democracy. The throne, the center of everything, remains the symbol of eternal transcendence, even over the city itself. This is to say that the vision remains a vision and not a map or a timetable. There is a realm beyond even the vision of the new Jerusalem, beyond the new creation. This realm is quite appropriately described as the throne. Creation proceeds outward and downward from this invisible center; toward it the life of the new creation is oriented upward and forward. But the prophet rightly refused to describe this invisible center of glory; he was content to speak the names of God and of the Lamb.

Can we ever comprehend in more objective terms that ontological perspective which is implicit in the vision? Probably not. The very meaning of the word transcendence denies that possibility. John does not use the terms heaven and earth with strict conformity to non-prophetic categories. Nevertheless, we can discern an inner logic which characterizes his thinking. His outlook stresses the intrinsic incompatibility of the old and the new, yet recognizes their compresence. Each is a structure of power, with claims to sovereignty and actions of obedience. The new creation elicits the hostility of the old and uses that hostility as an occasion for victory. The citizens of the two realms met daily in the streets of Philadelphia and Pergamum, yet they did not dwell on the same earth, although in their hearts as well as in their behavior the forces of the two realms met in combat. The only way for Christians to understand what was happening on the streets of the cities was to listen to what the Spirit was saying through this conflict between the old and the new.

We are left in the position of recognizing that neither of John's realms was spaceless, yet neither of them could be measured by the usual measures of space. His thought was not spacelessly transcendent, though it transcended the usual conceptions of space. Certainly we should not accuse him of holding a naive three-storied view of the world. His mind was far more sophisticated than that. Nor should we interpret his visions as announcing the end of history or of the world, since his vision was not controlled by our notions of a single world and an all-inclusive temporal process. This would destroy the integrity of his seeing and thinking. It would identify history as coterminous with the realm of Satan alone. It would confine the temporal world within the dominion of Babylon. To be sure, in doing this one might try to preserve the hope for redemption beyond history, but he would destroy the vocation of the Church in space and time, which to John could be accomplished through its daily contact with the earth-dwellers and its redemptive struggle with the powers of evil.

Most interpretations of Revelation err, I believe, in stating the options too simply. They fail to recognize the profundity of John's thought or the complexity of prophetic visions as a mode of communication. For example, it is easily assumed that John's thought was either historical (i.e., that he was concerned only with the situation in the seven churches in 95 A.D.) or timeless (i.e., that he had no concern for that concrete situation). Such a statement of the options evades the deeper problems. The real question is how John perceived the forces which were operating in that situation and how he related them to archetypal and final realities. For simple-minded folk, any mention of transcending space and time requires a stratospheric voyage into trackless and timeless realms. But to recognize a reality which transcends space and time need not empty space or time of significance; only the denial of transcendence can produce that result. John's visions conveyed to his Christian readers his conviction that they were themselves in touch with an order of reality which transcended space and time by revealing the eternal and universal significance of each day and place.

To be sure, this kind of transcendence required a substantial devaluation of men's measurements of temporal duration. Who was really dead, the Lamb or the Beast? The answer would determine the actions of Christian congregations in Pergamum and Laodicea. Time and space were essential to such actions, yet they did not determine the source or the result of those actions. When the prophet saw God's judgments operating in the first creation, he did not predict its end as something which could be noted on a calendar. Nor was he speculating on the arrival of a future day on which the final cosmic conflagration would take place. He saw the slain Lamb seated on the throne. The Lamb disclosed what had taken place in the cross and in many other events, along with what must soon take place, i.e., how the power released by God would continue to operate. He disclosed the decision of God to dwell with his people in a new city. That city was devoid of neither time nor space, since it bound together acts of human obedience with acts of divine sovereignty. Yet neither was it confined by space or regulated by time. It comes down "out of heaven from God." The vision of that city was not designed to tease men with ontological riddles, or to encourage them to set the date for coming events, or to construct elaborate charts covering the rise and fall of civilizations. It was rather designed to lead the congregations of Asia to worship God in ways conformable to his purpose as revealed in Jesus and thus to become as radical in their monotheism as Jesus had been. The validity of John's ontological outlook rested not so much on his pictures of heaven and earth as on his affirmations concerning God, and on the vocational corollaries of those affirmations. (See my essay, "Cosmology of the Apocalypse," in W. Klassen and G. Snyder, *Current Issues in N.T. Interpretation*, 23-37; also R. P. Martin, *Carmen Christi*, 249-278.)

8. The Clouds of Heaven

The prophetic perception of the divine transcendence is expressed not so much in abstract philosophical concepts as in very tangible symbols. One might choose many such symbols to illustrate the matter, but we have selected one for closer scrutiny—the symbol of the clouds. This choice may be defended by saying that in the minds of most modern readers the term cloud is a non-symbolic designation of a natural phenomenon, which demonstrates, if anything, the narrow naïveté and the mundane horizons of the seer. It it could be demonstrated that John actually used the cloud as a theophanic symbol expressing a profound perception of transcendence, this would show that John was a far more sophisticated thinker than is usually granted. I believe that such a demonstration is possible. R. B. Y. Scott has presented the case for Daniel, one of the sources of John's imagery (NTS 5 [1959], 127-132); an even stronger case can be made for *Revelation*.

Six times the prophet uses the term translated cloud, and quite naturally in connection with his descriptions of heavenly reality (1:7; 10:1; 11:12; 14: 14, 15, 16). In the use of this metaphor, the modern idiom is worlds distant from the biblical. To understand the prophet's use of the image, we should first scan a few of the key Old Testament narratives where clouds play a symbolic role.

The first picture should be familiar to everyone: it is that of the dark cloud that appeared after the great deluge had abated. In this cloud God sets his rainbow as a token of the covenant he has signed with all creation. Whenever people become apprehensive of the destruction of all life, they will see this rainbow and will recall this everlasting promise. God will not utterly destroy all flesh, a message perennially needed by people panicked by calamities (Gen. 9:8-17).

A second striking picture of the cloud appears in the story of God's covenant with Moses and the Israelite pilgrims at Mt. Sinai. To these refugees on their trek to freedom God wanted to disclose his promise of a glorious destiny and his commands of strenuous obedience. He came down in a cloud upon the mountain; Moses ascended the mountain into this cloud. The fateful meeting took place, surrounded by thunder and lightning. The dark cloud hid God from Moses and concealed their encounter from the people. Yet for all its darkness, this cloud disclosed the presence of God—his invisible glory, his sovereign purpose, his fearsome power, his invincible intention to guide and govern this people throughout the course of their wanderings. God spoke and his people heard. Yet the inmost nature of this revelation remained inaccessible to the prying gaze of earthbound eyes.

The Almighty, whose presence enveloped Sinai in clouds, was not an unmoving deity who remained seated on a mountain throne, but a Lord who led his people throughout their journey. The picture of his cloud is not a "still" but a "movie." At each turning in the weary wilderness trail his presence was marked by a pillar of cloud which went before the pilgrims, guiding and protecting them (Ex. 13:21, 22). At times, it moved around to the rear of the caravan, but only to protect them from their pursuers (ch. 14:19-25). Its main function was to show them the way in which they should march and to give the light by which to march (Ps. 78:14; 105:39). The whole course of their journey to the Promised Land was thus the scene of a miraculous providence that would not let them go, even when they worshiped the calf instead of their Deliverer (see Neh. 9:19, 20).

The same unearthly cloud signified God's presence (or absence) in the tent of meeting, where the people of Israel rendered their thanks to God and renewed their vows to serve him. Here in worship they recognized their dependence upon him and sought his guidance for the day. Whenever his glory filled the tabernacle, there the cloud overshadowed his encounters with them. God had chosen to dwell in thick darkness, but men could nevertheless know when he was present. If they sought to pene-

trate the cloud to see him face to face, they were punished. Out of
the cloud he could strike down the rebels. Within the cloud, on
the other hand, he could impart his Spirit to men, selecting
prophets and elders to minister to the people. As the Temple
became more elaborate and the liturgy more highly organized,
the cloud took up its place in the Holy of Holies, at the mercy
seat, where the relationship of God to his people was most intimate and most ultimate.

Because their ancient sagas so closely associated the glory
of God with the clouds, it is not strange that the poets should
have used this image in exalting the majesty of the Eternal (Ps.
104). Nor is it strange that the prophets should have described
their experiences in similarly vivid images. Ezekiel, for example,
encountered the glory of the Lord in a stormy wind blowing
from the north. There came a great cloud, permeated by fire
and radiant with brightness. From this nimbus emerged living
creatures and revolving wheels. From the cloud came a spirit
and a voice, commissioning the awestruck and prostrate prophet
to carry a message from the Most High to his rebellious people.
The Spirit endowed him with both the words and the courage
to proclaim them (Ezek. 1:4 to 2:7). On another occasion, the
same prophet depicted the brightness of God's glory as a cloud
that filled the house. In the midst of the cloud were the cherubim
and God's throne, the fires of heavenly judgment and angels who
do God's bidding. Out of the cloud spoke the voice of God
Almighty (ch. 10:1-8).

The later prophets who proclaimed the nearness of the
Lord's day utilized the same imagery. The day when God's
wrath would descend on man's sin would be "a day of clouds and
thick darkness," a day of trumpets and alarms, a day of devouring
fire and cowering fears (Joel 1:15 to 2:3; Zeph. 1:14-18). Most
famous of these prophecies, perhaps, was this word of Daniel:

I saw in the night visions,
      and behold, with the clouds of heaven
         there came one like a son of man,
      and he came to the Ancient of Days
         and was presented before him.

> And to him was given dominion
>> and glory and kingdom,
> that all peoples, nations, and languages
>> should serve him;
> his dominion is an everlasting dominion,
>> which shall not pass away,
> and his kingdom one
>> that shall not be destroyed (Dan. 7:13, 14).

It is clear, then, that the men of the New Testament had inherited a colorful and complex tradition concerning the clouds. This image had moved toward the center of their cluster of images. It evoked memories of God's decisive actions, his gracious promises, his continual guidance. It expressed the awe and dread appropriate to moments of visitation and calling. It effectively articulated the majestic paradox of the hiddenness of God in his self-disclosure. It carried profound associations of glory and power, judgment and blessing, distance and nearness. The image preserved the reality of God's abiding presence without denying the intermittent character of his disclosures. The image suggested that, like the cloud, God's purpose transcends earthbound space and time without annihilating those basic conditions under which the human caravan moved forward.

This tradition provides many clues to the meaning of New Testament stories. In some ways the most strategic of these stories narrates the transfiguration of Jesus (Mark 9:2-8; Matt. 17:1-8; Luke 9:28-36). This is the occasion when Jesus meets with Moses and Elijah, when the presence of the divine glory is manifested to fearful disciples, when a voice comes from the cloud: "This is my beloved Son . . . listen to him." The event is shrouded in mystery, the majestic mystery of God's meeting with men. This man Jesus holds an ultimate authority; his mission has a time-transcending significance; on this mountain a new covenant is sealed; here at a new turning in the exodus of God's pilgrims, the pillar of cloud descends again to guide them; here is a new compassionate concern for earth. In him God comes to men; along this man's road to the cross men may glimpse heaven's compassionate concern for earth. In him God comes to men, they have access to God. Many traits in the Old Testament epic thus recur in this episode that reveals "the glory of God in the face of Jesus Christ."

Another strategic event involving the cloud may be found in the narrative of the ascension (Acts 1:9). After the risen Lord had completed his commissioning of his disciples and had prepared them for their tasks, he was taken from their sight by a cloud. Two men in angelic garments, presumably from the same cloud, chided the disciples for looking into heaven and announced that Jesus would return again in the same fashion.

This same expectation concerning the return of Christ is common to other New Testament traditions. At the conclusion of the Synoptic apocalypse, after a prophetic vision of all the tribulations anticipated in the last days, a climactic accent is placed on this assurance:

> And then they will see the Son of man coming in clouds, with great power and glory. And then he will send out the angels, and gather his elect from the four winds, from the ends of the earth to the ends of heaven (Mark 13:26, 27; Matt. 24:30, 31; Luke 21:27, 28).

At the trial of Jesus before the Sanhedrin, when the high priest had asked Jesus directly if he were the Christ, he received a similar reply (Mark 14:62; Matt. 26:64; Luke 22:69). The clouds are an emblem of God's sovereign power and majestic glory moving toward the earth.

Having surveyed some of the key connotations of clouds in the biblical lexicon, we can now perhaps return to the Johannine passages. All belong to the language of divine majesty and mystery, intimating the presence of the divine power and glory. All stress the universal significance of the event at hand. They are ways of dealing with the final judgment and redemption, with an accounting that transcends earthly fortunes, and from which no one can escape. The atmosphere is one of numinous awe before manifestations of the divine intervention. To see these clouds requires a special kind of vision.

In four cases (1:7; 14:14, 15, 16) the clouds are associated with Christ. They portend that simultaneous and universal "recognition-scene" when all will know him. This scene will be especially traumatic to those who killed him, producing the grief and remorse of self-knowledge and the assurance of divine retribution (1:7). The picture is drawn from the tradition of Daniel and Ezekiel, and yet is wholly congenial with the accounts in the Synoptic Gospels. A fuller picture is found in 14:14ff., where the appearance of the cloud is an expression of Christ's approval and confirmation of the faithful endurance of the saints, the sign of the permanence of their works (vs. 12, 13). The cloud is white, symbol of transcendent purity and consummate glory. It supports the impression of regal glory, but this glory is chiefly exercised in the harvesting of the earth in accord with the demands of the heavenly temple.

In 10:1 an angel appears robed in a cloud; apparently this is one of the marks of the angel's power to institute judgment over earth and sea. The angel is acting for Christ, and therefore is described in much the same terms.

Only in 11:12 does the cloud appear in conjunction with human figures. This is very significant. The two prophets who have been faithful unto death share in Christ's resurrection after three and a half days. The cloud is a mark of heaven's verdict on their earthly career. But more important, their enemies will see them (like the enemies of Christ in 1:7). Final fear will fall on all, so that all will give glory to the God of heaven. The hour of their appearance on the cloud will be marked by a great earthquake, great judgment, great reversal of roles, great glory. Surely this is the same "cloud" as that on which their Lord comes. This notion brings John's thought close to that of Paul, where Jesus is joined in the clouds by his faithful saints (1 Thes. 4:16, 17). John's thought is thus imbued with images common to many apostolic writers and probably to Jesus himself.

The return of Christ with the clouds will be an event that belongs to the same order of reality as all the earlier visitations of God that have been accompanied by the cloud. Christian hope is a living forward toward that day when his transcendent glory will be seen by every man. The symbol of the cloud connotes the coming rendezvous of all those who in every age and place have given their faithful witness to God's covenant, their rendezvous with Christ and God. As such, it is a symbol of universal judgment and redemption, a symbol of the intrinsic catholicity of this community, and a symbol of the inseparability of earthly happenings and heavenly potencies. (Note: this essay is based in part on chapter 8 in my *Christian Hope and the Second Coming*.)

9. Comparable Patterns of Thought in Luke's Gospel

In the concluding pages of Part I we suggested as an area for further study the comparison of John's perspective with that of other early Christian authors. Only now do we undertake such a study, because each student must have a basic comprehension of John's perspective before he can effectively pursue the work of comparison. That work should not be considered marginal or optional. It is all the more necessary because it has been so long neglected. Whether one base his judgment on the use of Revelation in church lectionaries or in private reading, in pulpit preaching or in theological curricula, he will discover that the modern church is strongly disposed to treat the Apocalypse as atypical of New Testament thinking as a whole. Striking corroboration of this observation is provided by Guilford Dudley's survey of current lectionaries arranged for Sunday use. In the Methodist cycle only one of 52 readings is drawn from Revelation, and from this reading (19:1, 4, 6-8) the editors have deleted several verses which might be considered obnoxious. The Episcopalian cycle adopts 4:1-11 as the only example in 104 readings, a choice appropriate to the liturgical emphasis. The United Lutheran lectionary passes the Apocalypse by completely. Dudley is justified in concluding that there is a "national consensus" for treating Revelation as obsolete (*The Recovery of Christian Myth*, 22f.).

Current scholarship gives priority to the study of the Pauline letters and the Gospels, and only rarely does it appeal to the *Book of Revelation* as an aid in that study. Many readers assume that it is inferior in value because of late origin or limited relevance. Many are convinced that this document really belongs to millennial sectarians and not to the main-line traditions. In various quarters one finds assertions that it illustrates obsolete mythology, a ghetto mentality, or sub-Christian ethics. There is ample reason, therefore, to reopen the question whether Revelation is actually atypical of the New Testament; if it is not a-typical it may actually afford valuable help in interpreting the other books.

We cannot provide a full rehearsal of the evidence here, but we can indicate a sample of studies which should be pursued on a wider scale. Do we find in Luke's Gospel patterns of thought which are congenial to those in Revelation? We choose Luke because many exegetes place his Gospel at the opposite end of the theological spectrum from the Apocalypse. Many grounds are offered for this placement, some good and some bad. John's book seems to be ultra-Jewish in idiom, Luke's ultra-Hellenistic. John appears to voice a maximum of hostility toward Rome; Luke a minimum. Where John describes heavenly visions, Luke narrates historical happenings. To Luke the doctrine of the atoning power of Christ's death is marginal; to John it is pivotal, e.g., his emphasis on the image of the Lamb. The Apocalypse illustrates a futurist eschatology undiminished by despair over the delay of the Parousia; in Luke, the futurist reference is little more than a vestigial remnant of earlier enthusiasms, dulled by decades of disappointment. If an unprejudiced examination of the evidence should reveal a genuine homogeneity between these two authors, the implications would reach very far. We should be led to suspect that prevalent views of both books are based on unjustified stereotypes which exaggerate the differences between the two authors and neglect their common witness. We would also expect to find an even broader band of mutuality between the Apocalypse and other New Testament writings.

In calling attention to certain aspects of that homogeneity, we do not deny important contrasts. We do not present a full picture of the objectives or provenance of Luke, nor do we wish to argue the literary dependence of one author on the other, or the chronological priority of either. Both documents comprised a complex editorial process of weaving together earlier sources, both written and oral. Each writer had his own distinctive objectives and task. Luke's Gospel concluded with the resurrection of Jesus; John began with that event. Luke wrote as a theological historian in order to instruct such converts as Theophilus, to appeal to unconverted Jews and Gentiles, and to defend the Church against external adversaries. John wrote as a prophet, addressing the congregation for its "upbuilding, encouragement, and consolation" in such a way that by disclosing God's presence in their midst, he might enable them to worship him more fully (1 Cor. 14:3, 22-25).

Let us begin by observing that Luke, in full agreement with Paul and other apostolic writers, stressed the importance of the gift of prophecy. His Gospel gives central attention to the roles of two prophets, John the Baptist and Jesus. The relation of their *marturia* to the *logos* of God is as strategic to Luke as to John. Luke places their witness firmly in the long succession of the prophets, both those of the Old Testament period and such figures as Zechariah, Elizabeth, Simeon, and Anna. Just as the prophecies of Luke 1, 2 cover the events of the Gospel, so too do the prophecies of Pentecost in Acts 2, 3 cover the events of church history. In Acts 2:17-21 Luke uses a citation from Joel which would seem as apt if found in the *Book of Revelation*. For Luke, as for John, the chain of communication required five links: God, Christ, the angels and (or) the Holy Spirit, the prophets, the people of God (see p. 3f.).

Let us now draw a sharper focus upon certain structural elements in the thought patterns of John to see whether Luke shared those patterns to any significant degree. First we may recall the degree to which the prophet visualized the Gospel in terms of the Messiah's struggle with Satan, in which he vanquished God's chief adversary. Did Luke find this pattern of thought congenial? Fr. M. E. Boismard presents very persuasively the affirmative argument, "Luke and the Apocalypse" in *Synoptische Studien*. The fundamental ideas underlying the Lucan edition of Jesus' temptation (4:1-11) are the same as those in *Revelation* 13. In fact, Luke varies the synoptic story of the trial of the Messiah in the direction of conforming it to the apocalyptic conception (compare Lk. 4:6 and Rev. 13:4). The central test is whether Jesus is to be a false prophet or true. As a true prophet, Jesus must not only win this initial battle with Satan; he must also face and win the final battle. This entails a watchfulness (in the upper room, and at Gethsemane) to discern deceptions and to accept apparent defeat and death. Satan enters Judas as a way of launching his last assault on the Messiah. Satan uses the power of the state, the synagogue, and "false prophets" to surround, to arrest, and to execute Jesus. But Jesus responded to "the power of darkness" by remaining faithful to death (22:53). This became his hour of victory in which "the accuser of our brethren has been thrown down" (Rev. 12:10). During his ministry Jesus had been invulnerable to the violence of the adversary (Lk. 4:29, 30). Note that this invulnerability had been achieved by refusing to claim immunity (4:10, 11); but when his ministry had been completed in Jerusalem, that invulnerability had been removed (Lk. 22), and every effort by the disciples to save him from the final trial was condemned as faithlessness. Luke's pictures of Jesus as prophet conform to John's picture in almost every detail (Rev. 11:3-13). Luke fully recognizes the power of the devil, as ruler of all the kingdoms of the world (4:5; *oikoumenē* is equivalent to John's *gē*), to bestow his authority and glory on those who worship him. But Luke recognizes also that Jesus belonged to quite another kingdom which afforded him sufficient power to evict Satan from his throne. Jesus exercised this other kind of authority and glory. He could therefore proclaim the arrival of the acceptable year (4:18, 19) on the basis of his vision of Satan "fallen like lightning from heaven" (10:18; compare Rev. 12:12).

Luke described the victory of holy men over Satan in ways comparable to the Apocalypse, and with literary forms which reflect the same moods and motifs. The hymns in the nativity stories, for example, and in the account of the Pentecostal church, are all hymns of triumph (compare Lk. 1:50-54; 1:68-75; Acts 4:24-26 with the songs in Rev. 7 and 15). As in Revelation, the Lucan hymns are located at strategic places in the narratives, and they articulate the victory of the whole Church as well as the faith of specific individuals. The songs of angels and the doxologies of men are comparable in both form and function to the songs in Rev. 4 and 5. Angels proclaim the eternal Gospel in both documents (Lk. 1:19; 2:10; Rev. 14:6). The roles in redemption of Gabriel and Michael are analogous (Lk. 1:19, 26; Rev. 12:7), though far from identical. There are important affinities between the struggle and victory of the messianic mother in Rev. 12:1-6 and Mary's humility and trust in Lk. 1, 2. The Lucan image of virginity (1:27) is similar to the apocalyptist's image; so, too, Mary's vulnerability to the sword and her sharing in the judgment upon Israel (Lk. 2:34-35) are akin to the struggles between the woman and the devil in Rev. 12. The power which flows from the patience and the prayers of the righteous Zechariah, Mary, Simeon, and Anna is comparable to the power which emanates from the heavenly altar in Revelation. In both documents the coming of salvation provoked a far-reaching warfare between the messianic community (the Messiah, his mother, the prophetic witnesses, the holy ones) and the demonic community. Moreover, each victory of the former community presaged the coming of a final battle which would be won only by loyal endurance to the end.

Luke and John present similar attitudes toward the basic duties of Jesus' followers. In the Gospel as much as in the Apocalypse the pictures of the Messiah's struggle provide a paradigmatic norm for the community of disciples. The beatitudes and the woes in Luke 6 would sound entirely appropriate if found in Revelation—the poor and the rich (see Rev. 2:9; 3:17), the hungry and the sated (7:16), those who weep or rejoice (7:17; 21:4), those who are persecuted or praised (2:10; 6:10). So, too, the same beatitude is assured to those who hear and obey the word of God (compare Lk. 11:28 and Rev. 1:3; 22:7). Along with the other synoptists, Luke makes normative for every disciple a participation in "Jesus' agony, his royal power, and his loyal endurance."

Father Boismard presents an extensive analysis of the account of the mission of the 70 in Luke 10, showing its marked congruities to John's thinking. Sent as lambs in the midst of wolves, they are given authority over serpents and scorpions, an authority made possible by the fall of Satan from heaven. The demonic spirits are now subject to them and nothing can hurt them. Thus is overcome the curse of Gen. 3:15 (compare Rev. 11:4-8 and 12:5, 13-17). Their names have been written in heaven, and consequently the sharpest assaults of the enemy can be met with joy. Moreover, the response of Bethsaida or Chorazin to their prophetic work placed those cities in the immediate company of Tyre, Sidon, and Sodom. The portrait of the apostles' authority, their work and their conflict parallels precisely that of the two olive trees in Rev. 11. The story of John and James wishing to call down fire from heaven to destroy unrepentant cities (Lk. 9:52-56) requires for full intelligibility some such context as that provided by Rev. 11:5. But if one adopts that context, why does Jesus rebuke the two brothers? Because they do not yet understand the character of the fire? Because they are not yet entitled to exercise authority? Because only after Jesus has completed his mission of fire-casting can they begin theirs? Or because they want to use this power against their human adversaries rather than against the demonic sponsors? Whatever the answer, Luke had reason for locating the story on the way leading to Jerusalem, immediately after the announcement of Jesus' destiny. And that reason is wholly congenial to the mission of the witnesses in Rev. 11.

In both Gospel and Apocalypse one encounters the paradox of apostolic vulnerability and invulnerability. This paradox is particularly plain in Lk. 21. The disciples would be hated "by all" and would receive a violent death (21:16, 17); yet not a hair of their heads would perish (21:18). Luke resolved this paradox by distinguishing two deaths, one under Satan's control and one under God's (12:4-9), although he did not, like John, label these the first and the second deaths. The coming of the final woes will provide an opportunity for apostles to give their witness, to win their lives by their loyal endurance, and to rejoice over their redemption (21:13, 19, 28). By their watchfulness and prayer they will escape God's judgment on the earth-dwellers and will take their stand before the Son of Man (21:35, 36). This chapter conveys virtually the same understanding of the churches' situation as John's, in the Church's task of obeying Christ's commands. They were to remember with confidence their first love and their first victory; they should be alert to a coming test of their loyalty which would be as rigorous as that of Jesus and of the twelve, after Satan had received permission to sift them (22:31-38; see my essay on this text in Nov. Test. VII [1964], 128-134; also Boismard, *op. cit.*).

We have noted how central in Revelation was the view of Jerusalem both as the holy city (ch. 21, 22) and as the place of conflict with babylonic idolatry and adultery (11:8; see above, p. 99f.). We find a similar pattern of thinking in Luke. The holy city is the place where the messianic prophecy must be delivered, be rejected, and be vindicated. This city will be trodden down by the nations (Lk. 21:24; Rev. 11:1, 2). In the final battle, Satan will gather all his strength and will "surround the camp of the saints and the beloved city" (Rev. 21:9), a vision which is basically the same as that in Lk. 21:20-24. (Neither in *Revelation* nor in Luke does this prediction require interpretation as a conscious allusion to the Jewish war of 66-70 A.D.) The congruity is strengthened when we realize that the Babylon whose desolation John promised was present in the Jerusalem which killed the prophets (11:8), and that the Jerusalem whose desolation Luke promised embraced babylonic realities (Lk. 18:31-34; 19:41-44). Both Luke and John combined within a single expectation the desolation as well as the redemption of Jerusalem, recognizing thus the compresence in that city of the divine purpose and of its parodic enemy. In other words, Luke as well as John could visualize many cities as present in Jerusalem, thus expressing that type of transcendence of space which permeates the Apocalypse. A study of Luke's use of the term *today* indicates a similar sense of how specific times are transcended in the Kingdom of God. Luke visualized one judgment day as embracing God's final verdict on Nineveh, Egypt, Tyre, Sidon, Sodom (11:30-32; 11:50, 51; 17:25f.).

We may now compare the two perspectives with regard to their views of the nearness of the end and of the character and length of the interim. Do we find convincing evidence for the usual view that John's eschatology reflects a higher pitch of apocalyptic excitement than Luke's? Revelation gives this impression with its oft-repeated "I am coming soon." This formula is not found in Luke. Yet should we expect such a message from the enthroned Christ in the case of a writer who was telling the story of Jesus' earthly ministry? In relating Jesus' message concerning the Kingdom of God or the coming of the Son of Man, Luke does not hesitate to speak of its nearness. It is true that on occasion Luke protests against the expectation of a speedy denouement (19:11), but so does John (6:11). Luke also warns against the assumption that the day will tarry (21:34-36). The Lucan parables could be said to fulfill some of the same functions as John's warnings (Lk. 12:35-46; 17:25-30; 18:1-8).

John used other formulas as well to describe "things to come," such as "the season is at hand" (1:3; 22:10) or "only a short time" (6:11; 10:7; 12:12). Luke continued the synoptic tradition of expressing the urgency of the prophetic announcements by using an even greater variety of formulas (3:9, 17; 4:19-21; 9:27; 10:9, 11; 11:51; 12:20; 12:35-40). All of these formulas, whether in Luke or John, served to fix the eyes of the disciples of Jesus upon the coming fulfillment of God's promises and threats. They set the horizon of the community's expectation in a rendezvous with its master. They defined the present situation as an interim, with a duration to be determined by the master. In view of all this evidence, we conclude that it is not at all certain that whereas John expected an imminent end of history, Luke had relaxed into a less alert readiness, encouraging his Church to adjust itself to long-term expectancies.

How do John and Luke describe the character of the interim? We have already commented on the character of Christian existence during the interim. It is a period of unremitting conflict between the messianic community and its demonic adversary in which the former community is both persecuted and protected, both vulnerable and invulnerable to the designs of the Enemy. In this respect there are intriguing parallels between the stories of the mothers in Luke 2 and Revelation 12; between the destiny of the two prophets in Revelation 11 and the apostles in Luke 10 and 21; between the struggle of the Messiah in Gospel and Apocalypse; between the prosperity and adversity of the Church in Acts and in Revelation. In the main, the beatitudes of the Gospel and Apocalypse are addressed to the same community fighting the same warfare, and the woes are likewise shaped to disclose the enemies whose wills were exerted through pressures both internal and external to the Church.

What can be said about the length of the interim? It is altogether obvious that many of the symbolic estimates of duration which John employs are foreign to Luke. There seems to be nothing comparable to the 3½ times of Rev. 12:14; the 1260 days of 12:6; the thousand years of 20:4; or the ten days of 2:10. There should not be the slightest hesitation in recognizing the fact that Luke sees little value in such estimates of duration. Does this fact, however, indicate a vast shift in perspective? One may doubt it. Let us observe Luke's use of two measurements of duration which are not wholly alien.

The first of these appears in those archetypal events which Luke describes at the very beginning of Jesus' ministry, a description which is itself prophetic of the entire mission. In the temptation which took place in the wilderness (Lk. 4:1-11), Jesus was forced to struggle with the devil for the authority and glory of all the kingdoms of the world. All were assumed to be under the devil's control and all could be seen "in a moment of time." But the key to this authority was devil-worship, and Jesus refused it. In doing so he accepted to the full his own vulnerability to hunger, to accident and death. Then, in the opening episode in Nazareth, Jesus faced the sharpest kind of opposition from "all in the synagogue." They tried to cast him from "the hill on which their city was built," but divine protection prevented the success of this plan. (Note the images so common to the *Apocalypse*: the synagogue of Satan, the hill, the city of

Babylon, 4:20-30). When he announced "Today has this scripture . . . ," Jesus compared his mission to that of Elijah. In this comparison Elijah's prophecy coincided with a drought, heaven-sent, which lasted *42 months*. Is it a coincidence that the only other New Testament use of this measure of duration is found in the apocalyptic estimate of the interim? (Rev. 11:6). It is remarkable that this figure does not appear in the Old Testament narratives (1 Kings 17) or in other legends about Elijah earlier than Luke (unless one so dates James 5:17). It is also probable that it is mentioned by Luke because he saw some connection between the duration of this famine and the length of the Messiah's mission. There are numerous links between Elijah and Christ in this paragraph. There are also numerous terms which convey apocalyptic symbolism: e.g., famine, land, widow, city, mountain, etc. It is significant, therefore, that when Luke does use a figure to express the duration of a prophet's ministry it is the very figure adopted by John.

The second measurement of duration adopted by Luke (and by the other Synoptists as well) is conveyed by the word "generation." We should not press the verbal evidence unduly. Luke can and does use *genea* in the normal sense to convey a specific span of time (Acts 13:36), so that past epochs can be described as a sequence of many generations (Acts 15:21). This temporal conception is usually assumed to be operative in the prophecy adopted from Mark, "This generation shall not pass away" (21:32), in such a way as to make this an explicit measurement of time: "before forty years have passed." Yet Luke's use of the term generation is not usually dependent upon the temporal constituent. Those who heard Peter's message in Acts 2:40 were quite able to save themselves from "this evil generation." That is, not every one alive belonged to the same generation. The evil generation was in fact constituted by its rejection of the prophetic message of John the Baptist and Jesus (Lk. 7:31). At stake was the question of paternity and sonship, which could only be answered by voluntary choice. The gluttons and drunkards who followed Jesus manifested a different paternity or generation

(7:4). They were "sons of light," not "sons of this evil age" (Lk. 16:8; 20:34). It is the character of its response to Jesus that marks the cohesion of a generation (9:41). It is this response that makes this evil generation one with men of Nineveh and with men of Solomon's day (11:29-32). In fact, Luke understands the saying to signify that "this generation" must be judged for the blood of all prophets which had been slain from the earth's foundation (11:48-52). Men's response to God's messengers determined their paternity, their responsibility, their fate. By its rejection of the Son of Man, "this generation" demonstrated its unity with the men of Noah's day and of Lot's, and thereby brought upon itself the same sudden, unexpected judgment (17:25-30). In short, this category serves a function in Luke's discourse entirely similar to that of the earth-dwellers in the Apocalypse. The Evangelist and the Apocalyptist announce a verdict on these faithless men, which is as sure and speedy in the Gospel as in the Apocalypse. For both authors, the category serves to represent the solidarity of men from various countries and centuries in an inheritance as ominous and sudden as the great flood.

Luke is also as forthright as John in declaring the separation of "the sons of light" from this evil generation (or the earth-dwellers). Even though heaven and earth pass away (Lk. 21:32 relates the demise of the generation to the transiency of the first creation), the words of the Messiah do not. As the woes fall on the evil generation, so redemption draws near to the faithful. The boundary between the two communities is to be discerned where Jesus' disciples obey his command and adopt his example of prayer, watchfulness, and endurance (21:32-36).

(Note: Further links between the time-consciousness of Luke and John may be discerned in their use of the term *oikoumenē* [compare Lk. 4:5; 21:26; Acts 17:6, 31; 19:27 with Rev. 3:10; 12:4; 16:14] and the use of the phrase *those who sit on the earth* [compare Luke 21:35 with Rev. 14:6].)

Let us comment finally upon one of these frontier markers, the presence of endurance, *hupomonē*. The real test of the kinship of Luke and John is not whether the language of one expressed greater imminence than that of the other, but whether their concepts of Christian duties were compatible, for it was the dialectics of inner decisions which was embodied in their description of temporal dynamisms.

A full examination would of course entail a search for the Lucan attitude towards such key Johannine imperatives as remember, repent, conquer, be faithful unto death, awake, watch, worship, hear, hold fast. I believe that Luke, along with many other New Testament writers, gave ample attention to such commands. For our purpose it may be sufficient to indicate a special affinity between Luke and John in their conception of *hupomonē*—loyal endurance. John's conception has been presented elsewhere; let us note here the gallery of examples of patience provided in the Gospel. Included are Zechariah, Elizabeth, Simeon, and Anna, the woman seeking redress before an unrighteous judge (18:1-8), and others. Then let us note the Lucan stress on certain teachings of Jesus. In his version of the parable of the seed, for example, Luke gave both common and distinctive nuances to the seed which is "the word of God" (8:11-21). In common with the other synoptists, he suggested that an understanding of the parables is equivalent to knowledge of the mysteries of God's kingdom (8:10; compare Rev. 10:7; 17:7). Such knowledge required the listening ear (8:8; Rev. 2:7), and separated the blind eye from the seeing (8:10; Rev. 3:18). The Lucan edition understood that persecution is a time of trial for the Christian (8:13), and stressed the conviction that fidelity to the word must take the form of loyal endurance (8:15). We must not ignore the change which Luke alone makes in the parable in its climactic point (8:15). What vindicates the fruitfulness of those who have received the seed in a good heart is their *endurance*. Elsewhere Luke makes it clear that the believer preserves and claims his own soul by his endurance (21:19). Here he makes it equally clear that God's word becomes fruitful for others only through his own endurance. It is quite possible, of course, that endurance meant something quite different for Luke. H. Conzelmann believes that this duty had lost its eschatological "fever" in Luke's concentration on the ethical requirements of continuing life in the world (*The Theology of St. Luke*, 231-234). And in our day, as Helen Corke has said, endurance has become "the Christian term for inertia." But I believe that Conzelmann has drawn too sharp a disjunction between the eschatological and the ethical. In Luke, as in John, it is the character of *hupomonē* which conditions and controls the temporal accent upon futurity and imminence.

PART III

Translation with Annotations

1:1 *THIS BOOK IS THE REVELATION WHICH GOD*
ENTRUSTED TO JESUS CHRIST, SO THAT HE COULD
ENABLE[1] HIS SLAVES[2] TO SEE WHAT MUST HAPPEN
2 *SOON.[3] JESUS CHRIST SENT THIS REVELATION*
THROUGH HIS ANGEL[4] TO HIS SLAVE JOHN WHO,
TELLING WHAT HE SAW, CONFIRMED GOD'S SAVING
PURPOSE AS IT HAS BEEN CONFIRMED[5] BY JESUS
CHRIST.

3 *God bless the Reader. God bless all who hear this prophecy[6] and*
who obey it, for the season is at hand![7]

4 *To the seven Asian congregations John sends grace and peace*
from the God who now rules,[8]
who has always ruled,
and who is coming to rule,
from the seven spirits[9] before his throne

---

1. See H. Schlier, TWNT, II, 26-30.
2. K. Rengstorf, TWNT, II, 264-283; Minear, *Images*, 156f.
3. Dan. 2:28, 29, 45; Isa. 48:6; Rev. 1:19; 2:16; 3:11; 11:14; 22:6, 7; Mt. 24:6; Lk. 18:8; Rom. 16:20; p. 179f.
4. See J. Michl, *Engelvorstellungen;* van der Waal, 55-86; below, p. 84.
5. Rev. 1:9; 6:9; p. 222f.; Vos, *Synoptic Traditions*, 196-207.
6. See Bieder, TZ, 10 (1954), 13-30; Vos, 54-59.
7. Rev. 11:18; 12:12; 22:10; Dan. 7:22; 12:4; Mk. 1:15; Mt. 3:2; 10:7; 13:30; 21:34; 26:18; Lk. 19:44; 21:8, 36; I Peter 1:5, 11; 4:17.
8. Lit., "who is and who was and who is to come." Here and in the other instances of this formula I have chosen the stronger verb *rule*, because the key issue was more one of effective power than of mere existence. Rev. 1:18; 4:8; 11:17; 16:5; Exod. 3:14; Isa. 41:4; 43:10; 44:6. R. M. Grant, *Gnosticism*, 70; W. C. van Unnik, NTS, 9 (1963), 87-94.
9. Rev. 3:1; 4:5; 5:6; Zech. 3:9; 4:2, 10; Isa. 11:2; Tob. 12:15. A. Skrinjar, Bib. 1935, 1-24, 113-140; J. Michl, *Engelvorstellungen*, 112-157; S. Langton, *Angel Teaching*, 187-192; E. Schweizer, Ev. Th 11 (1951-52), 502-512.

5   *from Jesus the Messiah,*
        who loyally confirmed[10] God's work,
        who became the first of the dead[11] to be reborn,
        and who is now the ruler of earth's kings.

    "To him be glory and power forever,
            for he loves us,
            he has freed us[12] from Sin's bondage by his death,
6   *he has formed us into a kingdom[13]*
                to serve God, his Father, as priests.
            Amen."

7   *"There! He is coming with the clouds.[14]*
            Everyone will see him,
            even those who pierced him.
            All earth's tribes will mourn over him,
    I vouch for this!"

            "Amen."

8   *This is what God the Lord says:*
        "I the All-Powerful,[15] am the A and the Z.
        I now rule, I have always ruled, I am coming to rule."

---

10. Lit., "testified" . . . Rev. 2:3; 3:14; 6:9; 11:7; 12:11, 17; 19:11; 20:4; p. 222f. Psa. 89:38; Isa. 55:4; Jer. 42:5; N. Brox, *Zeuge und Martyrer,* 98f.; M. Rissi, TZ, 21 (1965), 85f.
11. Psa. 89:27; Col. 1:18; Rom. 8:29; Heb. 12:23.
12. Psa. 130:8; Isa. 1:18; 40:2; I Cor. 6:11; Tit. 2:14. An alternate reading: "cleansed us," see Rev. 7:14; Psa. 51:4; Isa. 1:16.
13. Exod. 19:6; Isa. 61:6; Dan. 7:22, 27; 2 Sam. 7:14; I Peter 2:5, 9; Rev. 5:10; 20:6; Minear, *Images,* 96-104; 119-134; van der Waal, 87-122.
14. Zech. 12:10; Dan. 7:13; Isa. 40:5; 52:10; Mt. 24:30; Mk. 13:26; Lk. 21:27; John 19:34, 37; I Th. 4:17; Langenberg, BA 278-279; R. B. Y. Scott, NTS 5 (1959), 128-132; Vos, 60-71; above, p. 279f.
15. Amos 3:13 (LXX); 4:13 (LXX); Isa. 44:8; Rev. 4:8; 11:17; 15:3; 16:7; 19:6, 15; 21:22. S. Laeuchli, ThZ 16 (1960), 359-366; Delling, Nov T 3 (1959), 107-137.

I

^{1:9} I am John, your brother and full-partner with you in Jesus'
agony, in his royal power, and in his loyal endurance. I was
on Patmos Island because of God's saving purpose as confirmed
¹⁰ by Jesus. It was the Lord's Day[1] when the Spirit came upon me.
Behind me I heard a majestic voice like a trumpet calling:
¹¹   "Write what you see in a scroll.
        Send it to the seven congregations:
        Ephesus, Smyrna, Pergamum, Thyatira,
        Sardis, Philadelphia, Laodicea."

¹² When I turned to see what voice was speaking to me,
I saw seven gold candelabra,
¹³ and in the center a figure like a man:[2]
        a robe came down to his feet
        a gold scarf[3a] encircled his shoulders
¹⁴   his head and hair were white as snow,[3b] or as wool
        his eyes flashed like flames of fire
¹⁵   his legs[4] like burnished bronze, fired in a furnace
        his voice[5] had the sound of rushing rivers
¹⁶   in his right hand[6] he held seven stars
        from his mouth came a double-edged sword,[7]
            razor-sharp
        his face blazed like the sun in full strength.

¹⁷ And when I saw him, I fell like a corpse at his feet. But
touching me with his right hand, he said:
        "Have no fear![8]
        I am the First and the Last,[9] the Living One.
¹⁸   I became a corpse, but look—I am alive forever.
        I now hold the keys[10] to Death and to Hades.

19   Write down what you have seen, things present and
            things to come.
20   You saw seven stars[11] in my right hand
            and seven gold candelabra;
                    this is the secret:[12]
            those seven stars are angels of the seven congregations;
            those seven candelabra are the seven congregations.

2:1   "Take down this letter for the angel of the congregation in
        Ephesus:[13]
        'This is dictated[14] by the One who with his right hand controls
        the seven stars, who walks among the seven gold candelabra:
2   I know what you have accomplished, your toil and
                your loyal endurance.[15] I know you did not tolerate
                evil-doers, but put to the test those self-styled apostles
3   and found them to be liars, as indeed they are. You
                suffered because of me, yet you endured and did not
                grow weary.
4   But this is what I am counting against you: You have
                forsaken your first devotion.[16]
5   Remember the height from which you have fallen.
                Repent.[17]Accomplish again what you did at first.
                If you do not repent, I will come to you and will shift
                your candelabra from its place.
6   (You have this to your credit: You hate the deeds of
                the Nicolaitans,[18] which I also hate.)
7   Let everyone who can hear[19] listen to what the Spirit
                is telling the congregations.
                I will give to the victor[20] food from the Tree of Life[21]
                    in God's Paradise.' "

8   "Take down this letter for the angel of the congregation in
        Smyrna:[22]
        'This is dictated by the First and the Last, who was killed
        and came alive:[23]

9   I know your agony and your poverty (in reality, you
     are wealthy!)[24] I know the blasphemy of those
     self-styled Jews, who are not Jews but Satan's[25] own
     synagogue.

10   Do not fear what you will soon suffer. Look! The
     Devil, to put you to the test, is about to throw some
     of you into prison, where the agony will last ten
     days.[26] Be loyal to death, and I will give life to you
     as a crown.[27]

11   Let everyone who can hear listen to what the Spirit
     is telling the congregations.
     The victor will not be injured by the second
     death.' "[28]

12   "Take down this letter for the angel of the congregation in
     Pergamum:[29]
     'This is dictated by the One who wields the double-edged
     sword,[30] razor-sharp:

13   I know that you dwell where Satan has his throne,[31]
     and yet you remained loyal to me and did not spurn
     my own loyalty, even at the time when Antipas, who
     faithfully confirmed my work,[32] was killed there
     among you, where Satan dwells.

14   Yet I am counting a few things against you. Some of
     you adhere to Balaam's[33] teaching, who persuaded
     Balak to set a stumbling-block before the sons of
     Israel, leading them into idolatry[34] and fornication.

15   Some of you adhere also to the Nicolaitan teaching.

16   Repent. If you do not, I am coming to you soon and
     I will fight against them with the sword of my mouth.

17   Let everyone who can hear listen to what the Spirit
     is telling the congregations.
     I will give to the victor the bread of heaven,[35] and a
     white amulet[36] inscribed with a new name[37] known
     to none but the recipient.' "

18   "*Take down this letter for the angel of the congregation in
Thyatira:*[38]
'*This is dictated by the Son of God, whose eyes flash like
flames of fire,*[39] *whose legs are like burnished bronze:*

19   *I know what you have accomplished: your love, your
faithfulness, your service and your loyal endurance.
Lately you have accomplished even more than before.*

20   *But this is what I am counting against you. You
tolerate that woman Jezebel,*[40] *self-advertised
prophetess, who deceives my slaves and persuades*

21   *them to commit fornication*[41] *and idolatry. I have
given her time to repent of her fornication, but she
will not.*

22   *Look! I am hurling her on to a couch. Those who
consort with her I am hurling into great agony unless
they repent of her deeds. Her children I will smite*

23   *with death.*[42] *To each of you I will give whatever your
deeds merit. All the congregations will learn that I
am the One who discerns the innermost secrets.*[43]

24,25   *Until I come hold firm to what you have achieved.
I add no other obligation for you Thyatirans who do
not follow Jezebel's teaching and who do not claim
knowledge of what they call Satan's secrets.*[44]

26   *To the victor who loyally continues my work to the
end,*

                    I will give authority[45] *over the nations,
                    just as I received it from my Father.*

27   *The victor will rule them with an iron rod,
                      he will smash them like broken dishes.*

28   *To the victor I will also give the dawn-star.*[46]

29   *Let everyone who can hear listen to what the Spirit
is telling the congregations.' "*

3:1   "*Take down this letter for the angel of the congregation in
Sardis:*[47]

'This is dictated by the One who controls the seven spirits[48]
of God and the seven stars:[49]

> I know what you have accomplished. Men think of
> you as alive, but actually you are dead.[50]

2

> Wake up![51] Rouse what is about to die, those deeds
> of yours which I have found unworthy to offer to my

3

> God. Remember what you have received and heard.
> Hold fast to that and repent.
> If you do not awaken, I will come like a thief and
> you will be unable to know the hour of my coming.

4

> Among you in Sardis, however, are a few who have
> not soiled their clothing. They will walk with me in
> white,[52] for they have proved themselves worthy.

5

> So the victor will walk clothed in white,
> nor will I cross out his name from the book of life.[53]
> I will vouch for him[54] in the presence of my Father
> and his angels.

6

> Let everyone who can hear listen to what the Spirit
> is telling the congregations.' "

7

"Take down this letter for the angel of the congregation in
Philadelphia:[55]
'This is dictated by the One who is holy and true, who holds
the key of David.[56] No one can lock what he opens, or open

8

what he locks. There! I have opened to you a door which no
one can close.

> I know what you have accomplished. Even
> in your weakness you held fast to my
> purpose and did not deny my name.

9,10

> Because you held fast to the purpose of my own loyal
> endurance, I will bring members of Satan's synagogue,
> who falsely claim to be Jews, to worship at your feet[57]
> and to admit my love for you. I will shield you
> from that trial[58] which is soon to test the earth-
> dwellers[59] throughout the world.

11   *I am coming soon. Hold fast! Let no one seize your*
          crown.

12   *I will set the victor up as a pillar in my God's*
          sanctuary;
                  never again will he leave it.
          On him I will inscribe the name[60] of my God,
                  the name of my God's city,[61]
                      (the new Jerusalem which comes down
                          from heaven, from my God)
                  and my own new name.

13   *Let everyone who can hear listen to what the Spirit*
          is telling the congregations.' "

14   *"Take down this letter for the angel of the congregation in*
      Laodicea:[62]
      'This is dictated by the Amen,[63] the True and Faithful
      Guarantor, the Model[64] of God's creative work:

15   *I know what you have accomplished. You are neither*
16   *hot nor cold, when you ought to be one or the other.*
17   *Because you are tepid, neither hot nor cold, I will*
          spit you out. Because you say 'I am wealthy.[65] I lack
          nothing.' and do not see that you are miserable,
          pitiable, poor, blind, naked.

18   *This is my advice to you:*
                  Buy from me gold[66] which has been refined by
                      fire,
                      so that you may become wealthy.
                  Buy and wear white clothing,
                      to hide the disgrace of your nakedness.[67]
                  Buy salve for your eyes,
                      so that you can see.

19   *I discipline[68] and punish all whom I love. Be zealous.*
          Repent.

20   *Look! I have taken my stand at the door. I am*
          knocking.[69] To anyone who hears me calling and

who opens the door, I will come in. I will dine[70]
with him; he will dine with me.

21   *I will give to the victor a seat on my throne with me,*
just as, by my victory,
I have taken a seat with my Father on his throne.

22   *Let everyone who can hear listen to what the Spirit is*
telling the congregations.' "

---

1. Eze. 3:12; W. Stott, NTS 12 (1965), 70-74; K. Strand, NTS 13 (1967), 174-181; *Neotestamentica et Patristica* (O. Cullmann), 272-281; J. Danielou, *Bible and Liturgy*, 242-261; M. Shepherd, 81.

2. Dan. 7:13; 8:15; 10:16; Eze. 1:26; 8:2; Zech. 4:2; Mt. 16:27; Rev. 14:14; R. P. Martin, *Carmen Christi*, 205-211.

3a. Rev. 15:6; Dan. 10:5; Eze. 9:2, 11; 44:17f.; Exod. 28:39f.; 29:9; Lev. 6:3; 8:7.

3b. Mt. 17:2; Dan. 7:9; Enoch 14:20; Slav. Enoch 1:5; 37:1; H. Langenberg, BA, 226f.; Simon, ENY, 168f.

4. Rev. 2:18; Eze. 1:7 (LXX).

5. Rev. 14:2; 19:6; Eze. 1:24; 43:2; Psa. 93:4; H. G. May, JBL 74 (1955), 9-21.

6. Rev. 1:17; 2:1; 10:5; 13:16; 20:1, 4; H. Langenberg, BA, 85f.

7. Rev. 2:16; 19:15, 21; Heb. 4:12; Lk. 2:35; Isa. 11:4; 49:2; Wis. Sol. 18:15; Enoch 14:20; Simon, ENY, 168; H. Feret, 76f.

8. Rev. 2:10; 19:10; 22:8; Dan. 8:17f.; 10:8-12, 17-19; Jos. 5:14; Eze. 1:28; 3:23; 43:3; 44:4; Isa. 44:2 (LXX); Mt. 17:6; J. K. Kuntz, *Self Revelation of God*, 59-71.

9. Rev. 2:8; 22:13; Isa. 41:4; 44:6; 48:12; Psa. 90:2; John 8:58.

10. Rev. 3:7; 9:1; 20:1; 21:25; Mt. 16:19; 23:13; John 20:19, 26; Isa. 22:22; Psa. 9:14; Job 38:17; J. Jeremias, TWNT I, 146-149; Simon, 173; Minear, *Christian Hope*, 175-188; F. Dölger, *Sol Salutis*, 346ff.

11. Rev. 2:1, 28; 3:1; 22:16; H. Langenberg, BA, 251-254; S-B, III, 790f.

12. Rev. 10:7; 17:5, 7; R. E. Brown, Bib. 39 (1958), 431-434.

13. A. Fabre, RB 7 (1910), 161-178, 344-367; J. Keil, *Ephesos*, 1955; Forschungen in Ephesos, österreichen archäologischen Institut (1906-1953); D. Magie, I, 446f.; 577f.; II, 1432f.; also above, p. 52f.

14. For the origin of the pattern of seven letters, see J. M. Rife, JBL, 60 (1941), 179-182; and for literary analysis, above, p. 41f.
15. Above p. 23f.
16. Jer. 2:2; Hos. 1-3; Rev. 2:5.
17. Rev. 2:16; 21f.; 3:3, 19; 9:20f.; 16:9f., above p. 216f.
18. Rev. 2:15; H. Zimmermann, 191f.; P. Janzon, SEA, 21 (1956), 82-108.
19. Rev. 13:9; 21:7; 22:2; Mk. 4:9, 23; 7:16; Mt. 11:15; Lk. 8:8; 14:35; Horst, TWNT, V, 557 M. Dibelius, Th STK, 83 (1910), 461-471; Vos, 71-75.
20. Rev. 11:7; 12:11; 13:7; 15:2; 17:14; 19:11; O. Bauernfeind, TWNT, IV, 941-945; Leivestad, 212-238; F. Dölger, SS, 210; above p. 170f.
21. Rev. 22:2, 14; Gen. 2:9; 3:22; Eze. 47:12; Enoch 24:3-6; 25:4-6; Slav. En. 8:2-4; TL, 18:10, 11; Psa. Sol. 14:2, 3; Lk. 23:43; H. Zimmermann, 177; J. Dupont, 152; S-B, III, 792; F. Dölger, SS, 220-226.
22. C. J. Cadoux, *Ancient Smyrna*, 228-366; Wm. Ramsay, *Letters to Seven Churches*, ch. 19, 20; P-W, III A1, 1927, 730-765.
23. For use of contrapuntal motifs of death and life, see Rev. 1:5; 18; 2:10, 11; 3:1; 11:7, 11; 12:11; 13:3, 12, 14; 14:13; 20:4, 5, 12.
24. For similar use of motifs of poverty and wealth, compare Rev. 3:17f.; 6:15; 13:16; 18:3, 15, 16; Mt. 19:21f.; Mk. 10:21; 12:42f.; Lk. 4:18; 6:20, 24; 14:21; 2 Cor. 6:10; 8:9; James 2:5.
25. Rev. 3:9; Num. 20:4; 31:16; 2 Cor. 11:14; Hans Bietenhard, *Die himmlische Welt*, 209-221; H. Schlier, *Principalities and Powers;* K. Heim, *Jesus the Lord*, Ch. 9-15; W. Frend, *Martyrdom and Persecution*, 15f.
26. Dan. 1:12, 14; B. Gerhardsson, *The Testing of God's Son*, 25-42.
27. Rev. 3:11; 4:4, 10; 6:2; 9:7; 12:1; 14:14; James 1:12; 1 Peter 5:4; 2 Tim. 4:8; 1 Cor. 9:25; H. Langenberg, BA, 99f.; J. Dupont, 150ff.; Vos, 192; R. Leaney, 152.
28. Rev. 20:6, 14; 21:8; S-B, III, 830f.; above p. 174f.
29. See above pp. 000; *Altertümer von Pergamon*, Vol. 1-8 (1885-1930); E. V. Hansen, *The Attalids of Pergamon* (1947); D. Magie, *Roman Rule in Asia Minor*, I, 1-33, 446f., 564, 582f.; P. Wood, Exp T 73 (1961-62), 263f.; H. Kähler, *Der grosse Fries von Pergamon* (1948); *Pergamon* (1949).
30. See note on 1:16, above p. 252f.
31. Notice variety in the uses of this motif: 1:4; 2:13; 3:21; 4:2-10;

7:9-17; 12:5; 13:2; 16:10; 20:11f.; see H. Langenberg, BA, 125-128; L. Mowry, JBL 71 (1952), 75-84.

32. The Greek phrase describing Antipas is identical with the phrase describing Christ in 1:5. Compare Psa. 89:38; see N. Brox, 92-105.

33. Rev. 2:20; Num. 22:1f.; 31:16; 25:1f.; Jude 11; S-B III, 793; K. G. Kuhn, TWNT, I, 524f.; R. Leaney, 74.

34. Lit., "Food sacrificed to idols." Rev. 2:6, 20; Jude 11; 2 Peter 2:15; Acts 15:20, 29; 21:25; C. Barrett, NTS, 11 (1965), 138-153. The term is closely related, if not identical, to the more general "idolatry," Rev. 9:20; 21:8; 22:15, and the worship of the beast, Rev. 13:14f.; 14:9, 11; 15:2; 19:20; 20:4; Patai, 140-157.

35. John 6:31-49; Psa. 78:24; Ex. 16:13-15; Bar. 29:8; Mt. 6:11; Mk. 14:22; 1 Cor. 10:1-5; P. Borgen, *Bread from Heaven;* S-B, II, 481-485; III, 793f.; J. Daniélou, *Bible and Liturgy,* 147ff.

36. The symbolism of white is important. See note on 1:17; the significance of the amulet is less certain and less common. Beckwith, 461-463; Charles, I, 66f.; Caird, 42; Lohmeyer, 27.

37. For importance of the symbol of the name, Rev. 2:3, 13, 17; 3:1, 5, 8, 12; 6:8; 11:18; 13:1, 6, 8, 17; Isa. 62:2; 65:15; S-B III, 794; J. Pedersen, *Israel,* I, 245-259; H. Bietenhard, TWNT, V, 269-283; R. Harrisville, *Newness in the N.T.,* 93f.; F. Dölger, Sp, 56-60; 149f.

38. See biblio. on the seven cities, p. 61f. Thyatira is the site of the modern Akhisar. There have been very few archaeological results of significance for N.T. study. P-W, VI A1, 1936, 756ff.

39. The prominence of fire and the range of connotations may be seen in the following: Rev. 1:14; 3:18; 4:5; 8:5; 9:17f.; 11:5; 13:13; 14:10, 18; 18:8; 19:12, 20; cp. Mk. 9:43-49; Lk. 12:49; 1 Cor. 3:13, 15; Acts 2; 1 Peter 1:7; Heb. 12:29.

40. Rev. 2:6, 14, 15, 20, a symbolic name based on 1 Kings 16:31; 18:19; 2 K. 9:22ff., probably to be associated with the Balaamites and Nicolaitans. See note on 2:14.

41. See note on 2:14; also 1 K. 16:31; 21:25; 2 K. 9:22; Num. 25:1f.; 31:16; this image has major importance for John: Rev. 9:21; 14:8; 17:1-16; 18:3, 9; 19:2; 21:8; 22:15. H. Langenberg, BA, 56; Hauck, TWNT, VI, 594f.; above p. 217f.

42. Patai, 140-149. Compare the death of the sons of Ahab, 2 K. 10:7.

43. Jer. 11:20; 17:10; 20:12; Psa. 7:10; Psa. 26:2; 1 Sam. 16:7; Prov. 17:3; 21:2; Lk. 16:15; P. Borgen, *Bread from Heaven,* 72.

44. Perhaps the special "advantage" claimed by the Nicolaitans, H. Zimmermann, 193.

45. Psa. 2:8, 9.

46. Isa. 14:12; 2 P. 1:19; A. Fabre, RB (1908), 227-240.

47. G. M. A. Hanfmann, BASOR, 154 (1959), 1-35; P-W, IA2, 1920, 2475ff. H. C. Butler, Publications of the American Soc. for Excavation of Sardis, Part I; P. Wood, Exp. T 73 (1961-62), 263f.; D. Magie, I, 500f.

48. See note on 1:4; Isa. 11:2; Zech. 3:9; 4:10.

49. See note on 1:20.

50. See note on 2:8, also Dupont 150f.

51. Lit. "watch," 16:15; Mt. 24:42f.; 25:13; 26:38-40; Mk. 13:37; Lk. 12:37-39; 1 Cor. 16:13; Col. 4:2; 1 Th. 5:6-10; 1 P. 5:8; cf. E. Lövestam, 95-107; P. Minear, Christian Hope, 128-138; Vos, 75-84; above p. 148f.

52. Rev. 3:18; 4:4; 6:11; 7:9, 13; 19:14; Mt. 17:2; 28:3; John 20:12; Acts 1:10; Enoch 71:1; J. Z. Smith, HR 5 (1966), 217-238; S-B, III, 794f.; Allo 59-61; Langenberg, BA, 90-94.

53. Ex. 32:33; Psa. 69:29; 1 Sam. 25:29; Dan. 12:1; Lk. 10:20; Heb. 12:23; above p. 83.

54. Mt. 10:32; Lk. 12:8; Vos, 86-94.

55. See biblio. on Asian cities and churches p. 61f., the modern city is Alasehir. P-W XIX, 2, 1938, 2091f.; W. Calder, BJRL 7 (1922), 309-354.

56. See note on 1:18; Isa. 22:22; Job 12:14; S-B, I, 736, 741; Simon, ENY, 173; Minear, Christian Hope, 175-187; L. Brun, 97f.

57. Isa. 43:4; 45:14; 49:23; 60:14; Psa. 72:9; Lk. 14:25.

58. See S. Brown, JBL, 85 (1966), 308-314.

59. See above p. 261f. Isa. 24:17; Hos. 4:1; Joel 1:2; 2:1; Psa. 24:1; 33:8; 49:1; Enoch 37:5; 54:9; 55:1; 60:5; 65:6, 12; 66:1.

60. See note on 2:17.

61. Rev. 21:2; Isa. 56:5; 62:2; 66:15; Eze. 48:35; Enoch 90:29; S-B III, 795.

62. See above p. 56f.; S. E. Johnson, BA 13 (1950), 1-18; P-W, XII, 1, 1924, 722-724; M. Rudwick & E. Green, Exp. T. 69 (1957-58), 176f.; W. Ramsay, Cities and Bishoprics, I, 32-82; D. Magie, I, 577f.

63. 2 Cor. 1:20. See A. Stuiber, JAC 1 (1958), 153-158; L. Silberman, JBL, 82 (1963), 213-215; J. Danielou, Jewish Christianity, 337f.; H. Schlier, TWNT I, 341.

64. Prov. 8:22; John 1:1-3; Rom. 8:29; Col. 1:15.

65. See note on 2:9; Hosea 12:8f.; Zech. 11:5; Rev. 17:7.

66. See Concordance for frequent use; compare esp. 1 P. 1:7, 18; H. Langenberg, BA, 111-114.
67. See note on 3:4, 5 and on 1:13.
68. Prov. 3:12; Heb. 12:7f.; 1 P. 1:7; 4:12; Rom. 5:1f.; 1 Cor. 11:32; James 1:2.
69. Song of Songs, 5:2; R. P. C. Hanson, 34.
70. Jas. 5:9; Luke 12:35-37; A. Ehrhardt, Ev Th, 1957, 431-445; J. Behm, TWNT, II, 33-35; Charles I, 100f.; Swete, 63; Hadorn, 64; Vos, 94-100.

II

4:1   *Afterward I looked: There!*
A door into heaven had been thrown open.[1]
Again I heard the first trumpet-voice[2] *telling me:*
    "Come up here.[3]
    I must help you see what must happen."
2   *At once I was filled with the Spirit.*

    There!
    In heaven a throne[4] *had been placed.*
3   *Sitting on it One whose appearance*
        resembled jasper and carnelian.
    Encircling the throne a rainbow, bright as emerald.
4   *Surrounding the throne twenty-four thrones,*
    twenty-four elders[5] *enthroned, in white robes with gold*
        crowns.
5   *From the throne came lightning, voices, thunder;*[6]
    in front of the throne seven blazing torches (the spirits of
        God);
6   *in front of the throne, a lake of glass, clear as crystal.*
    At the center,[7] *around the throne, four living creatures*[8]
        full of eyes on all sides,
7   *the first like a lion, the second an ox,*
        the third with human face, the fourth like an eagle
            in flight.
8   *Each of the four had six wings,*
        Each was full of eyes, inside and out.
        Day and night, without ceasing they sang:
            "Holy, holy, holy,[9]
            God, all-powerful Lord,
                who now rules
                who has always ruled
                who is coming to rule."

9   *As these living creatures give glory, praise and thanks*
         to the Enthroned who is forever alive,

10   *the twenty-four elders prostrate[10] themselves before the*
         Enthroned, worshiping him who is forever alive,
    they throw their crowns before the throne, singing:

11   *"You are worthy[11] our Lord, our God,*
         to receive glory, praise, power,
         because you created everything.
         You willed everything to exist as your
         creation."

5:1   *In the right hand of the Enthroned I saw a scroll,*
    with script inside and out, fastened with seven seals.

2   *I saw a powerful angel, shouting with mighty voice:*
         "Who has earned the right to break the
         seals,
         to open this scroll?"

3   *No one had the power to open the scroll[12] and to look*
         inside,
    no one in heaven, on earth or beneath the earth.

4   *I was in tears because no one[13] had been found*
         who had earned the right to do this,

5   *but one of the elders said to me:*
         "Stop crying! Look!
         David's son, the lion from Judah's tribe,[14]
         is the victor.
         He has earned the right to open the scroll
         and its seals."

6   *Between the throne and the four living creatures,*
         in the midst of the elders, I saw a Lamb![15]
         He stood as one slaughtered.[16]
         He had seven horns and seven eyes
         (the seven spirits of God assigned to the whole
         earth).

7   *He came and took the scroll from the right hand*
8   *of the Enthroned.*

At that moment
the four living creatures and the twenty-four elders
prostrated themselves before the Lamb.
Each carried a harp and gold bowls full of incense[17]
    (the prayers[18] of holy men).

9   They chanted a new hymn:[19]
        "You have earned the right
            to receive the scroll and open its
            seals,
        for you were slaughtered,
            with your blood you purchased for
            God
        men from every race and language, nation
            and people;

10   you created them priests,[20] a kingdom for
            our God,—
        as kings they will rule over the earth."

11   Surrounding the throne, around the living creatures and
        the elders,
    I saw many angels, angels by the thousands and the tens
        of thousands.

12   I heard them singing loudly:
        "The slaughtered Lamb has earned the right
        to receive power and wealth, wisdom and
            strength,
        honor and glory and blessing."[21]

13   I heard the song of every creature in heaven,
    on earth, under the earth, in the sea:
        "Eternal blessing and honor, glory and
            power
        To the Enthroned and to the Lamb."

14   "Amen" shouted the four living creatures.
    The elders prostrated themselves in worship.

6:1   I saw[22] the Lamb break one of the seven seals;
    I heard one of the four living creatures shout like thunder,
    "Come!"

I looked
2   There! A white horse—
      its rider carried a bow,
      a crown was given him,
      as victor he rode out to win the victory.

3   When the Lamb broke the second seal,
    I heard the second living creature shout, "Come!"
4   Another horse came, fiery red—
      its rider was given a huge sword,
      he was given power to take peace[23] from the earth,
      to make men slaughter one another.

5   When the Lamb broke the third seal
    I heard the third living creature shout, "Come!"
    I looked
      There! A black horse—
      its rider carried a pair of scales in his hand.
6   I heard what sounded like a cry from the midst of the
            four living creatures:
         "Charge a day's pay for a quart of wheat or
            three quarts of barley,
         but do not harm the olives or the wine."[24]

7   When the Lamb broke the fourth seal,
    I heard the fourth living creature shout, "Come!"
8   I looked
      There! A pale horse—
      its rider's name is Death;
      Hades rides with him.[25]
    Authority was given to them over a quarter of the earth
    to slaughter with sword, famine, death,
         and by the earth-beasts.[26]

9   When the Lamb broke the fifth seal,
    I saw beneath the altar[27]

 the souls of men who had been slaughtered
 because of God's saving purpose and the confirmation they
  gave to it.

10 *They shouted with a loud voice:*
  "O Master, holy and true,
  how long until you judge and avenge
  our slaughter[28] by the earth-dwellers?"

11 *A white robe was issued to each of them.*
 They were instructed to rest a little while longer
 until the count was complete of fellow-slaves and brothers
 who would soon be slain as they had been.

12 *When the Lamb broke the sixth seal,*
 I looked
  There came a great earthquake:[30]
  the sun turned black [31] as funeral smoke,
  the whole moon became like blood,
13 *stars fell from sky to ground*
  like a fig tree, hurricane-driven, scattering its figs.
14 *The sky was rolled up like a scroll.*
  Every mountain and island was dislodged.
  Taking cover[32] in caves and mountain crevices,
15 *the earth's kings, potentates, generals,*
  millionaires, bosses, freemen, slaves,
  begged the mountains and the rocks:
16   *"Fall on us![33]*
   Hide us from the face of the Enthroned!
   Hide us from the anger of the Lamb!
17   *The great day[34] of their anger has arrived.*
   Who has the power to stand against them?"

7:1 *Afterward I saw four angels standing at earth's four corners,[35]*
 controlling the earth's four winds, lest they blow on earth or
 sea or trees.

2   *I saw another angel, rising from the east,*[36]
     carrying the brand[37] *of the living God.*
     It shouted to the four angels
     Who had received power to hurt the earth and sea:
3   *"Don't hurt the earth or the sea or the trees*
        until we have branded
        the forehead of the slaves of our God."
4   *I heard the count of those who were branded: 144,000.*
     There were 12,000[38] *from every tribe*[39] *of the sons of Israel,*
     12,000 branded from
5   *the tribe of Judah, the tribe of Reuben,*
6   *the tribe of Gad, the tribe of Asher,*
        the tribe of Napthali, the tribe of Manasseh,
7   *the tribe of Simeon, the tribe of Levi,*
8   *the tribe of Issachar, the tribe of Zebulon,*
        the tribe of Joseph, the tribe of Benjamin.

9   *Afterward I looked. There!*
       A huge crowd, too huge to be counted,
       from every nation, tribe, tongue, people,[40]
       standing before the throne,
       standing before the Lamb,
       wearing white robes,
       palm branches[41] *in their hands,*
10   *shouting with tremendous voice:*
          "Salvation to our enthroned God!
          Salvation to the Lamb!"

11   *All the angels surrounded the throne, the living creatures, the*
     elders—
     they prostrated themselves before the throne,
     they worshiped God, and sang:
12   *"Amen!*
       Blessing and glory
       wisdom and gratitude
       praise and power and majesty

to our God forever.
Amen!"[42]

13 *One of the elders asked me, "Who are those who are wearing*
    the white robes? Where do they come from?"
14 *I replied, "My master, that is something you know."*
    Then he told me:
        "These are coming from the great agony,
        they washed their robes,[43]
        bleaching them white in the Lamb's blood.
        That is why they now stand before God's throne,
15   *worshiping him night and day in his temple.*
        That is why the Enthroned dwells[44] *with them.*
16   *Never again will they hunger or thirst.*
        The sun does not scorch them, nor any fire,
17   *for the Lamb at the throne will be their shepherd.*[45]
        He will guide them to the fountain of living water.
        God will brush every tear from their eyes."

8:1 *When the Lamb broke the seventh seal, there was dead silence*[46]
     in heaven for half an hour. . . .

---

1. Rev. 3:8, 20; 9:2; 11:19; 15:5; 19:11; Mt. 3:16; John 1:52;
    10:3; Acts 10:11; Exod. 19:16, 20, 24; W. van Unnik in *Apopho-
    reta*, 269-280.
2. Rev. 1:10; Josh. 6; Judges 7; Num. 10:1-3; Isa. 27:12f.; 1 Cor.
    15; 1 Thes. 4:16; Mt. 24:31; Heb. 12:19; *War of Sons of Light*,
    M. Burrows, 392f.; Caird, 107-110.
3. Dan. 2:28, 29, 45; Exod. 19:16, 24; Rev. 11:12; R. E. Brown,
    CBQ 20 (1958), 420f.
4. For use in Rev. see H. Langenberg, BA, 125-128; also Bieten-
    hard, *Himmlische Welt*, 53-99; also 1 Kings 22:19; Isa. 6:1;
    Eze. 1:26; 10:1; Dan. 7:9; 2 Chron. 18:18; Psa. 11:4; 47:9;
    103:19; Sirach 1:8; Enoch 14:18, 20; Slav. En. 20:3; 22:1; S-B
    I, 974f.
5. See above p. 83

6. Rev. 4:5; 6:1; 10:3, 4; 11:9; 14:2; 16:18; 19:6; Exod. 19:16-20; Deut. 5:22; 32:41; Psa. 18:7-15; 29:3-9; 77:18f.; Eze. 1:4-28; Dan. 7:9; Enoch 59; Bar. 21:6.

7. See R. R. Brewer, JBL 71 (1952), 227-231.

8. See above p. 83f.

9. Isa. 6:3; Slav. En. 8:8; 17; 19:6; 21:1; 22:3; J. Horst, 274f.; Proksch, TWNT, I, 100-115; N. Walker, NTS 5 (1958-59), 132f.; biblio. on liturgical context, above p. 26.

10. Rev. 3:9; 5:14; 7:11; 9:20; 11:1, 16; 13:4-15; 14:7-11; 15:4; 20:4; 22:8; J. Horst, 269-291.

11. Rev. 5:12; 7:12; 12:10; 19:1; 1 Chron. 29:11, 12; Psa. 62:12; Acts 4:24; Rom. 4:17; L. Brun, 48-68.

12. Eze. 2:9f.; Isa. 29:11; Dan. 7:10; 8:26; 12:4; Enoch 89:70; 90:20; Rev. 10:2; IV Ez. 6:20; above p. 83; R. P. Martin, *Carmen Christi*, 252-255.

13. Ex. 20:4; Psa. 146:6; Dan. 7:2; Enoch 47:2; 90:20; Mk. 13:32; H. Müller, ZNTW 54 (1963), 254-267.

14. Gen. 49:9, 10; Isa. 11:1, 10; Rev. 22:16; Lk. 2:34; Rom. 15:12; Mt. 1:1; Sib. Or. III, 396; S-B III, 801.

15. For the dominance of this image, see Rev. 5:12, 13; 6:1, 16; 7:9-17; 12:11; 13:8, 11; 14:1-10; 15:3; 19:7f.; 21:9-27; 22:1f.; Isa. 53:7; Zech. 4:10; Ex. 12:3, 6; Jer. 11:19; Acts 8:32; 1 P. 1:19; John 1:29, 36; W. Köster, in *Vom Wort des Lebens*, 152-174. Compare biblio. on christology, above p. 33f.

16. The prophet uses the same Greek word to apply to several figures: 5:9, 12; 6:4, 9; 13:3, 8; 18:24. Compare above p. 201f. This is the word used in the LXX for Abraham's sacrifice (Gen. 22:10), for the Passover Lamb (Ex. 12:6), and for the peace offering (Lev. 17:5).

17. Psa. 141:2; Lk. 1:10; Rev. 8:3, 4; Langenberg, BA, 188-190; Simon, ENY, 186f.

18. What prayers? The familiar Lord's Prayer takes on new meanings when placed in such a context. R. E. Brown, *N.T. Essays*, 217-252; G. Caird, 145.

19. Rev. 14:3; Psa. 144:9; 33:3; 40:4; 96:1; 149:1; Isa. 42:10; Psa. Sol. 3:2; Judith 16:1, 13; Harrisville, 96f.; L. Brun, 48-68; S-B III, 801; J. Horst, 276f.

20. See note on 1:6, also biblio. on liturgy, p. 26.

21. See L. Brun, 48-68.

22. On the interpretation of the four horsemen. See A. Feuillet, ZNTW, 57 (1966), 229-260; M. W. Müller, ZNTW 8 (1907), 290-316; J. S. Considine, CBQ 6 (1944), 406-422; M. Rissi, Int. 18 (1964), 407-418; E. Lohmeyer, 59f.; W. Baldensperger,

RHPR (1924); Allo, 92-102; Simon, ENY, 166. For possible use of Wis. Sol. 11-19, see R. Hanson, 70f.; for relation to synoptic parallels, Mk. 13, Charles, I, 158-160; Vos, 181-191; Zech. 1:8; 6:2-6; Eze. 5:12-17; above p. 266f.

23. Mt. 10:34; Lk. 12:51; Jub. 23:19; Eth. Enoch 56:7; 4 Esdras 5:5; Vos, 113-117.

24. H. Schlier, TWNT II, 468-471; J. Moffatt, Expos. 1908B, 359-369; S. Krauss, ZNTW, 1909, 81-89; D. Magie, I, 581; II, 1444; E. Lohmeyer, 61.

25. Rev. 2:23; 20:14; Hos. 13:14; Prov. 5:5; Eze. 33:27; 14:19; Jer. 21:7; Psa. Sol. 15:8.

26. Jer. 14:12; 15:3; Eze. 5:12, 17; 14:21; Rev. 11:7; 13:1-18; 19:19f.; 20:4, 10; see above p. 265f.

27. Rev. 8:3; Ex. 29:12; Lev. 4:7, 18, 34; 5:9; 8:15; 17:11; Heb. 12:23; S-B, III, 803.

28. Lit., "blood." Gen. 4:10; 2 Macc. 8:3; Deut. 32:43; 2 K. 9:7; Psa. 79:5, 10; Zech. 1:12; Mt. 23:35; Lk. 11:51; Heb. 11:4; 12:24; J. Behm, TWNT, I, 172-177; H. Jahnow, Leichenlied, 54f.

29. See note on 3:4.

30. Bar. 70:2f.; Am. 8:8; Hag. 2:6; Rev. 8:5; 11:13, 19; 16:18; Mk. 13:8; Mt. 27:51f.; 28:2; Lk. 21:11; H. Langenberg, 277; P. Minear, Christian Hope, 163-174; G. Caird, 88-93.

31. Joel 2:10, 31; 3:15; Isa. 13:10; Eze. 32:7, 8; Acts 2:20; Mk. 13:24, 25; Mt. 24:29; Lk. 21:25; Jahnow, 18, 231.

32. Isa. 2:10, 19, 21; 34:4, 12; Jer. 4:29; 14:3; Enoch 62:3, 5; Rev. 16:20; 20:11. See above p. 237f.

33. Hos. 10:8; Lk. 23:30; Rev. 9:6; Vos, 117-120.

34. Joel 2:11; 3:4; Nahum 1:6; Mal. 3:2; Isa. 13:16; Zeph. 1:14, 18; 2:3; Eze. 9:15; Psa. 76:8; 130:3; Enoch 22:11; 54:6; Jubilees 24:28, 30.

35. Jer. 49:36; Eze. 37:9; Dan. 7:2; Zech. 2:10; 6:5; Mt. 24:31; Slav. En. 69:22; 60:12; Jub. 2:2.

36. The East quickly developed a liturgical significance; F. Dölger, SS, 137, 215; M. Rissi, TH, 45f.

37. Eze. 9:4f.; Rev. 9:4; Exod. 12:23; Psa. Sol. 15:8, 10; John 3:33; 6:27; 2 Cor. 1:22; Eph. 1:13; 4:30; Danielou, Bible and Liturgy, 54-69; Theol. of Jewish Christianity, 147-163; G. Lampe, Seal of the Spirit, 16f.; F. Dölger, Sp, 34f., 56-71; 149f.; M. Shepherd, 90.

38. Rev. 14:1, 3; S-B III, 804; M. Rissi, TH, 89-104.

39. Rev. 21:12, 13; C. H. Harpold, Twelve Tribes of the Apoc.

40. This fourfold division of mankind is common in Rev. 5:9; 10:11; 11:9; 13:7; 14:6; 17:15.
41. The symbolism of this scene is strongly reminiscent of the Feast of Tabernacles, Danielou, *Primitive Christian Symbols*, 1-24; S-B, II, 789.
42. See biblio. on liturgy, p. 26f.; also L. Brun, 49, 57f., 64; A. Stuiber, JAC 1 (1958), 153-158; P. Glaue, ZKG 44 (1925), 184-198; H. Schlier, TWNT I, 339-342; S-B I, 242f., III, 456-471; J. Horst, 279ff.
43. Exod. 19:10, 14; Dan. 12:1; Gen. 49:11; Mt. 24:21; Rev. 2:9, 10, 22; 3:4, 5; 19:13; 22:14; Charles, I, 186.
44. Eze. 37:27; 43:7; Isa. 4:5; Joel 4:21; Zech. 2:14; 8:3; Lev. 26:11; Psa. 68:17; En. 45:4; compare Y. Congar, *Mystery of the Temple*, 204-248.
45. See biblio. on Christology, p. 33f.; these two verses illustrate how John fuses together echoes from many sources. Isa. 49:10; John 6:35, 37; P. Borgen, 166; Psa. 23:2; 121:6; Isa. 25:8; Eze. 34:23; Enoch 48:1f.; John 10; Eze. 37:24; Jer. 2:13; John 7:37; Isa. 25:8; Jer. 31:16; Psa. 126:5, 6.
46. Heb. 2:20; Zech. 2:17; M. Rissi, TH, 3-6.

III

8:2 I saw the seven angels[1]
who have taken their stand before God.
Seven trumpets[2] were given to them.

3　　Another angel came and took his stand before the altar.
He was holding a gold censer.
A large supply of incense[3] was given him
that he might offer the prayers of all the holy ones
at the gold altar before the throne.
4　　The smoke of the incense with the prayers of the holy
　　　　ones
billowed up before God from the hand of the angel.
5　　The angel grasped the censer,
filled it with fire from the altar,
hurled it on the earth.
Thunders rolled, shouts,
bolts of lightning, an earthquake.

6 The seven angels raised their trumpets
and got ready to blow.
7 The first blew:
hail came,[4] and fire mixed with blood;
it was hurled on the earth.
A third of the earth was burned,
a third of the trees were burned,
all the green grass was burned.

8 The second angel blew:[5]
something like a great mountain on fire
was hurled into the sea.

9   A third of the sea turned into blood,
         a third of everything alive in the sea died,
         A third of the ships foundered.

10   The third angel blew:[6]
         a great star, burning like a torch, fell from heaven,
         fell on a third of the rivers,
         fell on a third of the springs of water
11   (its name was Wormwood).
         A third of the waters turned into wormwood.
         Hosts of men died from the waters,
         for they were poisoned.

12   The fourth angel blew:[7]
         a third of the sun was plagued,
         a third of the moon, a third of the stars;
         a third of their light was quenched,
         a third of the daylight failed,
                   likewise the night.

13   I saw an eagle flying in mid-heaven.
             I heard him shout with a loud cry:
                   "Woe, woe, woe!
                Three angels are about to blow the three
                   last trumpets—
                these are the three woes against the
                   earth-dwellers."[8]

9:1   The fifth angel blew:
             I saw a star[9] which had fallen from sky to earth;
             to it was given the key to the shaft of the Abyss.
2   When it opened the shaft of the Abyss,
             smoke poured from the shaft as from a huge furnace;

sun and air were darkened by the smoke from the Abyss.

3 *From the smoke came locusts*[10] *over the earth,*
   Authority was given to them, like the authority of earth's
         scorpions.[11]

4 *They were ordered not to injure earth's grass, shrub or*
         tree,
   but only men who lack God's brand on their foreheads.

5 *They were ordered not to kill them*
   but only to torment them for five months—[12]
   a torment like the torment of scorpion stings.

6 *In those days men will long for death*[13]
            but will not find it;
       they will desire to die
            but death will flee from them.

7 *The locusts resembled horses*[14] *groomed for battle;*
          on their heads crowns like gold,
          their faces like human faces,

8   *their hair like woman's hair,*
          their teeth like lion's teeth,

9   *their breastplates like breastplates of iron,*
          the clatter of their wings like chariots,
             drawn by many horses, rushing to battle.

10 *They had tails and stingers like scorpions;*
          in their tails lay their power to wound men for
             five months.

11 *Over them as King is the angel of the Abyss.*
   His name in Hebrew is Abaddon,[15] *in Greek*
          Apollyon.

12   This one woe has gone.
                      Attention!
                      Two woes are yet to come!

13   The sixth *angel blew:*
from the corners of the gold altar before God,

14   *I heard a voice command the sixth angel with the*
trumpet:

"Set loose the four angels who are bound at the
Euphrates,[16] the great river."

15   *The four angels were set loose. They had been kept ready*
for the hour, the day, the month and the year, to kill one

16   *third[17] of mankind. I heard the count of the cavalry:*
two hundred million. This is how I saw the horses
and their riders in the vision:

17   *Breastplates were fiery red, blue, yellow;*
the horses' heads like lion's heads,
from their mouths poured fire, smoke, sulphur.

18   *A third of mankind was killed by these three*
plagues,
                    by fire, smoke, sulphur pouring from
their mouths.

19   *The authority of the horses is in their mouth*
and tails;
their tails are like serpents,
tails with heads with which they wound.

20   *The rest of mankind, not killed by these plagues,*
refused to repent[18] their handiwork.
They went on worshiping demonic forces,
idols of gold, silver, bronze, stone, wood,
which have no power to see, hear or walk.

21   *They refused to repent their murders,*
their sorcery, their fornications, their thefts.

10:1   *I saw another powerful angel*
            coming down from heaven
            wrapped in a cloud.

> *On his head a rainbow,*
> *his face like the sun,*
> *his legs like pillars of fire,*
2   *holding a lttle scroll, unrolled.*
> *His right foot he planted on the sea,*
> *his left foot on the land.*
3   *He shouted with a roar like a lion.*
> *When he shouted, the seven thunders[19] added*
>   *their own voices.*
4   *When I heard what the seven thunders said,*
> *I was about to write it down,*
> *but I heard a heavenly voice saying,*
>   *"Don't write that!*
>   *Seal up what the seven thunders said!"*

5   *The angel whom I had seen*
> *standing on sea and land*
> *raised his right hand to heaven,*
6   *took an oath by the One who lives forever,*
> *who created the heaven and everything in it,*
> *the earth and everything in it,*
> *the sea and everything in it.*
7   *"The time for delay[20] has passed.*
>   *In these days of the seventh angel,*
>   *when he will blow his trumpet,*
>   *the mystery[21] of God will be accomplished*
>   *as he promised the prophets,[22] his own slaves."*

8   *The heavenly voice which I had heard*
> *commanded me again*
>   *"Go. Take the unrolled scroll[23]*
>   *from the angel's hand,*
>   *who stands on sea and land."*
9   *I went up to the angel,*
> *asking for the scroll.*

He said:

> "*Take it. Eat it.*[24]
> *It will turn your stomach sour,*
> *but in your mouth it will be honey-sweet.*"

10   *I took the scroll from his hand and ate it.*
It was honey-sweet in my mouth,
but when I swallowed, my stomach turned sour.

11   *They said:*

> "*Again you must prophesy*[25]
> *to peoples, nations, tongues*
> *and many kings.*"

11:1   *A reed like a rod*[26] *was given me with the command:*

> "*Rise. Take the measure*[27] *of God's temple,*
> *of its altar, and those who worship there.*

2   > *Exclude the court outside the temple.*
> *Don't measure it, for it was given to the*
> *Gentiles.*
> *For forty-two months*[28] *they will despoil*[29] *the*
> *Holy City.*

3   > *I will give authority to my two witnesses*
> *and they will have power to prophesy,*
> *clothed in sackcloth, for 1260 days.*

4   > *They are two olive trees,*[30] *two lamps,*
> *who now confront the earth's master.*

5   > *When anyone tries to wound them,*
> *fire*[31] *bursts forth from their mouths*
> *and devours their enemies.*
> *When anyone tries to wound them,*
> *he must be killed in this way.*

6   > *They hold authority to shut up the sky*[32]
> *so that no rain fall during their prophecy.*
> *They hold authority over the waters*
> *to turn them into blood.*[33]

They have authority over the earth
to smite it with plague[34]
as often as they wish.

7   *When they have completed their testimony*
the beast[35] *which ascends from the Abyss*
will fight against them, conquer and kill them,

8   *their corpse on the street of the Great City,*[36]
called in prophetic language Sodom and Egypt,
where also their lord was crucified.

9   *Men from peoples, tribes, tongues and nations*
will stare at their corpse for three days and a
*   half*
and refuse to allow them burial.

10   *The earth-dwellers*[37] *will gloat over them,*
celebrating, sending gifts to one another,
for these two prophets had been a torment[38]
to the earth-dwellers.

11   *But after three days and a half*
a spirit of life from God entered them.
They stood on their feet.
Terror laid hold of the onlookers.

12   *They heard a loud command from heaven:*
*   'Come up here.'*
They ascended[39] *to heaven on the cloud.*
Their enemies stared at them.

13   *In that very hour came a great earthquake;*[40]
a tenth of the city was shattered,
seven thousand men perished in the earthquake.
The rest were struck with terror
and gave glory to the God of heaven."

14   The second Woe has passed. Attention!
                          The third Woe comes quickly.

15   *The seventh* angel blew.
    Loud voices in heaven began to shout:
        "The kingdom of the world has now become
        the kingdom of our Lord and of his Messiah.
        He will rule forever."[41]

16   *The twenty-four elders,*
    seated on their thrones before God,
    prostrated themselves.
17   *They worshiped God:*
        "We thank you, Lord, all-powerful God,
        you who now rule and have always ruled,
18   *you have used your great power,*
        you have established your rule.
        The nations were enraged
        when your fury came,
        the time for the dead to be judged,
        the time for rewarding your slaves,
        the prophets, the holy ones, those who
            worship your name, both small and great,
        the time to destroy earth's destroyers."[42]

---

1. S-B, III, 805f. See biblio. on angels p. 84.
2. See note on 4:1. U. Simon, 186f.; Minear, *Christian Hope;* Sellers,
    BA 4 (1941), 40.
3. See note on 5:8; R. Leaney, 133.
4. Four of the plagues are directly related to those of the Exodus:

hail	Rev. 8:7	Ex. 9:18-26
blood-sea	8:8	7:17-21
darkness	8:12	10:21-23
locusts	9:3-11	10:4-15

    hail—other allusions, Joel 3:3; Isa. 28:2; Wis. Sol. 5:22; Eze.
    38:22; S-B, III, 808.
5. Jer. 51:25; Psa. 78:44; Hos. 4:3; Isa. 2:16; E. Hilgert, 148f.
6. Isa. 14:12; Dan. 8:10; Jer. 9:14; Deut. 29:17; Am. 5:7; 6:12;
    Sib.Or. 5:158f.
7. Am. 8:9; Joel 2:10; 3:4; Isa. 13:10; Am. 5:18, 20; Mt. 24:29.

8. See above p. 261f.; H. Feret, 99f.
9. Isa. 14:12; Dan. 8:10; Enoch 86:1; Gen. 19:28; 29:2; Ex. 19:18; Rev. 16:10; 20:2, 3.
10. Ex. 9:4; 10:12-15; Wis. Sol. 16:9.
11. Deut. 8:15; 1 K. 12:11, 4; 2 Chr. 10:11, 14; Isa. 2:6; H. Feret, 120f.
12. S-B III, 461f.; M. Rissi, TH, 25-27.
13. Job 3:21; 7:15, 16; Jer. 8:3; Rev. 6:16, 17; Mark 9:49, 50; Lk. 23:30.
14. Joel 1:1-2:11; J. Michl, BZ 23 (1935-36), 266-288; Bib. 23 (1942), 192f.
15. Rev. 20:2, 3; Job 18:14; 26:6; 28:22; 31:12; Psa. 88:12; Prov. 15:11; 27:20; S-B III, 810.
16. Gen. 15:18; Deut. 1:7; Jos. 1:4; Rev. 16:12.
17. Zech. 13:8, 9; Eze. 5:2; Charles, I, 233.
18. Isa. 17:8; 43:7, 9; Psa. 106:37; 115:4-7; 135:15-17; Dan. 5:23f.; Acts 17:29; Deut. 31:29; 32:17; Micah 5:12; Enoch 90:7; see above p. 261f. It may be noted that all the sins are infractions of the Decalog (Ex. 20:4, 5, 13-15).
19. See note on 4:1; Dan. 8:26; 12:4, 7; Hab. 2:3; Rev. 5:1; 22:10; notice the close correlation between the thunders, the trumpets, and the angels. Is this command to silence similar to the silence of 8:1?
20. Lit., "time is no more." Compare 1 Cor. 15:52; I Th 4:16; Mt. 24:31; G. Delling, TWNT III, 460-463; J. Barr, *Biblical Words for Time*, 76. Is this promise fulfilled in 11:15?
21. Isa. 27:13; Amos 3:7; Zech. 1:6; Dan. 9:6, 10; Mt. 24:31; Rom. 16:25; cf. R. E. Brown, Bib. 39 (1958), 426-434; W. van Unnik, NTS 9 (1963), 86-94.
22. The central motif of this vision 10:11; 11:3, 18; cf. A. Satake, *Gemeindeordnung*, 47-87; H. Langenberg, BA, 130-133; above p. 97f. Does John allude to so many O.T. prophets because of this conviction of a single mystery?
23. See biblio. on p. 83.
24. Eze. 2:8f.; 3:1-3; Zech. 5:2; Jer. 15:16f.; Isa. 3:14; J. Michl, Bib. (1942), 192-193; K. Schmidt, Th Z 3 (1947), 161-177.
25. Jer. 1:10; 25:30; Dan. 3:4; 7:14; Rev. 5:9.
26. Symbols of ruling, judging, shepherding: compare Psa. 2:9; Mk. 6:8; 15:19; Mt. 27:29; 1 Cor. 4:21; Heb. 1:8; Rev. 2:27; 12:5; 19:15; 21:15, 16; H. Langenberg, BA, 96.
27. Zech. 2:5f; 14:1-11; Eze. 40:3, 47; 41:13; 43:13; Jer. 31:39; 2 Sam. 8:2; 2 K. 21:13; Isa. 34:11; Amos 7:7f.; Mark 13:1f.; J. Horst, 255f.

28. Rev. 12:6; 13:5; Dan. 7:21, 25; 9:27; Lk. 4:25; James 5:17; see above p. 294f.
29. Lit., "trample"—Zech. 12:3; Isa. 63:18; Psa. 79:1; Lk. 21:24; Vos, 120-125.
30. Olive trees; see biblio. above p. 103f.; M. Rissi, TH 87.
31. See note on 2:18; n.b. esp. Luke 9:54; 12:49; also 2 Sam. 22:9; 2 K. 1:10f.; Psa. 97:3; Jer. 5:14; 4 Ez. 13:8; Enoch 14:8-22; 2 Th. 2:8; S-B III, 812; E. Watson & B. Hamilton, RSLR 2 (1966), 84-92; above p. 124f.
32. 1 K 17:1; Lk. 4:25; Vos. 125-130.
33. Ex. 7:27-11:10; Rev. 6:12; 8:7f.; 14:20; 16:3f.
34. 1 Sam. 4:8; Acts 16:23; Lk. 10:30; Rev. 9:18; 13:3; 15:1, 6f.; 16:9, 21; 21:9.
35. Dan. 7:3; Rev. 13:1; 17:8; 20:2,3; above p. 174f.
36. Isa. 1:9f.; 3:9; Eze. 16:48; 23:3-27; Mt. 10:15; Rom. 9:29; see P. Minear, NTS 13 (1966), 93-97; S-B, III, 812.
37. See above p. 262f.
38. A mark of the final conflict between the messianic and the demonic: Mt. 8:6, 29; Mk. 5:7; Lk. 16:23, 28; Rev. 9:5; 12:2; 14:10f.; 18:7, 10, 15; 20:10.
39. 2 K 2:11; Ass. Moses 38; Rev. 4:1; the extent of the analogy to the death and resurrection of Jesus (11:8) is an important issue.
40. Compare the earthquake in Mt. 27:51f. to signal the resurrection. Also Eze. 38:19-20, also note on 6:12.
41. Rev. 12:10; Ex. 15:18; Psa. 10:16; 22:28; Dan. 2:44; 7:14; Zech. 14:9; Obad. 21; Psa. Sol. 17:4; Lk. 1:32f.; J. Horst, 284f.; J. Marsh, ch. 8.
42. Psa. 2; 46:7; 99:1; 110:5; 115:13; Acts 4:25; Rom. 2:5; Rev. 10:7; 12:10; L. Brun, 61-70.

IV

11:19   The temple[1] of God in heaven was opened;
in his temple the ark[2] of his covenant appeared;
lightnings came—voices—
thunderings—huge hail-stones—earthquake.

12:1   In heaven appeared a spectacular sign:
        a woman[3] robed in the sun,
        the moon beneath her feet,
        a crown of twelve stars on her head.
2   Pregnant, she cries out,
        tormented by her birth-pangs.

3   In heaven appeared another sign: There!
        A colossal fiery dragon[4]
        with seven heads and ten horns;
        on the heads, seven crowns.
4   His tail swept up and cast to earth
        a third of heaven's stars.

The dragon took his stand before the pregnant woman,
        to devour her child at birth.
5   She gave birth to a son, a male child,[5]
        destined to rule all the nations
        with an iron rod.
Her son was snatched up to God, to God's throne.
6   The woman escaped to the wilderness,[6]
        where she receives from God a place prepared,
        where they will feed her for 1260 days.

7   War broke out in heaven:
        Michael[7] and his angels fought with the dragon;
        the dragon and his angels fought,

8   *but they did not prevail.*
   No longer was there room for them in heaven.
9   *Cast down was the colossal dragon, the primeval Snake,[8]*
   called the Devil or Satan,
   who seduces the whole world.
   He was cast down[9] to the earth,
   cast down with him his angels.

10   I *heard a loud voice in heaven:*
   "Now has come the salvation and the power,
              the kingdom of our God,
              the authority of his Messiah,
   for cast down is the accuser of our brothers,
   who accuses them day and night before our God,
11   *for they have conquered[10] him by the Lamb's blood*
              and by their own work of confirmation,
              for even in death they did not yield to self-love.

12   *So be merry,[11] you heavens!*
              Be merry, you whose homes are there!
              Woe to the earth and the sea,
              for the Devil has come down to you!
              He is furious, for he knows
              his time is short."

13   *When the dragon saw that he had been cast down to the earth,*
              he pursued the woman who had borne the male child.
14   *To the woman were given the two wings of the huge eagle,[12]*
              so that she could fly to her own place, to the wilderness,
              where she is fed for three years and a half,[13]
              out of the Snake's reach.
15   *The Snake spouted water from his mouth like a river[14]*
              after the woman, to sweep her away in the flood,
16   *but the earth came to the woman's help; it opened its mouth*
              and drank the river which the dragon's mouth spouted.

17   *Furious with the woman, the dragon went away to wage war*

> *on the rest of her children,*
> *on those who obey God's commands*
> *and hold fast to Jesus' work[15] of confirmation.*

18 *And so the dragon took his stand on the seashore.*

13:1 *I saw a beast rising from the sea[16]*
> *with ten horns and seven heads;*
> *on its horns ten crowns,*
> *on its heads the name 'Blasphemy.'[17]*

2 *Like a leopard was the beast I saw,*
like the feet of a bear its feet,
like the jaws of a lion its jaws.
> *To it the dragon gave his own power,*
> *his throne and great authority.*

3 *One of its heads was as slaughtered[18]*
but the plague of its death was healed.
The whole earth was hypnotized by the beast;

4 *they worshiped the dragon because he gave authority to the beast;*
they worshiped the beast, saying:
> > *"Who is its equal?*
> > *Who has power to resist it?"*

5 *It was given a mouth to speak arrogant blasphemies;*
it was given authority to operate for forty-two months;

6 *it opened its mouth in blasphemies against God,*
> > *it blasphemed his name,*
> > *it blasphemed his temple,*
> > *those who dwell in heaven.[19]*

7 *It was given power to fight against the holy men[20] and to conquer them;*
it was given authority over every tribe, people, language and nation.

8 > *All the earth-dwellers will worship it,*
> > *all whose name appears not in the Life-Book[21] of the Lamb*

who was slaughtered ever since the world
  began.

9   *Let everyone who can hear listen to this:*
10   *"Whoever goes into slavery, into slavery[22]*
    must go.
    Whoever kills with a sword, with a sword must
    be killed."
This is the key: the loyal endurance, the faithfulness of
  holy men."

11   *I saw a second beast[23] rising from the earth;*
    it had two horns like a lamb, but it spoke like a dragon.
12   *It exercises the whole authority of the first beast in its*
    presence;
    it causes the earth and the earth-dwellers[24] to worship
    the first beast, whose death plague was healed;
13   *it works spectacular signs,[25] even making fire[26a] descend*
    before men from heaven to earth;
14   *it deceives earth-dwellers by the signs it was allowed to*
    work in the beast's presence,
    inducing earth-dwellers to make an idol to the beast,
    who received the sword-plague and yet came alive.
15   *It was allowed to impart breath to the idol of the beast,*
    so that the beast's idol might speak
    and sentence to death as many
    as would not worship the beast's idol.
16   *Unknown and famous,*
        rich and poor,
        free men and slaves,
    it causes them all to be branded on their right hand or
    on their forehead,
17   *so that no one is able to buy or sell unless he has the*
    brand,[26b]

> *the beast's name or the number of its*
> *name.*

18
> *This is the key:* Wisdom
> Whoever has intelligence should calculate
> the number of the beast.
> It is a human number. Its number is 666.[27]

14:1   I looked:
> *There! The Lamb has taken his stand on Mt. Zion*[28]
> *with him a hundred and forty-four thousand,*[29]
> *having his name and his father's name*
> *inscribed on their foreheads.*

2   I heard a voice from heaven:
> *like the voice of many rivers,*[30]
> *like the voice of great thunders,*
> *a voice like harpists playing on their harps.*[31]

3
> *They sing a new hymn before the throne,*
> *before the four living creatures and*
> *the elders.*
> *No one is entitled to learn that hymn,*
> *but the hundred and forty-four*
> *thousand*
> *whom he purchased from earth.*

4
> *These are virgins,*[32] *they have never been defiled*
> *with women.*
> *These are men who follow the Lamb*[33] *wherever*
> *he goes.*
> *They have been purchased from men as a first*
> *installment*[34] *for God and the Lamb.*

5
> *They are blameless; no false confession*[35] *was*
> *found on their lips.*

6   *Flying in mid-heaven I saw another angel*
    with an eternal gospel[36] *to proclaim to the earth-dwellers*
7   *and to every race, tribe, language and people,*
    shouting loudly:
             "*Fear God! Give glory to him!*
             The hour of his judgment has come!
             Worship him who created[37] *the heaven, the*
                 earth, the sea, and
                         the sources of the rivers!"
8   *A second angel followed, shouting:*
             "*Great Babylon*[38] *has fallen, fallen.*
             All nations have drunk the wine
                 of [*God's*] *fury*[39] *on her fornication.*"[40]

9   *A third angel followed them, shouting loudly:*
             "*Whoever worships the beast and its idol*
             whoever receives its brand on forehead or hand,
10   *he will drink the wine of God's fury*
             poured out straight in the cup of his wrath.
             He will be tormented by fire and sulphur
                 before holy angels, before the Lamb.
11   *The smoke of their torment rises forever,*
                 day and night they have no rest,
             those who worship the beast and its idol,
             who receive the brand of his name."

12   *This is the key:* The loyal endurance[41] of the
                         holy ones,
                             who obey God's commandments,
                             who hold to the faithfulness of Jesus.[42]

13 *I heard a command from heaven:* "Write!
                     From now on, blessed[43] are those who die in the
                         Lord.

> *They shall now receive rest from their travail, for*
> *their works accompany them.*
> *The Spirit says 'I guarantee it.' "*

14 *I looked:*
> *There! A white cloud!*
> *On the cloud sits a figure like a man*
> *with a gold crown on his head,*
> *a sharp scythe in his hand.*

15 *Another angel came from the temple,*
>> *shouting loudly to the one who sat on the cloud:*
>>> *"Send your scythe! Harvest!*[44]
>>> *Harvest time has come,*
>>> *the crops of earth are withered."*
16 *He who sat on the cloud sent his scythe to the earth,*
> *and the earth was harvested.*

17 *Another angel came from the temple in heaven,*
> *he also had a sharp scythe.*

18 *Another angel came from the altar*
> *who held authority over the fire.*
> *He shouted loudly to the one with the sharp scythe:*
>>> *"Send your sharp scythe!*
>>> *Gather the grapes from earth's vineyard*[45]
>>> *for the bunches are ripe."*
19
>>> *And the angel sent his scythe to the earth;*
>>> *he gathered earth's grapes;*
>>> *he cast them into the great wine-press*[46] *of God's*
>>> *fury.*
20
>>> *The wine-press was trampled outside the city.*
>>> *Blood flowed from the wine-press, as deep as*
>>>> *horses' bridles, for two hundred miles. . . .*

15:2   *And I saw what looked like a crystal sea,*[47] *mixed with fire.*
       Standing at the crystal sea, the victors over the beast,
                           its idol, and the number of its name.
   3   *They play God's harps and sing the hymn of Moses,*[48]
       God's slave, and the hymn of the Lamb:

                       "Lord God of all power,
                   your works are majestic and marvelous.
                       King of the nations,
                   your ways are just and trustworthy.
                   Lord, who will not fear you?
   4   *Who will not glorify your name*
                           for you alone are holy?
                   All nations will come and worship before you
                           for your justice has been
                           vindicated."[49]

---

1. As beginning of new vision, see above p. 115f.; Heb. 8:2-4; 9:24; Ex. 25:40; Wis. Sol. 9:8; Bar. 4:5; 6:7-10; Acts 7:44; 1 K 8:1-6; 2 Macc. 2:4-8.
2. 1 K. 8:1, 6; 2 Chron. 5:7.
3. Isa. 26:17-27:1; 54:5; Jer. 3:6-10; Eze. 16:8; Hos. 2:21f.; Psa. 104:2; Gen. 37:9; LeFrois, 74-146; B. Rigaux, RB, 61 (1954) 179-182; all study of the woman of ch. 12 must consider the intended contrasts with the woman of ch. 17. Cf. J. E. Bruns, CBQ 26 (1964), 459-463; see biblio. above p. 127f.
4. Dan. 7:7; 8:10; Isa. 27:1; 29:3; Psa. 91:13; Rev. 12:4-13:4; 16:13; 20:2; H. Wallace, BA 11 (1948), 61f.; Halver 96-98; Bietenhard, *Himmlische Welt*, 205-221; Le Frois, 146-159; R. P. Martin, *Carmen Christi*, 157f.
5. Isa. 66:7; Psa. 2:9; Jer. 20:15; Isa. 7:14; 9:5; F. Boll, ZNTW, 1914, 253; Rev. 2:27; Le Frois, 162-175.
6. Rev. 12:14; 17:3; 17:16; 18:16, 19; Mt. 12:25; Mt. 3:3; 4:1; Lk. 15:4; Acts 7:30-44; U. Mauser, *Christ in the Wilderness*, Ch. 1-4; G. Williams, *Wilderness and Paradise*, 10-27; Le Frois, 175-187; R. Leaney, 221f.; B. Gerhardsson, 40.
7. Dan. 10:13, 21; 12:1; Heb. 2:5; Jude; W. Lueken, *Michael*; S-B III, 813.

8. Gen. 3:15, 16. For convincing evidence that the vision of ch. 12 is based on this Genesis passage, see L. Cerfaux, ETL (1955), 21-33.

9. Luke 10:18; Dan. 2:35 (Theod.); Gen. 3:1, 13f.; Job 1:7f.; Zech. 3:1; Enoch 40:7; Jub. 48:15; Slav. En. 29:5; John 8:44; Rev. 20:2, 9, 11.

10. The importance of the words for victory can hardly be overstressed: Lk. 11:22; I John 2:13; 5:4; John 16:33; Rev. ch. 2, 3; 5:5; 6:2; 11:7; 13:7; 15:2; 17:14; 21:7; Leivestad, 212-238; O. Bauernfeind, TWNT IV, 941-945.

11. Isa. 5:8-22; 44:23; 49:13; Psa. 96:11; Jer. 51:48; L. Brun, 84-90; note contrast of 12:12a with 11:10.

12. Ex. 19:4; Deut. 32:11; Isa. 40:31; Dan. 7:4; Eze. 17:3, 7.

13. Lit: "time and times and half a time." Based on half the sacred number 7 and on the prophecies of Dan. 7:25; 12:7, this is the same symbol as 42 months (11:2; 13:5) or 1260 days (12:6; 11:3).

14. Isa. 59:19; Eze. 29:3; 32:2; Psa. 18:5; 42:8; 74:15; A. Wikenhauser, BZ, 1908, 171; 1909, 48.

15. Lit: witness or testimony. This characterization links the followers of Jesus to the formula of 1:2, 9; above p. 222f.; they are united by *their* share in *his* work; for other key descriptions cf. 7:14f.; 12:11; 14:1-5; 22:14.

16. Dan. 7:1-7; Isa. 27:1; Job 40, 41; Eth. Enoch 60:7-9; II Esdras 6:49-53; the horns and heads link the beast to the dragon (12:3); seven and ten suggest the complete incarnation of blasphemy, i.e., of claim to ultimate power and majesty. O. Kaiser, *Die mythische Bedeutung des Meeres*, 92-159.

17. False claims to sovereignty. Dan. 7:8, 11, 20, 25; 11:36; Psa. 12:4; Isa. 11:6f.; Hos. 13:7f.; Jer. 5:6; 2 Th. 2:4; L. Brun, 118; see above p. 228f.

18. Lit: wounded to death. See above p. 247f. The verb is the same as that used for the Lamb, see note on 5:6.

19. Note the implication regarding the holy men (usually translated saints). They are God's dwelling, they live in heaven and bear God's name (3:12); the exercise of blasphemy against God takes the form of claiming power over his people.

20. There is no escape from using a misleading or archaic English word for *hagioi*. The reader must learn how these terms for holiness and sanctity derive their meanings from the ancient contexts, and are vastly different from modern concepts: H. Langenberg, 133f.; A. Satake, 26f.; O. Procksch, TWNT I, 100-115.

21. Life-book: see biblio. above p. 83; J. Marsh, 147f.

22. Jer. 15:2; 43:11; Mt. 26:52; Charles I, 357; Vos, 104-109.
23. Later identified as a false prophet 16:13; 19:20; 20:10. Cp. Mt. 7:15; 24:11; Lk. 6:26; 1 John 4:1; Vos, 130-136; B. Murmulstein. TSK 101 (1929), 447-457; U. Simon, 163f.; E. Lohmeyer, 113; H. Wallace, BA 11 (1948), 61f.
24. See note on 3:10; above p. 123f.
25. Deut. 13:1-5; Mt. 24:24; 2 Th. 2:9.
26a. See note on 11:5 and on 2:18. 1 K. 18:38; 2 K. 1:10, 12; Ex. 7:11; Mt. 24:24; Isa. 24:17; Hos. 4:1; Enoch 54:6; 57:7.
26b. Dan. 3:5f.; Eze. 9:4; Isa. 44:5; Rev. 14:9, 11; 16:2; 19:20; 20:4; above p. 256f.
27. See special biblio. p. 128.
28. Psa. 125:1; Eze. 9:4; Zech. 14; Heb. 12:22; Joel 2:32; 2 Esdras 13:35; E. Lohmeyer, 121f.; M. Rissi, TH, 90f.
29. Rev. 7:4; 21:17; K. Rengstorf, TWNT II, 323f.; Langenberg, 216.
30. Eze. 1:24; 43:2; Rev. 1:15; 19:6; H. G. May, JBL, 74 (1955), 9-21.
31. Psa. 33:2; 81:3; 92:4; 149:3; 150:3; Eze. 1:5; Isa. 24:23; Rev. 5:8; 15:2; 18:22; Langenberg, 189f.; Sellers, BA, 4 (1941), 37f.
32. Mt. 25:1f.; note sharp contrast to prostitutes: Rev. 2:14, 20; 17:1-18:9; 21:8; R. Devine, Scrip. 16 (1964), 1-5; Cerfaux & Cambier, 125; Boismard, 61; Delling, TWNT V, 835; Minear, *Images*, 52f.; Legrand, 46f., 134-140.
33. Lk. 9:57; Mk. 8:34f.; Mt. 10:38; Jn. 12:25f.; E. Schweizer, *Lordship and Discipleship*, 77-85; E. Power, Bib. 4 (1923), 108-112; L. Vos, 136-144.
34. Isa. 53:7; James 1:18; Rom. 11:16; 16:5; 2 Th. 2:13; P. Minear, *Images*, 111f.
35. Psa. 32:2; Isa. 53:9; Zeph. 3:13; Rev. 3:9; 21:27; 22:15; John 8:44; Rom. 1:25; 1 John 2:21, 27; note that the antonym "blameless" is frequently associated with the lamb-sacrifice: Heb. 9:14; 1 P. 1:1; and with fearless confession: Phil. 2:15; Col. 1:22; Eph. 1:4.
36. See Masson; in *Hommage et reconnaissance*; R. Hanson, *op. cit.*, 351-356; L. Cerfaux, ETL 39 (1963), 672-681; Vos, 152-156.
37. Ex. 20:11; Psa. 146:6; Acts 4:24; Neh. 8:6; Rev. 4:11; 5:10; 21:5; see above p. 270f.
38. Isa. 21:9; Jer. 50:2; 51:8; Nahum 3:4; Dan. 4:27; Psa. Sol. 8:15; Rev. 16:19; 17:5f.; 18:2ff.; S-B, III, 816; K. Kuhn, TWNT, I, 512-514; above pp. 156f., 236f.
39. Mt. 20:22f.; 25:41; Psa. 75:8f.; Isa. 51:17-23; Jer. 25:15f.; above, pp. 152-156.
40. See above p. 217f.

41. See above p. 24f.
42. One may well notice how often it is to *Jesus'* faithfulness or endurance or confirmation that the believer holds fast; e.g., 2:13, 26; 3:8, 10; 7:14; see above p. 194f.
43. Heb. 4:10; S-B III, 817; the seven beatitudes may be studied together. Rev. 1:3; 14:13; 16:15; 19:9; 20:6; 22:7, 14. Compare W. Bieder, TZ 10 (1954), 13-30; L. Brun, 39-47; 58-69; E. Käsemann, 98f.
44. Isa. 17:5; 63:2f.; Jer. 51:33; Psa. 68:24; Enoch 100:3; Vos, 144-151.
45. Mk. 12:1-12; P. Minear, *Images*, 43f.
46. Joel 3:14; Isa. 63:1-6; Lam. 1:15; Enoch 100:3; Rev. 19:13, 15.
47. Rev. 4:6; 21:18, 21; 2 Macc. 38:8; 1 K 7:23, 44; 2 K 16:17; 2 Chron. 4:2, 15; for baptismal connotations, see Lundberg, *La Typologie Baptismale*, 116-135; also Langenberg, 13f.; 115f.; Danielou, *Bible and Liturgy*, 316.
48. Ex. 15:1, 11; Psa. 86:9; 92:5; 111:2; 139:14; Jer. 10:6, 7; Mal. 1:11. Here one detects strong echoes of the Exodus typology. A. N. Wilder, *Language*, 97f.
49. Deut. 32:4; Psa. 145:17; Jer. 10:10; Hos. 4:10; Psa. 119:75; Rom. 9:14; J. Horst, 286f.; see above, p. 172f.

V

15:1   *I saw another sign in heaven, great and spectacular—seven angels with seven plagues, which are the last, because with them God's fury is ended. . . .*

5   *Afterward I looked:*

> *thrown open was the sanctuary of the Tent of Witness*[1] *in heaven,*

6   > *out of the sanctuary came the seven angels with the seven plagues,*
> *robed in shining white linen, with gold scarves around their chests.*

7   > *One of the four living creatures gave to the seven angels seven gold bowls full of the fury of the God who lives forever.*

8   > *The sanctuary was so filled with smoke*[2] *from God's glory and power that no one was able to enter the sanctuary until the seven plagues*[3] *of the seven angels were ended.*

16:1   *From the sanctuary I heard a loud command to the seven angels:*

>> *"Go! Empty over the earth the seven bowls of God's fury."*[4]

2   >> *The first went and emptied his bowl over the earth.*
>> *A foul, devilish ulcer appeared on those men who bore the brand of the Beast, who worshiped his idol.*

3   >> *The second emptied his bowl over the sea.*
>> *it turned to blood, like the blood of a corpse.*

344

Every living thing died,
everything in the sea.

4   The third *emptied his bowl over* rivers *and*
                 water-springs.
               They turned to blood.
5   *I heard the angel of the waters say:*
                      "*You are just[5] in condemning these*
                      things, O holy one,
                             you who now rule and have
                             always ruled.
6   *They have poured out the blood of*
                      holy men and prophets,
                             so you have given them blood
                             to drink.
                      They deserve it!"

7   *I heard the altar approve:*
                      "*Yes, O Lord, all-powerful God,*
                      your verdicts are reliable and just."

8   The fourth *emptied his bowl on the* sun.
               It was allowed to scorch men with fire;
9   *men were seared with great blisters.*
               They blasphemed the name of God
                      who authorized these plagues;
               they would not repent by giving glory to him.

10   The fifth *emptied his bowl on the* Beast's
                 throne.
               His kingdom was plunged into darkness.
               They gnawed their tongues with pain.
11   *They blasphemed the God of heaven for their*
                 pains and ulcers,
               but they did not repent of their deeds.

12   *The* sixth *emptied his bowl over the* Euphrates,
      the great River.
    Its water was dried up to prepare the road
    for the kings to come from the East.[6]

13   *I saw three polluted spirits like frogs*[7]
      from the mouth of the Dragon
      from the mouth of the Beast
      from the mouth of the false
        prophet.

14   *These are demonic spirits, working*
      miracles,
    sent to summon the kings of the whole
      world
    to battle on the Great Day of God,
      the all-powerful. . . .

15   *(Attention!*
    I am coming like a thief![8]
    Blessed is the alert watchman
    who guards his clothing,
    lest he walk naked
    and men stare at his shame.)

16   . . . *and they gathered them at the*
      place called Armageddon[9] *in*
      Hebrew.

17   *The* seventh *emptied his bowl over the* air.
    From the throne, out of the sanctuary, came
      a loud voice;
        "It is ended."

18   *Lightnings, voices, thunders, a great earthquake*
      came.
    Never since men have lived on earth has any
      earthquake been so violent.

19   *The Great City broke into three parts.*
     The cities of the Gentiles fell.
     Great Babylon was remembered before God;
     he gave her the cup
        with the wine of the fury of his anger.
20   *Every island fled; every mountain vanished.*
21   *Hailstones, heavy as hundred-weights, fell on*
       men from heaven.
     They blasphemed God for the plague of hail,
       so terrible was that plague.

17:1 *One of the seven angels with the seven bowls came to me and said:*
2   *"Come. I will enable you to see the verdict on the great prostitute,[10] who sits on the many waters. Earth's kings[11] have committed adultery with her. The earth-dwellers[12] have got drunk on the wine of her adultery."*
3 *He carried me in the Spirit to a wilderness[13] where I saw*
    a woman sitting on a scarlet Beast,[14]
    which was full of the names of blasphemers,
    with seven heads and ten horns.
4   *The woman was robed in purple and scarlet;*
    she was gilded with gold, jewels, pearls.[15]
    She carried in her hand a gold cup[16]
    filled with abominations,
    the pollutions of her adultery.
5   *On her forehead was inscribed a name, a mystery:*
      "Babylon the Great,
       mother of prostitutes,
       mother of earth's abominations."
6   *I saw her drinking the blood[17] of holy men,*
    the blood of Jesus' guarantors.

7 *On seeing her I was astounded, but the angel asked:*
      "Why this astonishment?
      I will explain to you the mystery of the woman

and the mystery of the Beast[18] which carries her,
with his seven heads and ten horns:

8   "The Beast which you saw did rule,[19] but rules no longer.
He is about to ascend from the Abyss and to go to
        perdition.
When they see the Beast, that he ruled but rules no
        longer and is to come,
the earth-dwellers will be astonished,
those whose names have not been inscribed
in the Book of Life[20] since the world began."

9   (This is a call for the intelligent man to use his wisdom.)

"The seven heads[21] are seven mountains, on which the
        woman sits.
They are also seven kings—
10   five have fallen,
              one is ruling, the other has not yet come;
              when he comes he must remain a short while—
11   The Beast which did rule, but rules no longer,
is himself an eighth, yet one of the seven;
he is going to perdition.

12   "The ten horns you saw are ten kings[22]
which have not yet received a kingdom.
With the Beast they will receive authority
to rule as kings for one hour.
13   They agree in a common cause, to give
to the Beast their power and authority.
14   They will wage war on the Lamb
but the Lamb will conquer them,
for he is Lord of lords, King of kings.[23]
Those on his side are the called, the chosen, the loyal."
15   He said to me:
The waters[24] which you saw,

where the prostitute is sitting,
are peoples, crowds, nations and tongues.

16 *The Beast and the ten horns which you saw—*
they will hate the prostitute,
they will make her a wilderness,
they will strip her naked,
they will devour her flesh,[25]
they will consume her with fire.

17 *For God planted his purpose in their hearts*
to join in a common cause,
to give their kingdom to the Beast
until God's purposes are realized.

18 *The woman which you saw is the Great City*
which exercises sovereignty over earth's kings."

18:1 *Afterward I saw another angel coming down with great*
2 *authority from heaven. The earth was alight with his glory.*
With a powerful voice he shouted:
"Babylon the Great has fallen, fallen.[26]
She has become the haunt of demons,
the prison of every polluted spirit,
the cage of every polluted, hateful bird,
3 *for all nations have drunk the wine*
of the fury of her adultery.
Earth's kings have committed adultery with her,
earth's merchants have fattened on the power
of her affluence."

4 *I heard another voice calling from heaven:*
"O my people, come out of her,[27a]
5 *lest you share in her sins*
and receive a share of her plagues,
for her sins have risen to heaven
and God has remembered her injustices.

6   *Give her tit for tat!*[27b]
       Whatever she has done; double it!
       Pour her a double portion of the cup she mixed!

7   *Give her as much torment and grief*
       as she gave herself of arrogance and luxury.
       Because she gloats in her heart:
             'I now rule as queen,
             I am no widow,
             I shall not know grief,'

8   *therefore her plagues will fall in a single day:*
             famine, grief, death.
       She will be consumed by fire,
       for mighty is the Lord God who condemns her."

9   When they see the smoke from her burning, earth's kings,
       those who shared her adultery and affluence, will weep and
10   wail over her. Standing far off from dread of her torment,
       they will cry:
             "Woe to you! Woe to you![28]
             O great city, O mighty city, Babylon!
             In a single hour your condemnation has come."

11   Earth's merchants will weep and grieve over her, for no one
       buys their merchandise any more:
12   gold and silver, jewels and pearls,[29]
          cloth of purple and silk and linen,
          scented wood and ivory dishes,
          precious carvings, bronze, iron and marble,
13   cinnamon, spice, incense, perfume and frankincense,
          wine and oil, flour and wheat,
          cattle and sheep, horses and chariots,
          the bodies and souls of men.

14   *"Fled from you are the objects of your soul's lust;*
       vanished from you all the glamour and splendor,
       never again to be found."

15 Traders[30] in these things, who had grown rich off the city,
stood far off from dread of her torment, weeping and grieving:
16   "Woe to you! Woe to you!
        O great city!
        City robed in linen, purple, scarlet,
        city gilded with gold, jewels, pearls,
17   in a single hour so much wealth was made
           wilderness."

18 Pilots, travelers, sailors and all who worked at sea
stood far off when they saw the smoke of her burning.
They kept wailing:
        "What other city is like the great city?"
19 Weeping and grieving they threw dust on their heads, wailing:
        "Woe to you! Woe to you!
        O great city,
        where all ship owners
        grew wealthy from her splendor!
        In a single hour the city was made wilderness."

20   "O heaven,[31] O you holy men.
        O you prophets and apostles,
        rejoice over her, for from her
        God has claimed justice for you."

21 A mighty angel lifted a stone, heavy as a millstone,[32] and
hurled it into the sea, saying:
        "With such violence as this
        will the great city, Babylon, be hurled down,
        no longer to be found.

22   No longer in you will be heard
           the music of harps and singers,
           of flutes and trumpets;

> No longer in you will be found
>   the artists of any craft;
> No longer in you will be heard
>   the sound of a mill;

23

> no longer in you will be seen
>   the light of a lamp;
> no longer in you will be heard
>   the voice of bride and groom,[33]
> for your merchants were earth's potentates,
> by your sorcery all nations were deceived,

24

> in you was found the blood of prophets and
>   holy men,
> the blood of all who have been slaughtered on
>   the earth."

19:1 Afterward I heard what sounded like the roar of a great multitude in heaven:

> "Alleluia![34]
> The salvation, the glory, the power of our God!

2

> His verdicts are just and sure.
> He has brought to judgment the great prostitute,
> who polluted the earth with her adultery;
> from her hand he has claimed justice
> for the blood of his slaves."

3 Again they shouted:

> "Alleluia!
> Her smoke is rising forever."

4 The twenty-four elders and the four living creatures prostrated themselves and worshiped the God who is enthroned, saying:

> "Amen! Alleluia!"

5 A message came from the throne:

> "Praise our God
> all his slaves,
> you who fear him,
> whether unknown or famous."

6 *Like the roar of a huge multitude,*
  like the rushing of many rivers,
  like the rolling of mighty thunders,
  I heard them shouting:
          "Alleluia!
          Our Lord, the all-powerful God
          has established his kingdom!
7   *Let us rejoice, let us celebrate,*
          let us give him the glory,
          for the wedding of the Lamb has come!
          His bride has prepared herself;
8   *she has been given pure white linen to wear;*
            this linen is the vindication of holy men."

9 *He said to me:*
        "Write this down: Blessed are those invited to the
        Lamb's wedding supper!"
    Again he said:
        "This is the sure purpose of God."

10 *When I fell at his feet to worship him, he said to me:*[35]
          "Don't worship me. Worship God!
          I am your fellow-slave,
          fellow-slave of your brothers,
          who verify Jesus' work of confirmation.
          That very work is the spirit of prophecy."

---

1. Ex. 38:21; 40:34; compare Acts 7:44, another definite link to the worship of Israel during the wilderness sojourn. John thinks of this as the place where God dwells with his people. Rev. 7:15; 12:12; 13:6; 21:3.
2. Isa. 6:4; Eze. 10:4; 44:4; Ex 29:43; 40:34; Lev. 16:2; Num. 9:15; I K 8:10, 11; 2 Chron. 5:13f.
3. Lev. 26:21; Psa. 75:8; Isa. 22:31; 51:17, 22; 66:1; Jer. 25:15; Eze. 10:2; H. P. Muller, ZNTW 51 (1960), 268-278.
4. E. Hühn has shown the correlation between this passage and Exodus (*op. cit.*, 257):

Rev. 16: 2	ulcers	Ex. 9:8-11	also Deut. 28:35; Job 2:7f.
16:4-6	bloody rivers	7:17-21	
16:10	darkness	10:21-23	also Psa. 105:28; Isa. 8:22
16:13f	frogs	8:2-7	
16:18f	hail, thunder, etc.	9:18-26	

5. Mt. 10:32f.; Rom. 9:14; Deut. 32:4; Psa. 79:2f.; 145:17; 92:16; 119:75, 137; 2 Chron. 19:7; Job 8:3; 34:10; Isa. 34:7; 49:26; Wis. Sol. 11:16; 12:23; 16:1; Psa. Sol. 2:7, 17, 38f.; 17:10.

6. Isa. 41:2, 25; 46:11; Rev. 9:14; 20:7-10.

7. Jer. 14:14; 27:14; 29:8f.; Eze. 22:28; Micah 3:5; F. Steinmetzer, BZ 10 (1912), 252-260.

8. P. Minear, *Christian Hope*, 128-138; E. Lövestam, 95-107, J. Z. Smith, HR 5 (1966), 217-238; E. G. Selwyn, 375-382, 439-458; see above p. 148f.

9. Judges 5:19; 2 K 9:27; 23:29f.; Zech. 12:11; J. Jeremias, ZNTW 31 (1932), 73-77; H. Gunkel, 263-266; J. Michael, JTS (1937), 168-172; C. C. Torrey, HTR (1938), 237-248.

10. Jer. 51:13; Isa. 1:21; Nah. 3:4; Jer. 2:20; J. E. Bruns, CBQ 26 (1964), 459-463. Notice in this whole chapter the parodic contrasts with the women of ch. 12 and the city of ch. 21, 22, as well as the use of diverse phrases from the O.T. prophets.

11. See above p. 235f.

12. Isa. 23:17; Jer. 51:7; Nah. 3:4; above p. 261f.

13. Wilderness, see note on 12:6.

14. This connects this vision directly to 13:1f.

15. This vision should be contrasted throughout with the jewels of Jerusalem, 21:9f.

16. Jer. 51:7; Mt. 23:25f.; Lk. 11:39; Kuhn, TWNT I, 513; E. Lohmeyer, 140f.

17. Isa. 34:7; 49:26; see note on p. 156; Mt. 23:35; Lk. 11:50; L. Vos, 162f.

18. Dan. 7:3; Rev. 11:7; 19:19; 20:2, 7; see biblio. on Antichrist, p. 128.

19. Lit: "he was, and is not and is coming." See explanation of translation of 1:4 above p. 300.

20. See above p. 83.

21. See above p. 283f.; A. Strobel, NTS (1963-64), 433-445.

22. Dan. 7:20, 24.

23. Deut. 10:17; Dan. 2:47; 2 Macc 13:4; 3 Macc. 5:35; Enoch 9:4; I Tim 6:15.
24. See note on p. 000.
25. Psa. 27:2; Mic 3:2f.; Lev. 21:9; Jer. 50:32; Nahum 3:15; Isa. 16:37f.; Hos. 2:12. It is essential to notice this warfare between beast, horns, and harlot.
26. In this whole chapter we find a series of funeral laments, with both form and content based on O.T. models, especially Eze. (ch. 19, 26, 27, 28, 32) although other prophets as well. Jer. 50:39; Isa. 13:21; 14:23; 34:11, 13. For thorough analysis see Jahnow, 219ff., 243f.; 253f.; also L. Brun, 88f.
27a. Jer. 50:8; 51:6; Isa. 48:20; 52:11; Mt. 24; 2 Cor. 6:17; Eph. 5:11.
27b. It is not clear who is now speaking and to whom. Is the heavenly voice speaking to "my people" as in vs. 4? It is more likely that the heavenly voice is speaking to the beast and the ten horns of 17:16, for they are the agents of God's verdict in this vision.
28. Mt. 11:21; 23; Isa. 5:8-22; see pp. 154-157. Contemporary idiom offers few expressions with comparable weight: "Curses! Damned! Damnation!" Only novelists have preserved the sense of total devastation or fulfilment as dependent on the present decision in the primordial battle between God and Satan.
29. A rather inclusive and accurate list of major items of commerce in John's day, commerce which poured through the cities to which he was writing as a source of their prosperity.
30. A. D. Knox, JTS (1915), 77, 78.
31. Note whom John includes in the term heaven. Isa. 44:23; 49:13; Psa. 96:11; Jer. 51:48; Deut. 32:43; 2 K 9:7.
32. Jer. 51:63; Lk. 17:2; Mt. 18:6; I Clem. 46:8.
33. Notice sharp contrast with 19:7f.; S-B III, 822.
34. See the Hallel Psalms 113-118, which were prominently used at the Passover. Tob. 13:18; S-B III, 822; J. Horst, 288f.
35. An extremely strategic verse. Notice the implications concerning the identity of the angels in the whole book, the centrality of worship as newly defined by Christ, the character of prophecy and the historical thrust of the prophetic charisma. In fact, a conclusion like this demythologizes the very myths which the prophet has used. J. Horst, 257f.

VI

19:11   I saw heaven[1] thrown open:
      There! A white horse!
      Its rider, loyal and trustworthy!
      He judges and fights with justice,
12   his eyes[2] like flaming fire,
      on his head many crowns,—
      no one else knows what Name is inscribed—
13   wearing a robe spotted with blood.
      He is God's saving purpose in person.
14   The armies in heaven follow him
      riding white horses,
      wearing pure white linen.
15   From his mouth comes a razor-sharp sword[3]
      with which to smite the nations;
      he will rule them with an iron rod;
      he will tread the wine-press
      of the fury of the anger of God the all-powerful.
16   On his robe[4] and on his thigh
      his name[5] is inscribed:
      "King of kings. Lord of lords."

17   I saw an angel standing in the sun. He shouted with a loud
     voice to all the birds[6] flying in mid-heaven:
18   "Come! Gather for God's great feast,
      to eat the flesh of kings and generals and armed men,
      the flesh of horses and their riders,
      the flesh of free men and slaves,
      the unknown and the famous, all of them."

19   I saw the Beast gathered with earth's kings and their armies to
     do battle against the rider and against his army. The Beast

20 *was taken prisoner, and with him the false prophet who faked signs before him, by which he deceived those who accepted the brand of the Beast and worshiped his idol. Both were hurled alive into the fiery lake[7] burning with sulphur.*

21 *The rest were slaughtered by the sword coming from the mouth of the rider. All the birds were glutted with their flesh.*

20:1 *I saw an angel descending from heaven*
carrying in his hand the key of the Abyss and a great chain.

2 *He captured the Dragon, the primeval snake who is the devil or Satan,*
      he chained[8] him for a thousand years,[9]

3   *he threw him into the Abyss;*
      he shut and locked the door on him
      so that he would no longer deceive[10] the nations
      until the thousand years are over.
      Afterward he must be released for a short while.[11]

4 *I saw thrones, and enthroned I saw[12]*
      the souls of those who had been murdered
      for their loyal witness to Jesus, to the saving purpose of
         God;
      they worshiped neither the Beast nor his idol;
      they refused his brand on their foreheads and arms.
      They were installed as judges;
      they came to life and shared Christ's royal power
      for a thousand years.

5   *(The rest of the dead did not come to life*
      until the thousand years were over.)

6   *This is the first resurrection.*
      Those who share this first resurrection
      are blessed and holy;
      the second death wields no authority over them.
      They will be priests of God and priests of Christ,
      sharing his royal power for a thousand years.

7 *When the thousand years are over, Satan will be released from*
8 *his prison. He will come out to deceive the nations at earth's*
   four corners,—Gog and Magog,[13]—summoning them to
9 *battle. They are as numerous as the sand of the sea. They*
   ascended to the broad surface of the earth. They built
10 *siege-camps[14] around the beloved city, the holy ones. But fire*
   came down from heaven and devoured them. The devil who
   deceives them was hurled into the lake of fire and sulphur, to
   join the Beast and the false prophet.[15] Day and night will they
   be tormented forever.

11 *I saw a great white throne,[16] and One enthroned*
        from whose face earth and heaven fled away,
        they vanished utterly.
12 *I saw all the dead, the famous and the unknown,*
        standing before the throne.
        The books[17] were opened.
        (Another book, the Book of Life, was opened.)
        The dead received verdicts according
              to their accomplishments in the books.
13   *The sea surrendered its dead,*
        Death and Hades surrendered their dead;
        each received a verdict according to his
              accomplishments.
14   *Then Death and Hades were hurled into the burning lake.*
        (This is the second death, the burning lake.)
15   *Into that lake was hurled everyone*
        whose name was not entered in the Book of Life.

21:1 *I saw a new heaven and a new earth![18]*
        The first heaven and the first earth had disappeared,
        the sea had lost its power.
2   *I saw the Holy City,*
        New Jerusalem descending from heaven, from God,
        like a bride,[19] beautiful for her husband!

3   *I heard a loud voice from the throne:*
        "There! God's home is with men;
        he will dwell[20] with them,
        they will be his people,
        God will himself live with them.
        He will end their weeping:[21]
4   *no more death, no more grief,*
        no more wailing or suffering,
        for the first things have vanished."
5   *The Enthroned spoke:*
        "There! I am making everything new. . . .
        Write it down. This saving purpose is faithful and
          reliable."
6   *Then he told me:*
        "It is done.
        I am the A and the Z, the beginning and the end.
        To the thirsty I will freely give water[22]
        from the fountain of life.
7   *These things the victor will inherit:*
        to him, I will be 'God';
        to me, he will be 'Son.'
8   *But the second death,*
                inheritance in the lake afire with sulphur,
                will be for cowards and traitors,
                perverts and murderers,
                prostitutes and sorcerers,
                idolators and all liars."

9   *Then came one of the seven angels with the seven bowls full*
    of the final plagues. He called to me:
        "Come! I will show you the virgin-wife of the Lamb."

10   *In the Spirit he took me away to a huge, high mountain.*
    He showed me the Holy City Jerusalem[23] descending from
    heaven, from God.

11   *God's glory filled it;*
            its light like a precious jewel,
                like crystal jasper.
12   *It had a broad high wall with twelve gates,*
            at the gates twelve angels,
13   *to the east three gates,*
                    to the south three gates,
                    to the north three gates,
                    to the west three gates,
            inscribed the names of the twelve tribes of
                Israel.
14   *The city wall rested on twelve foundations,*
                on them twelve names,
                    the twelve apostles of the Lamb.

15   *The angel who spoke to me was carrying a gold rod to*
16   *measure[24] the city, its gates, its walls.*
            The city had four corners,
            its length equal to its width.
            The city measured twelve hundred kilometers,
17   *its length, width and height were equal,*
            its wall measured one hundred forty four times
                the length of the forearm
18   *(This is a man's measure, an angel's measure).*
            The walls were constructed of jasper.
            The city itself was pure gold,
                transparent as crystal.
19   *The foundations of the city-wall were beautiful*
                    with all kinds of jewels:
20   *the first foundation jasper, the second*
                        sapphire,
                    the third chalcedony, the fourth
                        emerald,
                    the fifth agate, the sixth carnelian,
                    the seventh yellow topaz, the eighth
                        beryl,

the ninth topaz, the tenth apple-green
quartz,
the eleventh blue sapphire, the twelfth
amethyst.

21 The twelve gates were twelve pearls,
each of the gates made out of one pearl.[25]
The city's street was pure gold,
like transparent crystal.

22 Within the city I saw no temple,
for its temple is the Lord,
23 the all-powerful God and the Lamb.
The city has no need for sunlight or
moonlight,[26]
for God's glory floods it with light,
24 with the Lamb as its lamp.
In its light the nations walk.
25 Into it the earth's kings bring their glory
with the glory and praise of the
nations.
There is no night,
26 so the gates are never closed day or night.
27 Into it will come nothing unclean,
nothing corrupt, nothing false;
only those included in the Lamb's Book of Life.

22:1 He showed me a river,[27] flowing from the throne of God and
the Lamb,
the water of life, sparkling like crystal.
2 The tree of life,[28] in the middle of the city
street,
on both sides of the river, producing twelve
harvests,
every month yielding its harvest.
3 The tree's leaves give health to the nations.
(No longer will anything be damned.)

In it God and the Lamb will be enthroned.
His slaves will worship him;

4   *they will look on his face,*
his name will be on their foreheads.

5   *There will be no more night,*
no need for lamplight or sunlight,
for the Lord God will shine on them,
and they shall be kings forever.

6   He said to me:

"These promises are trustworthy and true!
The Lord, God of the prophets' Spirit,
sent his angel to show his slaves
what must happen soon"

7   *"There! Soon I am coming.*
Blessed is the man who obeys
the prophetic commands of this book."

---

1. Eze. 1:1; Zech. 1:8; 6:3, 6; see note on Rev. 6:2. Note how in this passage John brings together into a new focus both the chief O.T. books and the cardinal features of Christ's work. See biblio. on christology, p. 33f.; also M. Russi, *Die Zukunft der Welt*, which is an extension of TZ 21 (1965), 81-95.
2. Dan. 10:6; Rev. 1:14; 2:18; 5:6.
3. Psa. 2:9; Rev. 1:16; 2:12, 16; 19:21.
4. Isa. 63:1-6; Rev. 3:4f., 18; 4:4; 16:15; 19:16.
5. Deut. 10:17; Dan. 2:47; P. Skehan, CBQ 10 (1948), 398; see note on Rev. 2:17.
6. Eze. 39:4, 17-20; Isa. 34:6; Jer. 46:10; Jer. 12:9; I Sam. 17:44; 2 K. 9:36; Lev. 26:29; Rev. 17:16; 18:2; Lk. 17:37.
7. Rev. 3:5; 14:10; 20:9, 14f.; 21:8; Mt. 25:41; Dan. 7:11; Eze. 38:22; Isa. 34:9f.; 30:33; Gen. 19:24; Lev. 10:2; Num. 16:35; Psa. 21:10; Enoch 48:9; Slav. En. 10:2-6.
8. Isa. 24:21; Mt. 12:29; 13:30; 16:19; 18:18; Rev. 9:14f.; Rev. 1:5.
9. Enoch 54:5f.; see above p. 174f.; S-B III, 823-831; R. Hanson, 344-347.

10. This is one of the most frequent and important words in John's vocabulary, and in the broader Jewish-Christian pictures of demonic temptation. Rev. 2:20; 12:9; 13:14; 18:23; 19:20; 20:8, 10; also Mt. 18:12f.; 24:4-24; Lk. 21:8; John 7:47; I John 3:7; 4:6; I Cor. 15:33; Eph. 4:14; I P 2:25; Heb. 11:38; James 5:19f.

11. A technical apocalyptic term: compare Rev. 6:11; John 7:33; 12:35.

12. In this paragraph one might well survey the other N.T. writings for similar motifs, but it is better first to see how every phrase is anticipated in early chapters, by using a concordance.

13. Eze. 38:2, 9, 15; 39; S-B III, 831-840; K. Kuhn, TWNT I, 789-791; Bietenhard, 43f.

14. 2 K 1:10-12; Lk. 21:20-24; Rev. 11:2, 5.

15. This paragraph forces the exegete to distinguish the Devil from the two beasts, all the while grasping their interdependence.

16. See note on 4:1; also Dan. 7:97f.; Psa. 114-3, 7; Mt. 25:31-46.

17. See biblio. on this motif p. 83.

18. Isa. 66:22; see above p. 271f.; R. Hanson, 70; S-B III, 840-847; R. Leaney, 16of.; P. Reymond, 195f.

19. 2 Cor. 11:1; Eph. 5:22-31; John 3:29; see Minear, *Images*, 54ff.; Vos, 163-174; J. Daniélou, *Lord of History*, 214-240; H. de Lubac, 29-54; Rev. 22:17; Matt. 22:1-10; 25:1-13; Lk. 12:36.

20. Ex. 6:7; 25:8; Lev. 26:11, 12; Deut. 28:1-14; Eze. 37:27; 43:7; John 14:23; 2 Cor. 6:16; Rev. 7:15; E. Hühn, 181; van Unnik in *N.T. Essays*, 270-305; B. Gerhardsson, 26.

21. Isa. 25:8; 35:10; 51:11; I Cor. 2:9; 15:54; Mt. 5:3-12; Acts 3:20; Enoch 25:6; Slav. En. 65:9; Patai, 202f.

22. Isa. 55:1; Psa. 23; Daniélou, *Symbols*, 42-57; S-B III, 854f.

23. Eze. 40:2; 48:30-35; Ex. 28:21; Harrisville, 99-105. The liturgical mood again becomes dominant: see biblio. p. 26 and J. Comblin, ETL (1953), 5-40.

24. Rev. 11:1, 2; Eze. 40:5; S-B, III, 849.

25. E. Burrows, JTS (1942), 177-179; G. Caird, 271-278.

26. Isa. 30:26; 60:19f.; Mal. 4:2; F. Dölger, SS, 216, 406-410; Patai, 83-94; Simon, ENY, 168f.

27. Gen. 2:10; Psa. 46:4; Eze. 47; Slavonic Enoch 8:5; A. Wünsche, *Lebensbaum und Lebenswasser*; P. Reymond, 242f.

28. See note on 2:7; J. Daniélou, *Symbols*, 25-41; S-B, III, 856f.; R. Patai, 86f.; P. Reymond, 236.

22:8   *This is John[1] speaking. I am the one who heard and saw these things. When I heard and saw them, I fell down to worship at the feet of the angel who showed them to me. But he said:*

9   *"Don't do that! Worship God![2]*
          I am only a slave along with you and your brothers,
          the prophets and all who obey the commands of this book."

10   *Then he said to me:*
          "Don't seal up[3] the prophetic commands of this book for the season is at hand.

11   *"Let the unjust go on doing injustice,[4]*
          Let the filthy go on being filthy;
          Let the just go on doing justice,
          Let the holy go on becoming holy."

12   *"There! I, Jesus, am coming soon*
          bringing my reward with me,
          to repay everyone according to his work.[5]

13   *"I am the A and the Z,*
          the first and the last.
          the beginning and the end.

14   *"Blessed are those who cleanse their robes,*
          in order to receive authority over the tree of life,
          and to enter the city through its gates.

15   *"Shut out are the dogs, sorcerers, prostitutes,*
          murderers, idolaters, and every one who loves and serves the Lie.

16   *"It is I, Jesus, who sent my angel to confirm these things to you, for the sake of the congregations.*
          I am of David's tree, its root and its fruit.[6]
          I am the bright star of the dawn."

17   *"The Spirit and the Bride say 'Come.'*
Let the man who hears say 'Come.'
Let every thirsty man come.
Let every one who wishes receive free
the water of life."

18 I *promise every hearer of the prophetic commands of this*
book:
    if any one adds to them,
        God will add to him the plagues[7] described in
        this book;
19   *if anyone subtracts from the prophetic commands of*
    this book,
        God will subtract his share in the tree of Life
        and in the holy city, as described in this book.

20 *It is one who confirms these things who says*
    "I vouch for it.
    I am coming soon."*

        "Amen! Lord Jesus, come!"[8]

21 *The grace of the Lord Jesus be with all.*

---

1. 1:1, 9; see p. 19.
2. Rev. 19:10.
3. What should be made of the contrast with 10:4?
4. Compare with Dan. 12:10; Rev. 13:9; E. Käsemann, *Exegetische Versuche,* II, 91-98.
5. The Apocalypse has a quite distinctive view of reward; see Rev. 2:2, 5, 6, 19, 22-26; 14:13; 15:3; 16:11; 18:6; 20:12.
6. Rev. 2:28; 5:5; Num. 24:17; Isa. 11:1, 10; Mt. 2:2; see A. Fabre, RB 5 (1908), 227-240; S-B, III, 851.
7. B. Olsson, ZNTW 31 (1932), 84-86; L. Brun, 109f; G. Caird, 287.
8. I Cor. 16:22; Didache 10:5; O. Cullmann, *Early Christian Worship,* 13ff.; F. Dölger, SS, 135, 198-219.

Bibliography

I. Commentaries

Allen, C. H., *The Message of the Book of Revelation* (Nashville: Cokesbury, 1939).

Allo, E. B., *L'Apocalypse de St. Jean* (Paris: Gabalda, 3rd ed., 1933).

Beasley-Murray, G. R., in *The New Bible Commentary* (London: Intervarsity Fellowship, 1953).

Beckwith, I. T., *The Apocalypse of John* (New York: Macmillan, 1920).

Behm, J., *Die Offenbarung des Johannes* (Göttingen: Vandenhoeck & Ruprecht, 1949).

Boismard, M. E., O.P., *L'Apocalypse* (Paris: Du Cerf, 1950).

Bonsirven, P. J., *L'Apocalypse de St. Jean* (Paris: Beauchesne, 1951).

Bousset, W., *Die Offenbarung Johannis* (Göttingen: Vanderhoeck & Ruprecht, 1906).

Bowman, J. W., *The Drama of the Book of Revelation* (Philadelphia: Westminster, 1960).

Brütsch, C., *Clarté de l'Apocalypse* (Geneva: Labor et Fides, 5th ed., 1967).

Burnet, A. W., *The Lord Reigneth* (New York: Scribners, 1947).

Caird, G. B., *The Revelation of St. John the Divine* (London: A. C. Black, 1966; New York: Harpers, 1966).

Carrington, P., *The Meaning of the Revelation* (London: S.P.C.K., 1931).

Case, S. J., *The Revelation of John* (Chicago: University of Chicago, 1919).

Cerfaux, L. and Cambier, J., *L'Apocalypse de St. Jean* (Paris: Lectio Divina, 1955).

Charles, R. H., *Revelation*, 2 vols. (Edinburgh: T. & T. Clark, 1920).

Farrer, A. M., *A Rebirth of Images* (Westminster: Dacre Press, 1949).

———, *The Revelation of St. John the Divine* (Oxford: Clarendon Press, 1964). (RJ)

Glasson, T. F., *The Revelation of John* (Cambridge: University Press, 1965).

Hadorn, W., *Die Offenbarung des Johannes* (Leipzig: Deichert, 1928).

Hartenstein, K., *Der wiederkommende Herr.* (Stuttgart: Missionsverlag, 3rd ed., 1954).

Hoskier, H. C., *The Complete Commentary of Oecumenius on the Apocalypse* (Ann Arbor: University of Michigan, 1928).

Kepler, T. S., *The Book of Revelation* (New York: Oxford, 1957).

Ketter, P., *Die Apokalypse.* (Freiburg: Herder, 3rd ed., 1953).

Kiddle, M., *The Revelation of St. John* (New York: Harpers, 1941).

Läpple, A., *Die Apokalypse nach Johannes* (Munich: Don Bosco, 1966).

Laymon, C. M., *The Book of Revelation* (New York: Abingdon, 1960).

Lilje H., *The Last Book of the Bible* (Philadelphia: Muhlenberg Press, 1957).

Loenertz, R. J., O.P., *Apocalypse of St. John* (London: Sheed & Ward, 1947).

Lohmeyer, E., *Die Offenbarung des Johannes* (Tübingen: J. C. B. Mohr, 1953).

Lohse, E., *Die Offenbarung des Johannes* (Göttingen, Vandenhoeck & Ruprecht, 1960).

Loisy, A., *L'Apocalypse de Jean* (Paris: E. Nourry, 1923).

Milligan, Wm., *The Revelation of John* (London: Macmillan, 1886).

Moffatt, J., *The Revelation of St. John the Divine* (London: Expositor's Great Testament, 1910).

Niles, D. T., *As Seeing the Invisible* (New York: Harper, 1961).

Peake, A. S., *The Revelation of John* (New York: Doran, 1922).

Poellot, L., *Revelation* (St. Louis: Concordia, 1962).

Preston, R. H. and Hanson, A. T., *The Revelation of St. John the Divine* (London: S.C.M. Press, 1949).

Richardson, D. W., *The Revelation of Jesus Christ* (Richmond: John Knox, 1939).

Rist, M., *The Revelation of St. John the Divine* in *Interpreter's Bible* XII (New York: Abingdon, 1957).

Rossetti, C. G., *The Face of the Deep.* A Devotional Commentary on the Apocalypse (London: S.P.C.K., 1907).

Scott, C. A., *Revelation* (Edinburgh: T. C. & E. C. Jack, 1902).

Sickenberger, J., *Erklärung der Johannesapokalypse* (Bonn: Hanstein, 1942).

von Speyr, *Apokalypse* (Wien: Herold, 1950).

Strack, H. L. and Billerbeck, P., *Kommentar zum Neuen Testament aus Talmud und Midrasch,* Vol. III München: C. H. Beck, 1954). (S-B)

Summers, R., *Worthy is the Lamb* (Nashville: Broadman, 1951).

Swedenborg, E., *The Apocalypse Revealed*, 2 vols. (New York: Swedenborg Foundation, 1949).

Swete, H. B., *The Apocalypse of St. John* (London: Macmillan, 1909).

Torrey, C. C., *The Apocalypse of John* (New Haven: Yale, 1958).

Turner, N., *Revelation in Peake's Commentary on the Bible* (London: Nelson, 1962).

Victorinus' Commentary on the Apocalypse of the Blessed John. Trans. R. E. Wallis. Ante-Nicene Fathers, Vol. VII (Buffalo: 1886).

Weiss, J., *Die Offenbarung des Johannes* (Göttingen: Vandenhoeck & Ruprecht, 1904).

Wikenhauser, A., *Offenbarung des Johannes* (Regensburg: F. Pustet, 1949).

Zahn, Th., *Die Offenbarung des Johannes*, 2 vols. (Leipzig: A. Deichert, 1924-26).

II. Books Devoted Wholly to the Apocalypse

Barclay, Wm., *The Letters to the Seven Churches* (London: S.C.M. Press, 1957).

Boll, F., *Aus der Offenbarung Johannis* (Berlin: Teubner, 1914).

Büchsel, F., *Die Christologie der Offenbarung* (Halle: Kaemmerer, 1907).

Burch, V., *Anthropology and the Apocalypse* (London: Macmillan, 1939).

Charles, R. H., *Studies in the Apocalypse* (Edinburgh: T. & T. Clark, 1913).

Comblin, J., *Le Christ dans l'Apocalypse* (Paris: Desclée, 1965).

Dallmayr, H., *Die sieben Leuchter* (Köln, Hegner, 1962).

Dehn, G., *Urchristliche Gemeindeleben* (Witten/Ruhr: Luther, 1954).

Féret, H. M., O.P., *The Apocalypse of St. John* (Westminster: Newman, 1958).

Feuillet, A., *L'Apocalypse. État de la question* (Paris: Brouwer, 1962).

Le Frois, B. J., S.V.D., *The Woman Clothed with the Sun* (Rome: Herder, 1954).

Giet, S., *L'Apocalypse et l'histoire* (Paris: Univ. de France, 1957).

Gutzwiller, R., *Herr der Herrscher* (Einsiedeln: Benziger, 1941).

Halver, R., *Der Mythos im Letzten Buch der Bibel* (Hamburg: H. Reich, 1964).

Haring, P., *Die Botschaft der Offenbarung des Heiligen Johannes* Munich: Pfeiffer, 1953).

Harpold, C. J., *Twelve Tribes of the Apocalypse* or *Roman Citizenship among the First Century Jews of Asia Minor* (Ann Arbor: Edwards, 1937).

Haugg, D., *Die Zwei Zeugen: Eine exegetische Studie über Apokalypse 11:1-13* (Münster: Aschendorffschen, 1936).

Herrmann, L., *La Vision de Patmos* (Bruxelles: Collection Latomus, vol. 28, 1965).

Holtz, T., *Die Christologie der Apokalypse des Johannes* (Berlin: Akademie, 1962).

Hort, F. J. A., *The Apocalypse of St. John*, I-III (London: Truebner, 1861).

Hoskier, H. C., *Concerning the Text of the Apocalypse*, 2 vols. (London: Bernard Quaritch, 1929).

Kamlah, W., *Apokalypse und Geschichtsbewusstsein* (Göttingen, 1931).

Langenberg, Heinrich, *Die prophetische Bildsprache der Apokalypse* (Metzingen: Ernst Franz, [n.d.]).

Langenberg, H., *Schlüssel zum Verständis der Apokalypse*, Pt. I (Metzinger: Ernst Franz, [n.d.]).

Lattimore, R., *The Revelation of John*. A Translation (New York: Harcourt, Brace & World, 1962).

Lawrence, D. H., *Apocalypse* (Florence: 1931).

Lévitan, J., *Une Juive Conception de l'Apocalypse* (Paris: Debresse, 1966).

Martin, H., *The Seven Letters* (Philadelphia: Westminster, 1955).

Michl, J., *Die Engelvorstellungen in der Apokalypse* (München: Hueber, 1937).

———, *Die 24 Ältesten in der Apokalypse* (München: Hueber, 1938).

Munck, J., *Petrus und Paulus in der Offenbarung Johannis* (Copenhagen: Rosenkilde & Bogger, 1950).

Poirier, L., *Les Septs Églises* (Washington: Catholic University, 1943).

———, *L'Église dans l'Apocalypse* (Montreal: Facultés S.J., 1962).

Prigent, P., *Apocalypse 12: Histoire de l'éxegese* (Tübingen, Mohr, 1959).

Ramsay, Wm., *Letters to the Seven Churches* (New York: Armstrong, 1905).

Reisner, E., *Das Buch mit den 7 Siegeln* (Göttingen: Vandenhoeck & Ruprecht, 1949).

Rissi, M., *Time and History: A Study on the Revelation* (Richmond: John Knox Press, 1966).

———, *Die Zukunft der Welt* (Rev. 19:11-22:15) (Basel: Reinhardt, 1966).

Satake, A., *Die Gemeindeordnung in der Johannesapokalypse* (Neu-kirchen: 1966).

Schlatter, A., *Das A. T. in der Offenbarung Johannes* (Gutersloh: C. Bertelsmann, 1912).

Schmid, J., *Studien zur Geschichte des griechischen Apokalypse-Textes*, 3 vols (München: Zink, 1955-1956).

Schmidt, K. L., *Aus der Johannesapokalypse* (Basel: H. Maser, 1945).

Schütz, R., *Die Offenbarung des Johannes und Kaiser Domitian* (Göttingen: Vandenhoeck & Ruprecht, 1933).

Scott, E. F., *The Book of Revelation* (New York: Scribners, 1940).

Scott, R. B. Y., *The Original Language of the Apocalypse* (Toronto: Univ. of Toronto, 1928).

Torrance, T. F., *The Apocalypse Today* (Grand Rapids: Eerdman, 1959).

Touilleux, P., *L'Apocalypse et les cultes de Domitien et de Cybele* (Paris: Geuthner, 1935).

Trench, R. C., *Commentary on the Epistles to the Seven Churches* (New York: Scribners, 1861).

Vos, L. A., *The Synoptic Traditions in the Apocalypse* (Kampen: Kok, 1965).

Waal, C. van der, *Oudtestamentische priesterlijke Motieven in de Apocalyps* (Goes: Oosterbaan, 1956).

Wishart, C. F., *The Book of Day* (New York: Oxford, 1935).

III. Essays in Journals, Symposia, and Dictionaries

Allo, E. B., A propros d'Apocalypse XI et XII, RB 31 (1922), 572-583.

Aune, D. D., Ecclesiology in the Apocalypse, EQ 38 (1966), 131-149.

Bailey, J. W., The Temporary Messianic Reign, JBL 53 (1934), 170-187.

Baldensperger, W., Les cavaliers de l'Apocalypse, Rev. 6:1-8, RHP (1924), 1-31.

Barrett, C. K., Things sacrificed to idols. NTS 11 (1965), 138-153.

Bauer, W., *Chiliasmus*, Lexicon für Antike und Christentum, XV, 1073-1078.

Bauernfeind, O., *Conquer*, TWNT, IV, 941-945.

Behm, J., *Blood*, TWNT I, 172-177.

————, Das Geschichtsbild der Offenbarung des Johannes, ZST 2 (1924), 323-344.

Bieder, W., Die sieben Seligpreisungen in der Offenbarung des Johannes, TZ 10 (1954), 13-30.

Boismard, M. E., L'Apocalypse ou les Apocalypses de S. Jean, RB 56 (1949), 511.

Bornkamm, G., Die Komposition der apokalyptic Visionen, ZNTW (1937), 132-149.

Bowman, J. W., The Revelation to John, Int. 9 (1955), 436-453.

Braun, F. M., La Femme vêtue du soleil, RT (1955), 639-669.

Brewer, R. R., Revelation 4:6 and Translations Thereof, JBL 71 (1952), 227-231.

Brown, R. E., Mystery, Bib. 39 (1958), 426-448; 40 (1959), 70-87; CBQ 20 (1958), 417-443.

Brown, S., The Hour of Trial, JBL 85 (1966), 308-314.

Bruns, J. E., The Contrasted Women of Apocalypse 12 and 17, CBQ 26 (1964), 459-463.

Bruston, C., La tête égorgée et le chiffre 666, ZNTW 5 (1904), 258-261.

Bultmann, R., History and Eschatology in the New Testament, NTS 1 (1954), 5-16.

——, Ist die Apokalypse die Mutter des urchristlichen Theologie? *Apophoreta* (E. Haenchen), Berlin, 1964, 64-69.

Caird, G. B., On Deciphering the Book of Revelation, Exp T 74 (1962-63), 13-15, 51-53, 82-84, 103-105.

Calder, Wm., Philadelphia and Montanism, BJRL 7 (1922), 309-354.

Cambier, J., Les images de l'A.T. dans l'Apocalypse, NRT (1955), 113-123.

Causse, A., *Le Mythe de la nouvelle Jérusalem*, RHP 18 (1938), 377-414.

Cerfaux, L., La Vision de la Femme et du Dragon, ETL (1955), 7-33.

——, Le Conflit entre Dieu et la Souverain divinise dans l'Apocalypse, Numen, Supplement 4 (1959), 459-470.

——, L'Évangile éternel (Apoc. 14:6), ETL 39 (1963), 672-81.

Clemen, C., Die Bildlichkeit der Offenbarung Johannes, in *Festgabe für J. Kaftan* (Tübingen, 1920), 25-43.

Comblin, J., La Liturgie de la Nouvelle Jerusalem, ETL 29 (1953), 5-40.

Considine, J. S., The Rider on the White Horse, CBQ 6 (1944), 406-422.

——, The Two Witnesses: Apocalypse 11:3-13, CBQ 8 (1946), 377-392.

Dahl, N. A., Christ, Creation and the Church, in C. H. Dodd, *The Background of the New Testament and its Eschatology* (Cambridge, 1956), 422-443.

Delling, G., Zum Gottesdienstlichen Stil der Johannes, Nov T 3 (1959), 107-137.

Devine, R., Virgin Followers of the Lamb, Scr 16 (1964), 1-5.

Dix, G. H., Heavenly Wisdom and Divine Logos in Jewish Apocalyptic, JTS (1925), 1-12.

Dubarle, A. M., La Femme couronnée d'étoiles (Apoc. 12), in A. Robert, *Melanges biblique* (Paris, 1957), 512-518.

Dugmore, C. W., Lord's Day and Easter, in O. Cullmann, *Neotestamentica et Patristica* (Leiden: Brill, 1962), 272-281.

Ehrhardt, A., Das Sendschreiben nach Laodizea, Ev Th (1957), 431-445.

Fabre, A., The Dawn Star, RB 5 (1908), 227-240.

———, L'Ange et le Chandelier de l'Église d'Ephèse, RB 7 (1910), 161-178, 344-367.

Feuillet, A., Les vingt-quatre Vieullards de l'Apocalypse, RB 65 (1958), 5-32.

———, Le Messie et sa Mère d'apres le ch. XII de l'Apocalypse, RB 66 (1959), 55-86.

———, Le premier cavalier de l'Apocalypse, ZNTW 57 (1966), 229-260.

Forster, W., Die Bilder in Offenbarung 12 und 17, Th STK 104 (1932), 279-310.

Gaster, T. H., *Angels*, IDB I, 128.

Giet, S., Retour sur l'Apocalypse, RSR 38 (1964), 71-92, 225-264.

Goppelt, L., Heilsoffenbarung und Geschichte nach der Offenbarung des Johannes, ThLZ (1952), 513-522.

Grelot, P., L'eschatologie de la Sagesse et les Apocalypses Juives, in A. Gelin, *A la Rencontre de Dieu* (Le Puy: 1961), 165-178.

Gry, L., Les chapitres XI et XII de l'Apocalypse, RB 31 (1922), 203-214.

Hadorn, W., Die Zahl 666, Ein Hinweis auf Trajan, ZNTW 19 (1919-20), 11-29.

Hanfmann, G. M. A., Excavations at Sardis, BASOR 154 (1959), 1-35.

Hopkins, M., Historical Perspective of Apocalypse, 1-11, CBQ 27 (1965), 42-47.

Hubert, M., L'architecture des lettres, RB (1960), 349-353.

Janzon, P., Nikolaiterna i Nya Testamentet och i fornkyrkan, SEÅ 21 (1956), 82-108.

Jeremias, J., Har Magedon, ZNTW 31 (1932), 73-77.

———, Hades, TWNT I, 146-149.

Johnson, S. E., Laodicea and its Neighbors, BA 13 (1950), 1-18.

————, Early Christianity in Asia Minor, JBL 77 (1958), 1-17.

Kallas, J., The Apocalypse—an Apocalyptic Book? JBL 86 (1967), 69-80.

Kassing, A., Das Weib und der Drache, BK 15 (1960), 114-116.

Klassen, Wm., Vengeance in the Apocalypse of John, CBQ 28 (1966), 300-311.

Knopf, R., Die Himmelstadt, in G. Heinrici, *Neutestamentlichen Studien* (Leipzig, 1914).

Koester, W., Lamm und Kirche in der Apokalypse, in M. Meinertz *Vom Wort des Lebens* (Münster, 1951).

Kuhn, K. G., Babylon, TWNT, I, 514-7.

————, Balaam, TWNT, I, 524, 525.

————, Gog and Magog, TWNT I, 789-791.

Ladd, G. E., Revelation 20 and the Millennium, RE 57 (1960), 167-175.

Laeuchli, S., Eine Gottesdienststruktur in der Johannesoffenbarung, Th Z 16 (1960), 359-378.

Lohmeyer, E., Die Offenbarung des Johannes 1920-1934, ThR 6 (1934), 269-314; 7 (1935), 28-62.

Lohse E., Die alttestamentliche Sprache des Sehers Johannes, ZNTW 52 (1961), 122-126.

Masson, Ch., L'Évangile éternel de l'Apocalypse 14:6, in K. Barth, *Hommage et reconnaissance* (Paris, 1946).

May, H. G., Some Cosmic Connotations of Mayim Rabbìm, "Many Waters," JBL 74 (1955), 9-21.

McNeile, A. H., The Number of the Beast, JTS 14 (1913), 443f.

Meinertz, M., Dieses Geschlecht in Neues Testament, BZ N.F. 1 (1957), 283-289.

Michl, J. E., *Chiliasmus*, Lexicon für Theologie und Kirche, II, 1058.

————, Zu Apk. 9:8, BZ 23 (1935-1936), 266-288.

————, Zu Apk. 9:8, Bib. 23 (1942), 192-193.

————, Die Deutung der Apokalyptischen Frau in der Gegenwart, BZ (1959), 301-310.

Minear, P., Babylon, IDB, I, 338.

————, Eschatology and History, Int 5 (1951), 27-39.

————, The Wounded Beast, JBL 72 (1953), 93-102.

————, The Time of Hope in the New Testament, SJT 6 (1953), 337-361.

————, Christian Eschatology and Historical Methodology, in *Neutestamentlichen Studien für R. Bultmann* (Berlin: 1957), 15-23.

————, The Cosmology of the Apocalypse, in O. Piper, *Current Issues in N.T. Interpretation* (New York: Harper, 1962), 23-37.

————, New Starting Point, Int 19 (1965), 3-15.

————, Ontology and Ecclesiology in the Apocalypse, NTS 13 (1966), 89-105.

Mitten, D. G., Sardis, BA 29 (1966), 38-68.

Molner, A., Apocalypse 12 dans l'interpretation hussite, RHP 45 (1965), 212-231.

Momigliano, A., Nero, in *Cambridge Ancient History*, Vol. X (Cambridge University, 1934), 702-742.

Mowry, L., Revelation 4-5 and Early Christian Liturgical Usage, JBL 71 (1952), 75-84.

Müller, H. P., Die Plagen der Apokalypse, ZNTW 51 (1960), 268-78.

————, Formgeschichtliche Untersuchungen zu Apokalypse 4f., TLZ 88 (1963), 951f.

————, Die Himmlische Ratsversammlung Revelation 5:1-5, ZNTW 54 (1963), 254-267.

Müller, M. W., Die apokalyptischen Reiter, ZNTW 8 (1907), 290-316.

Murdoch, W. R., History and Revelation in Jewish Apocalypticism, Int. 21 (1967), 167-187.

Mürmulstein, B., Das Zweite Tier in der Offenbarung Johannis, Th STK 101 (1929), 447-457.

Neuss, W., Apokalypse, in *Reallexicon zur deutschen Kunstgeschichte*, I, 751-782 (Stuttgart, 1937).

Newman, B., The Fallacy of the Domitian Hypothesis, NTS 10 (1963-1964), 133-139.

Nikolainen, A. T., Der Kirchenbegriff in der Offenbarung des Johannes, NTS 9 (1963), 351-361.

Oepke, A., *Kalupto*, TWNT, III, 573-597.

Olsson, B., Der Epilog der Offenbarung Johannis, ZNTW 31 (1932), 84-86.

Pfeiffer, R. H., Apocalypses, IB, I, 427-432, 435f.

Piper, O. A., The Apocalypse of John and the Liturgy of the Ancient Church, CH 20 (1951), 10-22.

Porteous, N., Jerusalem-Zion, The Growth of a Symbol, in W. Rudolph, *Verbannung und Heimkehr* (Tübinger, Mohr, 1961), 235-252.

Power, E., A Pretended Interpolation in the Apocalypse (14:4, 5), Bib 4 (1923), 108-112.

Ramsey, P., A Letter from Canon Rhymes to John of Patmos, RL (1966).

Repp, A. C., Ministry and Life in the Churches, CTM 25 (1964), 133-147.

Rife, J. M., Literary Background of Revelation 2, 3, JBL 60 (1941), 179-182.

Rigaux, P., La Femme et son lignage dans Gen., 3:14, 15, RB 61 (1954), 321-348.
Rinaldi, G., La porte aperta nel cielo, CBQ 25 (1963), 336-347.
Ringgren, H., Apokalyptik, RGG I, 463-466.
Rissi, M., Das Judenproblem, TZ (1957), 241-259.
──────, The Rider on the White Horse, Int. 18 (1964), 407-418.
──────, Die Erscheinung Christi nach Offenbarung 19:11-16, ThZ 21 (1965), 81-95.
Rist, M., Antichrist, IDB, I, 140-143.
──────, Apocalypticism, IDB I, 157-161.
──────, Millenium, IDB III, 381.
Rohmer, J., L'Apocalypse et le sens chrétienne de l'histoire, RSR (1952), 265-270.
Roller, O., Das Buch mit sieben Siegeln, ZNTW 36 (1937), 98-113.
Rudwick, M. and Green, E., The Laodicean Lukewarmness, Exp T 69 (1957/58), 176f.
Rühle, Arithmos, TWNT I, 461-4.
Ruotolo, L. P., A New Apocalypse, motive 27 (Dec. 1966), 21-36.
Sanders, H. A., The Number of the Beast in Revelation, JBL 37 (1918), 95-99.
Sanders, J. N., St. John on Patmos, NTS 9 (1963), 75-85.
Sasse, H., Gē, TWNT I, 332f.
Sattler, W., Das Buch mit sieben Siegeln, ZNTW 21 (1922), 43ff.
Schlier, H., Die Engel nach dem N. T., ALW 6 (1959), 43-56.
──────, Deiknumi, TWNT II, 26-30.
──────, Amen, TWNT I, 339-342.
──────, Elaion, TWNT II, 468-471.
Schmidt, K. L., Die Bildersprache in der Johannes-Apokalypse, ThZ 3 (1947), 170f.
──────, Jerusalem als Urbild und Abbild, Eranos Jahrbuch 18 (1950), 207-248.
Schrenk, J., Biblos, TWNT I, 615-620.
Schütz, R., Apokalyptik, RGG I, 467-469.
Schweizer, E., Die 7 Geister in der Apk., Ev Th 11 (1951-52), 502-512.
Scott, R. B. Y., The Clouds of Heaven, NTS 5 (1959), 127-132.
Seierstad, I. P., Erlebnis und Gehorsam beim Propheten Amos, ZATW 52 (1934), 22-41.
Sellers, O. R., Musical Instruments of Israel, BA 4 (1941), 33-47.
Silberman, L., Farewell to O AMHN, JBL 82 (1963), 213-215.
Simon, M., Retour du Christ, in M. Goguel, Aux Sources de la tradition chretienne (Neuchatel, 1950), 247-257.

Skehan, P. W., King of Kings, Lord of Lords, Rev. 19:16, CBQ 10 (1948), 398.

Skrinjar, A., Les sept Esprits, Bib. (1935), 1-24, 113-140.

Smith, J. Z., The Garments of Shame, HR 5 (1966), 217-238.

Snyder, J., A Reconstruction of an Early Cycle of Illustrations for Revelation, VigC 18 (1964), 146-162.

Staritz, K., Zu Offenbarung Johannis 5:1, ZNTW 30 (1931), 157-170.

Stauffer E., Das theologische Weltbild der Apokalypse, ZST 8 (1930), 203-205.

————, 666, in Coniectanea Neotestamentica (A. Fridrichsen) XI (1947), 237-241.

Steinmetzer, F. X., Das Froschsymbol in Offb. 16, BZ 10 (1912), 252-260.

Stendahl, K., The Called and the Chosen, in A. Fridrichsen, The Root of the Vine (New York: Philosophical Library, 1953).

Stott, W., A Note on the word Kuriakē in Revelation 1:10, NTS 12 (1965), 70-74.

Strand, K., Another Look at Lord's Day in Revelation 1:10, NTS 13 (1967), 174-181.

Strobel, A., Abfassung und Geschichtstheologie der Apokalypse, 17:9-12, NTS 10 (1964), 433-445.

Stuiber, A., Amen, JAC 1 (1958), 153-158.

Summers, R., Revelation 20, An Interpretation, RE 57 (1960), 176-183.

Thomas, R. L., The Glorified Christ on Patmos, Bib. Sac. 122 (1965), 241-247.

Torrance, T. F., Liturgie et Apocalypse, VC 11 (1957), 28-40.

Tribble, H. W., The Christ of the Apocalypse, RE 40 (1943), 167-176.

Trudinger, P., Some Observations concerning the Text of the Old Testament in the Book of Revelation, JTS 17 (1966), 82-88.

van Unnik, W. C., Dominus vobiscum, in T. W. Manson, New Testament Essays (Manchester, 1959), 270-305.

————, A Formula describing Prophecy, NTS 9 (1963), 87-94.

————, Die Geöffneten Himmel in der Offenbarungsvision des Apokryphons des Johannes, in E. Haenchen, Apophoreta (Berlin: Töpelmann, 1964).

Vanhoye, A., L'utilisation du livre d'Ezéchial dans l'Apokalypse, Bib 43 (1962), 436-476.

Vischer, E. and Corssen, P., Die Entstehung der Zahl 666, ZNTW 5 (1904), 84-88.

Walker, N., Origin of the Thrice Holy, NTS (1958), 132-133.
Wallace, H., Leviathan and the Beast in Revelation, BA XI (1948), 61f.
Watson, E. and Hamilton, B., Lumen Christi-Lumen Antichristi: The Exegesis of Apocalypse 11:5 and 13:13 in the Mediaeval Latin Fathers, RSLR 2 (1966), 84-92.
Wikenhauser, A., Ein weiterer Beleg für potamophoretos, BZ 1908, 171; 1909, 48.
Wilder, A. N., Kerygma, Eschatology, and Social Ethics, in C. H. Dodd, *The Background of the New Testament and Its Eschatology* (Cambridge, 1956), 509-536.
————, Social Factors in Early Christian Eschatology, in S. J. Case, *Early Christian Origins* (Chicago, 1961).
Wood, P., Local Knowledge in the Letters of the Apocalypse, Exp T 73 (1961-62), 263f.
Zimmermann, H., Christus und die Kirche in den Sendschreiben der Apokalypse, in L. Jaeger, *Unio Christianorum* (Paderborn, 1962), 176-197.
————, Heilsgeschichte und Weltgeschichte in der Johannes-apokalypse, BL 1 (1960), 75-86.

IV. Other Books Consulted

Balthasar, Hans Urs von, *A Theology of History* (New York: Sheed Ward, 1963).
Barr, J., *Biblical Words for Time* (London: SCM, 1962).
Barrett, C. K., *Jesus and the Gospel* (London, S.P.C.K., 1967).
Beasley-Murray, G. R., *Jesus and the Future* (London: Macmillan, 1954).
Bernanos, G., *The Star of Satan* (New York: Macmillan, 1940).
Bietenhard, H., *Die Himmlische Welt im Urchristentum und Spätjudentum* (Tübingen: Mohr, 1951).
————, *Das Tausendjahrige Reich* (Zurich: Zwingli, 1955).
Bonhöffer, D., *Letters and Papers from Prison* (London: SCM, 1953).
Borgen, P., *Bread from Heaven* (Leiden: Brill, 1965).
Bousset, W., *The Antichrist Legend* (London: Hutchinson, 1896).
Braun, F. M., *Der christliche Altar in seiner geschichtlichen Entwicklung* (Munich: 1924. Vol. I).
————, *La mère des Fidéles* (Tournai: Casterman, 1953).
————, *Jean le Théologièn* (Paris: Gabalda, 1959).
Brown, R. E., S.S., *New Testament Essays* (Milwaukee: Bruce, 1965).
Brox, N., *Zeuge und Martyrer* (München: Kösel, 1961).

Brun, L., *Segen und Fluch im Urchistentum* (Oslo: J. Dybwad, 1932).

Buechner, Frederick, *The Final Beast* (New York: Athenaeum, 1965).

Bultmann, R., *Primitive Christianity in its Historical Setting* (London: Thames and Hudson, 1956).

————, *History and Eschatology* (Edinburgh: University, 1957).

Burrows, M., *The Dead Sea Scrolls* (New York: Viking, 1955).

Butler, H. C., *Publications of the American Society for the Excavation of Sardis*, Part I, 1910-14 (Leyden: Brill, 1922).

Cadoux, C. J., *Ancient Smyrna* (Oxford: Blackwell, 1938).

Caird, G. B., *Principalities and Powers* (Oxford: Clarendon, 1956).

von Campenhausen, H., *Die Idee des Martyriums in der alten Kirche* (Göttingen: Vandenhoeck & Ruprecht, 1936).

Carzou, J. M., *L'Apocalypse* (Paris: A. Sauret, 1959).

Case, S. J., *The Millennial Hope* (Chicago: University of Chicago, 1918).

Cassirer, E., *Philosophie der symbolischen formen* (Darmstadt: 1958).

Congar, M. J., O.P., *Mystery of the Temple* (Westminster, Md.: Newman, 1962).

Conzelmann, H., *The Theology of St. Luke* (London: Faber, 1960).

Cullmann, O., *Early Christian Worship* (London: SCM, 1953).

————, *The State in the New Testament* (New York: Scribners, 1956).

————, *Christology of the New Testament* (Philadelphia: Westminster, 1959).

Daniélou, J., *The Bible and the Liturgy* (Notre Dame: University of Notre Dame, 1956).

————, *From Shadows to Reality* (London: Burns & Oates, 1960).

————, *Primitive Christian Symbols* (Baltimore: Helicon, 1961).

————, *Theology of Jewish Christianity* (London: Darton, Longman & Todd, 1964).

Delisle, L. et Meyer, P., *L'Apocalypse en Français au XIIIᵉ Siècle* (Paris: Didot, 1901).

Dillistone, F. W. ed., *Myth and Symbol* (London: S.P.C.K., 1966).

Dodd, C. H., *The Coming of Christ* (Cambridge: University Press, 1951).

Dölger, F. J., *Sphragis: Eine altchristliche Taufbezeichnung in ihren Beziehungen zur profanen und religiösen Kultur des Altertums* (Paderborn, 1911). (Sp)

————, *Sol Salutis: Gebet und Gesang im christlichen Altertum* (Münster i.W., 1925). (SS)

Dudley, Guilford, *The Recovery of Christian Myth* (Philadelphia: Westminster, 1967).

Dürer, A., *Die Apokalypse* (Dresden: Verlag der Kunst, 1956).

Dürr, J., *Die Stellung des Propheten Ezechiel in der israelitischen-judischen Apokalyptik* (Münster: 1923).

Durrwell, F. X., *The Resurrection* (New York: Sheed & Ward, 1960).

Dupont, Jacques, *La christologie de Saint Jean* (Bruges: L'abbaye de S André, 1951).

Dvorak, W., *Dürer's Apokalypse in Kunstgeschichte und Geistesgeschichte* (München: 1924).

Eliade, M., *The Myth of the Eternal Return* (New York: Pantheon, 1954).

——, *The Sacred and the Profane* (New York: Harcourt, Brace, 1959).

——, *Images and Symbols* (New York: Sheed & Ward, 1961).

Emonds, H., *Geistlicher Kriegsdienst. Der Topos der militia spiritualis* (Münster: 1938).

Forét, J., *Catalogue de L'Apocalypse Musée d'Art Moderne de la Ville de Paris* (Paris: 1961).

Frend, W. H. C., *Martyrdom and Persecution in the Early Church* (Oxford: Blackwell, 1965).

Frimmel, T., *Die Apokalypsis in den Bilderhandschriften des Mittelalters* (Vienna: 1865).

Frost, S. B., *Old Testament Apocalyptic* (London: Epworth, 1952).

Gerhardsson, B., *The Testing of God's Son* (Lund: Gleerup, 1966).

Goodenough, E., *Jewish Symbols in the Greco-Roman Period*, 12 vols. (New York: Pantheon, 1953-65).

Grant, R. M., *Gnosticism* (New York: Harper, 1961).

Gunkel, H., *Schöpfung und Chaos in Urzeit und Endzeit* (Göttingen, 1921).

Hansen, E. B., *The Attalids of Pergamum* (1947).

Hanson, A. T., *The Wrath of the Lamb* (London: S.P.C.K., 1957).

Hanson, R. P. C., *Allegory and Event* (London: SCM, 1959).

Harrisville, R., *Newness in the New Testament* (Minneapolis: Augsburg, 1960).

Heim, K., *Jesus the Lord* (London: Oliver and Boyd, 1959).

——, *Jesus the World Perfecter* (Edinburgh: Oliver & Boyd, 1959).

Hennecke, E., *New Testament Apocrypha* (ed. W. Schneemelcher), Vol. II (Philadelphia: Westminster, 1965).

Hilgert, E., *The Ship and Related Symbols in the N.T.* (Assen: Van Gorcum, 1962).

Hooke, S. H., *Alpha and Omega* (London: Nisbet, 1961).

Horst, J., *Proskunein* (Gutersloh: Bertelsmann, 1932).

Hühn, Eugen, *Die messianischen Weissagungen des israelitischen-jüdischen Volkes bis zu den Targumin*, Vol. 2 *Die altestamentlichen Citate und Reminiscenzen im N. T.* (Tübingen: Mohr, 1899, 1900).

Jahnow, H., *Das hebraische Leichenlied im Rahmen der Völker dichtung* (Giessen: Töpelmann, 1923).

James, M. R., *The Apocalypse in Art* (London: Oxford University, 1931).

Jones, A. H. M., *Cities of the Eastern Roman Provinces* (Oxford: Clarendon, 1937).

Juraschek, F., *Das Rätsel in Dürer's Gotteschau* (Salzburg, 1955).

Kähler, H., *Der grosse Fries von Pergamon* (Berlin, 1948; Pergamon, Berlin, 1949).

Kaiser, O., *Die mythische Bedeutung des Meeres in Ägypten, Ugarit und Israel* (Berlin: Töpelmann, 1959).

Käsemann, E., *Exegetische Versuche und Besinnungen*, Vol. II (Göttingen: Vandenhoeck & Ruprecht, 1964).

Kassing, A. Th., *Die Kirche und Maria* (Düsseldorf: Patmos, 1958).

Keil, J., *Ephesos, Ein Fuhrer durch die Ruinenstatts und ihre Geschichte* (1955).

Kierkegaard, S., *The Gospel of Suffering* (Minneapolis: Augsburg, 1948).

Kitamori, K., *Theology of the Pain of God* (London: S.C.M., 1966).

Koch, K., *Was ist Formgeschichte?* (Neukirchen: 1964).

Koep, Leo, *Das himmlische Buch im Antike und Christentum* (Bonn: Peter Hanstein, 1952).

Kristeller, P., *Die Apokalypse älteste Blochbuchausgabe in Lichtdrucknachbildung* (Berlin, 1916).

Kümmel, W. G., *Introduction to the New Testament* (New York: Abingdon, 1966).

Kuntz, J. K., *The Self-Revelation of God* (Philadelphia: Westminster, 1967).

Laeuchli, S., *The Serpent and the Dove* (New York: Abingdon, 1966).

Lagerlof, S., *The Miracles of Antichrist* (Boston: Little, Brown, 1899).

Lampe, G. W. A., *The Seal of the Spirit* (London: Longmans Green, 1951).

Langton, S., *The Angel Teaching of the New Testament* (London: Jas. Clarke, 1940).

Leaney, A. R. C., *The Rule of Qumran and its Meaning* (Philadelphia: Westminster, 1966).

Legrand, L., *The Biblical Doctrine of Virginity* (New York: Sheed & Ward, 1963).

Leivestad, R., *Christ the Conqueror* (New York: Macmillan, 1954).
Lövestam, E., *Spiritual Wakefulness in the New Testament* (Lund: Gleerup, 1963).
Lossky, V., *Mystical Theology of the Eastern Church* (London: J. Clarke, 1957).
Lourcat, J., *L'Apocalypse d'Angers* (Paris: 1955).
de Lubac, H., S.J., *Splendour of the Church* (New York: Sheed & Ward, 1956).
Lueken, W., *Michael* (Göttingen: Vandenhoeck & Ruprecht, 1898).
Magie, D., *Roman Rule in Asia Minor*, 2 vols (Princeton Univ. Press, 1950).
Marsh, J., *Fulness of Time* (London: Nisbet, 1952).
Martin, R. P., *Carmen Christi, Phil. 2:5-11* (Cambridge: University Press, 1967).
Mauser, U., *Christ in the Wilderness* (London: SCM, 1963).
van der Meer, F., *Maiestas Domini: Theophanies de l'Apocalypse dans l'Art Chrétien* (Roma, 1938).
Minear, P., *The Kingdom and the Power* (Philadelphia: Westminster, 1950).
———, *Christian Hope and the Second Coming* (Philadelphia: Westminster, 1954).
———, *Horizons of Christian Community* (St. Louis: Bethany, 1959).
———, *Images of the Church* (Philadelphia: Westminster, 1960).
———, *Eyes of Faith* (2nd ed.) (St. Louis: Bethany, 1966).
Moffatt, J., *Introduction to the New Testament* (New York: Scribners, 1917).
Moltmann, J., *Theology of Hope* (London: SCM, 1967).
Moody, D., *The Hope of Glory* (Grand Rapids: Eerdmans, 1964).
Morris, L., *The Biblical Doctrine of Judgment* (Grand Rapids: Erdmans, 1960).
Mowinckel, S., *He That Cometh* (Oxford: Blackwell, 1956).
Müller, W., *Die heilige Stadt: Roma quadrata, himmlische Jerusalem und die Mythe vom Weltnabel* (Stuttgart: 1961).
Neuss, W., *Die Apokalypse in altspanischen und altchristlichen Bibel-illustration* (Münster: 1931).
———, *Das Buch Ezekiel in Theologie und Kunst zum Ende das XII Jahrhunderts* (Münster, 1912).
Newton, Isaac, *Observations upon the Prophecies of Daniel and the Apocalypse of St. John* (London, 1733).
Niebuhr, H. R., *The Kingdom of God in America* (Chicago: Willett, Clark, 1937).

Niebuhr, R. R., *Resurrection and Historical Reason* (New York: Scribners, 1957).

Noack, B., *Satanas und Soteria* (Copenhagen: Gad, 1948).

Oesterley, W. O. E., *The Jewish Background of the Christian Liturgy* (Oxford: Clarendon, 1925).

Patai, R., *Man and Temple in Ancient Jewish Myth and Ritual* (London: Nelson, 1947).

Petit, M., *Les apocalypse manuscrites du Moyen Age et les Tapisseries de la Cathedral d'Angers* (Paris, 1869).

Porter, F. C., *Messages of the Apocalyptical Writers* (New York: Scribners, 1905).

Pury, R. de, *Journal from My Cell* (New York: Harpers, 1946).

von Rad, G., *Old Testament Theology*, 2 vols. (New York: Harper, 1965).

Rahner, K., *Mary, Mother of the Lord* (New York: Herder, 1963).

Ramsay, Wm., *Cities and Bishoprics of Phrygia*, 2 vols. (Oxford: Clarendon, 1895-97).

Reymond, P., *L'eau, sa vie, et sa signification dans l'ancien Testament* (Leiden: Brill, 1958).

Richardson, A., *Introduction to the Theology of the New Testament* (New York: Harper, 1958).

Rigaux, B., *L'Antechrist et l'Opposition au Royaume messianique* (Paris: Gembloux, 1932).

Robinson, J. A. T., *In the End, God . . .* (London: Jas. Clarke, 1950).
———, *Jesus and His Coming* (London: SCM, 1957).

Rowley, H. H., *The Relevance of Apocalyptic* (New York: Harper, 1955).

Russell, D. S., *Method and Message of Jewish Apocalyptic* (Philadelphia: Westminster, 1964).

Schlier, H., *Die Zeit der Kirche* (Freiburg: Herder, 1956).
———, *Principalities and Powers in the New Testament* (New York: Herder, 1961).
———, *Besinnung auf das Neue Testament*, Vol. II (Freiburg: Herder, 1964).

Schmidt, K. L., *Die Polis in Kirche und Welt* (Basel: 1939).

Schnackenburg, R., *God's Rule and Kingdom* (London: Herder, 1963).
———, *The Moral Teaching of the New Testament* (London: Burns & Oates, 1965).

Schubert, P., *The Form and Function of Pauline Thanksgivings* (Berlin: Töpelmann, 1939).

Schütz, P., *Gesammelte Werke*, III (Hamburg: Furche, 1966).

Schweizer, E., *Lordship and Discipleship* (London: SCM, 1960).

Selwyn, E. G., *First Epistle of Peter* (London: Macmillan, 1946).

Semmelroth, O., *Mary, Archetype of the Church* (New York: Sheed & Ward, 1963).

Shepherd, Massey H., Jr., *The Paschal Liturgy and the Apocalypse* (Richmond, Va.: John Knox Press, 1960).

Simon, U. E., *Heaven* (New York: Harper, 1958).

———, *The End is Not Yet* (Aberdeen: University Press, 1964). (ENY)

Sitwell, E., *The Collected Poems of Edith Sitwell* (New York: Vanguard, 1954).

Smits, C., *Oud-Testamentische Citaten in het N.T.*, Vol. 2 (S-Hertogenbosch: Malmberg, 1955).

Soloview, V., *Die Erzählung vom Antichrist* (Luzern: 1946).

Stauffer, E., *Christ and the Caesars* (London: S.C.M., 1955).

———, *New Testament Theology* (London: S.C.M., 1955).

———, *Jerusalem und Rom im Zeitalter Jesu Christ* (Bern: Francke, 1957).

Streeter, B. H., *The Primitive Church* (New York: Macmillan, 1929).

Thurian, M., *Mary, Mother of All Christians* (New York: Herder, 1963).

Weiss, J., *History of Primitive Christianity*, 2 vols. (New York: Wilson-Erickson, 1937).

Wikenhauser, A., *Introduction to the New Testament* (New York: Herder, 1958).

Wilder, A. N., *Healing of the Waters* (New York: Harper, 1943).

———, *Eschatology and Ethics* (New York: Harper, 1950).

———, *The Language of the Gospel* (New York: Harper & Row, 1964).

Williams, G. H., *Wilderness and Paradise in Christian Thought* (New York: Harper, 1962).

Winklhofer, A., *The Coming of His Kingdom* (Freiburg: Herder, 1963).

Wölfflin, K., *Die Kunst A. Dürers* (München, 1920).

Wünsche, A., *Die Sagen vom Lebensbaum und Lebenswasser* (Leipzig: Pfeiffer, 1905).

de Young, J. C., *Jerusalem in the New Testament* (Kampen: Kok, 1960).

Photo Credits

ST. JOHN THE THEOLOGIAN—*courtesy of Mr. S. Papadopoulos of Athens.*

"THE ADORATION OF THE LAMB"—*copyright A. C. L. Bruxelles.*

THE PROPHET JOHN AND CHRIST—*The Metropolitan Museum of Art, New York. Gift of Mortimer L. Schiff, 1918.*

STATUE OF ARTEMIS—*courtesy of Mustafa Kapkin, Izmir, Turkey.*

"BLESSED ARE THE DEAD WHO DIE IN THE LORD"—*Archives Photographiques, Paris.*

THE OPENING PARAGRAPH OF THE APOCALYPSE—*Yale University, Beinecke Library.*